AN IMPERFECT GOD

ALSO BY HENRY WIENCEK

The Hairstons: An American Family in Black and White

National Geographic Guide to America's Great Houses
(with Donna M. Lucey)

Old Houses

The Smithsonian Guides to Historic America:
Southern New England and *Virginia and the Capital Region*

Mansions of the Virginia Gentry

Plantations of the Old South

AN IMPERFECT GOD

George Washington, His Slaves, and the Creation of America

Henry Wiencek

FARRAR, STRAUS AND GIROUX

NEW YORK

Farrar, Straus and Giroux
19 Union Square West, New York 10003

Distributed in Canada by Douglas & McIntyre Ltd.
Printed in the United States of America
Published in 2003 by Farrar, Straus and Giroux
First paperback edition, 2004

The Library of Congress has cataloged the hardcover edition as follows:
Wiencek, Henry.
      An imperfect god : George Washington, his slaves, and the
creation of America / Henry Wiencek.— 1st ed.
          p.   cm.
      Includes bibliographical references and index.
      ISBN 0-374-17526-8 (alk. paper)
          1. Washington, George, 1732–1799.   2. Washington, George,
      1732–1799—Views on slavery.   3. Washington, George,
      1732–1799—Relations with slaves.   4. Presidents—United
      States—Biography.   5. Slavery—Political aspects—United
      States—History—18th century.   6. United States—Politics and
      government—1775–1783.   I. Title

E312.17.W6 2003
973.4'1'092—dc21

                                                    2003006984

Paperback ISBN-13: 978-0-374-52951-2
Paperback ISBN-10: 0-374-52951-5

Designed by Robert C. Olsson
Map designed by Lili Wronker after Beverly Runge. Reprinted
with permission of the University of Virginia Press

www.fsgbooks.com

3   5   7   9   10   8   6   4   2

For my son

Contents

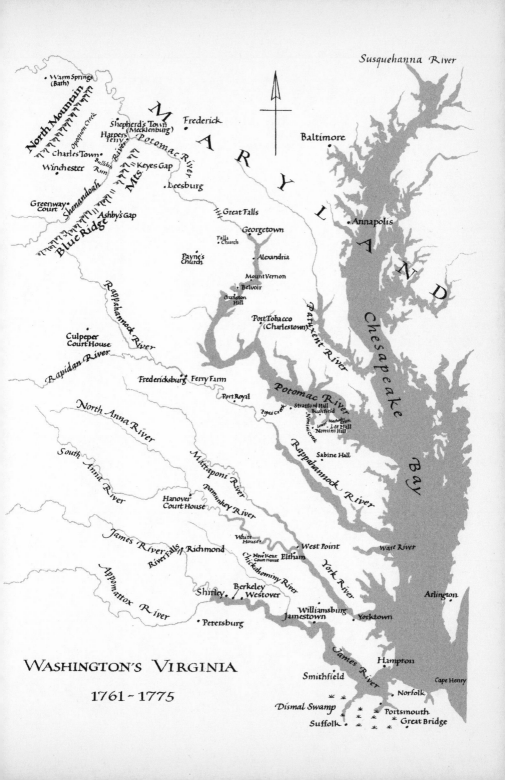

Susquehanna River

MARYLAND

North Mountain

Warm Spring
(Bath)

Opequon Creek

Shepherd's Town
(Mecklenburg)

Frederick

Harpers
Ferry

Charles Town

Potomac River

Winchester

Bullskin Run

Keyes Gap

Baltimore

Shenandoah River

Leesburg

Greenway
Court

Ashby's Gap

Blue Ridge Mts.

Great Falls

Georgetown

Annapolis

Falls
Church

Payne's
Church

Alexandria

Mount Vernon

Belvoir

Gunston
Hall

Port Tobacco
(Charlestown)

Patuxent River

Chesapeake

Rappahannock River

Culpeper
Court House

Rapidan River

Fredericksburg Ferry Farm

Potomac River

Port Royal

Popes Creek

Stratton Hall
Bushfield

Nomini Creek

Lower
Machodoc Lee Hall
Nomini Hall

Bay

North Anna River

Sabine Hall

Rappahannock River

South Anna River

Mattaponi River

Pamunkey River

Hanover
Court House

White
House

James River

River Falls Richmond

New Kent
Court House Eltham

West Point

Ware River

Chickahominy River

York River

Appomattox River

Shirley

Berkeley
Westover

Williamsburg

Jamestown

Arlington

Yorktown

Petersburg

James River

Hampton

WASHINGTON'S VIRGINIA

1761~1775

Smithfield

Dismal Swamp

Suffolk

Norfolk

Portsmouth
Great Bridge

Cape Henry

AN IMPERFECT GOD

The General's Dream

$\mathcal{B}$EFORE DAWN one summer morning at Mount Vernon, George Washington awoke from a troubling dream. It was 1799, the last year of the general's life, and he was finally savoring the fruits of retirement. But the serenity of that summer was abruptly shaken by the dream.

Martha had awakened first, and had just risen from the bed when Washington stirred and spoke to her. She could tell at a glance that an uncharacteristic sadness had settled upon her husband in the night.

He had dreamed, he told her, that they were sitting and talking about the happy life they had spent together and the many more years they would have in each other's company. In the dream "a great light" suddenly surrounded them; and from the light there emerged the barely visible figure of an angel, who stood at Martha's side and whispered in her ear. As the angel spoke, Martha "suddenly turned pale and then began to vanish from his sight and he was left alone."

The dream seemed to foretell that Martha would be taken from him, but Washington grasped a different meaning: he said to her, "You know, a contrary result indicated by dreams may be expected. I may soon leave you."[1]

Alarmed, Martha tried to comfort him by forcing a laugh at "the absurdity of being disturbed by an idle dream," but her efforts were in vain. The dream became "so deeply impressed on his mind that he could not shake it off for several days."

Washington was a fatalist; he feared nothing, not even death. If his time had come, then it had come. The grimness Martha discerned arose not from fear but from a seriousness of purpose. He took the dream as a sign that he had to settle certain accounts before time ran out. From some scraps of paper she came across in his study, Martha soon discovered that, in the wake of his troubling dream, her husband had begun to write his last will.*

"In the name of God amen I George Washington of Mount Vernon—a citizen of the United States, and lately President of the same, do make, ordain and declare this Instrument; which is written with my own hand and every page thereof subscribed with my name, to be my last Will & Testament, revoking all others." The document was eventually to run to twenty-nine pages and would carefully enumerate bequests to some fifty relatives—a tangled family tree that Washington, like all Southern patriarchs, kept committed to memory.[2]

In the first, one-sentence item, he provided for the needs of "my dearly beloved wife Martha Washington" for as long as she might live. But after this customary clause, Washington turned to the subject that clearly was uppermost in his mind, to which he had given a great deal of thought for a long time. With his next words George Washington renounced the system that had nurtured him and given him wealth: "Upon the decease of my wife, it is my Will & desire that all the Slaves which I hold in my *own right*, shall receive their freedom." After writing that plain declaration, Washington filled almost three pages with explicit instructions for the manner in which his slaves should be freed. He specified that the children should be educated and trained so that they could support themselves as free people.

It was an astounding decision. As he sat in his study—a room that one visitor called "the focus of political intelligence for the new world"—Washington felt the isolation of the man who can see what others cannot or will not. He was a man who had discovered that his

---

* He had written a will almost twenty-five years before, as he was preparing to take command of the Continental Army, and may have written another one. The final will was published several months after his death.

moral system was wrong. He had helped to create a new world but had allowed into it an infection that he feared would eventually destroy it.[3]

No other Founding Father would set his slaves free, and certainly none of them contemplated educating slaves as Washington did. The traditional planter's definition of benevolence presumed holding the slaves in humane but firm bondage, and the schooling that some favored slaves received was intended not to fit them for independence but to make them more useful to the master. To understand how extraordinary Washington's decision was, one has only to look at the pronouncements of other Southern Founding Fathers on the subject of slavery. A fellow Virginian, Patrick Henry, wrote of the slaves, "let us treat the unhappy Victims with lenity, it is the furthest advance we can make towards Justice." Thomas Jefferson scoffed at the very notion of emancipation: "To give liberty to, or rather, to abandon persons whose habits have been formed in slavery is like abandoning children." Washington thought otherwise.[4]

In his last months, Washington struggled with the paradox that continues to vex us today: how is it that the nation—conceived in liberty and dedicated to the proposition that all men are created equal—preserved slavery? The word "paradox" suggests abstraction, a debate in a gathering of bewigged white gentlemen. But Washington's will reveals that, in the stately chambers of Mount Vernon, his struggle over slavery was played out in a sharp family conflict.[5]

The emancipation clause stands out from the rest of Washington's will in the unique forcefulness of its language. Elsewhere in it Washington used the standard legal expressions—"I give and bequeath," "it is my will and direction." In one instance he politely wrote, "by way of advice, I recommend it to my Executors . . ." But the emancipation clause rings with the voice of command; it has the iron firmness of a field order: "I do hereby expressly forbid the Sale . . . of any Slave I may die possessed of, under any pretence whatsoever." This plainly implies that Washington expected that pretenses would be made and slaves would be sold once he was gone. Furthermore, Washington commanded his family "to see that *this* clause respecting Slaves, and every part thereof be religiously fulfilled . . . without evasion, neglect or delay" (the emphasis is Washington's). Nowhere else in the document did he speak with such vehemence. The force of his commands makes it clear that within his own family Washington was entirely alone in his thinking about slavery. He expected that the emancipation would come as a shock to his family and, moreover, he expected them to resist it. Washington was positioning himself as the protector of his slaves.*

Washington's emancipation of his slaves at Mount Vernon has long been dismissed as a mere parting grace note, of little significance except as a mark of his inherent benevolence. But the will hints at a profound moral struggle; indeed, his decision to free his slaves represented a repudiation of a lifetime of mastery. For his entire life he had been conditioned to be indifferent to the aspirations and humanity of African-Americans. Something happened to change him and to set him radically apart from his peers and his family.

Crossing the barrier into the past is treacherous, but the journey is doubly difficult if one is seeking to understand a man as elusive, as contradictory, but as critically important as George Washington. "As to the inner man we are strangely ignorant," one historian wrote, "no more elusive personality exists in history." A French visitor remarked, "an atmosphere of silence envelops the deeds of Washington." Even in his own time, Washington's achievement surrounded him with a blinding, almost divine radiance that made the man himself seem unapproachable. Watching him as he merely walked down the street, Abigail Adams could almost feel the ground tremble under the shoe of the man who appeared "as awful as a god." Once when he en-

---

* In any family the last will and testament is the ultimate instrument of control that one generation wields over another. Washington brandished it as effectively as anyone. Writing in September 1799 to a nephew, Lawrence Lewis, who was in line for a large bequest, Washington said, "I have not the most distant idea that any event will happen that could effect a change in my present determination, nor any suspicion that you [would] incur my serious displeasure." But he took care to point out that he had his will on the table beside him, readily available for emendation in case any serious displeasure arose.

tered a room full of his step-granddaughter's friends, apparently eager
for an informal chat, all conversation instantly ceased. The step-
granddaughter recalled that because of "the awe and respect he inspired . . . his own near relatives feared to speak or laugh before him."
On the occasions when his presence chilled a social event, "he would
sit a short time and then retire, quite provoked and disappointed."
Then and now his unique eminence arises from his sterling personal
qualities, from the inescapable fact that we Americans owe everything
we have to him, and from the eerie sense that, in him, some fragment
of divine Providence did indeed touch this ground.[6]

Washington's home on the Potomac, Mount Vernon, has been a
place of pilgrimage since his lifetime. More than a million people
come to Mount Vernon every year, seeking some clue to understanding the character of the distant figure at the core of the American endeavor. Washington designed Mount Vernon himself. The house and
every foot of its gardens and grounds present a view of the inner man
and the workings of his mind. (One visitor of Washington's time said
as much, remarking that "the good Order of its Masters Mind appears
extended to every Thing around it.") The house is the perfect mirror
of the man: it presents one puzzle after another. And it embodies a
basic contradiction—Mount Vernon is not the humble abode of a
democrat, but the manor house of a colonial potentate. Washington
lived privately in some grandeur and rural pomp, with a decidedly
British flavor; and yet he was the man who refused to be king, who in-
fused the ceremonies of republican government with plainness, who
left a legacy of presidential modesty.

When you approach Mount Vernon from its gate today you are
seeing it as a visitor would have in 1799. You are also seeing it the way
Washington wanted you to—from a distance, set back behind a long
greensward, the whole view framed by groves, which a visitor described as a "labyrinth of evergreens where the sun cannot . . . pene-
trate." The first view of the house was designed to impress the
onlooker, and it surely does. The numerous outbuildings that sur-
round the mansion call to mind the variety of labors that maintained
this estate—kitchen, storehouse, smokehouse, washhouse, stable,

coachhouse, overseer's quarters, ice house, greenhouse, and, farther off from the house, a gristmill and even a distillery. In itself this scene reveals the power of the occupant, who commanded so much work. Even in colonial times the scope of a planter's ownership could surprise outsiders, as it did a Frenchman who visited a Virginia plantation and remarked, "When I reached his place I thought I was entering a rather large village, but later was told that all of it belonged to him."[7]

The exterior surface of the house strangely has the texture of sandpaper. Washington ordered wooden weatherboarding to be cut, painted, and dusted with sand so that the boards would look exactly like blocks of stone. Stone was what British potentates used. He could not afford stone, but he wanted the look, and he got it, even if the monumental effect fades on close inspection and if the scheme is surprisingly un-American in its taste. One modern historian rather unkindly describes the house as "pretentious" and opines, "when Mount Vernon was seen in a haze of nostalgia after a bottle or two of Madeira, the woodwork turned to stone in the eyes of homesick Englishmen." Washington never visited England, but British style did form his frame of reference.[8]

The requirements of modern tourism compel visitors to enter the house in an apparently unusual but historically correct way, not through the front door but through a side door into a large dining room. This is just how guests at a semipublic event would have entered the house in Washington's time. The dining room is two stories in height, with an impressive Palladian window dominating one wall of the room. Washington chose to adorn the ceiling of this public room not with some heroic relief or constellation of classical symbols, but with images of tools. One looks up at his ceiling to find plaster scythes, shovels, and picks. The size of the room tells something about the owner's social station, but the room's real significance is that it symbolizes his unshakable optimism. Work had begun on the dining room, along with other improvements and enlargements around the house, just before Washington rode off to command the Revolutionary army. Like many, he hoped the war would be a short one; but even as the conflict dragged on year after dreary year, he sent orders for the work on his house to be kept up. He expected to see it again, larger and more handsome than it was when he left it. It was six years before he laid eyes on it again.

From the dining room one gets only a peek at a jewel-box chamber painted, at Washington's own choice, in an eye-popping shade called "Prussian blue." Now closed off by a velvet rope, this room was the family's West Parlor, where with special guests they sipped tea and played cards under the frowning brows of heavily carved paneling. Washington chose the patterns from British architectural books; the paneling added historical heft to his colonial outpost and created a room-sized frame for his gallery of family portraits. Here he placed the portrait of himself—done at Martha's earnest request—by Charles Willson Peale. This is the face which should, by rights, be on the dollar—it shows Washington in the uniform he wore as frontier commander in the French and Indian War, with marching orders stuffed in his pocket and a look of jaunty courage. Here he is every inch the man who wrote to his brother, "I heard Bullets whistle and believe me there was something charming in the sound." On another wall is a portrait of Martha at the age of twenty-six, done in dowdy fashion by the society painter John Wollaston, the favorite of the Virginia gentry for his ability to render in oils their importance, though their charm eluded him. Here also are the Custis children, Jacky and Patsy, whom Martha brought to Mount Vernon and whom Washington adopted as his own. Despite its museumlike atmosphere, Mount Vernon in its day was always home to young children—first the Custis children and then the grandchildren.[9]

This room neatly encapsulates Washington's social history—one might call it his Virginia Genealogy Room, though the grandest family connections belonged not to him but to Martha. As a Virginia historian wrote, "not even retroactively, not even after George became the absolute number one citizen of Virginia and the new nation, were the Washingtons ever included in the aristocracy."[10] His forebears were middling planters, but Washington's architectural tastes show his yearning to gain entry to the top tier for himself. His wife and her children, however, were already at the top. Martha's first husband was a Custis, whose mother had been a Parke: two names at the peak of colonial Virginia society. Martha's children and grandchildren carried the middle name Parke as a badge of their lineage and, no less important, to qualify them as heirs to an old Parke estate.* George Washington presided over a household of wealthy aristocrats, inheritors of a tradition that excluded Washington himself, no matter how grand his mansion might be. Another aspect of his life revealed in this room is the absence of portraits of Washington's own children. He and Martha were childless, and that failure saddened him.

Mount Vernon occupies two landscapes and straddles, as far as that is possible, two realms of time. The key to grasping the vision behind Washington's plan is the enormous view that unfolds from the piazza at the rear of the house. The land falls away below you into a massive landscape, with the Potomac River winding to infinity and forests stretching to the horizon. This was Washington's favorite spot, where he sat every afternoon, and this was the place one visitor, Abigail Adams, called Mount Vernon's "greatest adornment."[11] Behind you, forgotten now, is the clipped and calculated paradise of the colonial Virginia gentleman. Before you stretches an open and endless prospect, encompassing anything the world could send it—a view not of the past but of the future. The genius of the house and of its builder is most fully felt here; this eighteenth-century artifact, and its creator, still speak so powerfully today because they frame this view of the future.

The future Washington envisioned for this house, after he was gone, was one without slavery. That is the ultimate contradiction of Mount Vernon. The place we see today, beautifully restored, is a place Washington wished to see, in part, dismantled. Of course he wished that it would endure, but on a different foundation.

There is a spot at Mount Vernon where one can stand today and see a revealing remnant of the system that Washington rejected. I had

---

* Pride in one's lineage crossed racial boundaries: a mixed-race family descended illegitimately from the Custises also used Parke as a middle name.

passed the place many times without realizing what I was looking at. Like so much about slavery, something important was carefully concealed while standing in plain sight, because it had been disguised. While strolling through the elegant garden at Mount Vernon, I paused to admire the majestic Greenhouse that Washington designed himself. Here, Washington grew oranges, so exotic and precious they were regarded as "the fruit of kings." In his time, "possession of a greenhouse [implied] that we have scaled the heights of power . . . that we have almost allegorical control over the natural universe," as the garden historian Mac Griswold has written.[12] On one side, the Greenhouse faces the Upper Garden, where Washington liked to take guests for a stroll down paths bordered with boxwood and flowerbeds. Then and now, someone walking through the elegant garden and admiring the majestic Greenhouse would not know that the wings extending from the sides of the building, providing architectural balance and harmony, were slave barracks.

The barracks opened to the rear, and on the garden side there were no doors nor windows large enough to afford a glimpse at the interior. So when Washington's guests strolled past the Greenhouse they saw no sign that these long, handsome brick wings housed the plantation's slaves. Washington had devised an architecture that rendered slavery invisible, while at the same time weaving slavery into the fabric of his grand design. It was a brilliant, chilling stroke of architectural inspiration.

Built of brick and attached to one of the most prominent buildings on the estate, the barracks signify the permanence of slavery. At one time Washington envisioned that slavery would be part of the fabric of Mount Vernon's future and America's future. Slavery would be not merely accommodated but embraced and transformed into a beautiful, imposing symbol of status and "control over the natural universe." The Greenhouse is a vestige of the system Washington eventually rejected. He built it and then he emptied it.

In our time Mount Vernon has felt the reverberations of the thunderclap that struck Monticello, Thomas Jefferson's mountaintop home to the south, when DNA testing of Jefferson's descendants and descendants of his slave Sally Hemings indicated that Jefferson was most likely the father of Hemings's children. To many people, that revelation in 1998 came with as much shock as the discovery of a new continent. If we thought we had fully mapped our world, we were wrong. In the wake of the Jefferson-Hemings revelation, descendants of Washington's slaves came forward to ask for their own DNA testing. Their oral tradition, they said, had long held that their black forebear, a slave named West Ford, was the son of George Washington and a slave named Venus. While this information was not exactly new—it had long been known to the Ford descendants and to some scholars— it emerged forcefully into public view at a moment when it seemed that a single new nugget of information could, overnight, completely change our view of a major historical figure.

Oral history is very difficult to interpret, and while a story may contain obvious errors, that does not mean that it can be summarily dismissed. In the matter of West Ford, the documentary evidence is ambiguous, but there is virtually no doubt he was kin to the first president.

George and Martha Washington had other relatives in their slave community as well. A few months into my research on Washington I came across information that Martha had a half sister who was black, whose family remained close to the Washington and Custis families at least until the 1850s. The relationship was hardly secret—it was described in detail in a Congressional document published in 1871. Some might see such revelations as scandalous; I see them as windows into a past we are struggling to understand.

To consider Washington in connection with slavery challenges the myth of Washington as the perfect secular god. The biographer Douglas Southall Freeman wrestled with this issue when he wrote in 1948, "The integrity of the United States was assumed, for some reason, to presuppose the flawlessness of Washington's character. Complete faith in him was part of the creed of loyalty."[13] On the one hand, the myth of Washington hides a great deal—his pride, his ambition, his acquisitiveness (some might call it greed), and his willingness to subordinate the weak to his ambition. But on the other hand, the myth does not do him justice, for he transformed himself, shedding his ambition and his self-seeking, to bring liberty to a people who were exasperatingly indifferent and reluctant to share sacrifice. It has been said that he was bedeviled by feelings of inadequacy, perhaps resulting from his difficult relationship with his mother and the absence of a father. Certainly he was keenly aware of his lack of education. But against this he threw a relentless drive for attainment and a habit of discipline. In his young adulthood this drive had no other object beyond his own aggrandizement. When he committed himself to the patriot cause, this drive, this discipline, this single-mindedness helped win the nation its independence. Toward the end of his life he grappled with the problem of slavery. His wrenching private conflict over race and slavery was a microcosm of the national struggle—one that is not yet over.

CHAPTER ONE

Home Ground

*H*ARDLY HAD I BEGUN my research when I discovered that collateral descendants of Washington still live in Virginia. There is almost always something to be learned from meeting descendants of your subject—they have fragments of lore to pass on, documents bypassed by other researchers, echoes of old mannerisms. So when this family extended an invitation to visit I leaped at the opportunity. Like many ancient Virginia families, this branch of the Washington clan remains rooted to the soil. They live on an estate called Blenheim adjacent to the spot where George Washington was born. The birthplace is a National Monument, a weighty designation that lies like a tombstone over the past, but almost within shouting distance Washington's relatives are still there, doing what he would be doing, farming the land.

George Washington is so firmly associated with Mount Vernon that many people assume he was born there. In fact his birthplace lies some sixty-five miles downriver in a part of Virginia known as the Northern Neck, a finger of land fifty-two miles long and ten miles wide between the Potomac and Rappahannock rivers. At the time of Washington's birth in 1732 the Neck was one of the most important regions in the colony—home to some of its richest and most influential families—but it began to lose population in midcentury as its tobacco fields became depleted. By the late 1700s the population of Westmoreland County, where Washington was born, had dwindled to about half of what it had been at the end of the 1600s. As in so many parts of the South, economic decline preserved the world of long ago. Today the land is still rural, the houses of the colonial tobacco barons still stand, and descendants of the original families still live on the ancestral acres.

As I drove east from Fredericksburg toward Blenheim, the suburbs dwindled and the road shrank to a two-lane blacktop fringed with fields and forests, the landscape of Washington's time. Today we travel alone, at high speed, encapsulated in vehicles that take us to our destinations with minimal interaction with anything outside the glass. Not so in Washington's time. Travelers, if they seemed a decent sort, were eagerly welcomed at private homes as bearers of news or, at least, breakers of the rural monotony. Virginia hospitality was such, said one visitor, that it was "possible to travel through the whole country without money." If one offered to pay one's hosts for the night's stay, they were "rather angry, asking whether one did not know the custom of the country." An eighteenth-century English traveler named Andrew Burnaby described the effect that the heat and lushness of the American southland had on his former countrymen: "the climate and external appearance of the country conspire to make them indolent, easy, and good-natured: extremely fond of society, and much given to convivial pleasures."[1]

In the 1700s a traveler of the common sort would doff his hat and bow if he encountered a well-born gentleman on horseback. Such gentlemen stood out not only because of their fine clothes but because of their peculiar, damn-you-get-out-of-the-way gallop. There were many such potentates on the Neck, but none could match Robert Carter, who bounced along the road in a gilded carriage. The possessor of a thousand slaves and 300,000 acres of land, Carter was easily the wealthiest man in Virginia. His power earned him the appellation "King" Carter. Though Carter's enormous house on the Northern Neck, Corotoman, is long gone, he did leave behind one of Virginia's most enigmatic architectural treasures: the jewel-like Christ Church near the eastern end of the Neck. No one knows who designed it, but the anonymous architect created a profoundly spiritual structure—an apparently simple brick construct whose soaring interior makes the mind leap toward the eternal.*[2]

Churches such as this one also served as the focus of temporal power. Attendance at Sunday services was required of all by law, and all heads of households were taxed to support the church. The church's governing body, the vestry, had quasi-public functions, including unusual police powers. The churchwardens, naturally, kept an eye out for those who neglected to attend services. These miscreants were reported to the county court (reporting was simple because vestrymen usually served as the county justices as well) and fined, with the proceeds going to the support of the church. Since churches provided support for orphans and abandoned children, churchwardens were always alert for the births of illegitimate children who might become an expense for the church. The wardens hauled the mothers into court, where they were duly fined. The churches, formally and informally, were depots of local gossip, news, and official pronouncements. Runaway slaves could be "outlawed," meaning that they were thenceforth outside the protection of the law and could legally be killed with impunity, because they had ceased to exist as far as the law was concerned. Notices identifying outlaws were customarily nailed to the door of the church where all would see them, and where they became a sharp symbol of the distinction between the saved and the damned.[3]

One aspect of Christ Church's design is deeply symbolic of the era. The seating does not consist of rows of pews, but of twenty-two rectangular, high-backed stalls, each designated for a particular family, with the Carters having the largest one. Families came in with their servants and slaves and sat together in isolation from the other congregants. The minister preached from a raised pulpit that allowed him to look down on his flock while they gazed up at him. In Washing-

---

* One local man spent years measuring the building, the shadows it casts, and the movement of sunlight through it at the various seasons, concluding that the structure had been designed according to abstruse Masonic formulas. Armed with tape measure and notepad, he was an intriguing figure; tourists took him for a staffer and asked questions, prompting off-the-cuff disquisitions on the curious history of the place that would inevitably attract a knot of listeners, to the annoyance of the officials who ran the site. Eventually they banned him from the property.

ton's Virginia, family determined one's place and one's identity, even in relation to the Creator. The family was the engine of wealth and power. The Carters had their stall enclosed in a curtain so that ordinary folk could not even lay eyes on them as they worshiped.

In Washington's time Virginians were already obsessed with what we might call practical genealogy. This grew out of the need for keeping mental track of distant cousins for legal purposes. All these people had to be kept in mind when one was drawing up a deed or a will, or dividing slaves (recall that Washington made mention of more than fifty relatives in his will). Kinship with an old-line family of substance and influence conferred prestige on the lesser relations. Thus, as one historian wrote, "the gentry of Virginia studied one another's genealogies as closely as a stockman would scrutinize his stud books." When an English visitor asked for advice on getting along in the colony, a Virginian strongly cautioned him against offending any "person of note." By way of explanation he added, "either by blood or marriage, we are almost all related, and so connected in our interests, that whoever of a stranger presumes to offend any one of us will infallibly find an enemy of the whole. Nor, right or wrong, do we forsake him, till by one means or other his ruin is accomplished." At the top level of Virginia society and government the entanglements were almost incestuous: in 1724 all twelve members of Virginia's Royal Council were related by blood or marriage.[4]

King Carter founded a dynasty numbered among the "FFVs"— First Families of Virginia. (Carter's son Landon became George Washington's political mentor.) His children intermarried with other leading families and established Carter outposts across the Tidewater. Alongside the Carters, the other pillar of the Northern Neck in Washington's time was the Lee family. The Lees lived in Stratford Hall, just a few miles east of the Washingtons. Their massive brick mansion, with the look of a fortress, still stands on its magnificent site atop bluffs over the Potomac. (The Lees' earlier home was burned to the ground in 1729 by convicts sent from England to be American servants.) Despite its formidable appearance, the house was designed for the lavish, large-scale entertainments of which Virginians were so fond. Parties lasted for days, featuring horse races, boat races, music, dancing, and reckless gambling.

The builder of Stratford was Thomas Lee (1690–1750), whose position as head of the colony's Royal Council allowed Lee to style himself "President of Virginia." With a sharp nose, high forehead, and piercing eyes, he possessed a visage that was both exceedingly handsome—he may have been one of the few men of the eighteenth century who actually looked good wearing the flowing wig of high office—and unbearably proud. He passed the Lee pride in abundance to one of his sons, who was said to possess "a haughtiness peculiar to himself . . . being in the superlative degree to any I had ever beheld, even in this Country," by which the speaker meant Virginia.[5]

In 1744 Lee journeyed from Stratford to Lancaster, Pennsylvania, to negotiate with the Iroquois for the purchase of an enormous inland empire—territory that would form the future states of Kentucky, Ohio, Indiana, Illinois, Wisconsin, Michigan, and part of Minnesota—all for about $400 in cash and gifts. With a group of other Virginians Lee founded the Ohio Company to settle and exploit this tract. Thereafter, Ohio Valley land speculation became the dream and the bane of Virginians, including George Washington. His half brother Lawrence served as president of the Ohio Company, and as a Virginia militia officer young George went into the wilderness to bully the French into leaving the territory that Lee had purchased, and ended up starting the French and Indian War. Two of Thomas Lee's sons signed the Declaration of Independence (the only brothers to do so).

For generations the Lees did business with the Washingtons, competed with them for land, and intermarried with them. The Lee-Washington relationship is fraught with historical ironies. During the Revolution, Henry "Light-Horse Harry" Lee caught George Washington's eye with a dashing victory over British forces in New Jersey. The two became close friends, and Henry Lee delivered the famous eulogy of Washington before Congress: "First in war, first in peace, and first in the hearts of his countrymen." Lee and Washington shared a commitment to a strong national union and central government. After the Revolution Lee invested rashly in real estate and fell so catastrophically into debt that he chained shut the doors of Stratford Hall to keep out the creditors. At Stratford on January 19, 1807, Lee's wife, Ann, gave birth to their fifth child, Robert E. Lee, in an atmosphere of financial gloom—she left the house to reside with her relations. Ann was a Carter, a great-granddaughter of King Carter. Robert E. Lee connected the Lee and Carter lines with the Washington and Custis lineage when he married George and Martha Washington's great-granddaughter, Mary Custis.

Blenheim was hard to find. The only landmark I had to go on was a mailbox by the side of the road, and I sailed right past it. When I corrected my mistake I ended up on what seemed a road to nowhere, a narrow graveled trace that burrowed through a tunnel of trees and vines, curving this way and that as it followed the course of a stream. The outlines of a house reared up on the left. This was not the historic Washington house but a newer one (newer being nineteenth-century) occupied by the younger generation. Blenheim lay somewhere farther down the twisting road.

A man emerged from this house, and I watched closely as he approached. It was said by Ralph Waldo Emerson that "every man is a quotation from all his ancestors"; I wondered if this man quoted any inherited Washingtonian vestiges.[6] I was braced for a dose of the haughtiness I had experienced at other Southern ancestral homes. His family was descended in a female line from George's half brother Augustine "Austin" Washington, whose son William Augustine had built Blenheim (and was bequeathed a sword by George Washington). This property had passed into a female Washington line when William Augustine's great-granddaughter married a Latané. My host was Larry Washington Latané.

A trim, soft-spoken man in his thirties, Larry displayed no godlike traits at first glance or any patrician airs, but he quickly reverted to ancestral form by inviting me to have a look at his garden. George Washington's guests at Mount Vernon were invariably taken to see the general's garden; special guests were taken to the outlying farms.

Likewise, Larry gave me a tour of his plantings. He wrote for the *Richmond Times-Dispatch* but also cultivated a large organic garden, selling his vegetables to restaurants in Washington, D.C. Like his collateral ancestor, he could not separate himself from agriculture and had chosen the purest way of pursuing it. Unlike his ancestor, who depended on the labor of slaves, this Washington planted and tended the land himself.

Three generations of the Latané family, counting Larry's children, resided on the Blenheim property. In short order Larry's parents drove up from the Blenheim house down the road. A grizzled, stocky man, Lawrence Sr. spoke with the old Virginia accent, which has a Scottish tone that makes "outside the house" sound like "ootside the hoose." He outlined a Virginian's plan for a visit: we would go to see the family cemetery.

The Washington family cemetery was on a farm that had once been owned by another branch of the family, who had sold it some time ago while retaining title to the cemetery and the right to visit it. As we approached the graveyard, Lawrence Sr. told how they had almost lost it. The farm had been purchased by a family from up North who didn't like the idea that a patch of useful land was being taken up with a graveyard. He got wind of the new owner's intentions from a workman: "A man came to me and said, 'That new man that bought the place wants to bulldoze the cemetery.' So I had to go up there and get him straight." Having failed to bulldoze the Washington cemetery, the new owner then asked if he could be buried in it. Lawrence declined to extend him that honor and made a point of visiting the cemetery more often just to keep his eye on it.

An iron fence surrounded the graves, at the end of a large field. A house called Campbellton once stood just a short distance away, but it had burned down in the 1920s. A line of trees screened the field and the cemetery from view, so the gravestones had escaped the vandalism that often befalls isolated country burial grounds. Lawrence tugged open the iron gate. As he took me through the place I was struck by its evidence that the family of the Founding Father had firmly embraced the cause of the rebellion in the Civil War.

"Here is a son who lived at Blenheim," Lawrence said as we paused at the stone for Richard Washington, who died July 6, 1863. When we scraped some dirt from the bottom of the stone we unearthed the inscription: *Killed in Action at Hagerstown in the Retreat from Gettysburg.* Lawrence pointed to the next stone: "Here's another Civil War man, the son of Sarah Tayloe Washington. He was a lieutenant colonel, I think, in the Ninth Virginia Cavalry." Nearby was the stone for John Tayloe, whose story Lawrence also knew. "He was a prisoner held on a gunboat. They were coming down the Rappahannock and the captain saw that he was nearly dead, so they put him ashore opposite his house, which is a mile inland, and he died after he got home. Now here's a man who was a cadet at VMI in the Battle of New Market. And then he joined Mosby and stayed with him the whole war. Those Mosby men—they put up with something; it was tough." Mosby's cavalry was a legendary Confederate guerrilla unit. Mosby himself became known as the Grey Ghost, because the Union army could never figure out how to catch him after his devastating raids.

William Latané, a cavalryman killed heroically in 1863, also ascended into Confederate legend. His kinsman William D. Washington painted a sentimental scene of his funeral, titled *The Burial of Latané.* Engravings of the painting graced the walls of parlors throughout the postbellum South: its depiction of faithful slaves laying the fallen hero to rest perfectly expressed Lost Cause nostalgia for plantation life. It was not, however, painted from reality, but from a fantasy. William Washington depicted the scene in a Richmond studio during the war, recruiting a number of Richmond's society women to serve as his models. The completed canvas was displayed in the state capitol, becoming such an inspiration for Confederate patriotism that a receptacle was placed in front of it for people who wished to contribute to the war effort.

We stopped at the grave of a Washington who lived to be ninety. Lawrence remembered him from his childhood. "He was a real strong man, very powerful. All these old Washingtons were six feet four and weighed over two hundred pounds. They were tall and real powerful." That was a fair description of George Washington himself, who boasted that he had tossed a stone to the top of Natural Bridge, a stone arch in the Blue Ridge Mountains that is 215 feet above the ground. Washington was so enthralled by the bridge that he cut his initials into it, a manly *G.W.* still visible today.

But there were also graves of children. We found one who lived to the age of six, two others to the age of one. "They came down with typhoid and died," Lawrence said. "They died young in those days."

On the way back from the cemetery Lawrence Sr. abruptly began talking about something he had recently discovered. It was the kind of story one would expect the family to keep private, but looking at the grave markers seemed to have put him in a mood to bring certain things into the open. He had a conversation with a black man from the area, he said, someone he had known almost all his life. The man told Lawrence that he had inherited land given to his father by Lawrence's grandmother. Lawrence said the only conclusion he could draw was that one of his forebears had fathered a black child and that the family had given him land to help get him established. The black man, who had long been an acquaintance, was actually his relative. In Lawrence's mind there was no other explanation for the gift. No explanation was needed for Lawrence's belated discovery of his connection to a black family—such matters were seldom if ever spoken about in white families, though the black families knew the whole story and plain evidence of the connection could be found in the public land records at the courthouse, if one cared to look. As he related the story Lawrence betrayed no hint of resentment that this part of his family history had been revealed to him by a black man, and he obviously thought it important that I should know about this: he brought up the subject unasked.

We left the cemetery and drove to Blenheim, a plain two-story house in the common Virginia style of the Revolutionary era, but with large historic resonance. It was built from the bricks of the house where George Washington was born. His birth home burned on Christmas Day, 1779, when sparks from the chimney set fire to cotton stored in the attic. The owner at the time, George's nephew William Augustine Washington, had his slaves gather up the bricks from the ruined house and build a new home on this spot, farther inland. William Augustine built Blenheim a good mile from the Potomac, which seemed odd, since almost all their commerce and communication depended on the river. But as Lawrence Sr. explained, "they built it back in here because the British were shelling the houses along the river."

Blenheim went up at the same time George Washington was expanding Mount Vernon. When I saw the unadorned brick structure I realized just how far George Washington had come to be able to build Mount Vernon so lavishly. I was also struck by the rootedness of these old families. The Latanés had at one point sold this land and this house, but then Lawrence Sr. wanted it back, and when he acquired the house in the 1960s it had been reduced almost to a wreck. The walls still stood but the previous owners had left the interior in tatters. Latané went to work slowly rebuilding it all, though he carefully left one wall along a staircase unfinished so that he could always see the original beams put up by his ancestors. As we walked around the place we came upon a brick that bore a date, 1726, the year Washington's father expanded his house at Popes Creek in anticipation of the birth of more children.

"There was a slave house up in here, but it's long gone, all rotted away," Lawrence said. Larry pointed out a distant hedgerow where the cabin had once stood. Lightning had struck near this spot twice, Lawrence said, first blowing a chimney to bits and then splintering a walnut tree.

Inside, we were looking at family photographs when Mrs. Latané pulled out an old book. "Here's something I thought you might be interested in. See, they list some of the slaves."

We laid it out flat on the dining-room table and carefully turned the pages. It was the plantation's ledger from the 1850s. There were accounts of payments made to slaves for doing extra work, reports of the weather and of struggles with drought, notes on crop sales. One strange item stood alone. As we turned the pages we came to a sheet that was blank except for a few words written upside down at the bottom. We slid the book around and saw that it was a brief notation of a slave woman's giving birth. It was the only such record in the book. Records of African-American births and marriages had often been written that way by whites even after emancipation and even by public officials. They seemed to file black records upside down quite deliberately: they would keep the records in the same books as the white records but would not mix the two. It was as if they inhabited the same place, but existed in different dimensions.

Larry had another document he wanted to show me. Some years ago he had gone to the Westmoreland County courthouse in Montross to look at some of the old deeds and wills of the Washington family. All these records, which document the continuity of titles to land and property, are written into enormous books stored in the courthouse basement. Larry found the "Inventory and Apraisement of the personal Estate of William A. Washington deceased," submitted to the Westmoreland County Court in October 1811. It listed all his property, from a $100 cherry bedstead to a coffee pot worth 25 cents. The combined value of his personal property and livestock came to a little over $5,000. Then the assessors counted the slaves. They listed ninety-five people by name, giving their ages and values. In some cases the assessors listed the people by family units, such as Spencer, age 25, his wife Charity, age 30, and their two children Warner, age 6, and Billy, 2. The most valuable slave was the plantation's blacksmith, named Daniel, who was worth $600. The value of all the slaves came to about $21,800.

All of this was perfectly ordinary—the legal confirmation of the transfer of slaves and other personal property from one generation to another. I had seen many such documents in the papers of old Southern families. But in the margin the executor had scribbled an explanatory note about two of the slaves, and as I read it I began to understand the undertone of panic in George Washington's will.

James & Cary were exhibited for sale at Port Royal on 15th Jan~y 1811 but . . . no bidder could be found—James died 12th Feb~y at Haywood

I looked in the inventory for the names of James and Cary. I found that they were husband and wife, valued at $60 each, and that Cary was fifty-five years old and James was sixty. What the executor had done was to bring an elderly couple, who had given a lifetime of labor to the Washingtons, to the auction block. They were so old as to be worthless—"no bidder could be found"—and James was so feeble he died less than a month later. This was precisely the kind of act that George Washington so strenuously forbade in his will. I could begin to see that Washington had been so emphatic because he knew the hard-heartedness of the planters—even the people of his own family. He knew the flinty indifference that would allow someone to display two elderly people on the auction block in the hope of netting $120.

George Washington was indeed a quotation of his ancestors. The outlines of his early life bear a remarkable resemblance to those of his earliest American forebear, John Washington. George was a fourth-generation American whose family had built up a middling plantation enterprise on the Northern Neck with modest slaveholdings. His first American forebear was delivered to these shores in story-book fashion—washed up by a sudden squall on the Potomac. Washington's great-grandfather John was serving as a mate on the ketch *Sea Horse of London,* which plied a tobacco route from England to northern European ports (Danzig and Copenhagen) and thence to Virginia. After delivering cargoes to planters along the Potomac, the *Sea Horse* was heavily laden with tobacco for the voyage home when it grounded on a sandbar early in 1657. A storm blew in, capsizing the little vessel. John Washington set to work with the crew on the long task of righting and repairing the ship. In the meantime he made the acquaintance of Nathaniel Pope, who owned the spectacular cliffs on the Potomac's southern shore. John impressed both Nathaniel and his daughter Ann, so when the ketch was again seaworthy it left without its mate, who married Ann Pope a year or so later.

The young couple may have been smitten with one another, but the marriage choice of a wealthy Virginian's daughter was, at that time, not determined by love. The evidence points to a business arrangement advantageous to all the interested parties. John Washington could read and write; Nathaniel Pope could not. Washington knew the international tobacco trade firsthand; Pope was eager to increase his share in this commerce. As a wedding gift, Nathaniel bestowed 700 acres of land on his daughter, and he advanced John a loan of £80 to get him started. In this fashion, the Washington line planted its roots in Virginia.[7]

The machinery of English law was well established in colonial Virginia, and the records of the county courts present some of the richest documents we have for understanding the era. The proceedings of these local courts occasionally read like a racy crime blotter—especially since the courts often hauled in couples caught in fornication—but for the most part a county's judicial *Orders* are a mind-numbing catalog of real-estate transactions and suits for debt.

The profuse litigations over debt reveal a tight web of obligation among people high and low. No one could plant a crop without credit. Commoners went to the homes of their betters to obtain tools, seed, livestock, and other supplies, promising to pay in tobacco notes or wheat at harvest. The gentleman planters did the same thing on a larger scale with their London merchants. Year by year all grew more deeply obligated to each other in a great chain of debt. If a lowly tenant displeased the planter who had extended him credit he would suddenly find his loan had been called and he would lose all he had.[8]

The keys to prosperity were the tobacco leaf and the deed of land; producing the former was the means of obtaining more of the latter. With more people coming to Virginia all the time, land speculation was the real route to riches for the next century. George Washington himself said, "the greatest estates we have in this Colony" were acquired "by taking up and purchasing at very low rates the rich back lands which were thought nothing of in those days." Because "the rich back lands" largely came into the possession of wealthy planters, the western Virginia frontier did not beckon to the poor and landless as a place of opportunity.[9]

The method of land distribution in Virginia led to striking economic inequalities. About 10 percent of the adult males controlled 50–

75 percent of the colony's productive assets. The yeomen freeholders who owned their own land and worked it with one or two servants or slaves made up only 20–30 percent of the population. The economic and social bottom was very large: 60–70 percent of Virginia's males owned no land at all. They included tenant farmers, followed by the lowest stratum of slaves, servants, and poor white laborers. This pattern of land ownership contrasted sharply with the more equal ownership of property in New England. According to the historian David Hackett Fischer, "Throughout the Puritan colonies, the middle class of yeoman farmers and artisans made up the great majority of the population. Slaves, servants and tenants were very few." In Virginia, however, "a large proportion of land grants . . . were awarded by the Council to its own members and their kin. . . . In Massachusetts, access to the land was controlled by men of middling status who used it to reproduce families of their own rank. In Virginia, the distribution of land was dominated by an elite who employed it to maintain their own hegemony. The authority of Virginia's first families rested in part on this material base."[10]

John Washington combined a fortunate marriage with a head for real-estate speculation. In partnership with his brother-in-law, he imported sixty-three indentured servants. For each servant they brought in, the partners could claim a "headright" of fifty acres. In this manner, and by purchase, Washington himself became owner of a patchwork of tracts amounting to some five thousand acres. His largest single land acquisition, in 1674, was at Hunting Creek on the Potomac. This would later be Mount Vernon.

As John Washington was amassing his landholdings, Ann died in 1668, having borne five children. At that time life spans were so short and remarriages so common that Virginians devised the term "now-wife" to designate the current wife, as opposed to former or future wives.[11] The Washingtons had use for the term. In keeping with the custom of the time and place, John quickly remarried. He wedded a twice-over widow, Anne Brett, and when this second Anne died, he married her sister, the already thrice-married Frances Appleton. Thus the union of John and Frances Washington represented the culmination of eight marriages altogether. From his second marriage John had harvested a significant hoard of real estate, including ownership of the prison and court house of Westmoreland County. In those days, in the choice of a spouse, property trumped propriety: the sisters whom John married in succession had both been accused in county court (in a case heard by John—he could not plead ignorance) of whorish behavior. John himself came under a more serious cloud of suspicion: it was alleged he had allowed or actually participated in the murder of five Indians.[12]

John Washington began to acquire influence quickly, gaining entry to a class of colonials described this way by an English official: "in every river of this province there are men in number from ten to thirty, who by trade and industry have gotten very competent estates. Those gentlemen take care to supply the poorer sort with goods and necessaries, and are sure to keep them always in their debt, and consequently dependent on them. Out of this number are chosen His Majesty's Council, the Assembly, the Justices, and Officers of Government."[13] John fit the pattern almost exactly: he represented Westmoreland County in the House of Burgesses, served as a lieutenant colonel in the county militia, a county justice of the peace, and a vestryman of his parish, which was named after him. All of this presaged the early career of George Washington, who held the same local posts a century later—burgess, gentleman justice, and vestryman, with a colonelcy not in the county but in the Virginia militia.

This similarity was no accident. In every generation of the family, from the arrival of John to the ascendancy of his great-grandson George, Washingtons held prominent positions in the local government and parish. There existed an interlocking directorate of local governing bodies whose members all did business with one another and were very often related. Every son learned from his father the critical importance of keeping one's hand on the levers of local power. Whether the sons acquired this hereditary wisdom from observation or from plow-side chats, we don't know, but we do know that they absorbed the lesson well. George was literally schooled in the mechanics of government and plantation management in his early teen years.

His exercise book from that period survives, containing "Forms of Writing." Young George laboriously copied out twenty-eight "forms," all of which were legal or financial documents of one kind or another. They included a "Receipt for a Hogshead of Tobacco," "A General Release by a Minor to the Administrators on his father's estate," a land patent, a warrant, a bail bond, and a contract between a master and an indentured servant.[14]

George Washington had much in common with his ancestor John. Both were gifted, ambitious, restless young men eager to advance in the world. Both managed to improve their situation by marrying women of property from families more prominent than their own. John firmly established himself by his alliance with the Popes and then married, one after the other, the sisters who may have been "whorish" in their ways but had real estate to compensate. In his time George would catch the greatest prize in the bridal sweepstakes, the very wealthy widow Martha Dandridge Custis.

A string of tragic deaths nearly removed George Washington's line from these shores. John died, probably of typhoid fever, in 1677 at the age of forty-six. His will bequeathed the bulk of his estate to his firstborn child, Lawrence, who died in 1698 at age thirty-eight. These two relatively early deaths set a pattern that would later haunt George Washington—he knew that he came from short-lived people. Lawrence's widow remarried, departed for England with her three children and new husband, and promptly died, touching off a legal crisis. The new husband tried to claim his late wife's Washington inheritance and keep everything in England, but the late Lawrence's brother brought suit in Virginia to recover the Washington property and children. Now the Washingtons' local connections came into play. Undoubtedly moved by sympathy for the Washingtons, the justices of Westmoreland County set history back on its course by ordering that the three Washington orphans—including Augustine "Gus" Washington—be returned from England to Virginia. Either in 1715 or 1716 Gus married Jane Butler, daughter of a Westmoreland planter, who gave his daughter a dowry of 1,300 acres. In 1718 their first son, Lawrence, was born, followed two years later by Augustine, Jr., who would be known as Austin—both of whom would be important in George's life. After Jane Butler Washington died in 1729, Gus married Mary Ball, also of a Westmoreland County family. George, their first child, came into the world on February 11, 1732, at Popes Creek, the family's plantation on the Potomac.*

Gus Washington stood six feet tall and was remembered as being "of noble appearance, and most manly proportions, with the extraordinary development of muscular power for which his son was afterward so remarkable." His strength was such that he could "raise up and place in a wagon a mass of iron that two ordinary men could barely raise from the ground," and yet he gained a reputation "for the mildness, courtesy, and amiability of his manners."[15]

The Washington family moved among three different homes by the time George was seven years old, which might explain his later intense attachment to Mount Vernon. They left Popes Creek when George was three (but retained ownership of the place), lived for a while at the future site of Mount Vernon, and then settled in Fredericksburg at Ferry Farm. Augustine Washington died when George was only eleven, in circumstances eerily predictive of his son's death: he fell fatally ill in 1743 after catching a chill in a sudden downpour while riding his horse. The father's sudden demise, at the age of forty-nine, fit the pattern of early deaths among male Washingtons. Later in life George had but a foggy memory of his father. He was heard to say, "that he knew little of his father, other than a remembrance of his person, and of his parental fondness."[16]

Augustine's death left Mary Ball Washington with five children to look after. At age eleven George was the oldest child in the Ferry Farm household. Lawrence and Austin, the sons of Augustine's first wife, were off on their own. Upon George's shoulders would have fallen the tasks of keeping the household running and of keeping up his mother's spirits along with his own. His father's death ended any

---

* George was born while the so-called Old Style calendar was still in use; when the English calendar was reformed in 1752, all dates moved by eleven days and Washington's birthday fell on February 22.

hope George had of obtaining the English education his older half brothers had completed.

Mary Washington's influence on her son may be seen in Washington's strict self-discipline and abhorrence of waste—traits that might well have been drilled into him by a widowed mother suddenly left in pinched circumstances. One of the Washington cousins later gave a description of Mary and claimed that the general's daunting manner came from her: "Whoever has seen that awe-inspiring air and manner so characteristic in the Father of his Country, will remember the matron . . . the presiding genius of her well-ordered household, commanding and being obeyed." The cousin added, "of the mother I was ten times more afraid than I ever was of my own parents." In her presence, he said, the Washington sons, "proper tall fellows . . . were all mute as mice."[17]

One of Washington's early biographers, Mason Locke Weems (better known as Parson Weems), told the story of a very young George taking a whack at his father's prized cherry tree and then bravely admitting it with the immortal phrase *I can't tell a lie.* (Weems's sermonish version has been garbled in the endless retelling: Weems did not write that George cut down the cherry tree, only that he skinned off a bit of bark.[18]) Debunkers have swarmed over the tale, and we have been relentlessly taught that this story, the one thing everyone knows about the childhood of George Washington, is not true. But there is a twist: the most important part of the story might indeed be true.

A story was passed down in the Washington and Custis families that is remarkably close in spirit and theme to the account by Parson Weems. Martha's grandson, George Washington Parke Custis, wrote a series of magazine articles that were collected and published in 1860 as *Recollections and Private Memoirs of Washington.* Since Custis had grown up at Mount Vernon and had known the hero personally, this 600-page work remains a valuable source of information on Washington's life. Tucked into the *Recollections* is a story of a teenaged Washington who tested his strength and skill against a "vicious" horse, a sorrel with "a fierce and ungovernable nature" that no one could ride or even bridle.[19]

Early one morning Washington's friends decoyed the horse into a pen, tied him, and forced a bit into his mouth. George leaped on the horse's back and gave the word to release. The sorrel flew from the pen, bucking madly. In Custis's account, "the struggle now became terrific to the beholders," who regretted their rashness and began to fear that the struggle was "likely to be fatal to their daring associate." Fatal it was, but to the horse not the rider. "The gallant horse, summoning all his powers to one mighty effort, reared, and plunged with tremendous violence, burst his noble heart, and died in an instant."* No sooner had the struggle ended than the young men were summoned to breakfast by Mrs. Washington. Knowing that they had been rambling around the distant pastures of the farm, she asked them how her horses were doing that morning. The embarrassed silence at the table was broken by George: "Your favorite, the sorrel, is dead, madam. . . . I rode him, and in a desperate struggle for the mastery, he fell under me and died upon the spot." A flush of anger appeared on Mary's face, only to be replaced by tranquillity as she remarked, "while I regret the loss of my favorite, *I rejoice in my son, who always speaks the truth.*"

Custis obtained his information about the general's youth from two Washington cousins who had been the childhood companions of the chief.[20] Custis may have added an embellishment or two, but it is hard to believe that he would tell a lie about a story whose moral is not to tell a lie. Parson Weems also drew upon excellent sources. He knew Washington's close friend Dr. James Craik, who brought Weems to meet Washington at Mount Vernon in 1787; Weems lived for a while near Mount Vernon, preached at the church Washington attended, and spoke with members of the Washington family while doing his biographical research. It is plausible that he heard some version of the

---

* When asked if this sudden equine death was plausible, a group of Montana horse breeders said yes.

horse-breaking story, could not use the violent part of the tale in a book aimed at children, but realized the moral value of its punch line.

The account Custis wrote of the horse-breaking episode owes much to his skill as an author of historical melodramas, but the scene calls for a canvas more than a stage (Custis was also a painter of historical panoramas featuring the chief). A painting of the young Washington locked in mortal combat with a bucking steed would carry rich and accurate psychological symbolism. On the most superficial level the scene captures Washington's superb horsemanship—a skill that saved his life and steadied the nerves of others in Revolutionary battle. (During the retreat from Princeton, an American soldier could not help noticing how "the noble horse of General Washington . . . stood as firm as the rider, and seemed to understand that he was not to quit his post and station.")[21] But on a deeper level Custis had found an emblem of Washington's internal struggle. From his youth Washington struggled to attain control over himself.

The horse-breaking story reflects the attributes of the Virginia gentleman: it is manly to take risks; but when things go wrong you admit responsibility and accept the consequences. The ideal man has pride, willfulness, boisterous passions—all contained and controlled. He is "a complete sparkish gentleman."[22] A German traveler observed Virginia's rites of adolescence and wrote, "at fifteen, his father gives him a horse and a negro, with which he riots about the country, attends every fox-hunt, horse-race and cock-fight, and does nothing else whatever." The German rather ominously noted that "a Virginia youth of fifteen years is already such a man as he will be at twice that age."[23] Balancing "spark" and gentility required discipline. As the historian David Hackett Fischer writes:

> A gentleman of Virginia was expected to have boisterous feelings and manly passions and a formidable will. But at the same time he was also expected to achieve a stoic mastery of self. This vital tension became a coiled spring at the core of Virginia's culture, and a source of its great achievements during the eighteenth century. In the person-

ality of George Washington, Virginia's system of child rearing had a spectacular success.[24]

One might say that Washington trained himself to live "by the book," or more accurately, by three books—*The Rules of Civility,* Seneca's *Morals,* and Joseph Addison's tragedy *Cato.*[25] Describing the pervasive influence of the classical world and heroes on the Revolutionary generation, two historians noted, "everyone was more or less Roman. George Washington ranked first."[26] Seneca's sayings comprised a Stoic's guide to life:

> An honest man can never be outdone in courtesy.
> A good man can never be miserable, nor a wicked man happy.
> A sensual life is a miserable life.
> Hope and fear are the bane of human life.
> The contempt of death makes all the miseries of life easy to us.

By and large, Washington took to heart Seneca's denunciation of anger as "the most outrageous, brutal, dangerous, and intractable of all passions."[27] Reliance on philosophy, Seneca wrote, "gives us a veneration for God; a charity for our neighbor teaches us our duty to heaven. . . . refutes our errors, restrains our luxury, reproves our avarice." All of this was not veneer, but the struts and trusses of Washington's frame of mind.

Washington first read Addison's 1713 tragedy *Cato* as a young man, and he referred to it throughout his life. Addison based the play on the story of Cato the Younger, the first-century B.C. Roman statesman renowned for his Stoic virtue and devotion to republican principles. He opposed Caesar's imperial ambitions, and committed suicide rather than submit to him. Enormously popular in England and America, the play profoundly influenced Washington's generation. Men and women acted it out inwardly, in a Roman republican fantasy, dreaming of virtuous self-abnegation in service to a noble cause. Indeed, it is impossible to understand two of the most famous sayings of the Revolution without a knowledge of *Cato*. Nathan Hale went to his death on the gallows uttering the words "I regret only that I have but one life to give for my country"—a line from *Cato*. In his last moment Hale took comfort from knowing that he had lived according to the highest imaginable ideal. And when Patrick Henry electrified the Virginia Assembly by drawing his sword as he cried out, "Give me Liberty or Give me Death!" he was borrowing one of the most famous lines from *Cato*, knowing that everyone in the chamber had seen or read the play: the words are uttered by Cato himself at his suicide, by sword; Cato preferred death to being "a slave" in Caesar's hands.* By summoning the shade of Cato he was telling the chamber that not only had the Revolutionary moment arrived, but the moment when *Cato* would be reenacted in actuality. The moment was at hand when Virginians had to step into the role they had dreamed of, because events demanded a fresh generation of heroes.

When Washington wished to bestow the highest praise on an officer for achieving a victory (ironically, it was Benedict Arnold), he sent a message paraphrasing *Cato*: "It is not in the power of any man to command success, but you have done more—you have deserved it."[28] And in the darkest moment of the Revolution, at Valley Forge, George Washington assembled his officers to see a performance of *Cato*. Abigail Adams went further: she thought that George Washington *was* Cato. When she reached for a phrase to describe Washington, she grasped one from the play: "Cato is stern, and *awful as a god*."[29]

Another phrase from the play sums up the struggle and the ideal of the virtuous man Washington wished to make himself into: one had to be "severely bent against himself," to be master of himself most of all. His contemporaries recognized this virtue in Washington. A eulogist wrote: "His noblest victory / The *Conquest of Himself*."[30] For Washington's class, "the social creed was fundamentally a form of stoicism," as Fischer writes. The stoic ideal "cultivated a calm acceptance of life.

---

* The actual lines recalled by Hale and Henry are, respectively, "What a pity it is / That we can die but once to serve our country" (act 4, scene 4) and "It is not now a time to talk of aught / But chains or conquest, liberty or death" (act 2, scene 4).

It taught that one must fear nothing and accept whatever fate might bring with courage, honesty, dignity and grace."[31]

When he was about sixteen George Washington copied out, with great diligence and punctiliousness, 110 axioms intended to form habits of acceptable behavior. He copied them from a book called *The Rules of Civility & Decent Behaviour in Company and Conversation*. A tutor might have given it to him, but it is also possible that one of his half brothers thought it necessary to polish young George's bumpkin behavior to prepare him for encounters with polite society. Some of the rules were basic admonitions regarding table manners, such as rule 100, not to clean your teeth at the table with the table cloth, knife, or fork; and rule 107, "talk not with Meat in your Mouth." Others dealt with personal hygiene: "Rinse not your Mouth in the Presence of Others," "Kill no Vermin as Fleas, lice ticks &c in the Sight of Others," and "Spit not in the Fire."

Originally written in France more than a century earlier, the *Rules* traveled well in colonial Virginia, as both societies were built on deference to one's superiors, and in both societies one could easily offend a "person of quality" or a superior with thoughtless conduct. An especially elaborate rule was intended to prepare a young man for his first one-on-one conversation with someone of higher status. Oddly, it specifically describes an ambulatory conversation rather than a seated chat; the author may have been imagining the situation of a young traveler, on the road by himself for the first time, arriving at the home of a wealthy relative or family friend who takes him for a tour of the house:

> In walking up and Down in a House, only with One in Compan[y] if he be Greater than yourself, at the first give him the Right hand and Stop not till he does and be not the first that turns, and when you do turn let it be with your face towards him, if he be a Man of Great Quality, walk not with him Cheek by Joul but Somewhat behind him; but yet in Such a Manner that he may easily Speak to you.

Washington practiced rule 19 to perfection for his entire life: "Let your countenance be pleasant but in serious matters somewhat grave."

By following this and the other rules he learned the importance of being a social actor. It came down partly to control of the face: use facial expressions to mask the interior emotions; always look serene and controlled. Washington was shaken when a woman remarked to him that she could read in his face his joy at his impending retirement from the presidency. "You are wrong!" he barked. "My countenance never yet betrayed my feelings!"[32]

Two of the longer rules dealt with the intricate etiquette of "Pulling off your Hat to Persons of Distinction," a far more complex ritual than we would imagine ("he that makes too much haste to Put on his hat does not well, yet he ought to Put it on at the first, or at most the Second time of being ask'd"). Table etiquette followed social status: "It belongs to the Chiefest in Company to unfold his Napkin and fall to Meat first"; so the diner of low status had to hold still until the top person had filled his plate, and had to keep an eye on the progress of the top people at table because when they finished, all must lay down their forks: "In Company of your Betters be no[t longer in eating] than they are." Obligations were reciprocal, however. It would be rude for the "chiefest" to gobble his food and force the others to stop eating before they had their fill. The rules declared "the Slowest may have time allowed him."

The rules touched upon more than the niceties of deportment; at bottom they taught respect:

Every Action done in Company, ought to be with Some Sign of Respect, to those that are Present.

Speak not Evil of the absent for it is unjust.

Reproach none for the Infirmaties of Nature, nor Delight to Put them that have [them] in mind thereof.

Shew not yourself glad at the Misfortune of another though he were your enemy.

The long litany of rules concluded with the most important of all:

Labour to keep alive in your Breast that Little Spark of Ce[les]tial
fire Called Conscience.

George Washington became a man of rules. He was a man for whom
discipline, order, routine, and punctuality were liberating. When he began keeping a diary he headed the volume with the title "Where &
How my Time is Spent"; it was a tool most of all for keeping track of
himself. He governed himself by axioms in order to tame impulse. The
phrase "I make it a rule," unquestionably derived from his childhood
absorption of *The Rules of Civility,* runs throughout his letters, papers,
and conversations. If he had *made a rule* to do something then he was
immune to personal appeals, exceptions, and deviations. He would always do the right thing despite his personal inclination to do otherwise.

In 1756, as a young colonel of the Virginia militia, he received orders he did not like and wrote in response to Governor Robert Dinwiddie: "In order to avoid censure in every part of my conduct, I make
it a rule to obey the dictates of your Honor, the Assembly, and a good
conscience."[33] During the Revolution, when complaints of fraud were
made by lower ranks against a colonel Washington knew, the general
forwarded the charges for examination with the note: "The opinion I
have of Col Graytons honor induces me to believe the charges must
be ill founded; but I make it a rule to have every thing of this kind
carefully scrutinized." By this expedient, he removed his personal feelings from the issue.[34] When in 1781 he received intelligence about
British troop movements that might threaten a French position, he
wrote to the French duke in command: "I do not place much confidence in the Channels through which this report comes; but as I make
it a rule never to slight any intelligence of this nature, I think it my
duty to communicate it to you." Because he had this rule, Washington
didn't play hunches, and he also implied that if *he* had made it a rule
to evaluate such information seriously, then so should the duke. (The
further comment to the duke is a marvel—a command swathed in a
compliment: "Should this [report] be true, there is a remote probability that your Corps is their object, but it will be impossible for them
to accomplish their enterprise with the precautions you will naturally

take.")[35] And during his presidency, a French duke arrived at the Executive Mansion bearing letters of introduction from high-ranking people in England and the recommendation of Washington's intimate friend, Lafayette. Courtesy compelled receiving him, but the nobleman was turned away: "I knew the respect that I owed him. I could not, however, receive him at my house . . . I had made a rule not to admit to my house any Frenchman who was regarded as an emigree and who could not be represented by his Minister."[36]

Though Washington could resort to rules and procedures to guide him through misty moments in politics, warfare, and social life, his system broke down when it was applied to slaves. A household slave named Ona Judge made a successful escape to New Hampshire in the 1790s, and then sent word that she might come back if the general promised to free her later on. Washington found himself in the novel position of having to negotiate with a slave who held the high card—if she didn't get what she wanted she simply would not return. Washington fell back on his rules and precedents even in this instance, assuming that his reasoning would be as plain and persuasive to a slave as it had been to colonels and cabinet members. In his reply to Ona Judge, Washington wrote that an individual emancipation of the sort she requested would be, unfortunately, a violation of proper procedure: "however well disposed I might be to a gradual abolition, or even to an entire emancipation . . . it would neither be politic nor just to reward [you] with a premature preference."[37] Judge failed to be swayed by this argument, and Washington failed to understand that a slave would not see the justice of deferring her freedom because she should wait her proper turn.* The slaves and he did not inhabit the same logical universe.

When George Washington looked back on his youth, sharing his recollections with his first biographer, he spoke with surprising sharpness about the slave system and its corrupting effect on the masters. In 1787

---

* I will take up Ona Judge's extraordinary story in Chapter 9.

Colonel David Humphreys, who had served with the general in the Revolution, moved to Mount Vernon to research his biography. Humphreys, a Connecticut Yankee, knew nothing of conditions in the Virginia of Washington's youth except what Washington himself told him. After Humphreys wrote his narrative Washington reviewed and corrected it. The general let stand without correction a passage about the era of his youth, when the children of "Opulent families" were given "a horse & a servant to attend them, as soon as they could ride." The character of these people became "imperious & dissipated from the habit of commanding slaves & living in a measure without control."[38]

Though the institution existed in Virginia from the time the first Africans were brought to Jamestown in 1619, the slave system was slow to take shape. There was great confusion over what slavery meant, over who would be enslaved and who could become free, even over who was white and who was black. Some of these issues had been more or less settled by the time Washington was born in 1732, but not all.

To this day scholars disagree over the origins and fundamental nature of slavery, particularly over the question of which came first, racial prejudice or race-based slavery. Did racial prejudice lead to the enslavement of Africans, with resulting economic benefits that perpetuated slavery? Or did desire for wealth lead to enslavement, which created and perpetuated racial prejudice? Did whites despise slaves because they were black, or on a class basis, because they were slaves? Winthrop Jordan, in *White Over Black*, writes, "Rather than slavery creating 'prejudice,' or vice versa, they seem rather to have generated each other." David Hackett Fischer discounts the importance of economics and argues that Virginians originated slavery in their colony for cultural reasons, because they wished to re-create England's caste system: "Virginia's ruling elite . . . required an underclass that would remain firmly fixed in its condition of subordination. The culture of the English countryside could not be reproduced in the New World without this rural proletariat."[39]

During a war against the Indians that began in 1622, the Powhatan Uprising, the colonists enslaved the vanquished and quickly found ways to rationalize it. One Englishman said that the Indians were "apter for worke than yet our English are." The secretary of the colony wrote that the Indians could "most justly be compelled to servitude and drudgery" so that "even the meanest of the Plantation may imploy themselves more entirely in their Arts and Occupations ... whilest Savages performe their inferiour workes of digging in mynes, and the like." Another commented that the forge that "makes chaines for Savage Nation / Frees, feeds the rest." Enslavement could finance further conquests of the Indians, too, since after the men had been killed their families could be sold. In 1666 Governor William Berkeley wrote: "I think it is necessary to destroy all these northern indians. . . . it may be done without charge, for the women and children will defray it."[40]

Scholars still dispute the exact legal status of the Africans brought into Jamestown in 1619. The Spanish had previously baptized the Africans, and they bore Christian names. The Jamestown colonists put the blacks to work but shrank from making them slaves for life, which struck the English as a form of blasphemy. Many blacks became "Christian servants" for a set period of servitude; some were even set free by pious masters for having accepted Christianity. For a brief time belief in Christ overpowered slavery, but the Virginia Assembly began to close this religious loophole in 1667: "Whereas some doubts have risen whether children that are slaves by birth, and by the charity and piety of their owners made pertakers of the blessed sacrament of baptisme, should by vertue of their baptisme be made free; It is enacted . . . that the conferring of baptisme doth not alter the condition of the person as to his bondage or freedome."[41] For a few more years Africans who had been baptized before their arrival in Virginia could have the status of indentured servants, but the Assembly finally closed this loophole entirely in 1682 with a law proclaiming that, Christian or not, any "negroes, moors, mulattoes or Indians" imported to Virginia would be "slaves to all intents and purposes, any law, usage or custome to the contrary notwithstanding."[42]

Some whites and blacks continued to resist this tightening noose of laws, however: masters freed slaves, and whites and blacks married each other. So the legislature had to take more drastic steps. In 1691 the Assembly declared that a master who freed a slave had to pay to transport the freed person out of the colony within six months (a requirement that was later rescinded), and in the same session forbade white people from marrying blacks, on pain of banishment. The historian Philip D. Morgan writes, "in spite of the blacks' debased status, race relations in early Virginia were more pliable than they would later be, largely because disadvantaged blacks encountered a group of whites—indentured servants—who could claim to be similarly disadvantaged. . . . Not only did many blacks and whites work alongside one another, but they ate, caroused, smoked, ran away, stole, and made love together." Occasionally slaves and white servants joined up in escape attempts or uprisings.[43]

White indentured servants greatly outnumbered black slaves in seventeenth-century Virginia. (Washington's great-grandfather established himself in Virginia not by buying black slaves but by importing white servants.) In 1671 Governor Berkeley reported to the Board of Trade that Virginia's population was 40,000, of which 6,000 were indentured servants or "Christian servants for a short time" who had immigrated to Virginia in "the hope of bettering their condition in a growing country." (Others had been kidnapped and sent against their will, and still others were convicts.) There were only 2,000 blacks, most but not all of them slaves. Morgan writes, "in some counties, perhaps a third of the black population was free in the 1660s and 1670s." Though careful not to overstate his case and argue that a utopian, mixed-race society was possible in colonial Virginia, Morgan continues, "at least through the 1680s, Virginians came close to envisaging free blacks as members or potential members of their community."[44]

Though desperate for labor, Virginians complained about the mother country's policy of sending them "jailbirds." Perceiving England to be overpopulated by poor people, the British government encouraged the transportation of the indigent, unemployed, and criminals. Official thinking changed around 1700, when the government began to see a necessity to preserve the supply of cheap labor in the home country. The result of this policy change can be seen in the Virginia immigration figures: the 1680s saw the annual arrival of 1,500–2,000 white indentured servants, whereas only a hundred or so were arriving each year by 1715. Virginia had to make up the difference with slaves.[45]

The great planters rushed to import more and more slaves and to put ever larger acreages into the production of tobacco, which utterly changed the racial character of the colony. The slave system into which George Washington was born in 1732 was therefore created only about thirty years earlier; it was relatively new. As Winthrop Jordan writes, "By about 1700 the slave ships began spilling forth their black cargoes in greater and greater numbers. By that time, racial slavery and the necessary police powers had been written into law. . . . In 1705 Virginia gathered up the random statutes of a whole generation and baled them into a 'slave code' which would not have been out of place in the nineteenth century."[46]

The influx of slaves and the expansion of tobacco planting initially disrupted Virginia's economy, as planters went deeply into debt to acquire slaves just as tobacco prices were falling because of the sudden overproduction of the commodity. A colonial official wrote in 1708: "The people of Virginia will not now be so fond of purchasing Negroes as of late, being sensibly convinced of their error, which has in a manner ruined the credit of the country." Governor Spotswood echoed this sentiment three years later: "The great number of Negroes imported here and solely employed in making tobacco has produced for some years past an increase in tobacco far disproportionate to the consumption of it . . . and consequently lowered the price of it." But around the time of Washington's birth just twenty years later, the thinking in the colony had begun to change. The low price of tobacco in Europe had fed that continent's nicotine addiction, creating a great demand for the weed. A 1728 report to the Lords of Trade stated that " 'tis well known that the cheapness of Virginia tobacco in European markets is the true cause of the great consumption thereof."

Though white indentured servants became scarcer, their value fell while the value of slaves rose. The wealthy Virginia planter William Byrd II (a distant relative of Washington's by marriage) observed in 1739 that indentured servants in Virginia "are sold for four years and fetch from six to nine pounds," whereas slaves "sell for more than double." The fears about low tobacco prices disappeared as the great planters, with the means to import large numbers of slaves, were raising huge crops and reaping huge profits, despite the inferior quality of their harvests. Governor Gooch reported to London, "the rich man's trash will always damp the market and spoil the poor man's good tobacco which has been carefully managed."[47]

Byrd took note of the social transformation that Virginia was undergoing in 1736, when Washington was a small child, as a result of the growing population of black slaves: "I am sensible of many bad consequences of multiplying these Ethiopians amongst us. They blow up the pride and ruin the industry of our white people, who, seeing a rank of poor creatures below them, detest work for fear it should make them look like slaves." During a surveying trip along the Virginia–North Carolina border, Byrd recorded an extreme example of a lowly white laborer's fear that he would be looked upon as the equal of a black slave. On the frontier Byrd and his upper-crust companions dined on corn pone, the customary food of slaves, because it was all they had; but when Byrd offered it to a white worker the man was gravely insulted: "the boatwright was affronted that I gave him pone instead of English bread for breakfast, and took his horse and rode away without saying a word." Byrd's biographer comments, "those who were most punctilious about their social standing were generally those whose station approached the lowest level."[48]

By the time Washington was a young man, the slave system, after just fifty or so years, had taken over the colony to the degree that, as a minister wrote in 1757, "to live in Virginia without slaves is morally impossible." Because help could not be hired, he said, it had to be bought—a necessity "which of course draws us all into the original sin and curse of the country of purchasing slaves." In 1700 Virginia had 13,000 slaves; in 1730, 40,000; in 1750, 105,000, of whom nearly 80 percent were Virginia born.[49]

In the West Indies and South America, slaves were worked to death and replaced with fresh imports, but in the continental North American colonies of Great Britain the situation was the opposite. By about 1710, as Morgan notes, "Virginia's slave population began to grow from natural increase, an unprecedented event for any New World slave population. . . . Virginian slaveowners began to mention the value of having women in their labor forces." The fertility of the slave mothers meant that Virginia planters, including Washington, could "grow" their own labor force. One of Washington's distant cousins wrote to his manager in 1759, "the Breeding wenches most particularly, you must instruct the overseers to be kind and indulgent to." Thomas Jefferson's calculation of the economics of plantation slavery was chillingly blunt: "a woman who brings a child every two years [is] more profitable than the best man of the farm."[50] Washington family wills offer evidence of the increasing significance of slave property: Washington's father inherited just half a dozen slaves from his father's estate in 1715, and he bequeathed four dozen when he died in 1743; George Washington inherited ten of those slaves, and died in possession of 123.[51]

In his lifetime Washington was exposed to a variety of ways in which masters treated their slaves. There was the benevolent face, exemplified by a letter written by a distant relative of Martha Washington in 1697: "Be Calm and Obligeing to all servants, and when you speak doe it mildly Even to the poorest slave; if any of the Servants commit small faults yt [that] are of no consequence, do you hide them. If you understand of any great faults they commit, acquaint your mother, but doe not aggravate the fault."[52] But at roughly the same time, Robert "King" Carter was having his overseers cut off the toes of slaves to prevent them from running away. Of one slave Carter wrote, "dismembering will reclaim him. . . . I have cured many a Negro of running away by this means." This horrible practice, legalized in 1705, evidently became widespread, with much resultant butchery; it received further legal blessing in the tightening of the slave laws in 1723, when the Virginia Assembly absolved owners and surgeons of manslaughter if such "dismembering" resulted in the slave's death. The lawmakers assumed that no sane man would deliberately destroy his own very valuable property.[53] It is hideous to imagine that doctors would participate in such medical atrocities, but they did.[54] An overseer of one of the Lees devised a mechanism for questioning a slave: suspend the man from a hook in the ceiling so that his bare foot just touched a sharp stake set in the floor. It was best, said the overseer, if you began by giving the man a good spin on the rope.

As a child, Washington might have seen coffles of slaves being led down a road, offered for sale. (White convicts, shipped over from England, were also sold in this manner by "soul drivers.") The detestable business of selling slaves was not just the domain of professional traders. The potential for profit attracted planters with spare cash to invest. Thus John Carter, a son of King Carter, imported a large consignment of slaves in 1737 but was stunned to see the boat deliver mostly children, for which there was then slack demand. He was able to sell 145 of the Africans, at a loss, and to recoup as much of his investment as possible he considered turning the remaining children over to "those wholesale chaps."[55]

Cruelty and compassion coexisted in the same breast. Washington's own uncle, Joseph Ball, wrote explicit instructions to his overseer for the treatment of his favorite slave, a man named Aron. If Aron acted well he was to be allowed to ride a horse to church, was to be given a new house to live in, and was not made to work too hard. But in the event that Aron proved to be "unruly" or if he struck the overseer, Aron "must by tyed up and Slasht Severly, and pickled," by which Ball meant an excruciating process in which the bleeding victim was immersed in brine to increase the pain of the slashing. This was a *favored* slave. Ball warned the overseer that Aron might resist the punishment; so, he continued,

> If you have occasion to slash him get two or three Good White Men to help; and give it him heartily at once, and if he should Runaway, he must wear a Pothook about his neck, and if that won't bring him under, he must wear Iron spaneals upon his Legs till you are pretty sure he will be orderly; for as he is my slave he must and shall be obedient, but if he be orderly use him kindly. Shew him this letter.[56]

The relationships between masters and favored slaves present one of the deepest mysteries of that time and place. Washington's friend and mentor Landon Carter owned a man named Nassau, who acted as Carter's personal servant, plantation surgeon, apothecary, and companion. Nassau was an alcoholic. He would get so drunk, Carter wrote, that he could not tell "a chamber pot from a bottle of water." The two fought bitterly over Nassau's drinking, reconciled, fought again, and reconciled, in a cycle that went on for decades.

Nassau inspected Carter's crops, inventoried his livestock, whipped slaves when ordered, and dispensed medicines to slaves and whites. Their relationship was almost one of brothers: master and slave took walks together to look over the fields; they discussed the effectiveness of various medicines as affably as two planters in a parlor. In his diary Carter recorded his endless battle against Nassau's drinking. On one occasion Nasssau had "not been sensibly sober one evening since this day fortnight." Carter "begged him, prayed him," to stop drinking, urging Nassau to think of his responsibility to the sick people in his care. The master continued his pleading even when he began to think that Nassau was drinking deliberately "in order to spight him." At one point Carter actually put Nassau up for sale to frighten him, but he backed down, as Nassau probably knew he would. Their intense psychological battle reached a dramatic peak when Nassau was brought in by another slave, who had found him passed out on the ground "dead drunk." Carter threatened to hit him and Nassau charged into his master. Carter pushed him down the cellar stairs and had him tied up until he became sober. The next morning Carter ordered that Nassau be stripped and tied for a beating. With the overseer brandishing a stick in front of him, Nassau cried out for forgiveness and vowed before God he would never drink again. Carter relented, unable to bear the sight of his companion being beaten. "I forgave this creature," he wrote, "out of humanity, religion, and every virtuous duty." It was his hope, he continued, to "save one more soul Alive."[57]

CHAPTER TWO

On the Borderland

*O*N A JUNE MORNING IN 1815 a schooner called *Lady of the Lake* set sail from northern Virginia bearing George Washington Parke Custis, the grandson of George and Martha Washington, and a great admirer of the hero. Custis had already transformed his mansion, Arlington, into a virtual museum of Washington's life and career; and on that June day Custis headed down the Potomac with two companions in a further act of commemoration. They dropped anchor off the shore of Westmoreland County and clambered into a small boat. Once ashore they met up with two local gentlemen and a random party of fishermen, who, when told of the historic event about to unfold, fell in with Custis's group in its march to a spot not far from the water. Custis and his companions were bearing a slab of stone and an American flag. When they reached their destination they reverently wrapped the flag around the stone, which was then gently placed by four men—all descended from Revolutionary patriots—on a pedestal of rocks. The slab was engraved with the words:

HERE
THE 11TH OF FEBRUARY, 1732 (OLD STYLE,)
GEORGE WASHINGTON WAS BORN.

There were only ruins at the place, but Custis had been guided by a pile of bricks that he surmised "once formed the hearth around which

Washington in his infancy had played." After laying the stone, the party repaired to the schooner, fired a cannon in salute, and departed. Custis later wrote, probably correctly, that his marker was "the first stone to the memory of Washington."* His memorial itself became a valued relic. Curiosity seekers who tramped to the remote site over the years chipped off pieces of it as souvenirs until the entire stone had been whittled away by 1870.[1]

A new memorial rose at the behest of the federal government and the Commonwealth of Virginia in 1896. A forty-ton obelisk—a replica of the Washington Monument in the nation's capital, but one-tenth its size—was delivered via barge to the shores of Popes Creek and set in place upon what was thought to be the exact site of Washington's birth. In the early 1930s, as the two-hundredth anniversary of Washington's birth approached, a private group led by a Washington descendant moved the obelisk to construct a "Memorial House," a re-creation of an eighteenth-century Virginia planter's dwelling. Fortunately for history, the obelisk and the Memorial House that followed it were erected on the wrong spot. The builders missed the mark by about a hundred feet. Several years later archaeologists unearthed some 16,000 artifacts at the true site. The birth site, a family cemetery, and the surrounding 394 acres were officially designated the George Washington Birthplace National Monument under the administration of the National Park Service in 1932. Now set at the entrance of the park, the obelisk gradually rears up in the windshields of approaching visitors, creating the odd sensation that one has made a wrong turn and ended up on the National Mall.

I arrived at the Birthplace to the sound of clanging. The site was in full "plantation life" mode, with a blacksmith hammering away, costumed women cooking hoecakes in a fire, others washing laundry, and a woman pressing apples for cider. This spectacle of the plantation's daily round of chores presented an ironic tableau, for many of the on-

---

* The first public monument to Washington did not go up until twelve years later. On July 4, 1827, the residents of Boonsboro, Maryland, constructed a fifteen-foot tower of stones in his honor. At the Battle of Antietam during the Civil War the Union army used it as an observation post.

lookers that day were descendants of the women who had actually done that work on this very spot two and a half centuries earlier.

The Birthplace was hosting a gathering of Bowden descendants: three generations of Bowdens had been bound as indentured servants to two generations of the Washington family. This reunion had come about as the result of nearly twenty years of research by a California woman, Anita Wills, who had begun tracing her ancestors in 1980. She tracked the family line back to Virginia, where she discovered she was descended from Revolutionary War veterans. She sent her findings to the Daughters of the American Revolution and was duly inducted. Continuing her search, she discovered the Washington family connection from nineteenth-century documents in Fredericksburg that mentioned the family's service to the Washingtons at Popes Creek. The Park Service historian at Popes Creek was startled to get a phone call from a woman claiming to be descended from the plantation's servants. No one had ever been able to trace such a connection before; but he was convinced when he saw the documentation Anita Wills had gathered from county legal records and the Washington family's own papers.

George Washington had known the Bowdens well. In his teen years, when he spent long visits at Popes Creek with his brother Austin, he was waited on by Mary Bowden, who was three years older than Washington. Her daughter Patty was later willed by Austin to George's niece Elizabeth Washington Spotswood. An indentured servant could be sold, given away, or bequeathed in a will during the term of her contract, like a slave, though eventually she would be free.

Indentured servitude was a colonial version of the American Dream: if you hated the squalor and stink of London or the tedium of your father's pig farm in Yorkshire, America beckoned. If you were too poor to buy passage to the New World you could get there by signing a contract selling your labor to a planter for seven years. The labor and the conditions might be harsh, but at the end of your term you would get your freedom back and some cash, and you would be in the New World with the sky as your limit. I had never heard that blacks could be indentured servants, but somehow the Bowdens fit into this system.

The day's slate of events included music, a wreath-laying by the descendants, and tours of the plantation. (Park Service archaeologists have been looking for the site of the slave quarters there for some time, without much success. They have discovered artifacts and traces of buildings but nothing they can definitively identify as a slave dwelling.) Between stops on the walking tour the Bowden descendants traded family stories. A branch of the family had migrated to Pennsylvania, where they had been active in the Underground Railroad. Some Bowden descendants had served in the Revolutionary War on the American side; others had fought for the North in the Civil War. They had a rich oral history and an equally rich documented history. One man had brought with him a thick volume of photographs and historical records he had assembled in years of researching the family history.

I had a long talk with an elderly woman who told a family story not related to Washington, but so powerful and so poignantly evocative of the struggles of the enslaved people that I wrote it down anyway. The story was told to the woman by her grandfather, who had lived it. Her grandfather's mother, she said, was a slave on a plantation near Hilton Head in South Carolina before the Civil War. The overseer on the place was a cruel man. Even when she had recently given birth, the overseer "would make her jump over a fence on her way to work and then—maybe I shouldn't say this—*curse* her on her way to work. And then she overheard a conversation between the master and one of his overseers that if a woman beat a man they wouldn't do anything to her because it was a shame on the man." One day she was late getting to the fields because she was nursing her baby. "When she came she explained to the overseer and he picked up a stick and hit her on the head. My grandfather saw this when he was age seven. When she got herself together she saw this man standing over her, and she grabbed sand and threw it in his eyes, and gave him a beating." She had gotten her revenge on the overseer, but as a punishment the master sold her away, and kept her children. "All her children stayed there. My grandfather, being fair, was in the house training to be a butler. The mulatto children were very much in need for house servants."

Then came the Civil War. When Union troops swept through the area her grandfather escaped with them, joining up with the all-black Fifty-fourth Massachusetts Regiment. But after the war, he went back to look for his lost mother. He found his two half sisters, who told him he could find their mother on Hilton Head. He tracked her down, but after thirty years she did not recognize the man who had been just a boy when she last saw him. She had thought her child was dead. When she finally realized who he was, she cried out, "My son is alive!"—a cry of joy remembered for generations afterward.

The officials at the Birthplace had set up a large tent where Anita Wills would deliver her findings to a gathering of historians and officials. The chief historian of the National Park Service attended, as did a professor from Norfolk, an expert on slavery from Monticello, and local historians and genealogists from Fredericksburg and Charlottesville. The presence of the experts at this family gathering reflected a sea change that had occurred in American historiography, with African-American family historians, for the most part "amateurs," conducting research of prime importance. Keepers of mainstream American history had come that day to learn from someone who would have been dismissed as an interloper by a previous generation of scholars.

The Park Service's historian introduced Wills by invoking Alex Haley, whose book *Roots* had revolutionized the study of American history. Haley, he said, "showed us the way by digging deeper, by going into documents that nobody thought would reveal anything. It is significant that Alex Haley was not a historian; historians knew that you could not do what he wanted to do—and he was told that. But not being a historian, he wasn't aware of the cultural baggage that we brought to the discipline and he went about his work anyway, and the result, as we might say, is history."

A tall, dark-skinned, plainly dressed woman took the podium. Anita Wills spoke softly but with emotion as she methodically described her research, which she called "a spiritual quest that has opened my eyes to the lives and times of my ancestors." Her quest began in California, she said, when she simply asked her mother where the family had come from, and her mother said, Virginia. Her work proceeded very slowly until the Internet made distant records available online and put her in contact with other researchers. She found that her ancestors were mixed-race people, partly white, partly African, and partly Native American, a mixture not at all unusual in colonial Virginia. But her research offered a startling new view of George Washington. He came of age, and learned to be a master, on a racial borderland where the definitions and boundaries of race were dangerously fluid. Because they were mixed-race, Wills's ancestors lived on the margins of the borderland, enslaved but not quite slaves.

Female servants were especially vulnerable in colonial Virginia. Indenture contracts generally forbade servants to marry during the term of their indenture. The required celibacy was certainly burdensome, to say the least, because servant women were generally in their teens and twenties. If a female servant had a child during her indenture she was liable to be fined on two counts—the moral offense of having an illegitimate child and for introducing a financial burden to her master's household. The first penalty was officially imposed by the county court, acting on behalf of the vestry of the local parish, whose wardens were often the men who brought the women to the court. The church extracted a fine because it bore the responsibility and expense of caring for abandoned infants and orphans. The courts usually dealt with the second matter—the added expense to the master—by extending the term of the mother's indenture so that her extra unpaid labor would compensate the master for his expense.

George Washington's father sat as a justice of the Westmoreland County court. In the year of George's birth, 1732, and the year after, the court indicted twenty-eight women for "bearing a base born child." Twelve of them fled the county before the sheriff could get his hands on them and their children. All of them would have been young and probably destitute when they fled from Westmoreland to parts unknown with their infants to escape the authorities. Two women paid fines and had their cases dismissed, but two unfortunate mothers without money to pay their fines were hauled into court to hear the sentence: the sheriff was to administer "25 lashes well laid on at the publick whipping post."[2]

In 1751 Austin Washington appeared before the Westmoreland County court to inform the gentlemen justices that his indentured servant Mary had a mixed-race child, Martha, nicknamed Patty. He did not identify the father. By reporting Patty to the authorities, Austin gained a free servant for himself. A brief entry in the Westmoreland County *Orders* records the court's instructions to the churchwardens of Washington Parish "to bind out Martha Bowden a Mulatto Child Daughter of Mary Bowden to Augustine Washington, Gent. according to Law." Her term of indenture to the Washington family, as specified by law, would be thirty years from her date of birth; she would be freed on her thirty-first birthday. Patty was four years old.[3]

On two counts—because she was a mulatto and because her mother was an indentured servant—Patty Bowden fell afoul of the colony's race laws. In 1691 the Assembly had prescribed thirty-year servitude for the children of white women and black or Native American men. But this law was not enough to halt interracial births; so in 1723 the Assembly expanded the law to state, "Where any female mullatto, or indian, by law obliged to serve till the age of thirty or thirty-one years, shall during the time of her servitude, have any child born of her body, every such child shall serve the master . . . of such mullatto or indian, until it shall attain the same age the mother of such child was obliged by law to serve unto." By these laws, as one legal commentator has written, "the sins were visited on the next generation." Patty was indentured to Austin Washington because her mother was a mulatto. In an era when life spans ran only into the forties and fifties, a thirty-year indenture was servitude for much of one's life.[4]

Mary apparently tried to save her child from the indenture by running away, but Austin managed to find her and bring her back to Popes Creek. In addition to seeing her child bound for thirty years, the mother was punished by having her indenture extended to compensate Austin for his expenses in searching for her. Undeterred, she ran away a second time, only to be found and returned again. Mary's servitude was increased again by four years.[5]

As the law allowed, the indenture fell upon the next generation as well. In 1778 Patty had a daughter named Delphia, and she too was bound for thirty years. These transactions were so obscure, and so easy to overlook in the records, that no one had found them until the late twentieth century, when Anita Wills and a cousin came along, researching their family history.[6]

What Wills described was not the American Dream but the inversion of it, the imposition of thirty years of involuntary servitude on mixed-race children who were legally free. The Bowdens and people like them represented the thin edge of freedom inserting itself into the bricks and mortar of the slave system. As the daughters, one after the other, of nonslave women, they should have been free at birth. We can imagine what this would have created, very quickly: extended families of mixed race, some indentured, some enslaved, some free. Children such as Patty Bowden represented a threat to the slave system because their very existence was erasing the color line. If freed from indenture, they could have worked to purchase the contracts of their indentured relatives and thereupon set them free, and they could have done the same for their enslaved kin. Within two or three generations, in an evolutionary growth toward freedom, Virginia would have been home to a community of free mixed-race people with kinship ties to both the white and black communities.[7]

This may sound like an abolitionist fantasy, but it actually happened later on in Norfolk, Virginia. A researcher who looked at the manumission records for that city found that between 1791 and 1820, nearly 40 percent of the emancipations came about when blacks purchased freedom for themselves or family members. The names of three free African-Americans, a shoemaker, a baker, and a harbor pilot, turned up repeatedly in the records, buying other blacks to set them free.[8] They managed for a brief time to find a chink in the wall of slavery and exploit it. Such manumissions could have become a reality in Washington's youth if powerful local leaders such as his half brother had decided to look the other way, out of respect for privacy and the right of any person to chose a mate freely.

Austin Washington could have let the girl Patty remain free and allow her and her mother to leave as free people when the mother's indenture was finished, but he did not. He knew that such "new people," neither black nor white, neither fully slave nor fully free, threatened the foundation of his power. The third generation of indentured Bowdens, Delphia, was born in the possession of Washington's niece Elizabeth Washington Spotswood and her husband, Alexander. He set Patty and Delphia free because he recognized the danger of mixing freedom and slavery in the same community. Spotswood was explicit about his reason for the manumissions: he set the infant free to reward the mother "for faithful services," he said, but the mother went free because "I discharged her not wishing to have female Negroes entitled to freedom among my slaves."[9]

The laws and the writings of the planters suggest that racial mixing was extremely distasteful to all Virginians, but the rhetoric of the era is misleading. The rulers legislated for all, but they did not speak for all; they spoke for themselves. The very need for laws to prohibit interracial unions is powerful evidence that racial mixing was increasing; one does not forbid what does not exist. Perhaps it was distasteful to those who wrote the laws forbidding it, but certainly it was not an evil to the men and women of different races who had children together. The government of colonial Virginia represented the voices and opinions of a smaller number of men who were alike in their background and who had the same interests. They were all planters, they were all slaveholders; they spoke for their class, which consisted of themselves and people like them. The same men served in the General Assembly, in the county courts, and on the church vestries. The Washingtons offer an excellent example of this pattern. There was no Eugene Debs mounting an insurgent campaign for office on behalf of the slaves and the indentured.

Had the masters not been so vigilant in ferreting out mixed-race offspring and so dogged in their punishment of the mothers, the wall of slavery would have been breached. That was the implication of Anita Wills's research into her family; and that is what Washington grew up with. That was the borderland his father and brother stood watch over. Later, when the time came for Washington to assume his position in Virginia society, he too would find himself called upon to police the racial borderland. As the story of the Bowdens makes clear, Washington's society was still, at that late date, grappling with the question of what slavery was and who was a slave. The Bowdens tested the edges of that world.

When Washington's father died in 1743, young George's prospects changed utterly. Psychologically, the loss of his father affected him in ways we can only guess at. Financially, Gus Washington's death eliminated any chance that George could receive the English education that the father had bestowed on Lawrence and Austin, his half brothers. As the third son, George would not inherit enough land and slaves to establish himself properly, and there was evident confusion in the family over what to do with the boy as he entered his teen years. Lawrence came up with a solution: send him to sea.

Lawrence, who was fourteen years older than George, had tasted the naval and military life himself. In 1740 he had sailed from Virginia to Cartagena in the Caribbean as part of a British campaign against Spain. Though the campaign ended badly, Lawrence returned to Virginia full of admiration for his commander, Admiral Edward Vernon, after whom he named Mount Vernon. Like his forebears, Lawrence had advanced his financial and social prospects through a highly advantageous marriage. He courted and won Ann Fairfax, daughter of William Fairfax, who resided in the splendid Belvoir mansion not far from Mount Vernon. In Virginian terms, this was a celestial match—better even than an alliance with the Lees or Carters—for the Fairfax family controlled an enormous royal land grant whose extent today we can only gasp at. William acted as the agent for his cousin Lord Fairfax, who had inherited some five million acres, extending from the tip of the Northern Neck into the back country of the Shenandoah Valley, pursuant to a royal grant of 1649. King Carter, in his time, owed his wealth to his post as land agent of the Fairfaxes. By his marriage to Ann, Lawrence Washington leaped directly into the innermost circle of the most powerful family in the colony.

Mary Washington considered the question of George's future carefully and fretfully. She was loath to part with her oldest son when she most needed him, as Gus's death had left the Washingtons in pinched circumstances. Living with his mother at Ferry Farm, George was so poor he could not afford the corn for his horse to get to the dancing assemblies.[10] Mary sought advice on the navy question from friends in Fredericksburg and wrote about it to her half brother Joseph Ball in England. Meanwhile, George took up the eminently useful study of the science of surveying. In a chest at Ferry Farm he found his father's surveying instruments, and he set to work filling a copybook with mathematical exercises notable for their accuracy, clarity, and neatness.

At length a letter arrived for Mary Washington from England. Joseph Ball quashed any notion that George should go to sea. As for the Royal Navy, no one could gain any advancement there without patronage—"there are always too many grasping for it here, who have interest and he has none."[11] As for taking a berth in a Virginia merchant ship, that would be far worse. Ball wrote that on a merchant ship George would run the risk of being impressed into the Royal Navy as a common seaman, a fate worse than death. The navy, Ball wrote, would "cut him and staple him and use him like a Negro, or rather, like a dog." That comparison was enough to end all thought of the youth going to sea.

Many years later John Adams aimed a famous blast at Washington, proclaiming that the first president was "too illiterate, unread, unlearned for his station." Washington himself admitted to his "consciousness of a defective education." Whatever formal schooling Washington received ended by the age of fourteen or fifteen; thereafter he was self-taught.[12] But the autodidact did quite well for himself with an education that was part rough-hewing and part polish.

His skills as a surveyor did not go unnoticed by William Fairfax, who dispatched the teenager to the frontier to chart the lands Fairfax was selling to settlers. George's encounter with the frontier shaped him profoundly. In the first place his treks through the wilderness toughened him physically, until he could endure almost any trial brought by terrain or weather. Making his way on foot through the Pennsylvania woods in winter, he journeyed through snow for a week, then tumbled from a raft into an icy river. From all this he emerged intact, whereas his companion came down with frostbite.[13] He wrote wonderful letters from the frontier, full of joy at the adventure of it all:

> I have not slept above three nights or four in a bed but, after walking a good deal all the day, lay down before the fire upon a little hay, straw, fodder, or bearskin—whichever is to hand—with man, wife, and children like a parcel of dogs or cats, and happy's he that gets the berth nearest the fire.[14]

George found the people of the backwoods to be as crude as their surroundings. He was not favorably impressed by his first meeting with German settlers: "a great Company of People Men Women & Children that attended us through the Woods as we went shewing there Antick tricks. I really think they seem to be as Ignorant a Set of People as the Indians. They would never speak English but when spoken to they speak all Dutch."[15] Indians seem not to have cowed him at all, even when his surveying group was approached by some thirty warriors bearing a fresh scalp. Given liquor, the Indians commenced a dance, which he described in detail:

> They clear a large circle and make a great fire in the middle. Then seat themselves around it. . . . the best dancer jumps up as one awakened out of a sleep and runs and jumps about the ring in a most comical manner. He is followed by the rest. Then begin their musicians to play. The music is a pot half of water with a deerskin stretched over it as tight as it can, and a gourd with some shot in it to rattle, and a piece of a horse's tail tied to it to make it look fine. The one keeps rattling and the other drumming all the while the others are dancing.[16]

After this initial encounter he felt quite at ease. "Nothing remarkable . . . being with the Indians all day." His surveying work in the forest gave him the sense that even the wildest places could be made to yield to the rationality of the surveyor's chain and the deed book.

Back at Belvoir and Mount Vernon, George schooled himself in "the graceful arts" of dancing, fencing, and riding. William Fairfax handed him books to polish his manners and shape his intellect.

When Washington was nineteen his beloved half brother Lawrence came down with a persistent cough and fatigue that signaled the onset of tuberculosis. Lawrence sought relief at hot springs in western Virginia, taking George along with him. George also accompanied Lawrence on a voyage to Barbados in another fruitless attempt to restore his health. There, fortunately for history, George contracted a mild case of smallpox, just serious enough to leave a few slight pockmarks on his nose and to give him lifelong immunity to the disease. But the trip did Lawrence no good; he returned to Mount Vernon and died there in 1752 at the age of thirty-four, putting George in mind of the short life spans parceled out to his family.[17]

Lawrence's widow soon remarried, giving George the opportunity to rent Mount Vernon from her along with a portion of his late brother's slaves. He had already turned his surveying work into a profitable enterprise, and now he was a plantation master. Many men, having found a remunerative path, would have been content to remain on it for good; but not Washington. Lawrence's death had not broken George's ties to the Fairfax family. William Fairfax looked upon George as a son and pulled his formidable strings to advance the young man: the governor of Virginia, Robert Dinwiddie, chose Washington, at age twenty, to be adjutant of the Virginia militia.

In the fall of 1753 Dinwiddie dispatched Washington on a delicate mission out west. France and Great Britain were in dispute over ownership of the territory along the Ohio River system in western Pennsylvania and Virginia, known as the Ohio country. Washington went out to demand that the French abandon the region, which, coincidentally, prominent Virginians including Dinwiddie and the Washington family wished to develop.[18]

For more than fifty years Europe had been convulsed in a series of world wars, and North America became yet another theater in those wars. By the 1750s both the French and the British colonists came to view the Ohio Valley as the key to control of the continent. For the French, the Ohio River system was crucial in linking their Canadian holdings with those on the lower Mississippi Valley. For the British colonists, pushing farther westward in a quest for new land, the lush Ohio country seemed to be their natural birthright. When the French began building a series of forts along the Ohio River to gain control of that essential waterway, the Virginia land speculators demanded action. Believing they had legal control over some half a million acres in the region, they were not going to sit by and watch their investment vanish.[19]

Washington traveled west and met with the French. After a night of drinking with a group of French traders, the young envoy concluded that it was

> their absolute Design to take Possession of the Ohio, & by G[od] they wou'd do it, for though' they were sensible that the English cou'd raise two Men for their one; yet they knew their Motions were too slow & dilatory to prevent any Undertaking of theirs. They pretended to have an undoubted right to the river from a Discovery made by one La Sol [La Salle] 60 Years ago, & . . . [they intend] to prevent our Settling on the River or Waters of it, as they have heard of some Families moving out in order thereto.[20]

Though the French commander rejected Washington's demands, the expedition was not a complete failure. Having scouted the region, Washington returned to Williamsburg with invaluable information on the French presence in the Ohio country, a detailed map of the fort they had built near the Ohio River on French Creek, as well as intelligence on the size of the military force there and the number of canoes available to transport troops. Drawing upon his surveying skills he mapped the Ohio River system and pointed out the strategic im-

portance of the Forks of the Ohio—the site of present-day Pittsburgh, where the Monongahela and Allegheny Rivers join to form
the Ohio—writing in his journal, "I spent some time viewing the
rivers, and the land in the fork, which I think extremely well suited for
a fort, as it has the absolute command of both rivers." The expedition
brought Washington a wholly unexpected dividend—a continental
reputation. On his return to Williamsburg he presented his journal to
Dinwiddie, who ordered it published, instantly making the young officer "one of the most famous men in the colonies," as the scholar
Frank Grizzard has put it.[21]

Within months Washington was back in the Ohio wilderness. Appointed lieutenant colonel of the Virginia Regiment in 1754, Washington set out with some 140 men to protect Virginia workers
building a fort at the Forks of the Ohio. Before the militiamen could
get there, however, the French had taken over the site. While awaiting the arrival of the rest of the Virginia Regiment, Washington
would stride unexpectedly upon the world stage. He and his men
rashly ambushed a detachment of French soldiers they came upon in
the forest that spring. The commander, Jumonville, and nine others
fell dead in an incident that would be labeled an "assassination" by the
French, an interpretation bitterly disputed by the British. The bloody,
fatal firefight in the woods elated Washington; indeed he could barely
hide his exhilaration, writing to his brother two days later, "I can with
truth assure you, I heard Bullets whistle and believe me there was
something charming in the sound." (When the letter was later published in *London Magazine,* Washington's jaunty remark caught the
eye of King George II, who commented acidly that the young officer
would not have found the sound of bullets so charming "if he had
been used to hear[ing] many.") Those whistling bullets—charming or
not—turned out to be the opening shots in what American historians
call the French and Indian War, a savage struggle that would soon
turn into a global conflict.[22]

Despite his role in igniting a war, the twenty-two-year-old Washington found himself rewarded. Not long after the Jumonville inci-

dent, the colonel in charge of the Virginia Regiment broke his neck in a fall from his horse; Washington assumed command. The glory was short-lived, however; less than a month later, he and his regiment were attacked at their encampment, Fort Necessity, and forced to surrender. Despite the defeat he and his men received official praise from the House of Burgesses "for their late gallant and brave Behaviour in the Defense of their Country." When Dinwiddie reorganized the regiment in October 1754 Washington decided to resign his commission, but his energy and ambition remained undimmed.[23]

The following spring, General Edward Braddock arrived in Virginia with two regiments of British regulars to dislodge the French from the Ohio country. Seeing this as an opportunity to launch a career in the British army, Washington volunteered to serve as an aide to the general. The expedition resulted in disaster. Marching toward Fort Duquesne, which the French had built at the Forks of the Ohio, Braddock's 1,700-man column of British regulars and colonial militiamen was ambushed and routed by a smaller contingent of French soldiers and Native American allies. "We have been most scandalously beaten by a trifling body of men," Washington wrote. In the midst of the fray he took "4 bullets through my coat" and had "Two Horses shot under me." General Braddock was killed.[24]

News of the debacle spread panic among Virginia settlers, who anticipated raids by the French and their Native American allies. In response, Dinwiddie turned once again to Washington, naming him commander in chief of all of the military forces in Virginia. The twenty-three-year-old colonel faced a formidable challenge: he had to establish his authority over some fifty officers, many of whom were older than he and had more military experience; he had to raise a regiment of more than a thousand men; and he had to establish supply lines to support them in the wilderness. For the next three years, Washington was the supreme commander in this theater of the war, defending a 350-mile frontier against, in his words, "the cruel Incursions of a Crafty Savage Enemy."[25]

Out on the frontier Washington took on the daily exigencies of commanding in the field and, by letter, in the distant chambers of power, honing the political skills needed to placate both the governor, from whom he received his authority, and the legislature supplying his troops with funds. At a time when other Virginians his age and class were rioting about the countryside, gambling, drinking, and racing horses, Washington was set apart. "I am become in a manner an exile," he wrote plaintively. Yet that very distance from Virginia society during these formative years was crucial to his education. In part, it freed him from a Virginia provincialism that might have prevented his later transformation into a true nationalist during the Revolution. His imagination was fired by the frontier and the possibilities of the western lands. And he was forced to think on a grander scale than his peers back home. He had to, or he and his troops would not survive. On the frontier he forged the iron discipline that he imposed for the rest of his life on himself and on others. He hanged two soldiers for desertion and ordered other executions, but then second thoughts restrained him.[26]

Washington's authority began with his physical presence. To begin with, he towered over most of his men by about a foot. A comrade in arms set down a description of Washington that captures him better than any painted portrait:

> Straight as an Indian, measuring six feet two inches in his stockings and weighing 175 pounds. . . . His frame is padded with well-developed muscles, indicating great strength. His bones and joints are large, as are his hands and feet. He is wide shouldered but has not a deep or round chest; is neat waisted, but is broad across the hips and has rather long legs and arms. His head is well-shaped, though not large, but is gracefully poised on a superb neck. A large and straight rather than a prominent nose; blue gray penetrating eyes which are widely separated and overhung by a heavy brow. His face is long rather than broad, with high round cheek bones, and terminates in a good firm chin. He has clear though rather colorless pale skin which burns with the sun. A pleasing and benevolent though a commanding countenance, dark brown hair which he wears in a cue. His mouth is large and generally firmly closed, but which from time to time discloses

some defective teeth. His features are regular and placid with all the muscles of his face under perfect control, though flexible and expressive of deep feeling when moved by emotions. In conversation he looks you full in the face, is deliberate, deferential, and engaging. His demeanor at all times composed and dignified. His movements and gestures are graceful, his walk majestic, and he is a splendid horseman.[27]

In the winter of 1757–58 this "splendid" physical specimen was felled not by bullets but by an attack of dysentery so serious that he feared for his life. He recuperated at Mount Vernon and sought medical advice in Williamsburg, where a doctor told him that, as bad as things seemed, he would recover. In the spring of 1758 he returned to his regiment and took part in the final assault on Fort Duquesne. The French burned the fort and fled, leaving that prized location, the Forks of the Ohio, to the British. The war was effectively over and Washington could now turn his attention to his future. He was in possession of Mount Vernon, a relatively small establishment that could be expanded by a man of his energy and acumen. But there was a more rapid means of acquiring the cash and slaves he needed to build his realm. He could follow the path of his forefathers and seek an advantageous marriage. Word had reached him that there was a young widow, just recently bereaved, at a plantation on the Pamunkey River. She was the heiress to one of the largest fortunes in Virginia.

CHAPTER THREE

The Widow Custis

*M*ARTHA DANDRIDGE CUSTIS was just under five feet tall, with hazel eyes and dark hair. By her own account she had "beautiful" teeth and was "a fine, healthy girl." Except for her tiny hands and her rather prominent nose, almost everything about her was round and soft. Plain, plump, and short, she might have been invisible to male eyes in the vicinity of one of Virginia's tempestuous beauties except that she was vivacious—"good, sweet . . . loves to talk," said one European nobleman—and she was very, very rich.[1]

Her wealth came from her marriage to Daniel Parke Custis. His death in 1757 at the age of forty-six, probably from a heart attack, had left twenty-six-year-old Martha with two small children and an estate worth more than £40,000, as well as some 18,000 acres of land.[2]

The time and place of George and Martha's first meeting has been thoroughly debated by historians: did Washington deliberately seek out the widow Custis for her fortune, or did he happen to cross paths with her and receive, unbidden, Cupid's arrow? The family liked to believe the latter. A story passed down in the Custis and Washington families, transmitted by an old Custis slave and by Washington's white body servant, claimed that Washington was traveling to Williamsburg on military business when he crossed the Pamunkey River near the home of a friend who, in the usual Virginia fashion, insisted that Washington come in for a visit and meet his guests, among them the recently widowed Martha Custis. Smitten, Washington lingered at the house overnight, and soon thereafter asked Mrs. Custis for her hand. A close reading of Washington's diary, however, casts doubt. The slave and the servant were probably remembering a different visit.

The bare fact is that Washington's first mention of Martha occurs in his daily record of expenses: he noted how much he tipped her servants on a visit in March 1758 to her house.[3] (The tips were very large—he was making a great display of generosity.) Thus the evidence points to a planned call upon a rich widow (nine months older than himself) whose recent bereavement was well known in the upper echelon of Virginia society. Some calculation is apparent on the other side as well. Daniel Custis had been dead only nine months, but the widow was not so consumed by grief that she could not entertain a gentleman caller.

Washington would certainly have arrived looking resplendent in his uniform, full of stories of action on the frontier. He would, with equal certainty, have stated his intention to resign his commission in the event of a change in his marital status, since a young widow would not want to exchange the solitude of bereavement for the loneliness of being an officer's wife. The setting itself was romantic. Martha resided in a grand old Virginia house by the side of a lazy river.

A clue to their feelings can be found in their expense accounts. The month after they met both George and Martha were firing off orders to their London agents for something gay to wear. Washington, all atwitter, ordered, "By the first ship bound to any part of Virginia* . . . as much of the best superfine Blue Cotton Velvet as will make a coat, waistcoat and breeches for a tall man." Martha ordered a suit of clothes "not to be mourning" and, thinking *way* ahead, sent her favorite nightgown out to be dyed a "fashionable" color.[4]

The marriage went ahead very swiftly thanks to the absence of meddlesome fathers-in-law, who would have scrutinized the couple's

---

* This was unusual for him: he typically specified that his shipments had to arrive at the Potomac River. He was in such a hurry that he'd go anywhere in the colony or willingly pay the exorbitant rates of Virginia's teamsters to get his new suit promptly.

accounts and haggled over the marriage settlement. Negotiations over an earlier Custis marriage, for example, included this sharp communiqué from the father of the prospective bride: "I do not know your young gentleman, nor have you or he thought fit to send an account of his real and personal effects; however, if my daughter likes him, I will give her upon her marriage with him, half as much as he can make it appear he is worth."[5]

George and Martha married at the Custis mansion, named "White House," on the Pamunkey River on January 6, 1759. In his first order to his London merchant as a married man, George ordered a quantity of Spanish fly, the bitter aphrodisiac powder made from crushed beetles, useful for both sexes.[6]

Martha's order for a spruced-up nightgown and George's for the aphrodisiac hint at a physical attraction between the couple, but they were preeminently practical people. Financially and socially they possessed matching gears that meshed to power an engine of upward ascent. Martha needed a manager for her properties and a father for her children; Washington came from a family that married well, usually above its station. Altogether, it was a match made in Virginia. Washington resigned his commission in the Virginia militia largely because Martha's fortune enabled him to become a large-scale gentleman planter. Had Martha not entered the picture, he might have returned to the militia to pursue another dream, a commission in the regular army of His Majesty.

The fortune that George Washington sought and won in the person of Martha Custis had a baroque history. The two children Martha brought to her second marriage both bore the middle name Parke, which would also be the middle name of every child in the next Custis generation. Names bespeak tradition, but in this instance the names bore heavy legal and financial freight. Part of the fortune Martha conveyed to Washington originated with one of Virginia's most notorious figures, Daniel Parke II, a grandfather of Martha's first husband. George Washington inherited the man's assets and debts and raised two of his great-grandchildren. Even in the annals of Virginia, the Parke-Custis story stands out for its bizarre twists.

Born in Virginia in 1669, Daniel Parke II was exceedingly handsome, rich, and good with a sword. His skill at fencing unfortunately coincided with a short temper. He possessed "a quick resentment of every the least thing that looks like an affront or injury." One Sunday morning at church he angrily threw out a woman who was sitting in the wrong pew. He was in the habit of issuing challenges to duel, "especially before company," which was a serious breach of decorum. Parke managed to appall the gentry of two colonies at once when he took a horsewhip to the governor of Maryland and subsequently challenged him to a duel.[7] As gross a breach as this was, Parke was merely beginning his climb up the slopes of notoriety. He returned from a sojourn in England with a young woman whom he airily called his "cousin," openly installing her in the colony as his mistress, with their illegitimate son. He seemed to think that Virginians would close their eyes to the fact that he was already married to a high-ranking Virginia woman, whom he more or less abandoned, along with their two daughters.[8]

Parke grew bored with provincial society and sought excitement in England. He also tired of the complaints of his long-suffering wife; as he put it himself, he felt "obliged to be on one side of the ocean" with her on the other. Exquisitely adding insult to injury, he departed with his mistress, leaving his bastard son to be raised by his wife in Virginia.[9]

His charm, his fortune, and his connections wafted Parke aloft in the home country. He received a commission as a colonel in the British army, serving as aide-de-camp to the Duke of Marlborough with such distinction that he was given the honor of personally delivering news to Queen Anne of the army's great victory at Blenheim in 1704. As expected, the queen expressed her delight by offering the messenger the very generous gift of £500. Unexpectedly, Parke declined the gift, saying that his only wish was to have a portrait of Her Majesty. The court swooned, and the queen bestowed upon Parke a lavish, jewel-encrusted miniature of herself. Modesty and humility, strategically expressed, had their reward.[10]

Back in Virginia, Parke's two daughters attracted suitors of the highest rank, as Parke's ascent to celebrity and royal favor erased concerns about his morals. Lucy Parke married William Byrd II, while Frances was pursued by John Custis, scion of a wealthy landowning family and later to be a member of the topmost governing body in the colony, the twelve-man Royal Council. Custis won the hand of Frances after arduous long-distance negotiations between the fathers-in-law. They married in 1706 and celebrated the birth of their son, Daniel Parke Custis, in 1710. Young Daniel never laid eyes on his grandfather.

In death, Parke ascended simultaneously to the heights of notoriety and gallantry. Having been appointed royal governor of the Leeward Islands, he managed to provoke his constituents, both high and low, in Antigua by incessant philandering with the wives and daughters of prominent planters and harsh attempts to enforce the smuggling laws, while himself sipping bootlegged claret. Spurning demands that he leave the island, Parke found himself facing a mob one morning in 1710. Captured by the rioters, Parke was brutally tortured. Here his stoic training emerged for the ultimate test. In the midst of extreme agony he remained calm, uttering no curse upon his tormentors but only rebuking them as an aristocrat would, urging them to be quicker with their foul business: "Gentlemen, you have no sense of honor left, pray have some humanity." Sending up prayers, he died.[11]

Parke's sudden demise provoked a scramble among his heirs, who knew that he possessed enormous wealth but did not know that he also owed crushing debts. He gave handsome bequests to two illegitimate children, while requiring that anyone who wished to claim an inheritance had to adopt the surname Parke. John and Frances Custis took possession of a portion of the Parke land in Virginia, while beginning a legal wrangle over who would pay the Parke debts. The squabble enriched lawyers in Virginia and England until 1772.

Not only Parke's estate but his temperament endured as well. A family historian wrote that Parke's "reckless blood seems to have raced like wildfire through the veins" of his descendants, including his daughter Frances. The strife in the Custis-Parke marriage grew to legendary proportions, all over money. As the husband, John Custis had the legal right to manage his wife's properties, and he was so stingy that Frances was reduced to pawning pieces of the family silver. The couple argued violently and often, until they had to sit down with lawyers in Williamsburg and hash out an agreement by which Frances promised to forbear calling her husband "any vile names or give him any ill language, neither shall he give her any but to live lovingly together."[12]

Their quarrels culminated in a famous episode near their planta-tion, called Arlington, on the Eastern Shore of Virginia, the peninsula that separates the Chesapeake Bay from the Atlantic. Ostensibly de-claring a truce in their wrangling, John invited Frances to join him in a carriage ride to the shore. Instead of turning to drive along the beach John whipped the horses straight into the bay.

> "Where are you going, Mr. Custis?" Frances asked, with the water swirling around them.
> "To hell, Madam," came the reply.
> "Drive on," said Frances, "any place is better than Arlington."

Their quarrels ceased only with the death of Frances in 1715 from smallpox.[13]

After the death of his mother, Daniel Custis lived with his cantan-kerous father, alone except for their slaves; his older sister was sent away to be raised by her grandmother. The son seems to have been as docile as the father was demanding. His first attempts to establish a family of his own were quickly thwarted by the old man. At twenty-one Daniel courted a young woman who was already a widow (her name is known only as "Mrs. Betty"), but John Custis refused his ap-proval on the shaky pretext that the lovers were too young. At the age of thirty-one he was still courting, and was again frustrated because his father and the father of his intended could not agree on a marriage settlement. In the meantime Daniel did his duty as a son, managing properties he did not yet own so successfully that the Custises expanded without taking on a great deal of debt. They kept much of their profits in cash, locked away in a formidable iron strongbox that eventually made its way to Mount Vernon, a symbol of the solidity of wealth.[14]

Against all expectation, the two-man Custis household expanded around 1739 when the senior Custis, now about sixty-one, presented Daniel with a half sibling. He had fathered a son, whom he named John, with one of his slaves. One would expect an elder statesman of Virginia to keep such a development private. But the child, dark-skinned or not, was a Custis. In 1744 John Custis took the extraordinary step of petitioning the governor and the council, where he sat himself, to set a slave child free. The petition stated the boy was "Christened John but commonly called Jack, born of the body of his Negro Wench Young Alice." Though Jack was only about five years old, Custis had already bestowed property on him; now he wished the boy to be made free and specified that all Jack's descendants would be free people. The implication of this petition would have been quite clear to Custis's co-councillors; he did not ruffle the serenity of the council chamber with a bald statement that little John was his son. James B. Lynch, Jr., a Custis family historian, writes: "Although John . . . may have stretched the conventions of his age by treating Jack as a son, he did not defy them by *declaring* him one—such a manifesto would not only have been outside the bounds of tolerable behavior, it would have been unthinkable for a person of Custis' stature and position."[15]

Inured as he was to the demands, caprices, and the emotional distance of his father, Daniel must nevertheless have been flabbergasted by the gifts and the love John Custis bestowed on this mixed-race child of his old age. Lynch writes, "John's legitimate son Daniel often had reason to believe that his father preferred 'Black Jack' to him." In a letter to Daniel the father referred to the young mulatto half brother as his "dear black boy Jack," making no secret of his affection. He had a portrait made of the boy. When Jack became ill, Custis wrote, with evident deep feeling, "my dear black boy Jack [is] . . . sick; wch make me very melancholy." Custis said that if Jack were to die "I am sure I should soon follow him; it would break my heart, and bring my grey hairs with sorrow to the grave my lif being wrapt up in his."[16]

The recesses of John Custis's mind cannot be plumbed, but it is possible that his love for his black child came from a feeling that Jack was a true Custis, his black mother notwithstanding, whereas Daniel was a Parke, with the traits of John's late, unlamented wife. In a fit of anger at Daniel, John drew up a will disinheriting him and giving his entire estate to Jack. Friends intervened and Custis tore up the will; but he still intended that Jack would inherit a substantial estate.[17]

In his final will Custis reaffirmed his emancipation of Jack and wrote, "I hereby strictly require" that Daniel build for Jack "a handsome strong convenient dwelling house" furnished with feather beds, walnut tables, and leather-cushioned chairs. Jack was also to have "a good riding horse and two able working horses." To put a young black man on horseback was quite a declaration in Virginia. He gave him land and livestock, and set aside £500 sterling to provide a lifetime annuity and a yearly provision of food, clothing, and additional livestock, clearly intending that Jack should never have to work a day as long as he lived.[18]

Custis loved his black son but this did not make him an emancipator. He freed no other slaves, and gave several to Jack, who was allowed to choose four slaves his own age as companion-servants. In addition, into Jack's care Custis placed the enslaved mother, Alice, whom Jack was to own with all her "increase" (the plantation term for a slave woman's offspring). It seems that Custis felt no great love for Alice, else he might have set her free as well. To him, she may once have been a lover but she was still a slave. But Jack was different—Custis blood ran in his veins. Nothing, evidently, tormented old Custis more than to know that a Custis might be enslaved. In his will he carefully specified that all Jack's offspring "born of any free Woman" were to be free. This clause virtually commanded Jack to confine his love to free women, because any children he had with a slave would be enslaved. Custis specified that Jack was to live with Daniel until he reached the age of seventeen.[19]

Into this peculiar household came Martha Dandridge. Martha was seventeen and Daniel thirty-eight when the couple decided to marry. Given his age, he may have thought Martha represented his last chance at matrimony. The Custis and Dandridge families lived not far from each other on the Pamunkey River in New Kent County. Martha's uncle had served on the council with John Custis, but what should have been a mark in her favor was instead a point of contention, for the two politicians had quarreled in the past and the elder Custis continued to harbor a grudge. Worse, Custis was far richer than anyone in the Dandridge clan, "to whom he patently felt superior," as a historian wrote. Martha, he probably thought, was nothing but a gold digger.[20]

The couple tried to keep their betrothal a secret until Daniel figured out a way to broach the subject with his father, but word of the arrangement leaked out through friends. Old man Custis was furious, threatening to throw his silverware into the street before he would see any Dandridge get a hand on it. He wrote bluntly on the subject of money: Martha was "much inferior in point of fortune." High-ranking friends tried to intervene, as they had done before when Custis disinherited Daniel, but the father would have none of it.[21]

Clearly terrified of his father, Daniel could find no solution to the deadlock. Had he possessed some of the grit and temper of his Custis and Parke forebears, he might have bullied the bully into submission, but nearly four decades of his father's dominance had snuffed any spark of independence. So Martha, a mere teenager, stepped into the lion's den herself. She went to see old man Custis at Six Chimneys, as his grand Williamsburg mansion was called, and delivered "a prudent speech." The old man softened somewhat at the pleadings of the young woman, whom he now saw as "beautifull & sweet temper'd." But his irritation with his son remained, and he still refused to sanction the marriage. If Daniel and Martha proceeded with the nuptials without approval, in the hope that the old man would eventually relent, they ran the risk of provoking him into disinheriting Daniel a second time in favor of "Black Jack."[22]

Shortly after Martha's visit to Custis another negotiator arrived at Six Chimneys. A lawyer friend named James Power came bearing gifts, not for the old man but for his mulatto son. He presented young Jack with a horse, bridle, and saddle, and told Custis that the gifts were from Daniel. Custis melted at this display of affection from one brother to another; the kindness came wholly unexpected. All obstacles vanished—indeed Custis's effusiveness over the match knew no bounds. He told Power to convey the following to Daniel immediately:

> I am empowered by your father to let you know that he heartily and willingly consents to your marriage with Miss Dandridge—that he has so good a character of her, that he had rather you should have her than any lady in Virginia—nay, if possible, he is as much enamored with her character as you are with her person. . . . I stayed with him all night, and presented Jack with [a] horse, bridle, and saddle, in your name, which was taken as a singular favor.[23]

Since Power had brought the horse and its equipage with him, the gift had been planned in advance—but *not* by Daniel. Power had to tell him about the gift and that it had been bestowed in his name. One wonders if Power would have attempted such a bold and potentially hazardous stroke on his own, without the knowledge and approval of one of the principals. If Daniel did not know of the plan, Martha is the only one who could have been behind it. She understood the enigmatic John Custis better than his son did; she grasped that the father's affection for his son, though he was of mixed race, was genuine and deep.

John Custis died in November 1749, writing his last will only eight days before his death. To the end he harbored suspicion about Daniel's loyalty and obedience. He wrote that he wished to be buried on his ancestral plantation, Arlington, a long distance from Williamsburg. Conveying a corpse to the Eastern Shore would be bothersome, and

Custis feared that his son might be inclined to forgo the inconvenience. To ensure that Daniel would honor this wish Custis specified: "I strictly require it that as soon as possible my Real Dead Body and not a sham Coffin be carried to my plantation . . . and there my real Dead Body be buried [next to] my grandfather."[24]

The wedding of Martha Dandridge and Daniel Custis took place in May 1750,* probably at her family's home. Under the terms of his father's will Daniel was required to look after his younger mulatto brother until Jack turned seventeen. Virginia mansions were full of unacknowledged, dark-skinned half siblings acting as house servants, but the Custis situation was different. Jack had not been explicitly acknowledged as kin, but he had been freed and given property. As the Custis historian James Lynch writes, "One tries to visualize Daniel, Martha . . . and Jack living in a sort of ménage à trois at White House."[25]

The "ménage" did not last very long. One night in 1751 Jack, then about twelve years old, became violently ill. A doctor was summoned to bleed him, but he died the following night. The sudden death of a mulatto heir, who had caused much distress to his wealthy brother, would be cause for suspicion, except that the diary of a family friend records a significant symptom: "Col. Custis's Favorite Boy Jack died in ab[out] 21 hours illness . . . with a Pain in the back of his Neck." Localized neck pain, rapid onset, and rapid death in a young patient are all consistent with meningococcal meningitis.[26]

The early death of Jack rescued Martha and Daniel from the humiliating requirement of overseeing the welfare of a freed slave who had been granted a life of ease on their money. Even in death, Black Jack caused problems for his brother. His father had given him a 266-acre parcel of land with the stipulation that in the event of Jack's death it would go to a white man named Kendall. After Jack died Kendall took over the property, but Daniel went to court asserting that Jack

---

* This date is recorded in a Custis family Bible; some historians believe the marriage took place in 1749.

had never been free, that his father's manumission was defective on a technicality. The court disagreed, allowing Kendall to keep the land. Daniel had to buy it back.[27]

The story of the Custis fortune reveals the complexity of slavery, "the peculiar institution" Washington initially embraced and later contended against. Slavery began as a labor system, and we continue to think of it mainly in that narrow way, but in Washington's time it was evolving into an interlocking network of public and private systems. The need to control enslaved laborers and to regularize ownership of them created a legal system of slavery;* the web of daily interactions between free and enslaved made slavery into a social system; finally, blood ties linking slaves and free people made slavery into a family system.

Each system had its own customs and rules, which sometimes came into conflict with the rules and customs of another system. As one of the richest and most powerful men in Virginia, John Custis had believed that within his private realm he could bend the social and legal apparatus to suit the needs of his black son. Combining affection for his son with the traditional haughtiness of the Virginia aristocrat, he had believed that he could, by Custis fiat, abolish slavery in this one instance for the sake of his family feelings.

On the surface, the Custis story is an amusing, racy tale of illicit sex and big money. We have caught a wealthy slaveholder, a titan of Virginia politics, in bed with a slave. We could take this as a revelation of the hypocrisy of colonial society, which condemned racial mixing while avidly practicing it, but in our eagerness to assert our moral superiority we would miss the significance of the episode: human impulse was the great enemy of the slave system. John Custis put his family's wealth in danger when he acted out of sentiment, out of common humanity. He lost control of the situation, not in fathering an illegitimate child but in yielding to the fatherly impulse to recognize the child as his own. The legal and social rules of the time were de-

---

* British law offered few precedents. Lorena S. Walsh writes, "The idea of treating human beings as real property for purposes of inheritance was a novel legal practice that elite Virginians apparently borrowed from Barbados."

signed to eliminate these dangers caused by human weakness. If slaves could not own property, then no one would give them any; if slaves could not be free without sending them out of the colony, then no one would free them; if slaves could not marry, then no free person would marry an enslaved lover. Slavery's laws and customs constrained the free as well as the enslaved, but always with the purpose of preserving slavery.

History has been carefully shaped to suppress evidence of cracks in the slave system and distort the actions of the masters and mistresses who deviated from orthodoxy. In 1860 a biographer who worked closely with the Custis family, Benson J. Lossing, sought to explain Black Jack's unusual status by saying that John Custis "had taken a most violent fancy" to him, omitting any mention of a blood tie. A cover story was being put in place by the Custis family with the aid of a cooperative biographer. Yet the Black Jack episode remained so well known in Virginia that it was impossible to suppress it entirely, though it was easy to hide the truth by implying that the old gentleman was deluded or senile. No Southerner would actually believe that explanation, but it would be useful for outsiders, who knew so little of plantation ways that they might swallow it. In my previous research into the Hairston family of planters, I documented the story of Robert Hairston, who had a daughter with a slave, set her free, and bequeathed her his entire estate. Some of his relatives tried to overturn the will on the grounds that he was insane, and the insanity explanation was advanced by generations of white Hairstons who could not bear to admit that their forebear had a black child.[28]

In similar fashion, Washington's preeminent biographer, Douglas Southall Freeman, embellishes the Black Jack cover story by portraying Custis almost as a lunatic, writing that his "eccentricities were daily more marked and, in some ways, alarming. [He] had developed, in particular, an inexplicable fancy for a little slave boy named Jack, and once, after a madly unreasoning outburst of temper against Daniel, actually was believed to have made a will in which he left nothing to his children and his entire estate to the small Negro." Writing in 1965, the biographer James Thomas Flexner was able to acknowledge

Custis's paternity of Jack, but so obliquely that the reader might easily miss it: "He freed a colored boy born on his estate whom he had named after himself, and threatened, whenever his white son did not obey him, to make Jack his sole heir."[29]

The Black Jack story involved George Washington only tangentially, but it tended to cast a slight shadow of disrepute on Martha, by association, and a deeper one directly on the character of the Custis family. Lossing, author of several books about the Washington and Custis families, edited the memoirs of Martha's grandson George Washington Parke Custis, in which the Black Jack tale is told in a footnote. He probably got the "most violent fancy" explanation of the story from Martha's great-granddaughter Mary Custis Lee, the wife of Robert E. Lee; but the originator of the cover story was probably Martha herself, because there is a detail in the story that would have been known only to someone who had actually experienced the events in question. Only Martha could have conveyed the information that John Custis had written a will giving everything to Jack and then had torn it up; the will itself did not survive. That aspect of the story was the most unsettling one—it was a cautionary tale. Everyone knew that love could cross the racial boundary, but the real danger arose when property crossed it. Martha wanted it known that such people were mad, or nearly so.

The newly wed Washingtons arrived at Mount Vernon in April 1759, after a honeymoon, with Martha's children, at Williamsburg. In advance of their arrival Washington sent a hasty note by a slave to his manager, ordering him to put Mount Vernon in order for the arrival of the master and mistress. "Have the house very well cleaned," he wrote, "make fires in the Rooms [and] Air them—You must get two of the best Bedsteads put up. . . . get out the Chairs and Tables, & have them very well rubd & Cleand—the Stair case ought also to be polishd in order to make it look well. Enquire about the Neighbourhood, & get some Egg's and Chickens, and prepare in the best manner you can for our coming." Mount Vernon was in disarray on many counts—Washington was enlarging and renovating the house, which was cluttered with paints, tools, and construction debris. The farm itself was clearly in disorder if Washington felt he had to send out for eggs.[30]

Hardly had the Washingtons arrived when George got down to very pressing business, his assumption of control over the Custis estate. He settled at his desk with a large pile of Custis accounts and ran his eye over page after page of inventories from their six plantations in six counties. He wrote out lists of all the slaves, beginning with a roster of the eighty-four "dower slaves," worth almost £3,000, that represented Martha's share of the Custis slaves, the share he now controlled. He wrote to the Custis agents in London, Robert Cary & Company, informing them of the new arrangement of the family affairs:

> The Inclos'd is the Ministers Certificate of my Marriage with Mrs. Martha Custis, properly as I am told, Authenticated, You will therefore for the future please to address all your Letters which relate to the Affairs of the late Danl. Parke Custis Esqr. to me, as by Marriage I am entitled to a third part of that Estate, and Invested likewise with the care of the other two thirds by a Decree of our Genl. Court which I obtain'd in order to strengthen the Power I before had in consequence of my Wifes Administration.[31]

Under Virginia law, because Daniel Custis had died without leaving a will, his estate had been divided into three parts for his wife and two children. The value of Daniel Custis's Virginia estate, not counting his nearly 18,000 acres of land, was about £30,000, of which about £9,000 represented the value of his slaves. In addition he held about £10,000 in British accounts. His Virginia cash, bonds, securities, other liquid assets, and personal property were split evenly, with each heir receiving more than £7,000. Under the law, Martha's "dower" share became Washington's property immediately upon their marriage. By court order Washington became legal guardian of both children, with control over their finances. Two-thirds of the land and slaves went to Jacky in name, but under Washington's guardianship. Martha received the remaining third for her use during her lifetime only; these lands and slaves came under George Washington's management, but he could not sell them because after Martha's death they would revert to the Custis estate, earmarked for Jacky. Patsy received no land or slaves, her inheritance being entirely in cash and securities.[32]

Jacky and Patsy embodied the future of the Custis family. To ensure their position in their toplofty stratum of Virginia society, their fortune could not just be ample, it had to be splendid. When the time came, they would not find suitable marriage mates if the estate had declined. Martha would not want to see her children endure the rejection she had suffered at the hands of old John Custis, who spurned her because she was "much inferior in point of fortune." Thus Martha, her children, and Washington entered into a symbiotic relationship with the estate that supported them. As David Hackett Fischer observes: "The primary purpose of [inheritance] customs was not to serve the interest of individuals, but to promote the welfare of the family and even the estate. . . . More than one English gentleman believed that his estate did not exist to serve posterity; but that posterity existed to serve the estate."[33]

Indeed the Custis estate remained a legal entity unto itself until Jacky Custis came of age. The law required Washington to make regular reports of his stewardship to the court in Williamsburg. For more than a decade he had judges and lawyers looking over his shoulder as he recorded, in minute detail, every transaction involving the Custis children. If he summoned a doctor to treat Patsy, if he bought Jacky books, he had to write the expenditures in his ledger and report them annually. This complicated arrangement required that he keep the books carefully, since he was managing three distinct financial entities whose assets could easily become commingled and confused. In fact, this happened among the slaves. Custis slaves married Washington slaves, creating families that crossed the columns in Washington's ledgers. These intermarriages caused Washington enormous anxiety at the end of his life, as he faced the prospect of freeing part of a family while leaving the other part enslaved, unless he could persuade the Custis heirs of the justice of emancipation. But all of that was far in the future. Washington wrote to another business agent expressing the delight he was feeling as family life took root at Mount Vernon: "I am now I believe fixd at this Seat with an agreable Consort for Life and hope to find more happiness [here] than I ever experienc'd amidst a wide and bustling World."[34]

Though Washington could be aloof and distant among adults, he loved children. "He was rather partial to children," Martha's grandson G.W.P. Custis recalled, drawing from his own memories of gamboling about Mount Vernon; "their infantine playfulness appeared to please him."[35] Jacky and Patsy, aged five and three, had their own slaves at Mount Vernon. A ten-year-old boy named Julius "waits on Jacky Custis," according to the financial accounts Washington wrote out. Jacky shared with his sister the services of a nineteen-year-old maid named Moll, who "sews &ca for them." In addition, Patsy had her own maid, a twelve-year-old also named Moll. To Washington, who had spent his own teen years on the frontier, sleeping in the open and in vermin-ridden pest holes, the constant bustling of house servants tending to the every whim of children must have seemed like a mirage. Altogether, twelve house slaves tended the four Washingtons, including two waiters, a cook, scullion, ironer, washer, spinner, seamstress, and Martha's fifteen-year-old maid, Sally. Such a profusion of services would have been impossible without slavery.[36]

Although Washington adopted Martha's two children, they did not take their new father's name: their name remained "Custis." The children's personal slaves wore "livery," colorful "Babes in Toyland" uniforms with a customized design that signified their servitude not to the Washingtons but to the Custises. In ordering the livery from London, Washington specified: "let the Livery be suited to the Arms of the Custis Family." Clearly Martha wanted to impress upon her children their Custis bloodline over their acquired Washington lineage.[37]

With historical figures of George and Martha Washington's stature— people whose lives have been minutely researched—it would seem very unlikely that new material would surface that would change our view of them in any significant way. But in the archives at Mount Vernon and through contacts with slave descendants I came across quite startling new information about the Washingtons and their slaves. There was a slave child at Mount Vernon who was their relative; she was Martha's half sister and became George Washington's kin through his marriage to Martha.

Among the small slave children frolicking about Mount Vernon in the spring of 1759 was a girl named Ann Dandridge, who probably became a playmate of Jacky and Patsy. She was also their aunt, though they didn't know it. Ann was the daughter of Martha's father and a woman whose name is not known, of mixed white, Native American, and African blood. Ann's date of birth is unknown, but Martha's father died in 1756, at age fifty-six, so Ann would have been at least three when she came to Mount Vernon and may have been slightly older. Martha took her in after her father's death and made her part of the Custis household and then the Washington household. As far as I can tell Ann is not mentioned in any of the Mount Vernon records. This omission led me to think that Ann might not have been a slave, because Washington kept rather good accounts of the slaves at Mount Vernon, though there are many gaps (for one thing, no systematic record of slave births has been found). Tracing a slave or servant named Ann is problematic because the nicknames Anna, Nancy, and Nan were common. The question of Ann's legal status was resolved when, through a descendant of hers, I found a record of her manumission in 1802, carried out after Martha's death. Ann came into the possession of Martha's granddaughter Eliza Custis Law, whose husband arranged the manumission when Ann was in her forties. She was freed under her married name, Holmes, and the nickname Nancy.[38]*

The manumission record does not mention a blood tie to Martha. Ann's family history emerges, ironically, in a record of the most public sort—a Congressional report published in 1871, a survey of schools in Washington, D.C., whose authors interviewed Ann's granddaughter, a teacher. She gave an account of her family background: "Ann

---

* I will take up this story in more detail in Chapter 8.

Dandridge was the daughter of a half-breed, (Indian and colored,) her grandfather being a Cherokee chief, and her reputed father was the father of Martha Dandridge, afterwards Mrs. Custis, who, in 1759, was married to General Washington." This discovery struck me as highly important for many reasons: it completely undercuts the image of the Washingtons as radically separate and aloof from their slaves; it adds layers of questions to Washington's final decision to emancipate his slaves; and it takes us deeply into the psychology of mastery.[39]

In many respects Ann Dandridge existed in a kind of twilight. She was in fact a Dandridge and carried the name, but legally she was a nonperson, mere property. Ann's very existence presented Martha with a problem. Had Martha felt resentment or malice for her half sister, she would have sold her or found some other way of discreetly getting rid of her. We might speculate that to protect the child Martha believed she had to keep her a slave—it was her duty as a sister and as a Dandridge, whatever feelings she might have had. By the standards of that time and place Martha probably thought this enslavement was an act of benevolence. Looking at the situation from Martha's perspective, one can see that the Virginia of 1759 was an impossible place for a free black Dandridge female. Ann might have found a home as a servant girl to a genteel family, but her path would have been inexorably downward. No white man of any substance would have married her; she would probably have found a colored or black husband among the free or enslaved African-Americans. Her children—Dandridge children—would have been dark-skinned and possibly enslaved. So out of duty and perhaps out of affection Martha took her sister under her wing and kept her a slave indefinitely. But there is another perspective here as well: once Martha was dead, Eliza and her husband could not bear to have Ann's enslavement continue. So one is compelled to ask, if Eliza could see the humanity of her great-aunt and free her, why could Martha not see it when Ann was no longer a child in need of protection but a grown woman?

Unlike old John Custis, who could not abide keeping his son Jack in slavery, Martha had the mental steel to hold a half sister as a slave. Martha's act reveals the capacity of the masters and mistresses to tolerate profound psychological dislocation, the conversion of kin into property. The evolution of slavery from a simple labor system into a complex, multigenerational nexus of sexual entanglements, property rights, secret family ties, and inheritance customs had thrown their tight little world out of joint. They had constructed a society where one sister held another in slavery, or where a family might simply dispose of blood kin. To his surprise, Washington discovered in 1760 that a Mount Vernon slave was the offspring of another prominent white family: "I was informd that Colo. Cocke was disgusted at my House, and left it because he [saw] an old Negroe there resembling his own Image." As Catesby Cocke was then fifty-eight, the old slave might have been a half brother he never knew he had. In any case he was flabbergasted to encounter enslaved kin. Some slaveholders saw the moral contradiction and some did not; there were divisions even in the same household. Later on, when George Washington was strenuously, desperately seeking a way to free his slaves, Martha lifted not a finger to help. She had been schooled better than he in the rigid mental discipline of mastery.[40]

With his marriage to Martha Custis, Washington became personally engaged in a mode of slavery that required certain evasions, denials, and psychological cruelties. When I traced Ann Dandridge's later life, I suspected that her plight formed one of the major reasons George Washington ultimately decided to free his slaves. Her role in motivating his actions remains unclear because George and Martha Washington never mention Ann in their surviving papers; but she was there at Mount Vernon, a daily reminder of the paradox of slavery. For a man of Washington's character, the lies and emotional cruelties of the plantation became unbearable. In 1759, as the beneficiary of one of the greatest slave-based fortunes in Virginia, Washington had to acquiesce, to cooperate with a bizarre system. Ultimately it repelled him, but not now—not when the Custis slaves brought him his salvation.

CHAPTER FOUR

A Life Honorable and Amusing

$\mathcal{T}$HE CUSTIS FORTUNE SAVED Washington from financial ruin, at least temporarily. At the time of his marriage he was sinking deeply into debt. A brief note in his diary of 1760 reveals that he was so strapped for cash that he had been putting off one creditor for two years. The gentleman, running out of patience, came to Mount Vernon to ask for his money, and Washington was unable to pay him. This circumstance was so painful that when Washington recorded it in his diary, he soothed himself with the euphemism, "was unprovided for a demand of £90."[1]

Washington was "unprovided" at the moment because he was awaiting the sale in England of his 1759 tobacco crop, but those sales proved unfavorable. His London agent sold the tobacco for less than £12 per hogshead (a barrel holding about 850 pounds); he suspected incompetence on his agent's part as he had heard of other sale prices between £14 and £16. At the same time he was stunned to see a 25 percent increase in the prices he was paying for imports. "I cannot forbear ushering in a complaint of the exorbitant prices of my goods this year. . . . Let it suffice to say that woolens, linens, nails, &c are mean in quality but not in price."[2]

Though Washington shipped more than 93,000 pounds of tobacco to England in the fall of 1760, the rendering of accounts he received the following summer was sobering: he was almost £1,900 in debt to his merchant. Like many other Virginia tobacco planters in precisely the same fix, Washington believed that the solution to falling prices and sinking profits would be found not in cutting back his expenditures but in expanding his planting operations. To accomplish this he had to buy more slaves and put more acres into production. He took a cash advance of £259 from his London merchants to carry out the purchase of slaves. The Custis estate had a credit of more than £2,000, which enabled Washington to obtain his loan; otherwise his note might have been refused.[3]

After three years of bad tobacco crops in a row, Washington had reduced his debt to his London merchants by only a hundred pounds. In a letter of September 27, 1763, he complained to his agents of his "manifest disappointments and losses" in the tobacco market, that his last shipment had been lacking a trunk containing £25 of linens and other items for Patsy ("disappointed she greatly is"), and that the hoes sent him "are so small and sorry that [the overseer] cannot possibly use them for they are scarcely wider or bigger in any respect than a man's hand." The money he acquired from his marriage to Martha was gone in four years, "swallowed up," Washington wrote, by the expense of buying slaves, land, and provisions and by the cost of putting up new buildings at Mount Vernon. He was in debt for the sum of £1,800 in 1764.[4]

As a young man Washington had tasted the luxuries of Virginia plantation life at the mansion of the Fairfaxes, who possessed enormous wealth thanks to their control, handed to them by the crown, of vast territories in Virginia. Washington had also observed the agonies of those who wished to enjoy this lifestyle without the steady means to support it. When, at the age of nineteen, he accompanied his brother Lawrence to Barbados, he got to know the lifestyle of the large-scale sugar planters there. They did not live nearly so lavishly as he had expected, and the reason was their debt. He exclaimed in his diary how astounding it was to him "that such people shou'd be in debt! and not be able to indulge themselves in all the Luxurys as well as necessarys of Life." Washington did not absorb this lesson well enough.[5]

The tobacco culture Washington inherited suffered from a cycle of economic boom and bust. Between 1744 and 1759 the price of high-quality tobacco fluctuated between £42 and £11 per hogshead.[6] The planters adjusted for this as best they could, but when Washington entered the market in the 1750s the situation had changed, though Virginians did not yet know it. Before 1750, planters could comfortably take on debt in lean years, knowing that eventually a run of profitable years would enable them to reduce or eliminate their load; but after 1750 deep and prolonged depressions in the tobacco market made their debts permanent. At this same time the Virginia and Maryland planters developed a taste for consumer goods and did not care to delay their gratification in acquiring them. In the late 1750s Virginia was hit with a drought that ruined crops and brought a rise in interest rates. Despite an alarming number of bankruptcies in England and America, the planters viewed the problem as a temporary one.

The French and Indian War, which lasted from 1756 to 1763, was in effect a global conflict, during which the British and European economies suffered severe dislocation from the costs of prosecuting the war and the disruption of markets. The colonists expected a rapid recovery when the Treaty of Paris ended hostilities, but the opposite occurred. One Maryland newspaper reported in 1764 that "the bankruptcies in Europe have made such a scarcity of money, and had such an effect on credit, that all our American commodities fall greatly." Prices rose for a year and then sagged for the rest of the decade as an economic depression settled in.[7]

Virginia planters built up debts they could not repay because they expected, by rights, to live well. They created a consumer society where wealth was made visible in grand houses grandly furnished in a manner the previous generation would have gasped at. In a pattern that future generations would follow, luxuries were redefined as necessities. The pride of the planters demanded that no expense be spared to proclaim their status. British magazines fostered a taste for stylish goods, and Virginia planters followed fads with greater speed and avidity than their richer counterparts in England.[8]

In the 1760s a Virginian noted with amazement that debts of £10,000 were thought nothing of, whereas twenty years earlier a planter would have been alarmed if he owed a tenth of that. As an example of colonial extravagance he pointed to the great planters' new fondness for costly imported carpets. "In 1740," he said, "I don't remember to have seen such a thing as a [Turkish] carpet except a small thing in a bed chamber, Now nothing are so common." Houses glittered with "every Appearance of Opulence." He noted grimly that cash was not paying for all this conspicuous consumption, but rather "all this is in great Measure owing to the Credit which the Planters have had from England," and that the planters were so busy spending that they did not know where the money was coming from. The colony's governor reported to London in 1762 that Virginia's debt was rising daily because of the taste for expensive imports, a disagreeable truth "that they shut their Eyes against. . . . I fear they are not prudent enough to quit any one Article of Luxury."[9]

Despite his debts, Washington continued to purchase wine, ale, furnishings for Mount Vernon, slaves, and finally, the topmost image of a planter's status. The emblem of wealth in Virginia was the coach, or "chariot," "the unchallengeable emblem of a planter of the highest affluence," as Douglas Southall Freeman calls it.[10] The chariot carried exactly the social status message of a modern automobile. A Virginia merchant wrote to England, "our Gentry have such proud spirits, that nothing will go down, but equipages of the nicest & newest fashions. You'll hardly believe it when I tell you that there are sundry chariots now in the country, which cost 200 Guineas."[11] In June 1768 the Washingtons were in need of a new coach. To his agents in London Washington wrote, "My old Chariot havg. run its race. . . . The intent of this Letter therefore is to desire you will bespeak me a New one." He requested that it be a model "in the newest taste, handsome, genteel and light. . . . To be made of the best Seasond Wood, and by a celebrated Workman." He had seen a new arrangement of steel springs "that play in a Brass barrel, and contribute at one and the same time to the ease and Ornament of the Carriage," and he asked for this feature. He liked the color green, as he thought it a color that would not fade and was in addition pleasing or "grateful to the Eye." But he hastened to add that he would take another color if it was "more in vogue." He wanted a "light gilding" and other ornamentation "that may not have a heavy and tawdry look." As a finishing touch he asked, "On the Harness let my Crest be engravd." He sent along a drawing of the Washington coat of arms to be copied by the engraver.[12]

Just three months later the coach was shipped to him. The invoice conveys some of the glory of this "new handsome Chariot, made of best materials, handsomely carvd." There were arches and scrolls; the sides, roof, and back gleamed with polished japanned paint; painted flowers adorned the panels of the doors; the frame glittered with gilt. A green Morocco leather seat, trimmed with lace, cushioned the passengers, whose feet rested on carpeting. The whole interior was sumptuously lined with green and red leather, and the passengers could gaze at the passing landscape through plate-glass windows etched with diamond-cut designs. If they desired privacy, they could snap shut Venetian blinds fashioned with mahogany frames. There was a place for the finishing touch, the ultimate accessory, a postilion—a slave, dressed in livery displaying the family colors, clutching a rail as the carriage bounced along, and ready to leap to the ground and open the door. The cost for the chariot and shipping came to £315 and change.[13]

Washington's purchase was a mixture of financial foolishness and confidence. Unlike many other Virginia planters, he had the shrewdness to see that the tobacco trade would eventually destroy him, and he began shifting to wheat in the mid-1760s. In just two years his output of wheat shot up from fourteen bushels per slave to fifty. His profits rose in spectacular fashion, from more than £9 per hand to £20.[14]

Debt still hung above Washington's head. He was able, briefly, to wipe out his arrears to his British merchants in 1773 when a sudden death in the Custis family brought him a large inheritance.* But just a few years later he was again among the Virginia planters who owed heavy balances to English merchants. When American debts to English banks and merchants became a matter of negotiation after the Revolution, it was found that Virginians owed almost half of the total

---

* Young Patsy died at age seventeen. See p. 150.

American debt, £1.4 million out of £3 million—with George Washington on the list among the largest Virginia debtors.[15]

In Washington's ledgers I found frequent entries showing that he bartered with his white tenants when they had no cash to pay the debts they owed him for various goods and services, such as repairs his blacksmiths made on equipment. His tenants paid with eggs, seeds, a cow, a clothes iron, butter, and by providing midwifery to the Mount Vernon slaves. In 1757 Washington noted that he paid seven shillings to "my Negros for Potatos."[16]

We have the image of the Southern planter as a man of leisure, resting in the shade of his porch with a julep in his hand, but that is a character of a later age, and the opposite of George Washington. Washington always took a direct and personal approach to the management of his plantation. Indeed, he loved farming. It provided him the deepest satisfaction, and he wrote about it with feeling:

> I think . . . that the life of a Husbandman of all others is the most delectable. It is honorable—It is amusing—and with Judicious management, it is profitable. To see plants rise from the Earth and flourish by the superior skill, and bounty of the labouror fills a contemplative mind with ideas which are more easy to be conceived than expressed. . . . The more I am acquainted with agricultural affairs the better I am pleased with them. I can no where find so great satisfaction, as in those innocent & useful pursuits. In indulging these feelings, I am led to reflect how . . . delightful to an undebauched mind is the task of making improvements on the earth.[17]

But to attain this honorable and delectable state of delight required struggle and labor. It required most of all a sense of mastery over the land and people, because the earth does not yield up its fruits easily. A Southern writer captured this sense of struggle when she described a woman who ran a farm: "'Everything is against you,' she would say, 'the weather is against you and the dirt is against you and the help is against you. They're all in league against you. There's nothing for it but an iron hand!'"[18] In Washington's case, the land was definitely against him. Mount Vernon was hilly, and runoff led to gullying. The top soil was thin, and beneath it lay a stratum of hard and virtually impervious clay. He was farming in a tub that would not drain.

Washington rode through his farms almost every day and imposed on everyone an almost military discipline. A senator joked in 1799 that "the etiquette and arrangement of an army is preserved on his farm."[19] But the reverse may have been true: Washington was to convey his plantation discipline to the army. He was possessed by a rage for order and a horror of waste.

Washington had been personally managing Mount Vernon for less than a year when he received a lesson in slave management that he thought important enough to record in his diary for future reference. On a February morning in 1760 he wrote that he was "Passing by my Carpenters" who were hewing poplar logs for fences. He took note of the stack of finished pieces they had completed the previous day and measured them. Four men, he found, had hewn "only" 120 feet of timber, a figure that struck him as ludicrously low. He asked them when they had begun the day before, and was told ten in the morning. With that reference point in mind, he "Sat down therefore and observd" his men at work, with his watch in his hand, as if he were timing a horse race.[20] This is what slaves dreaded. In fact, the crew of carpenters had a special reason for anxiety. Before Washington had taken personal control of Mount Vernon, the estate had been managed by Humphrey Knight, who died in 1758. The carpenters had literally felt Knight's anger over lax performances, and on that February morning they were undoubtedly wondering if this unfamiliar master might employ the same techniques as his late manager. In one of his reports Knight had written, "as to ye Carpentrs I have minded em all I posably could, and has whipt em when I could see a fault."[21]

With the master's eye on them, the men suddenly set a splendid pace. Washington wrote, "Tom and Mike in a less space than 30 Minutes cleard the Bushes" from around a poplar, cut the poplar into ten-foot sections, and "hughd each their side 12 Inches deep." He watched as they manhandled the crosscut saw and the heavy logs, until after "one hour and a quarter they each of them from the Stump finishd 20 Feet of hughing." Based on this observation Washington made a quick calculation: "from hence it appears very clear that allowing they work only from Sun to Sun and require two hour's at Breakfast they ought to yield each his 125 feet while the days are at their present length and more in proportion as they Increase." In sum, four men working all day hewed 120 feet of timber when the master wasn't looking; when the master was sitting there with his watch, *each* man produced 125 feet of finished timber, a productivity more than four times greater. Washington made note of this number, and it became his benchmark of productivity for the hewers.

Washington headed his annual diary with the title "Where & How my Time is Spent." Though he kept a careful, almost obsessive accounting of his activities, Washington's diaries have been a disappointment to biographers. He recorded almost no intimate observations, wrote no reflections revealing of his inner thoughts, and composed no eloquent flights of prose. But the very flatness of the diaries reveals the man—he was practical, hardworking, and demanding of himself and others. Cultivating wheat demanded less personal attention from him than growing tobacco did, and in 1765 Washington hired his cousin Lund Washington to take over many of Mount Vernon's management duties. One biographer, comparing Washington's diary entries from 1760 and 1768, thinks he found evidence that Washington began to lead a life of relative ease after he hired Lund to run things: "he was spending a considerable part of his time . . . in foxhunting, shooting, fishing, and visiting." His life did get somewhat easier—he spent several days in August 1768 foxhunting, relaxing at home, and attending horse races—but in the previous month he had spent twenty-two days supervising the cradling of wheat, the hay harvest, and planting.[22]

He personally examined the wheat crop on July 4 and found it too green to harvest and stopped the hands. The next day he hired a white harvester named Palmer to inspect the wheat and tell him if it could be safely cut. This aspect of farming was obviously a tricky business that

Washington did not feel competent to judge himself, hence he needed Palmer's opinion. Then Palmer, three white men, and four slaves began to cut at Muddy Hole farm. Washington kept an eye on them and noted, for future reference, the output of the hands: "six and sometimes 7 cradlers, cut the remainder of the field (abt. 28 acres) on this side to day." Another day he wrote, "Three White men (Cradlers) cut down abt. 10 or 12 Acres." He liked Palmer and decided to hire him to work with his carpenters at coopering. A certain amount of dickering went on between these two farming men. As part of their deal Palmer asked Washington to buy his wagon, and Washington wrote in the agreement that he would take the wagon "if it is no older than he says."[23]

Washington's work life at Mount Vernon had a routine sameness that did not bother him in the least. He wrote, with contentment, that "the history of a day . . . will serve for a year."

> I begin my diurnal course with the Sun; . . . if my hirelings are not in their places at that time I send them messages expressive of my sorrow for their indisposition—then having put these wheels in motion, I examine the state of things farther. . . . By the time I have accomplished these matters, breakfast (a little after seven oclock . . .) is ready. This over, I mount my horse and ride round my farms, which employs me until it is time to dress for dinner.[24]

Washington was a man of regular habits, and he expected his workers, white and black, to exhibit similar discipline and good order. In a seven-page directive to a manager he wrote,

> To request that my people may be at their work as soon as it is light—work 'till it is dark—and be diligent while they are at it can hardly be necessary, because the propriety of it must strike every manager who attends to my interest, or regards his own Character, and who, on reflection, must be convinced that lost labour is never to be regained—the presumption being, that, every labourer (male or female) does as much in the 24 hours as their strength, without endangering their health, or constitution, will allow of.[25]

To be at work "as soon as it is light" required that the slaves arise in the dark, before sunup, and walk in the dark to their assigned places. There was no time for breakfast, which came later. Washington also began work before breakfast. The slaves were expected to work until the sun went down, and then walk home in the dark. During the workday they had a two-hour break. In the summer months, the slaves put in a workday of fifteen to sixteen hours, six days a week.

Washington kept a close eye on his white overseers as well, and coached them in the basics of management. He sought to inculcate the habit of forethought in them, directing that if an item needed to be carted some distance immediately, then do it, but if something else would have to be carted to the same place the next day or the next month, then carry both of them at the same time and save a trip. "These things are only enumerated," he wrote, "to shew that the Manager who takes a comprehensive view of his business, will throw no labour away." His injunctions could be boiled down to two basics: use your head and always be at your job:

> Forethought and arrangement which will guard against the misapplication of labour, and doing it unseasonably: For in the affairs of farming or Planting, more perhaps than in any other, it may justly be said there is a time for all things. Because if a man will do that kind of work in clear and mild weather which can as well be done in frost, Snow and rain, when these come, he has nothing to do; consequently, during that period there is a total loss of labour. . . . be constantly with your people. There is no other sure way of getting work well done and quietly by negroes; for when an Overlooker's back is turned the most of them will slight their work, or be idle altogether.[26]

Washington took direct control of his Mount Vernon estate at a time when British agriculture was about to undergo a modernizing revolution. A passion for improving agriculture extended to the height of British society—it was chic to be concerned with the muck of farming. George III, who became king in 1760, began to maintain his own experimental plots at Windsor Castle. He wrote articles on agriculture (published with his farm overseer credited as the author). The English agricultural scientist Jethro Tull promoted the use of manures, advocated pulverizing soil with horse-drawn plows, suggested planting crops in rows so that cultivating machinery could move more easily among the plants, and devised a drilling device to set seeds at regular intervals. Washington adopted all these methods.[27]

He displayed a remarkable grasp of the farm as a complex system, an interlocking organism made up of land, climate, livestock, crops, equipment, and labor. Part of this grasp was probably intuitive, but he also gained insights from other Virginia planters, notably his good friend Landon Carter. Both Washington and Carter took a scientific approach to plantation management. Carter wrote an observation that either man might have made: "This world has somehow been established upon the principles of number, weight, and measure." Washington was averse to anything that was "slovenly but easy," and he wrote, "I shall begrudge no reasonable expence that will contribute to the improvement & neatness of my Farms . . . for nothing pleases me better than to see them in good order, and every thing trim, handsome, & thriving about them; nor nothing hurts me more than to find them otherwise."[28]

When Washington shifted from tobacco to wheat in the 1760s he had to make numerous changes at Mount Vernon. He understood the fundamental but complex relation that large-scale cultivation required large numbers of draft animals, which required large amounts of fodder, which in turn required new crops and a new landscape at Mount Vernon. This he set about in methodical fashion to create. He drained swamps to create new fields, where he planted the usual corn fodder, but also experimented with other forage crops such as lucerne, timothy, sain foin, clover, and burnet. With his draft animals provided for, he could conduct his cultivation with plows rather than with men and women wielding hoes. He had to schedule the plantation's seasonal activities with care, lest one ripening crop go to waste while another was being tended. His hay had to be cut, for example, at the same time the wheat was ripening. By abandoning tobacco Washington freed up time and labor because tobacco required constant attention whereas wheat and corn did not. The dividends in time and labor he invested in new crops of grain, peas, potatoes, and grapes. Another dividend ripened—an increase in manure, which Washington collected and plowed back into his fields.

The new modes of agriculture at Mount Vernon created a need for new skills, and it also created a new pattern of work assignments. Women worked in the fields at some of the worst, most distasteful tasks that required less skill, such as gathering and spreading manure, clearing stumps from swamps (a task with the evocative name of "grubbing"), cleaning dirt from grain, building fences, cleaning stables, and breaking up ground with hand tools in places where the plows could not go. About 65 percent of the working field slaves were women, and Washington was demanding and punctilious in his instructions for them. He wrote to a manager: "when I say grub well I mean that everything wh. is not to remain as trees should be taken up by the roots; so . . . that the Plow may meet with no interruption, and the field lye perfectly smooth for the Scythe." The menfolk meanwhile handled the plows, harrows, and wagons, sowed and cut the grain, and dug and maintained ditches. The job of ditcher, which I initially took to be a low-level task, was actually considered a skilled position.[29]

In reviewing Washington's records, I was surprised to come across evidence that Washington knew his field slaves individually. I had assumed that when he gave orders in the fields he would address himself to "you there!" or "you, the fellow with the red scarf, yes, you!" But Washington's own words offered such detailed descriptions of four of his slaves that we can actually get the sense of gazing at their faces. He obviously observed these men closely, because he wrote these descriptions from memory:

Peros, 35 or 40 Years of Age, a well-set Fellow, of about 5 Feet 8 Inches high, yellowish Complexion, with a very full round Face, and full black Beard, his Speech is something slow and broken, but not in so great a Degree as to render him remarkable.

Jack, 30 Years (or thereabouts) old, a slim, black, well made Fellow, of near 6 Feet high, a small Face, with Cuts down each Cheek, being his Country Marks, his Feet are large (or long) for he requires a great Shoe.

Neptune, aged 25 or 30, well set, and of about 5 Feet 8 or 9 Inches high, thin jaw'd, his Teeth stragling and fil'd sharp, his Back, if rightly remember'd, has many small Marks or Dots running from both Shoulders down to his Waistband, and his Head was close shaved.

Cupid, 23 or 25 Years old, a black well made Fellow, 5 Feet 8 or 9 Inches high, round and full faced, with broad Teeth before, the Skin of his Face is coarse, and inclined to be pimpley.[30]

The most remarkable features are the scarring and filed teeth of two of these men—marks of their birth in Africa. The series of cuts on Jack's face and the network of dots cut into Neptune's back had meanings that Washington did not understand, but he took careful note of them. In fact, Neptune and Cupid had been brought to Virginia from Africa only two years before Washington wrote these descriptions in 1761. Washington noted that "they talk very broken and unintelligible English." Jack had been transported from Africa several years earlier and spoke "pretty good English."

Washington wrote the descriptions because these four men had run away. In August 1761 he placed an advertisement in the *Maryland Gazette* describing the men and offering a reward for their capture. The men had run away on a Sunday and had apparently planned their escape for that day of the week. Three of them disappeared wearing Sunday clothes, such as the "dark colour'd Cloth Coat, a white Linen Waistcoat, white Breeches and white Stockings" that Peros wore. Sunday being a day off for slaves, the four escapers would not have been missed until nightfall or the next day; and the sight of four men walking down a road in good clothing would not have aroused much suspicion because many masters allowed slaves to leave the plantation on Sundays to visit relatives or trade in Alexandria.

Washington knew Cupid well because Cupid had been deathly ill with pleurisy about a year and a half before running away, several months after his arrival from Africa. On his daily tour of inspection Washington had come upon him in bed and instantly realized the seriousness of his illness. He ordered that Cupid be carried in a cart to the main house "for better care of him" and personally checked on Cupid's condition during the day and evening, writing in his diary, "when I went to Bed I thought him within a few hours of breathing his last." Cupid recovered, but any gratitude he may have felt toward his owner for the care he received was outweighed by the desire for freedom. (Years later, a Mount Vernon house servant whose life was saved by costly medical care also subsequently laid plans to escape.) These four men represented about 10 percent of Washington's labor force: in 1760 he had forty-three slaves over the age of sixteen at Mount Vernon. All together the four runaways were probably considered to be worth about £200. Having grown up with slaves, Washington had carefully observed their patterns of behavior and he thought he could predict their moves. He wrote in the advertisement:

> As they went off without the least Suspicion, Provocation, or Difference with any Body, or the least angry Word or Abuse from their Overseers, 'tis supposed they will hardly lurk about in the Neighbourhood, but steer some direct Course (which cannot even be guessed at) in Hopes of an Escape: Or, perhaps, as the Negro Peros has lived many Years about Williamsburg, and King William County, and Jack in Middlesex, they may possibly bend their Course to one of those Places.

From Washington's words it would seem that slaves often ran off after a punishment or confrontation to "lurk about in the Neighbourhood" until they had cooled off and decided to return. But because

nothing untoward had happened with these men Washington suspected they had planned their escape to an area that Peros or Jack
knew well, where they could possibly lose themselves in a free black
community. He was probably trying to protect his reputation as a
master when he insisted that there had been no abuse.

Peros might have been the leader of the escape. He spoke English
fluently. His "yellowish Complexion" suggests that he was born in
America of mixed-race parents—he was a Custis slave who had come
to the Mount Vernon plantations after Washington's marriage, and he
had spent many years in and around Williamsburg. That town had a
community of free blacks who were notorious for helping runaways.*
Two things Washington said about him are revealing. In the first
place he said that Peros was "esteemed a sensible judicious Negro," a
phrase that expresses his surprise at the sudden flight. Washington
thought he understood Peros from his sensible and presumably docile
demeanor; in fact he knew nothing. He presided over a community of
consummate actors.

Secondly, Washington noted that Peros "speaks much better than
[the others], indeed has little of his Country Dialect left." But that
means that Peros had *some* of his "dialect" left—this American-born,
mixed-race slave had retained enough of his African language, probably from a parent, so that he could communicate with Neptune and
Cupid, who spoke only "very broken and unintelligible" English. This
vignette reveals a great deal about the slave community at Mount
Vernon: newly arrived Africans mingled with African-Americans;
some could barely speak English, and some bore the cultural marks
of their homeland, scars and filed teeth that may have made them
seem exotic to the American-born slaves. Even so, the Africans and
African-Americans made common cause and laid elaborate plans
together.

The escape did not succeed. All four men were recaptured and

---

* In 1773 an overseer on a Custis plantation near Williamsburg reported to Washington that it was useless to put leg irons on slaves because "the negro Blacksmiths in
town will soon file them off."[31]

brought back to Mount Vernon. Washington did not record how this came about, though he noted an expense for "Prison Fees in Maryld Neptune." His papers do not reveal the ultimate fates of these men. One by one, over the years, they simply cease being mentioned in Washington's records. They might have run away successfully, or died.[32]

Why did these men run away in the first place? Was Washington's regime a harsh one? How hard did his slaves work? From the records, I tried to get a sense of the amount of work done by George Washington's slaves. His diary entries are laconic, and it is impossible to get a sense of the difficulty of the slaves' lives from them. In an entry for February 1762, for example, he noted plainly, "Began Plowing for Oats. . . . Sowed a good deal of Tobo. Seed at all my Quarters." In March he wrote, "Finished Plowing for Oats—abt. 20 Acs. . . . Began Plowg. and Ditchg. the Meadow. . . . began Sowing & Harrowing in of Oats. . . . grafted Six trees in the Garden. . . . Burnt Tobo. Beds." Mixed in with these entries were equally spare accounts of disasters, such as: "a prodigious severe frost . . . 'tis to be fear'd the Seed all perished."

But at certain times of the year he entered cumulative tallies that give some sense of the scale of work he expected to be done. I did some simple arithmetic on these figures, and came up with numbers I found hard to believe. At his plantation in King William County in April 1763 he recorded the making of 190,000 corn holes and 170,000 tobacco hills.[33] His roster for that farm listed just fifteen slaves with two overseers—which meant that each slave made 24,000 hills and holes. This number seemed impossible. I sent out a query to Washington experts, one of whom wrote back to say, "If you set 24,000 plants in 30 days (800 per day), you would have to drop about one per minute average for 12 hours. That is not very strenuous work for farmers."[34]

But this arithmetical answer did not seem sufficient. It turned out that the administration of the Mount Vernon estate today was itself wrestling with this question, at the plantation's Pioneer Farm, which attempts to replicate Washington's farming techniques. I contacted the woman who supervised the farm, Jinny Fox, to put the question to her. She said that if I wanted to get an idea of the working lives of Washington's slaves, she would have to put some old-time tools in my hands and set me to work in the field. It seemed like a straightforward exercise in hands-on research.

A school bus disgorged a gaggle of middle-school children as I arrived at Mount Vernon's main gate on a cold, slate-gray day in January. Jinny Fox led me from the main gate and up the path in front of the mansion. I had seen it many times, but it remained an impressive, stirring sight. On that overcast day, its whitewashed presence seemed even larger and more imposing. It was 10:00 a.m., and it occurred to me that the master of Mount Vernon would have been out for hours by that time of morning, on his daily tour of inspection. He would have been casting his sharp, commanding eye over the very tasks Fox had in mind for me. I did not think I would want to see the figure of George Washington, astride a horse, suddenly looming over me as I wielded a hoe.

As Fox led me down a side path toward a corral, I asked what had brought her to Mount Vernon. She had grown up in California, where the schools had emphasized the region's Spanish history and barely touched on the Revolution. George Washington was little more than a distant historical figure in a powdered wig. But an interest in history led Fox to volunteer at Mount Vernon as an interpreter in the "hands-on history" tent, where staffers demonstrate eighteenth-century farming and cooking techniques for the tourists. She brought a great deal of enthusiasm to the task, and after two years as a volunteer she was offered a job. For a year her assignment was to don a period costume and interpret the character of Elizabeth Washington, wife of George Washington's cousin and farm manager, Lund Washington.[35] Then she moved to the Pioneer Farm, and when the supervisor resigned, Fox was offered his position.

We stopped at the corral, where several horses munched contentedly. One of them was in fact a mule by the name of Kit. Fox explained that Washington was the first person to breed mules in America, sterile beasts that are a cross between a male donkey and a mare. Kit and his equine cousins were on winter break from their duties in Washington's treading barn, where their task was to walk in endless circles, trampling wheat stalks to separate the grain from the chaff. "He was very particular about how they would be taken care of," Fox said. "He didn't want his mules used until they were at least three years old, and then he wanted them broken in gradually. He recognized the importance of taking good care of the livestock."

The introduction of mules was just one of Washington's agricultural innovations. Fox ticked off a few of his other achievements: "He rotates crops—first he tries buckwheat and later switches to clover . . . He builds the first dung repository in America to compost manure . . . He tries to reclaim marshland for meadows . . . He plants root vegetables as an experiment in cultivation . . . Experiments with feeding his livestock better and buying better sheep to breed. These were major agricultural experiments. His problem was the land wasn't very good to begin with. By the time Washington inherited this land it was pretty well exhausted. Even the additional land that he bought had been farmed for about one hundred years." She pointed out that on the fresher fields of central Virginia to the southwest, "Jefferson was able to grow tobacco for thirty years more than Washington."

I mentioned that the diary entries from the 1760s showed that Washington spent more and more time at his favorite sport of foxhunting and less at actually managing his farms. Fox quickly sprang to his defense.

"I think that Washington's character was set in stone from day one. Even though he might have been foxhunting a lot, he's got one eye on the farms. He was hunting over the territory where he had farms, and he's watching what's going on."

She added that Washington personally supervised tobacco planting and the extensive fishing operation on the Potomac. "What people don't realize is that the planters of tobacco were just as involved as the slaves. They were the artists. They knew exactly when things had to be done. They knew when the tobacco worms were going to appear, when the tobacco fleas were going to appear. And he watched over the hauling of the seines. In 1761 they pulled 1.5 million shad and herring out of the river in three weeks. That was a major enterprise he had to have his hand on, to make sure the fish were packed in salt quickly. They would gut them, take the heads off them, and wash them in a bath of brine, then they would pack them with rock salt and seal them in barrels. Washington set aside twenty fish per slave per month as an allowance, and then the rest was sold."

We stopped at a structure that looked exactly like a rough-hewn outhouse, except that it had a small fenced-in area in front where two chickens pecked at the ground. I hesitated to speculate why chickens would be ranging around an outhouse, but I had been misled by my ignorance of agricultural architecture.

"It's a chicken coop. We're trying to figure out if the chickens will survive; because if they do then we can bring in some of the rare breeds."

"Survive?"

"The foxes. It looks like we're down three chickens. I hope that's not a bad sign." She leaned over the chest-high fence to address the chickens directly. "I don't know if they've moved three, or if you guys are down three because somebody's gotten the rest of you." But we didn't see any feathers that would indicate the depredations of a predator.

"You grow used to the fact that livestock dies," Fox remarked as we descended a path through some woods and over a footbridge to the behind-the-scenes part of Mount Vernon.

I asked her what the slaves would normally be doing at this time of the year.

"In January they'd be chopping ice off the river, burning brush, hauling and cutting wood." The Pioneer Farm closes from December to February each year because the weather is too cold for the school groups. "The months in the winter are valuable to me because that's when I go through the records with a fine-toothed comb."

We descended into a ravine to a trailer by a dirt road. This was Jinny's headquarters in the woods. Inside she had an array of sickles in an overhead rack. Mallets and hoes with rough-hewn handles stood in a corner. A table was spread with miscellaneous hand tools and a cardboard filing carton that held a batch of long, slender wood shavings that looked like the makings of a basket. There was a large crosscut saw, sticks of various shapes and sizes that had been smoothed by long use, and underfoot here and there, wooden buckets coopered on the place.

Jinny pulled out a foot-long, heavy board embedded with nasty spikes. This was a hackle for shredding flax into strands that could be woven. She produced a wad of tangled flax, which she pulled through the hackle with her right hand while resting her left hand on the spikes to keep the hackle in place—a method I thought could shred her palm if she wasn't careful. I noticed she kept a bottle of antiseptic nearby.

As Jinny was demonstrating this risky procedure, her associate Mike Robinson came in. An archaeologist, Robinson split his time between Mount Vernon and Gunston Hall, the restored estate of Washington's friend George Mason, another of Virginia's eminent founders. Tall and bearded, Mike had the look of a genuine pioneer farmer.

The two of them rooted among the tools to select the right implement for me. Mike suggested the auger, used for digging post holes. "It's the most daunting tool," he said, but then he had a second thought: "We don't want to catch his finger." Jinny concurred: "I took out a quarter inch of flesh on that." Mike rummaged around again and came up with a froe and a mallet. I had never seen or heard of a froe, which sounded medieval and looked something like a hatchet except that its long, narrow blade was hung upside down on the handle and slid loosely up and down its length.

Jinny offered me an eighteenth-century-style woolen waistcoat, of the sort, Mike said, "worn by middling farmers." A slave would never have such a warm and comfortable garment for this raw January weather. Carrying our selection of eighteenth-century tools—froe, mallet, a pair of hoes, and a flail—we set off for the work shed.

Modern Mount Vernon has built a long shed where interpreters can display the typical tasks of an eighteenth-century farm. For nine months of the year this area swarms with tourists and school groups, but on this off-season day we had the place to ourselves. In front of the shed was a pile of straw. Jinny stepped over to the pile and began thumping it with a flail—two sticks, one long and one short, attached with leather straps. Jinny held the longer stick in a modified baseball-bat grip, with her hands apart, and swung hard so that the shorter, heavier stick mashed the straw. This was one method of threshing. Jinny handed the tool to me and I took a series of enthusiastic swings. Instantly, the tedium of the task became obvious—the same motion in the same place in endless repetition. I could not imagine doing this from the early dawn to the late dusk of a summer day.

Jinny led the way to a three-walled room in the work shed with a pair of rough-hewn contraptions whose function was not at all clear at first glance. She sat down at one of them, straddling a plank and placing her feet on a treadle underneath. A wooden bar, linked to the treadle, immediately snapped down in front of her. I was grateful that I had not sat down first because I would naturally have rested my hands on the precise spot where the bar slammed down. This was a coopering bench, which functioned as a large, man-powered vise. The cooper places a piece of wood on the shelf in front of him, steps on the treadle, and the bar snaps down to hold the wood firmly in place while the cooper shaves it into a stave. Jinny said they invited an old-time coopering expert from Nebraska to do a day of demonstrations. He said that in the old days coopers were apprenticed as early as age seven, and by the age of fifteen could turn out seven buckets a day.

The companion machine was a marvel of ingenuity—a lathe powered by a cut sapling that acts as a spring. The worker sits at the lathe, pushing a treadle. The treadle is attached by a rope to the sapling, fastened horizontally to a post behind the operator and extending over his head to the front of the lathe. Each time the worker pushes the treadle the sapling is pulled down; when he releases the treadle the sapling springs back into place, spinning the lathe. Mike said that the lathe was a vital machine for any farm estate because it was used for making handles, and "the handles for tools were particularly important because somehow they were always breaking." I commented that this "machinery" looked so antique and quaint—the perfect props for a Currier & Ives scene. Jinny responded, "With all the repetition it loses its charm."

They took me to the adjacent part of the shed, where I finally learned what a froe was for. Mike bent over a block of cedar, rested the blade near an edge of the wood, and tapped the froe with his mallet. The blade gently dug into the wood. Mike slipped the handle down a bit, gave the blade a twist, and with a splitting sound a neat sliver of cedar fell to the ground. "There's one shingle," Mike said. This is how roofs got made, one shingle at a time. Mike handed the tools to me, and I felt the pleasure of working with a tool perfectly suited to its task. I tapped and twisted, and soon had a small pile of shingles to show for my effort. I finished and leaned the froe against the block of wood, with its blade down, realizing quickly I was doing the wrong thing. I asked Mike how to put the tool away. "Would you put the froe on the ground with the blade down? Or would that dull it?" Mike replied, "That's what a slave would do."

His remark stunned me since it was so gratuitously insulting. Then Jinny jumped in and filled in the logic. "If it's dull you don't have to work. Wouldn't it be a shame if you came down here first thing in the morning and you found your blade was too dull for you to work?" Mike added, "How long would it take you to find another one?"

Now I realized the implication of Mike's earlier remark about tool handles always turning up broken. Jinny called it "passive resistance"—random and petty sabotage, malingering, tools missing and broken, rampant theft.

"Sheep are disappearing, wool is disappearing, grain is disappearing," Jinny said. "Washington is running himself ragged trying to stop it—lock this, lock that, only cut out enough fabric for one garment when you give it to them." Jinny had been reading the letters from Philadelphia written by Washington when he was president to his then manager at Mount Vernon, William Pearce. From Pearce's reports Washington had deduced that the slaves had figured out a way to steal wool without detection. It was his custom to allot to the slaves the dirty, least valuable portion of the wool at shearing time. "The best wool is from the back of the sheep's neck down his back," Fox explained. "The stomach wool was allowed the slaves because that's where all the vegetable matter and manure gets absorbed. Washington, who has figured out exactly how much wool he should be getting from these sheep, finds out that he is getting about two or two and a half pounds of wool instead of five pounds per sheep." When the slaves took their allotment of the fouled stomach wool, they were surreptitiously helping themselves to a large portion of the good wool.

To make matters worse, the shearers would toss some of the dirty stomach wool in with the batches going to the spinners at the mansion. The spinners were under orders, naturally, not to spin dirty wool. So when they received their allotments every week, they set aside the bad wool for themselves. In this manner, the thieving rippled through the Mount Vernon system. Washington, with his eagle eye, detected it from his meticulous reading of the weekly reports: "I perceive by the Spinning Report of last week, that each of the spinners have deducted half a pound of dirty wool. —to avoid this in the future (for if left to themselves they will soon deduct a pound or more) it would be best to let them receive none but clean wool."

The slave women at one of the Custis plantations that Washington had to manage from a distance were expert negotiators, and they took full advantage of the communications confusion that resulted from the master and mistress's absence. The overseer on that plantation wrote with exasperation to Washington in 1772 that a spinner had filled a quota of wool and stopped working, claiming that Mrs. Washington had agreed that three pounds a week of wool would be sufficient. Another slave refused to spin at all because Martha had agreed that she only had to sew, another because she said her only job was watching the children. The slaves had no qualms about refusing the overseer's requests, saying that Mrs. Washington did things differently. Confused and vexed, the overseer wrote to Washington to ask what Martha wanted done.[36]

Nails disappeared by the barrel; the stable boy was stealing the horse feed; Washington figured that half of his pigs were being stolen; and so much seed was walking off that Washington ordered the seed to be mixed with sand so it would be too bulky and heavy to steal. He railed against "the deception with respect to the Potatoes."[37] Washington went mad with frustration when he observed his wagoners at "work":

> There is nothing which stands in greater need of regulation than the Waggons and Carts at the Mansion House, which always whilst I was at home appeared to be most wretchedly employed—first in never carrying half a load; —2ndly in flying from one thing to another; and thirdly in no person seeming to know really what they did; and often times under pretence of doing this, that and the other thing, did nothing at all.

He complained that the wagons seemed to go off and "go to sleep." He watched as the carters pulled tiny loads they could carry on their backs, while his bricklayers stood idle because the carters hadn't delivered any bricks to them.[38]

From reading Washington's letters Fox came to a not-so-startling conclusion: "He obviously doesn't trust black people." I reminded her that Washington trusted several black men enough to make them overseers. "But they're picking him clean," she replied. "He was infuriated by Davy, whom he described earlier as being one of the best overseers, because the lambs were disappearing." She mentioned another slave named Isaac, one of the few slaves whom Washington allowed to have a gun for hunting. Isaac lost his hunting privilege when his carelessness with fire was thought to have caused the burning of the plantation's carpentry shop.

Washington struggled with his white overseers as well. When he was away from Mount Vernon during his presidency, the overseers drank and lazed about. "There was a man named Crow whose idea of overseeing was to entertain guests in his house, so he was never out in the fields," Jinny said. Naturally, the slaves simply stopped working. Jinny said that Washington found out about Crow's work habits from the slaves, "because when things fell behind Crow would pull out the whip." The slaves knew that Washington disapproved of indiscriminate whipping, so they complained to him. Jinny mentioned another overseer, Thomas Green, who was in charge of Mount Vernon's carpenters. He, too, did almost nothing, but he was able to get away with it for a long time.

"Green was smart. He let the slaves do what he did. They were getting drunk with him and they were not doing any work, but they weren't going to report on Green because Green wasn't whipping them. They had a sort of pact going, and that's what frustrated Washington. Washington wrote that the slaves under Green did nothing. He said it would take them longer to build a chicken coop than it would take the same number of carpenters in Philadelphia to build an entire house." But Washington worried that the man who replaced Green, James Donaldson, would prove equally unreliable. "He did not want Donaldson living with the slaves because he was afraid that Donaldson would corrupt them if he's a drinker. So his view of overseers isn't a whole lot better than his view of slaves." Washington gave Donaldson strict, almost military instructions not to get too familiar with his subordinates.

In his struggle to control his slaves Washington had to resort to violence. He regarded physical punishment as a necessity. But he also knew it was necessary to restrain his overseers in wielding the whip. "The overseers were supposed to petition him if a slave needed punishing. It was supposed to be written down why," Jinny said. He knew that Crow was a violent man—the slaves had told him—so when it became necessary to have a slave whipped, he sent instructions to Pearce to have it done, "but do not trust Crow to give it to him."[39] The issue of the whip forced Jinny to confront the morality of Washington's regime. "It's easy to say 'the overseers whipped the slaves.' But if Washington gave permission, he might as well have wielded the lash."

Fox had begun her close reading of Washington's letters and farm reports to reconstruct the reality of a working plantation as accurately as possible, but she was coming on something more valuable, a view of Washington's inner life, of his decades-long moral struggle with slavery. She found clues to it in many places, even in something as mundane as the weekly "sick bay" report from his manager. She found accounts of people who, with no clear excuse, did not show up for work for days on end. She noticed that Washington was often inclined to give these malingerers the benefit of the doubt. "Washington, being a fair enough individual, will entertain the idea that there might be a legitimate cause, which is amazing." He would direct the manager to visit the slave personally, examine him, and determine if a doctor's attentions were warranted.

This response to the thieving and malingering at Mount Vernon intrigued Jinny Fox. "He railed against it but didn't stop it. I think he could have stopped it. I think there were slaveholders who successfully stopped a lot of things, but they did it in a way that would have been unacceptable to Washington. If you keep people's flesh torn into shreds you can eventually break their spirit, or kill them. But that's where Washington stands out. I really like the man's character. He was a man with a keen sense of fairness and rightness. What's remarkable about Washington is there seems to be something carved out inside of him that is distinctly different." Yet as soon as Fox expressed this feeling about Washington's fair-mindedness, she qualified herself: "But he is a slave owner, and there's no way to sugarcoat that."

There is a particular incident in Washington's slaveholding career that is hard to sugarcoat. Some of his famous false teeth, celebrated in textbook lore, were yanked from the heads of his slaves and fitted into his dentures. Moreover, Washington apparently had slaves' teeth transplanted into his own jaw in 1784, in a procedure that did not succeed. At first, this seems to be the ne plus ultra of casual plantation cruelty; but Washington paid his slaves for the teeth, and the custom of the wealthy buying teeth from the poor was common in Europe. The dentist who performed the procedure at Mount Vernon was an itinerant Frenchman who transplanted teeth for many well-to-do clients, including acquaintances of Washington. It has long been known to specialists that some of Washington's false teeth came from the mouths of his slaves, but this inherently invidious tidbit of fact has not been widely circulated (despite enduring public interest in Washington's supposedly wooden dentures, which were mainly made of ivory) because it is impossible to rationalize it completely. Better not to know.[40]

I was standing at the edge of a field, staring at the dirt. Behind me, within running distance, flowed the Potomac River. In Washington's time the river carried a constant commerce of ships of all kinds. That view would surely have tantalized the slaves. The ships headed downstream were destined for the Chesapeake and the Atlantic, on routes to places where slavery did not exist. How many slaves imagined the run to the riverbank, a frantic swim to a passing vessel, a helping hand to pull a man aboard and take him away? In the history of Mount Vernon such a day came only once, and not exactly in that form. During the Revolution a British warship dropped anchor here, demanding supplies and offering passage to any slaves who wished to flee. Seventeen men and women scrambled aboard.

Jinny and Mike put a hoe in my hand and started me chopping at the clay. They explained that this earth had been plowed so often it was far softer than the hard clay the slaves would have confronted on an average January day. I was hoeing at a pretty brisk pace when Jinny began chanting a song.

> *Juba this, Juba that*
> *Juba killed a yellow cat.*

She timed her chant to my motions, and then began to slow down. I slowed down too, without thinking about it. She said that was how the slaves managed their own work: a leader would chant, setting a tempo that everyone could keep up with; if the overseer came into view, the leader would speed up, and once he departed the chant would slow down again.

I told Jinny and Mike that I had read that in one planting season, a slave would make more than 11,000 tobacco hills, and I asked them what that meant. Jinny took the hoe and pantomimed making a hill—the reality would have covered her with mud. A slave would set one foot on the ground and then hoe up the earth around it, heaping it against his or her leg—both men and women did this work—all the way to the knee. Then the slave would carefully lift out the leg, and the resulting hole, in a two-foot-high hill, would receive a tobacco seedling. Doing this several hundred times a day had to be one of the most arduous and filthy labors on a farm.

"They must have kept a frantic pace in planting season," I said. "There was probably no break for bad weather."

"Actually, tobacco planting is better in bad weather. The optimum time to transplant seedlings is in the rain, when they will have a better chance of surviving. They often planted tobacco in driving rainstorms. That's when you need to do it. You'd have one slave tending one to three acres, and you have three to five thousand holes per acre. The labor of tobacco was just tremendous, mind-boggling."

Mount Vernon's modern farm raises patches of tobacco and wheat, so visitors can get a sense, at any time of year except midwinter, of what kind of agricultural work was actually going on in Washington's time. And they can actually participate in the work. This "living history" approach to interpretation had been used for more than eighty years at other historic sites, but it was not inaugurated here at the Pioneer Farm until 1999.

"We had this pat little thing we did about hoecakes," she said. When visitors came to the fields they would find a costumed woman cooking a cornmeal cake on a hoe held over a fire. The visitors would be invited to have a bite of hoecake to give them a sense of how the slaves lived. "We would talk about the food the slaves ate and mention that they worked in the field and that would be it. We wouldn't get into any controversy. We had a lot of irritated, frustrated people who wanted to know the other side of the story. They wanted to know: *What were the slaves doing? What were their lives like?* And we were saying"—she mimicked in a jaunty tone—"'Oh, well, they got a quart of cornmeal, they got some salted fish.' You're almost making a mockery of what happened. It's a flippant approach. And it came off as Washington being 'good,' and that bothered me. It isn't that I want Washington to be bad. It's that I want people to understand what slavery was."

By trying to depict the lives of the slaves with some authenticity, Jinny Fox tumbled into the moral maze of slavery. The simple matter of re-creating a colonial farm scene had a paralyzing moral effect. Up North, ersatz Pilgrims can hoe and scythe all day long at Plimoth Plantation with no moral ambivalence, but in the South, simply to depict the working lives of slaves, without making any overt moral judgment, is to call the "goodness" of Washington into question.

"We began implementing the hands-on program because we wanted to produce a sense of what slavery really was, particularly for the groups of kids who come. If you do the work you begin to grasp the labor. In March, when it's still freezing here, they have an idea of what it's like to dig clay, cut rails, and split them. Anybody can do that in April and May, but they don't like to do it in March. Then, on a hot May day, cutting three bunches of wheat gives you a real idea of what it might be like cutting sixty acres. Only you get to quit. You can stop. *It's hot. I don't want to do this anymore.* But the slave is going to be there from five o'clock in the morning until the sun goes down.

"We raise about fifty tobacco plants per year and the kids are allowed to do a number of things with the plants. During the course of the year you have to sucker it, pull the worms off of it, watch it every day so that at the peak of ripeness you're going to be cutting it. Those plants are sticky; the leaves are covered with little hairs. When the kids handle those plants, we tell them to visualize about five thousand plants that they're responsible for, passing through every other day, checking for the worms.

"We work on a one-third-acre field. Sixty acres was the *smallest* of Washington's fields. He had fields of 120 acres. Imagine now, every six feet, another row of corn running the whole length of that acreage. And the only way to get the weeds out because of heavy rain is by hand. I can tell you, last summer, in our little, tiny one-third of an acre—and we didn't do it all day long because we rotate around—it took us four weeks to clear the weeds out. Once the vetch gets in there, you can weed it and two days later it's back up again.

"I don't know how people did it. I like hard work. I love working with my hands, I love being outdoors. But what if I were compelled to do that? What if the best I could hope for my child was that he might be light-skinned enough and clever enough to attract the attention of the master and be made a house servant rather than a field hand?" Promotion to "the big house" meant a somewhat easier life, but the enslavement continued. Perhaps the hardest thing about slavery was the eternity of it, to work in the fields and to see your children and grandchildren working beside you and know that this will be their life forever. There is never going to be any way out.

Next to the field where the work is demonstrated Jinny had a shed built where visitors can try grinding corn and taking part in a game the slave children played. Each day the slaves had two hours off at midmorning to make and eat their breakfast, and while the adults prepared the food the young ones played. Under the shelter (which the slaves actually would not have had), a table was set up with a large pestle with two long handles for crushing corn into meal. Jinny showed me how two people would stand at the mortar and methodically drop in the pestle, to a chant, to grind the day's corn. It takes about an hour to grind a cup of cornmeal, which is what they needed for a day's ration. This was a task the slaves actually wanted to do. It was part of their tradition. Washington wanted to give cornmeal rather than whole corn because it was easier to measure accurately and it saved time; but the slaves wanted the whole corn, and Washington reluctantly agreed. One reason the slaves wanted corn kernels instead of meal was that they were sharing their ration with their chickens.

Mount Vernon's archaeologists have been surprised at the variety of food remains they find in the foundation of the House for Families on the estate. "They were allowed to hunt and fish," Jinny said. The few slaves who were allowed to use a gun to hunt for Washington's table were hunting for their own food as well. But there was a time of year Jinny called "the starving season—the time when the meats are going bad, and there isn't the fresh game and the crops are not in yet and the vegetables the slaves were allowed to grow were not up yet. Probably between March and June." At that time of year poorer people, white and black, free and slave, were struggling to get enough food.

At another table under the shed Jinny and her staff have visitors play a plantation game, with four players standing around the table, sliding sticks to one another as someone chants. Players pass the sticks in time with the chant, which speeds faster and faster: the point of the game is to keep up the pace because the person chanting will stop abruptly, and you lose if you have two sticks in front of you. On a plantation, this game was meant for the littlest ones, slaves just three or four years old. The elders designed it so the children would learn as early as possible the rules of the slave life that awaited them: you need to work in unison with others; you need to keep up; if you fail to keep up, you'll get in trouble. Slave parents taught their children how to be slaves. They did not teach them to run away or fight back, which would have been suicidal; they taught their children how to survive. In the fields and in the mansion, the psychology of slavery was self-perpetuating.

Our final stop was Washington's threshing barn, an edifice far more interesting than its name implied. I did not think of Washington as an inventor, but his constant striving for efficiency led him, even in the midst of discharging the duties of the presidency, to take up a pencil and sketch out plans for an inspired piece of agricultural innovation. This new kind of barn was essentially a machine the size of a small building, where wheat would be threshed by horses and mules. The original barn stood until the 1870s, when it had to be torn down. In the 1990s Mount Vernon reconstructed it, based on Washington's original drawings and a glass-plate photograph taken about 1870. Round in appearance, the barn is actually a sixteen-sided polygon under a steeply pitched conical roof. (The caplike roof gives the barn a distinctly African appearance.) Jinny led the way up an earthen ramp to a wide opening. When I entered the barn I realized that I was on the second floor of a two-story structure. The lower floor, below grade, could not be seen from the front.

The slaves would haul the wheat up the ramp and spread it on the second-story floor to a depth of several feet. Then horses and mules would be brought in to trot around the circular floor, separating the wheat from the chaff under hoof. Washington had the inspiration to design this floor with gaps, so that the grain fell to the granary level below. He had his carpenter experiment with gaps of different widths to attain the perfect spacing that would allow the grain to fall through freely without letting straw fall along with it—a gap of 1.5 inches was found to be ideal. Once the grain had tumbled into the lower granary, there it would remain, safely stored, until wagons brought it to Washington's mill. The slaves would haul out the chaff, pile it up outside the barn, and begin the process again. It was an elegant solution to several problems, and to see the reconstructed barn today is to admire Washington's ingenuity.

Like so many aspects of plantation life, this barn had a subtext. Washington was inspired to build the barn after a long tug-of-war with the slaves over how threshing would be carried out at Mount Vernon. Washington wanted the slaves to thresh indoors on a threshing floor, so that rain would not ruin the wheat and so that the grain would not get mixed with dirt and then require time-consuming cleaning. For this purpose he originally built a one-story threshing barn, large enough to accommodate twenty to thirty threshers. But the slaves had their own agenda. Rather than flailing away at the wheat themselves, they preferred to have the horses do it for them; nor did they like the tasks of hauling the wheat into the barn and the straw out of it. The easiest way to thresh was still the old-fashioned way: to pile the wheat up in the field (as Mike remarked, "there are no doors in a field") and lead the horses over it. If the master didn't like it, too bad.

When Washington came to inspect the workers at his first barn, he found, to his astonishment, a threshing circle set up outside the barn. The slaves had simply ignored the building and spread the wheat on the ground, as before, and had set the horses to walking on it, as before. Washington knew when he was beaten. But from this defeat arose his inspiration: he would find a way to get the horses indoors.

The result was the ingenious two-story design with its carefully creviced floor.

Over all, however, Washington's attempts to increase efficiency, improve quality, and attain better profits were always hampered by the slave system. The slaves (and, to a great degree, the overseers) did not share his vision or his drive because they could never share in the results. Washington never quite grasped this idea because he had been brought up to be indifferent to what his inferiors thought and felt. He sensed the slaves' resistance to innovations, and it merely made him angry. Any innovation, he found, had to be very simple to be comprehensible to his overseers and slaves. A new type of English threshing machine caught his interest, but he despaired of getting any use out of it "among careless negros and ignorant Overseers," noting with sarcasm, "if there is anything complex in the machinery it will be no longer in use than a mushroom is in existence." Even a relatively simple device such as a new version of a plow would be of no use to him; he had learned "from repeated experiments, that all machines used in husbandry that are of a complicated nature, would be entirely useless . . . and impossible to be introduced into common use where they are to be worked by ignorant and clumsy hands, which must be the case in every part of the country where the ground is tilled by negros."[41]

Washington kept in his mind a simple formula as the governing principle of his life as a planter. Late in life he wrote it down in a letter to a manager. On his plantations he sought "tranquility with a *certain* income."[42] A great deal is expressed in this formula. Washington, like other planters, did not seek to be harsh or brutal; he wished for *tranquillity*. This is an eerie echo of a phrase in the Preamble to the Constitution, which states that the people ordain the Constitution to "insure domestic tranquility." That tranquillity was brought about by government and by the consent of the governed. Similarly, slaves had to accept government. They were not expected to consent, merely to acquiesce and to cooperate. The result would be "a certain income" for the owner. Tranquillity made the economic part of the formula possible, but the tranquillity of the plantation was entirely superficial, as it rested upon the constant threat of violence. The plantation could not function in turmoil and constant violence, so an atmosphere of harshness prevailed because economy always trumped human concerns. It is interesting that, unlike Jefferson, Washington never instituted a system of rewards for slaves who performed well; he expected that they would do their duty and that he owed them nothing extra.

In 1785 Washington had a conversation with a slave that shows how he kept his financial equations in mind. It was harvest time, when every man, woman, and child was needed to bring in the crop, so Washington was dismayed to spot someone not working. The man had injured his arm, which was in a sling. Washington thought that having the use of only one arm need not prevent a man from working, and he proceeded to demonstrate to his slave how to rake with one arm.

He grabbed a rake with one hand and tucked the other hand in his pocket. He then raked, saying to the slave, "Since you still have one hand free, you can guide a rake. See how I do it: I have one hand in my pocket and with the other I work. If you can use your hand to eat, why can't you use it to work?"[43] This man, though injured, was still consuming food. The one good hand that scooped up food could handle a tool.*

Another of Washington's basic equations expressed Virginia's governing economic principle: slaves equal land, and land equals wealth. The more slaves you had, the more land you could settle and cultivate. Washington spent about £2,000 buying slaves before 1772, but he ceased making purchases in that year. In July, making one of his last purchases, he wrote to the man who was carrying a consignment of Mount Vernon's flour and herring to the West Indies: "The Money arising from the Sales I would have laid out in Negroes, if choice ones can be had under Forty pounds Sterl[ing]." He specified what he wanted: "If the Return's are in Slaves let there be two thirds of them

---

* Though Washington complained about the difficulty of getting slaves to work effectively, it was not a problem confined to one race. He complained about white workers as well. He had to fire a white wagon driver who "behaved so remarkably ill . . . running me in debt in many places of the road he usd to travel." A house painter named John Winter "stole a good deal of my Paint & Oyl" and ran away. But Winter was caught and agreed to work off his theft, as he was "apprehensive of Justice."

Males, the other third Females—the former not exceeding (at any rate) 20 yrs of age—the latter 16—All of them to be strait Limb'd, & in every respect strong & likely, with good Teeth & good Countenances." He was thinking about Mount Vernon's future; he wanted teenaged slaves, including girls with a long period of childbearing ahead of them. Washington was growing laborers as if they were a crop, to make himself self-sufficient as a slave owner. The results of his planning are clear. Between 1760 and 1774 the number of his taxable slaves more than doubled from 49 to 135.[44]

The function of the slaves in Washington's financial equations— and the casual callousness of those equations—emerges clearly in the story of the slaves Nancy and London. In 1773 he dispatched these two slaves from Mount Vernon to a farm he was starting in western Pennsylvania. He had to begin cultivating it in order to reduce the taxes on the land—uncultivated land was taxed at a high rate to encourage settlement and to discourage holding land empty for speculation. Large landowners, such as George Washington, who was in fact engaged in a long-term real-estate investment, found it necessary to "settle" land with a small number of slaves, whose labor insured his investment.

Washington had a partner in this operation, Gilbert Simpson, who lived on the place. As his part of the bargain Washington sent the two slaves to clear the land and get a crop into the ground. Clearing virgin forest was perhaps the hardest of all farming tasks, requiring brute strength and a great deal of endurance to bear up under that labor for months at a time. Washington sent a crippled male slave and a house girl. They were useless to him at home, but they could earn their keep clearing distant land. The man named London was lame because he had lost some of his toes to frostbite. Washington knew well the extent of London's lameness—he could not even walk with ease, let alone perform hard labor. Washington himself wrote to Simpson, in explaining London's merits, that the loss of his toes "prevents his Walkg with as much activity as he otherwise would." But on the positive side Washington adjudged London to be "a good temperd quiet Fellow," meaning he was docile and would not disrupt the tranquillity of the operation.

As for Nancy, Washington knew she had a large family at Mount Vernon, which he later alluded to in a letter to Simpson, saying that they would be delighted to see her. When he sent her off from her family, Washington described Nancy as "a fine, healthy, likely young Girl which in a year or two more will be fit for any business—her principle employment hitherto has been House Work." So Nancy was little more than a child who had done housecleaning. Simpson described the work he had for them. He said he had never carried out harder work, and wrote, "the cutting is vastly heavy occasioned by the great number of old trees lying on the earth."

After putting London and Nancy to work for several months cutting and hauling enormous trees, Simpson was blunt in his report to Washington: "you furnish me with two hands as sorry as they could well be. The fellow is a worthless hand and I believe always will be so," partly because of his lazy nature and partly "occasioned by his feet." As for Nancy, "she knew nothing of work but I believe she will make a fine hand after two or three years."[45]

Washington's overriding concern with labor efficiency led him to divide his slaves in a way that greatly weakened their families. Later in life, he expressed great concern for the slave families, refusing to break them apart by sale and in his will expressing great anxiety lest families be broken up after his death. But he showed no concern for keeping families together day by day. He routinely separated husbands from wives and fathers from their children.[46]

Washington divided the Mount Vernon estate into five separate farms—an important management arrangement for the slaves. Every farm had its own slave quarters, which meant that the slave community was divided into five parts. Waste of any sort appalled Washington, and nothing irritated him more than wasting time. If he had only one central slave quarters, then the workers would expend valuable time "commuting" to work at outlying fields. As he wrote, he was determined to avoid losing "much time in marching and countermarching." But he needed the more skilled workers, who were male, at the main house, so the result of his division of laborers was that many families lived apart—husbands at the "Home Farm," wives and children on the outlying farms.

Washington was certainly aware of this effect when he formulated his work plans. The list of slave families he drew up as an appendix to the will shows that half of the married men at Mount Vernon did not live with their families. Thirty-two of the married women did not live with their husbands. In only eighteen families did husband and wife reside together. On one of the outlying farms there was not a single intact family. From time to time Washington responded to individual pleas and rescinded orders that would have separated spouses; but as a general management practice he institutionalized an indifference to the stability of the slave families.[47]

If Washington thought he had entirely solved the problem of "marching and countermarching" he was incorrect. He created a new problem he called "night walking"—men and women going out at night to visit family members. A man named Boson, who was twice caught running away in 1760, may actually have been night walking to visit his lover when he was caught. In Washington's later records Boson turns up as the husband of Myrtilla, who had been a house maid at Belvoir, the nearby Fairfax estate. Washington knew Myrtilla—after visits to the Fairfaxes in 1758 he noted in his account book the amount of the tips he'd given her. There is no record of Washington's buying her from the Fairfaxes, but then she appears suddenly in the Mount Vernon records as Boson's spouse and the mother of his children.[48] Romance accounted for some night walking, but there were more serious purposes as well. An overseer informed Washington of the extreme anxiety separations caused the families. During a measles outbreak a mother "begd to go up to see her Children," who were on a separate plantation. The separation of families, the overseer wrote, "seems like death to them."[49]

At the margins of the plantation formula, there could be certain deficiencies. Washington's own records indicate that the slaves were miserably clothed. A set of clothing was doled out just once a year, supplemented by a woolen jacket in winter. The set of clothes consisted, for the men, of "a jacket, breeches, 2 shirts, 1 [pair] stockings, 1 [pair] shoes each." Women got "a Petty coat, 2 shifts, a Jackett, [pair] stockings, & 1 [pair] shoes each." With no change of pants or petti-coat, these men and women were expected to carry out a year of field labor. Within months their clothing must have been reduced to mere rags. The slaves needed socks, could not get them from the master, and so they stole them, leading Washington to denounce their "vil-lany." And the slaves stole wheat sacks to mend their clothes by them-selves, sacks made of coarse fabric so close in appearance and texture to their normal clothing that repairs—and thefts—could not be de-tected. Washington's manager suggested purchasing sack cloth of a different design "which a [slave] could not mend his Cloaths with without a discovery." The clear meaning of this is that it was deemed preferable to have the slaves go about in tattered rags, and that dis-covery of a mended garment would bring down punishment.[50]

Washington complained about a seamstress making long pants for slaves rather than the regulation short breeches because he didn't want to expend the extra cloth. He was also very sparing of blankets. Moth-ers received a blanket for each newborn, but in the normal course of events people had to wait years to get a fresh blanket. These items, too, were reduced to filthy, insect-ridden rags because Washington or-dered the slaves to use their blankets not only for sleeping but to haul leaves to line the beds of the livestock.

> Let the People, with their blankets go every evening, or as often as occasion may require, to the nearest wood and fill them with leaves for the purposes abovementioned; bottoming the beds [of the stables and animal pens] with Corn Stalks and covering them *thick* with leaves.

This should be done, he said, "for the comfort of the Creatures. . . . Make the Cattle lay warm and comfortable. The Hogs also must be well bedded in leaves."[51]

The clothing shortage among the slaves was occasionally even more acute than the normal scarcity. In one year an overseer reported to Washington from an outlying Custis farm that the slaves had only one shirt each, instead of two, and that some of the shirts were too small to be worn. The following summer the overseer obliquely, gently chastised Washington because "you Sent for no Blankets . . . for the wenches with Child & those who have young children," so the overseer had to use the cotton allocated for clothes to make these blankets. The same overseer reported one December that the black children had no clothes at all—none—and it was already winter.[52]

Tranquillity had to be ensured with punishment. There was no other way, even at Mount Vernon. Washington took care of most offenses by slaves on the plantation with a whipping, carried out not by him but by the overseers. Only capital crimes merited the attention of the court: "If he should be guilty of any atrocious crime that would affect his life, he might be given up to the civil authority for trial; but for such offenses as most of his color are guilty of, you had better try further correction, accompanied by admonition and advice."[53]

One of Washington's overseers mentioned a whipping in one of his regular reports in 1773. James Hill, in charge of a Custis plantation that came under Washington's control after his marriage, wrote to him that he was having repeated trouble with a slave named Jemmy, "one of the Greatest Raschals I lookd after in all my life." In a fury with Jemmy for running away and stealing corn, Hill gathered a party of overseers and hunted him down with dogs. Hill prepared to give the man a severe lashing, but when Jemmy removed his shirt Hill was stunned—"he appeared as if he had been in time Past Severely Corrected." The scars Jemmy bore surprised even a hardened overseer. Nonetheless, some punishment had to be given; Hill reported, "I whipd him But very little."[54]

When one of his slaves ran away and was captured in 1793, Washington ordered a whipping with a euphemism and an admonition: "Let Abram get his deserts when taken, by way of example; but do not trust Crow [an overseer] to give it to him; —for I have reason to believe he is swayed more by passion than by judgment in all his corrections." Elsewhere Washington wrote that "flogging" by this overseer, Hyland Crow, had "in one or two instances been productive of serious consequences," apparently meaning serious injuries.[55] If Washington at times regretted the fierceness of his overseers, he also used it as a threat. When the productivity of the seamstresses at Mount Vernon fell off in 1792, Washington sent them a blunt warning through his manager: "tell them . . . from me, that what *has* been done, *shall* be done by fair or foul means . . . otherwise they will be sent to the several Plantations, and be placed as common laborers under the Overseers thereat." When a skilled laborer at the mansion, a bricklayer, was thought to be shirking, Washington threatened that he would be "severely punished and placed under one of the Overseers as a common hoe negro."[56] A slave named Sam ran away three or four times and was caught each time, prompting Washington to offer him for sale locally—he hired a town crier in June 1767 to call out the terms of the sale, but there were apparently no takers. Women ran away as well. When a runaway named Bett was caught, Washington had to pay the costs of her return, and he also paid to have Cloe released from prison.[57]

On a larger scale, Washington joined with his Virginia peers to monitor the tranquillity of the region. In the early 1760s Washington assumed the positions of regional authority that his family had traditionally held in the local church and county government. He was chosen for the Truro church vestry by the other members in 1762, and he was subsequently elected in a general vote by parishioners to the Fairfax parish vestry; in 1764 he was appointed a justice of Fairfax County. (In order to assume this office Washington had to take a religious oath, required of all civil officials, renouncing Roman Catholic beliefs regarding Holy Communion.) He served with his friends George William Fairfax, Bryan Fairfax, and George Mason. Washington did business with the other justices and vestrymen and with a number of the planters who appeared before him. It was a tight world.[58]

The records of the court's and vestry's proceedings, set down in ledger books in an antique handwriting hard to decipher, contain some entries we might find humorous today, such as the indictment of three men for "prophane swearing" and of another man for "keeping a disorderly house on the sabbath day,"[59] but much more common are the brief, spare entries suggesting a world of trouble and heartbreak. The county paid people who opened their homes to the needy, and poor people were sometimes given money to maintain their own children. The vestry records show expenditures to people "for keeping an Object of Charity . . . for keeping [a woman] in her sickness and burying her . . . for keeping a sick woman . . . for keeping a bastard child . . . for curing a sick woman . . . for keeping an orphan child . . . for maintaining a base born Child . . . for clothing . . . to Mary Hooper for keeping James Hooper a lame youth her son . . . to Matthew Bradly for the support of his son . . . to Mary Bryon for keeping Zephaniah Bryon her son."[60]

The churchwardens were responsible for counting up all the taxable slaves and indentured servants, a task that required visits to the parish's farms and homes. Many people were brought up on charges of failing to declare a servant for tax purposes. A man named John House was brought up in 1771 on just such a charge—he had failed to list his servant James McManning as taxable—but when the churchwarden paid a surprise call on the House residence looking for undeclared servants, he found other crimes as well. And given their nature, it seemed that John House was away from his home and had been for some time: "We present James McManning a servant belonging to John House . . . for living in Fornication with Margaret House." Mrs. House was brought up on charges of adultery.[61]

There were surprisingly few records of crimes by slaves. Two female slaves got a whipping for killing a hog; a slave convicted of stealing thirty-two Spanish dollars was sentenced to twenty-nine lashes on the bare back at the public whipping post and to be set in the pillory one hour; another slave, convicted of stealing, was sentenced to a half hour in the pillory and thirty-nine lashes. In some twenty years there was only one recorded murder case—a slave who had killed a white man and was condemned to hang. In August 1765 a slave named Nace was condemned to hang for stealing a horse, but he was apparently reprieved because five years later he was again brought to court for stealing. This time the justices decided to teach him a stern lesson. They ordered that Nace be put in the pillory with his ears nailed to it. He was to be released after a day, but without his ears, which were cut off. The order was signed in bold lettering by Washington's close friend George William Fairfax.[62] Such cases remind us that there were good reasons that the founders forbade "cruel and unusual punishments" in the Bill of Rights.

In the small world of Fairfax County, private interests inevitably intersected with public power. In 1765 Sampson Darrell, an acquaintance of Washington's and one of the justices sitting that day, brought into court his servant woman Catherine Blinston and charged her with having a bastard child. Blinston was a convict, one of the thousands of prisoners shipped over from England and Ireland to work as indentured servants. For her crime she was fined and had her term of service to Darrell extended. Either from stubbornness or, more likely, poverty, she did not pay the fine. Whatever the reason, the justices interpreted her nonpayment as insubordination, since a note to her case states, "the said Cath. refusing to pay her fine [it is ordered] that the Sheriff give her 25 lashes on the bare back."[63]

Washington was not present when that punishment was ordered, but he sat in judgment when Blinston's name was later called out in the Fairfax County court. As so frequently happened in these cases, Blinston continued to have children despite the penalties she risked. Her defiance cost her dearly, and it also redounded to the benefit of her master. At a court session in 1770 five years after Blinston's whipping, Justice Darrell called a brief halt to the regular proceedings and stepped off the bench. The court thereupon reconvened to grant a petition from Sampson Darrell, private citizen, ordering that "the churchwardens of Fairfax parish bind Sarah Blinston about three years old and Thomas Blinston about fifteen months old (base born children) apprentices to Sampson Darrell Gent according to Law." Darrell then stepped back to the bench to resume his duties, having gained Blinston's two children as his servants, no reason given.[64]

This was an extremely harsh world for poor women and their children. Washington was among the justices who ordered that "Mary Cameron be summoned to appear at the next court to shew cause why she refuses to bind out her children." A month later her two children, aged three and five, were taken from her and bound out. In other cases the court had allowed child support payments to poor mothers, but in Mary Cameron's case they did not. Race was apparently not a factor in this instance—the children were white—but Cameron must have done something to offend the sensibilities of the justices.[65]

Something akin to a mass roundup of mothers took place in the spring of 1770. On a single day the court brought indictments against eight women, ferreted out by two churchwardens, for having "base-born" children. We can imagine the anxiety of these young women as their pregnancies had advanced under the stern, unforgiving gaze of masters, neighbors, and the vigilant churchwardens. One warden sat in judgment as a justice; the other sat in the jury box. Seven of the defendants were white women who had borne white children, but one, a white servant named Jane Morrison, was brought up on the charge of "having a base born molato child." At a subsequent court session she was ordered to finish out her term of service to her current master, and then she was to be handed over to the churchwardens of Fairfax parish, Washington's vestry, to be sold for an additional term of five years, and the proceeds earmarked "for the use of the said parish." Four months later the court ordered the other vestry where Washington sat to "bind Hannah a molatto two years old Daughter of Sarah Manley & George a molatto one years old Son of Nan Manley apprentices to Paul Turley according to Law." It seems that two white sisters, the Manleys, both had mulatto children. The Manleys were Paul Turley's servants, so he got the labor of the children as well as the mothers. A basic distinction is maintained in these records: white orphans and "bastards" were taught reading, writing, and a useful trade; mulatto children were not taught anything—they were routed to the lowest rung of the laboring class.[66]

Washington sat in judgment when his acquaintance Joseph Moxley brought in his servant Isabella Livingston "for having a base born mulatto Child." Washington and the other justices fined her £15, an enormous sum utterly beyond the means of a servant. The fine was a mere pretext, because the judges ordered that if she could not pay it she would be sold, which was certainly their intention. As a further punishment she lost her twelve-year-old white son, who was taken from her and bound out. So the fate that "seems like death to them," the breakup of a family, befell this woman for the crime of having a mulatto child.[67]

Washington and his fellow justices punished racial mixing not because they were horrified by it on racial grounds but because it threatened the slave system by opening up the possibility of creating a growing class of free, mixed-race people. At the margin of Virginia society, race and sex acted as solvents on the carefully constructed authority of the hierarchy, blurring the definitions upon which the labor and social systems depended. To the masters, who were utterly dependent on mechanisms of control, women and blacks represented the irrational. Washington's friend Landon Carter remarked in 1777: "A negroe and a passionate woman are equal as to truth or falsehood; for neither thinks of what they say." In a rigidly hierarchical society the highest priority was maintaining the order of things. As a practical matter, white female sexuality was beyond the control of the masters, but they could impose their will on the offspring.[68]

Far from being appalled by miscegenation, Washington surrounded himself with its results. About the same time that he was sitting in judgment of Isabella Livingston "for having a base born mulatto Child" he was eagerly buying mulattoes himself. In October 1767 he traveled through his home county, Westmoreland, and found two mulatto boys being offered for sale. They were William and Frank Lee, brothers who were being auctioned at an estate sale after the death of their master. William and Frank apparently had special qualities that caught Washington's eye because he paid premium prices for them. Indeed, he bid more than three times as much for "Mulatto Will" as he did for a "Negro boy." Short of cash, he made the purchase with a promissory note payable eighteen months after the sale. He recorded the transaction in his account book:

[For] sundry slaves bot at y Sale and for w' I payd my bond payable y'
15th of April 1769—viz

> *Mulatto Will—£61-15
> *Ditto Frank   50
> Negro boy Adam 19
> Jack   19
> _____
> £149-15-0

Dark-skinned Adam and Jack were destined for the fields, but Washington brought William and Frank into the house. He had reached the point where he needed a particular kind of personal attendant, one who was almost white, and he paid dearly to obtain "yellow-skinned" people. William Lee became his valet and huntsman, Frank Lee the butler.[69]

At Mount Vernon, as in other great mansions across the South at that time, slavery had passed from being simply an economic system, a means of acquiring labor, into a new phase. In this final refinement, human beings were not just workers but living status symbols. Slavery offered not just labor but the psychological comfort of mastery itself. It was part of the mode of being to have people at one's command. That power could be intoxicating. Even George Washington felt it.

In June 1766 Washington noted in his ledger an expense of £2 for "taking up," or capturing, a runaway named Tom. Washington's reaction was swift and terrible. Less than three weeks later he wrote a letter to Joseph Thompson, captain of the schooner *Swift*, bound for the West Indies.

> Sir: With this Letter comes a Negro (Tom) which I beg the favour of you to sell, in any of the Islands you may go to, for whatever he will fetch, & bring me in return for him
>
> > One Hhd [hogshead] of best Molasses
> > One Ditto of best Rum
> > One Barrl of Lymes—if good and Cheap

One Pot of Tamarinds—contg about 10 lbs.

Two small Do of mixed Sweetmeats—abt. 5 lb. each.

And the residue, much or little, in good old Spirits.

That this Fellow is both a Rogue & Runaway (tho'. he was by no means remarkable for the former, and never practised the latter till of late) I shall not pretend to deny—But that he is exceeding healthy, strong, and good at the Hoe, the whole neighbourhood can testi-fie . . . which gives me reason to hope he may, with your good management, sell well, if kept clean & trim'd up a little when offerd to Sale.

I shall very chearfully allow you the customary Commissions on this affair, and must beg the favour of you (lest he shoud attempt his escape) to keep him handcuffd till you get to Sea—or in the Bay—after which I doubt not but you may make him very useful to you.

I wish you a pleasant and prosperous Passage, and a safe & speedy return, being Sir, etc.

Go: Washington [70]

Washington knew what fate was in store for Tom, who was at that moment undoubtedly in irons in a locked room at Mount Vernon. Tom also had to know what was coming, since Washington advised the captain to keep him handcuffed until safely out to sea. The West Indies plantations were disease-ridden pest holes, the preferred dumping ground for troublesome mainland slaves. Washington had visited Barbados and knew the horrors of the work-them-to-death sugarcane plantations there. Washington shipped off two other slaves to the West Indies, and as late as 1793 he was still using the threat of sale to the islands as a way of frightening his slaves into obedience.[71]

But beyond the cruelty of the sentence, a cruelty amply sanctioned by common practice on Virginia plantations of the time, is a deeply unnerving element in the letter—the jaunty tone, the airiness with which Washington consigns this man to perdition, with wishes of a pleasant and prosperous passage to the captain, and his "chearful" willingness to pay the normal fees. And for this transaction, Washington suspended his usual financial expectations. He was not seeking money for Tom. Here is a young planter taking pleasure in his power over the slave, his power to exchange a man for sweets and liquor, the makings of a fine party. You will trouble me no more.

Before he donned his Olympian raiments as Revolutionary commander and our first president, Washington was just another striving young planter, blithely ordering breeding wenches from his slave trader, blithely exiling a man to a likely death at hard labor.

CHAPTER FIVE

A Scheme in Williamsburg

*I*F TODAY an imaginary attorney of moral law wished to bring an indictment against the United States on the charge of slaveholding, the proper place to bring the proceeding would be Williamsburg, Virginia. Summoned from their graves, the defendants would include the great men—Washington, Jefferson, Patrick Henry—who, at the risk of their lives, helped to give this country independence and a government that protects the personal rights we enjoy today.

It is the capital of the American paradox, expressing the collision of slavery and freedom in the Revolutionary era. It is the place where the slaveholder Thomas Jefferson first uttered words that became, in slightly different form, our cornerstone: "Under the law of nature all men are born free."

It is also the site of a modern-day collision of past and present. The ambitious restoration project funded by the Rockefeller family, Colonial Williamsburg, vividly re-creates the birth of American liberty in the 1760s and early 1770s. The town was painstakingly restored and populated with costumed interpreters who enact scenes of colonial life with startling realism. This image of history presented by Colonial Williamsburg was for some decades incomplete and sanitized because it depicted slavery as a relatively benign, if unfortunate, social custom of the distant past. Beginning in 1979 Colonial Williamsburg began to conduct energetic research into slavery and then undertook to depict it with accuracy. The interpretation was controversial, and many veteran interpreters left in dismay at what had been done, while some African-American visitors, to this day, find the reenactments of slave life too painful to see. In any case, Williamsburg brings to life the paradox that otherwise remains distant and abstract.

In Williamsburg, as an elected member of the House of Burgesses, George Washington took part in the debates that led to the Revolution. He conducted personal business there; he attended banquets, balls, and the theater; he took his family to Williamsburg to break the monotony of plantation routine. Washington's many visits to Williamsburg have been thoroughly researched (we know his hotel bills to the farthing), but I was particularly interested in the aspects of slave life Washington would have encountered there. I came upon historical evidence that had not previously been considered, and it persuaded me that Williamsburg is a crucial place for understanding Washington as a slaveholder and his difficult private struggle with slavery.

The obvious objection to many modern inquiries into the morality of slaveholding is that they apply modern standards of ethics to the people of the past in a way that is manifestly unfair, illogical, and futile. To conduct a just inquiry, we would need an advocate of moral law from that time. In fact we have one. As we have done so many times in the past, we need only look to George Washington. He pronounced his judgment on this era, and upon himself, when he freed his slaves and declared slavery to be repugnant. Of all the great Virginia patriots, only Washington ultimately had the moral courage and the farsightedness to free his slaves. (Similarly, he was the very first of the Virginia patriots to foresee that British tyranny would be thrown off only by war.) But because so much about him as a slaveholder has been suppressed, his moral evolution has been obscured and his usefulness to us as a moral guide has been undermined.

When Washington began to turn against slavery later in his life, I believe that he had in his mind events in Williamsburg. He shrank in repugnance from the memory of what he had seen and what he himself had done there—an act so morally corrupt and of such stupefying cruelty that he vowed never to repeat it. No biographer has ever described what he did in the Williamsburg slave market—it contradicted the prevailing image of Washington and did not fit into a narrative of his life that would make sense.

Washington usually visited Williamsburg twice a year for the sessions of the House of Burgesses. After studying his diary I focused on a particular visit in 1769. It was a long stay, about six weeks; it was well documented; it came in the midst of important political events in the conflict with Great Britain. This visit also had a fascinating personal element. Washington brought his whole family with him, which he did not usually do. Many themes of his life coalesced in this single journey to the capital.

In November 1769, an elegant green coach, drawn by six horses, jounced along a road in New Kent County. People working in the fields by the road would have seen the recent passage of many such coaches, all heading to Williamsburg, carrying Virginia's elected representatives and their families to the session of the colonial Assembly. But this coach might have stood out from the others, not for the resplendent glint of its polished paneling and the glimmer of its cut glass, but for the strange noises it emitted. One can imagine a pair of slaves looking up from their work at the sound, doffing their hats and bowing—according to the established custom—and, when the coach had disappeared from sight, asking each other, "Do you think that coach will make it to Williamsburg?" For the noises coming from the coach of Colonel Washington were the cracks, groans, and snaps of an expensive contrivance in the process of breaking up. To his rage, Washington discovered that his beloved chariot "was made of wood so exceedingly Green that the Pannels slipped out of the Mouldings before it was two Months in use—Split from one end to the other— and became so open at the joints . . . that I expect very little further Service from it with all the repairs I can bestow." Washington had specified to his London merchant that he wanted the chariot fashioned of well-seasoned wood by a master workman. The irony was that when the British-made chariot began to disintegrate, Washington was on his way to Williamsburg for the Assembly's debate on the boycott of British goods.[1]

This costly, creaky chariot carried the Washington family— George and Martha, Jacky and Patsy—with two slaves clinging to the back and another at the reins. About a half-day's ride from Williamsburg, the coach came to a halt at Eltham, the estate of Martha's sister Anna Maria and her husband, Burwell Bassett. Martha and Patsy remained there while George and Jacky continued on to the capital. On reaching Williamsburg, they headed to Washington's customary place of lodging, a tavern run by a widow, Christiana Campbell, described wryly by another traveler as "a little old Woman, about four feet high; & equally thick, a little turn up Pug nose, a mouth screw'd up to one side."[2] The tavern stood but two blocks from the capitol, where the burgesses would be meeting.

For most of the year Williamsburg was a sleepy backwater. But twice a year the gentry thronged to the town for the occasions called "Publick Times," when the General Court sat in session. A traveler wrote in 1758, "At the time of the assemblies, and general courts, it is crowded with the gentry of the country. On those occasions there are balls and other amusements, but as soon as business is finished, they return to their plantations and the town is in a manner deserted." During "Publick Times" everyone of substance was in Williamsburg, so business could be transacted face-to-face, without the vexing delays inherent in the nascent postal system. Planters met to pay off debts to one another or to borrow money, as the case might be.[3] Washington was planning to recover at least part of a large debt owed to Jacky and Patsy by one of Virginia's biggest planters, Bernard Moore. Washington very likely kept his fifteen-year-old stepson informed of the details of the debt negotiations, since managing them was a skill Jacky himself would need later on.

On this trip Washington planned to take young Custis out on social occasions to introduce him to the capital's masculine society. The boy had to begin thinking about taking up the duties befitting a Custis and a Washington. Jacky would have been welcomed warmly, for the Custis name was already one to reckon with, and he himself would soon have to be reckoned with: he owned thousands of acres around Williamsburg and choice properties in the city itself.[4] During his time with Jacky in Williamsburg, Washington took him to see the colony's potentates. They enjoyed a candlelight dinner at the home of the speaker of the House of Burgesses, Edmund Pendleton, who also happened to be Jacky's lawyer. Pendleton would soon be presenting a legal question about Custis land to the General Court.[5] Washington also took his stepson to dinner at Governor Botetourt's palace.

For a provincial youth such as Jacky Custis, a sojourn in the capital taught a quick, intense lesson in the proper way to conduct oneself in society. Thomas Jefferson, who studied law at William and Mary in the 1760s and was elected a burgess in 1769, called Williamsburg "the finest school of manners and morals that ever existed in America," and said that in Williamsburg "I have heard more good sense, more rational and philosophical conversations, than in all my life besides."[6] An Englishman described Williamsburg as "delightful, healthful, and thriving," where the citizens "behave themselves exactly as the gentry in London."

Though it was styled a city in recognition of its status as the colonial capital, Williamsburg was but a small provincial town, with a permanent population of barely 1,800. It had been founded in 1699 when the newly arrived governor Francis Nicholson took one look at Jamestown and decided that Virginia needed a new capital. He chose the place a few miles inland from the James River, where the College of William and Mary had already been established. In his previous position as governor of Maryland, Nicholson had designed the capital of Annapolis, and he laid out Williamsburg in a similarly ambitious spirit. Baroque in character, Williamsburg boasted open spaces and sweeping vistas. The college and the imposing, H-shaped brick capitol building served as the intellectual, political, and architectural anchors of the town, facing each other from opposite ends of Duke of Gloucester Street, which Nicholson ordained to be ninety feet wide and a mile long. He placed the governor's palace, also of brick, at the center of town, set back from Duke of Gloucester Street on the broad

Palace Green. At the edge of the Green one of Nicholson's successors built Bruton Parish Church, which has been in continuous use since its consecration in 1715. Washington worshiped there—including on the historic "day of fasting, humiliation, and prayer" during the crisis over the Boston Tea Party—and Custis slaves were baptized there, with Washington's permission. It has been stated that Washington stood as godfather at these baptisms, but that is incorrect.

At the same time the church was going up, the colony was also building, within sight of the church, a sturdy brick octagon to hold gunpowder. When hostilities between Americans and the mother country finally broke out in April 1775, Governor Dunmore had his soldiers remove the powder by night, but they were observed by Revolutionary officers. Patrick Henry led a detachment of Virginia militia to reclaim the powder, which the governor claimed he needed to put down a rumored uprising of slaves. In fact the governor was planning to offer freedom to any slave who would side with Great Britain.

Williamsburg was a stage set for the pageant of royal government, embodied in the person of the governor, who symbolized the power emanating from across the sea. Virginia's House of Burgesses, though duly elected according to long-established law, served at the pleasure of the governor. Should the burgesses displease him, their assembly would be dissolved. Thus, the arrival in Williamsburg of a new governor called for maximum pomp and circumstance, elaborate expressions of courtesy and obeisance. Greeted outside the town by a delegation of the colony's leading men, he was solemnly conducted to the capitol for the oath of office and then to his palace. The night of his arrival would be marked by an Illumination—a great bonfire blazing at the center of town, and in every window of every house, candles twinkling in universal, joyous welcome for the sovereign's representative. As the colony's elite gathered at the palace for a formal ball, common folk assembled outside, where liquor was dispensed. As the revelers at the ball toasted the health of the king and each member of the royal family, cannons boomed in salute. The evening might culminate in a magnificent display of fireworks, with "caterine wheels, Italian candles, sea fountains, and sun flowers with the appearance of the sun and moon in their full lustre."[7]

The pageantry continued, on a smaller scale, on each day of Publick Times. In late morning the governor made a ceremonial progress from his palace to the capitol, riding in a carriage decorated with the coat of arms of Virginia, drawn by six horses. Precisely at noon he would alight at the capitol steps, where custom dictated that a knot of well-wishers be present to greet him. Inside, he would don the velvet robe of office and take his seat in the austere chamber of the Council.[8]

Duke of Gloucester Street, the location of Mrs. Campbell's establishment, where Washington and Jacky stayed, was the fashionable promenade for Virginia's gentry, who displayed themselves not on foot but on horseback. It was said that a Virginian would walk a mile to catch and saddle a horse for a ride of a hundred yards. Williamsburg suffered equine traffic jams, as no one wished to walk. A visitor found "saddled horses at every turn, and a swarming of riders . . . for a horse must be mounted, if only to fetch a prise of snuff from across the way."[9]

It was a town of music. Washington's friend and fellow planter Landon Carter, a notorious grump, wrote sarcastically in his diary, "I hear from every house a constant tuting upon one instrument or another." He added that the town's packs of dogs "will no doubt compleat the howl" made by the musicians.[10] The citizens of Williamsburg diverted themselves on violins, the spinet, harpsichord, oboe, trumpet, guitar, and many other instruments. The celebratory tones of Handel reverberated at Bruton Church; the taverns shook with bawdy ballads; fiddlers entertained at private parties as acrobats tumbled, clowns grimaced for the children, and a dancer gyrated on a tightrope. The soft beauty of a Virginia night could make people burst into song. A few weeks before the Washingtons arrived in November 1769, some of Martha's friends, the Dawson family, were leaving a house on Duke of Gloucester after a supper when, "everyone appearing in great spirits, it was proposed to set at the Steps and Sing a few songs which was no sooner said than done." In the midst of their singing a stranger approached out of the darkness with a small entourage. The "warblers" fell silent, at which the visitor called out, "Charming! Charming! Proceed for God sake." All recognized the voice of His Lordship Governor Botetourt, who refused an invitation to come inside, saying he would just settle down with them on the steps, which he did.[11]

Williamsburg had the first theater in the British colonies. Washington was a great fan of the drama, and while in Williamsburg he saw *The Beggar's Opera* and other plays. The town's theater also offered spectacles and wonders, such as "A Set of Water Works, representing the sea, and all manner of sea monsters sporting on the waves." One could view "A magnificent piece of Machinery, called Cupid's Paradise, representing seventy odd Pillars and Columns, with the appearance of Neptune and Amphrite," and another marvel known as "The Microcosm, or The World in Miniature," an attraction so well known "that a description would be needless, any more than it is the Microcosm."[12]

Perhaps the most important amusement at Williamsburg was horse racing, which Washington followed avidly. A modern horseman, having studied the races of eighteenth-century Williamsburg, has concluded that they raced animals of strength and stamina now unknown—"where can you now find horses to run three four-mile heats in a day?" Before each race the bookmakers raised a clamor, striding through the crowd shouting odds, and afterward the course echoed with "a tornado of applause from the winner's party . . . more especially if the horses had happened to jostle and one of the riders had been thrown off with a broken leg."[13]

Washington said that Williamsburg displayed "the manners and etiquette of a Court in miniature" and that the paramount social concerns were "precedance; dress, imitation." A Williamsburg historian who studied the social activities of this era writes that participation in Williamsburg society "*required* the unremitting performance of acts of civility and ceremony" and unwavering attention to "duty, courtesy, and manners." One was always being watched and measured. As an Englishman observed, Virginians tended to "read men by business and conversation." Dancing lessons taught ladies and gentlemen "to appear easy and amiable, genteel and free in person, Mien, Air and Motions, rather than stiff, awkward, deform'd and consequently disagreeable." When conversing one must carefully control "Gestures or Motions of the Body" and avoid nodding, looking to the side, or twisting one's mouth into a wry expression. Altogether, good breeding meant "the art of pleasing or contributing as much as possible to the ease and happiness of those with whom you converse." Despite the unremitting social pressure, the upper reaches of Virginia society still harbored a few out-and-out boors, such as the young man who had the nerve to make "prophane Jests against religion and things sacred" at a dinner at the governor's palace. Governor Gooch wrote a blistering letter to the gentleman who had brought the young man to the palace, informing him that the miscreant "had the assurance, in a most insolent manner, to affront my Wife and Sister, at my own Table."[14]

For Washington, a visit to Williamsburg brought to life the abstract laws he had painstakingly memorized as a youth in *The Rules of Civility*. Breaking the rules could have the most serious consequence: banishment from the corridors of power. The genial figure who had sat with the people singing on the steps, Lord Botetourt, was beloved as a good-tempered governor, but his immediate predecessor, Fauquier, had been extremely conscious of his position and the deference it required from His Majesty's subjects. A minister named John Camm, responsible for delivering some official papers to Fauquier, made the mistake of delivering the papers late and the more serious mistake of attempting to explain himself after the governor grumbled about being made to wait for the documents. In contradicting the governor, Camm had treated him "with great Indignity," and the result was political and social exile. When Camm and his companions prepared to leave,

With a commanding voice [the governor] bellowed to us to stop. We obey'd on the top of the Steps. He came out and called with great violence—Call my negroes, says he, call all my negroes, in high wrath.

When the negroes were come; look at him, mark him, says he, that you may know him again, & running his finger close up to my face: & if this Gentleman ever hereafter approach my Gates, take care that you do not suffer him to enter them.[15]

For years thereafter, Reverend Camm's behavior came under scrutiny by the governor, who later made a formal complaint to the Bishop of London that Camm violated the proper manner and procedure for doffing one's hat to a social superior. It made no difference that the infraction had taken place when Camm was on one side of a fence and the governor was on the other in a moving carriage—the rules had to be observed with great punctilio in Williamsburg. Camm had to write to the bishop to beg pardon:

> The Governor & His Lady once fancied Mr. Graham & me to have purposely Omitted the putting off of our Hats to them, when they passed by in a Chariot on the out side of the Pales of the College, while we were walking to & Fro in the gravel Walk within. And it was taken notice of, it seems, that I did not put off my hat to [the governor's sons] when I happened to meet them in the Streets. This compliment I never failed to pay the Governor so far as I can recollect; because custom here gave it to him from every body. But I did not extend it to his sons: because I thought it would be resented as a challenge of Acquaintance, from one who had never enjoyed the Honor of being introduced to them, & therefore could have no pretensions to make such a challenge.

For his part, Fauquier was quick to learn the intricacies of American courtesy, particularly the New World custom of the handshake. When Fauquier wished to put a Virginia planter in his place he did so by refusing to shake hands until he had finished rebuking the gentleman for a slight: "After some Observations and Remonstrances on his former Behaviour, I got up and took him by the Hand (a constant Token of good will in this Country which I had purposely omitted when he first entered my House)."[16]

When Washington described his early life to his first biographer, David Humphreys, he made some remarks about Williamsburg that his friend jotted down: "At Williamsburg a successive round of visiting & dinners—it was not possible for a man to retire sober." Virginians were notorious drinkers, and it is not surprising that Washington's remarks suggest the atmosphere of a fraternity house, with drunken gentlemen urging each other deeper into the bottle. Washington told Humphreys that a gentleman could not leave an event sober, "without incurring imputations which even a person of philosophic cast did not choose to merit."[17] Thomas Jefferson wrote of joining in the nightly revelry at the Raleigh Tavern as a twenty-year-old law student: "Last night [I was] as merry [as] agreeable company and dancing with Belinda could make me, I never could have thought the succeeding Sun would have seen me so wretched."[18]

Once night had descended and the governor was safely tucked away in his mansion, the gentry could freely indulge in both ferocious drinking and high-stakes gambling that astonished outsiders. "Gaming is amazingly prevalent in Williamsburg," a Northerner observed in the 1770s; a French visitor wrote, "Carousing and Drinking In one chamber and . . . dice in the other, which Continues till morning Commonly"; yet another remarked, "In the Day time people hurrying back and forwards from the Capitoll to the Taverns, and at night, Carousing." One planter, disgusted with himself over his gambling, wrote, "Burn me if I pay any more for such sport."[19]

One of the colony's richest and most distinguished planters, William Byrd III, gradually lost everything he had at the gambling tables in the 1760s and 1770s. A French traveler alighted at Williamsburg and fell in with a group of "professed gamesters" at the tavern where he was staying, a place, he wrote, "where all the best people resorted." One of the gamesters was Byrd himself, "who is never happy but when he has the box and Dices in hand. This gentleman . . . of the greatest property of any in America has reduced himself to that Degree by gameing, that few or nobody will Credit him for ever so small a sum of money. He was obliged to sel 400 fine Negroes a few days before my arival." The Frenchman recognized the compulsive nature of the Virginians' gambling—they all but physically forced him to play *something*: "there were many [attempts] made at me to get me in for the [dice] box but I had the good luck to Keep Clear of it, but could not avoid playing some rubers of whist notwithstanding my aversion to it."[20] The results were sometimes tragic: irretrievably in debt, Byrd shot himself on New Year's Day, 1777.

Washington's strong sense of personal discipline is evident in his diary. On many nights when he was alone in Williamsburg he noted that he stayed in his room all evening. Though he enjoyed Madeira and cards, he was moderate with both of these recreations. Sitting alone in his room on the second floor of a tavern, cloistered with business papers or a book, Washington must have been tempted by the din of carousing from the public room below, but he did not give in.

The diary also makes clear that Washington did not allow young Jacky Custis to indulge in card playing, perhaps because Washington's own luck at the table was running badly. On November 10 Washington noted that he lost more than a pound at cards that day. Washington wrote down every shilling of allowance he gave to Jacky and his accounts show no expenditure by the teenager on gambling.

Washington may have been coaching Jacky in habits of discipline and self-denial because young Custis certainly needed a bit of coaching in that regard. On this trip he was taking a break from his boarding school near Fredericksburg. Washington's correspondence with the headmaster, Jonathan Boucher, shows that both men were greatly concerned with Jacky's discipline and moral growth. The boy showed signs of being a normal young Virginia planter only more so—a "sparkish" Virginia gentleman veering out of control. He loved horses, girls, and the finer things of life that the Custis fortune could bring him. At Jacky's age Washington had been out on the frontier learning a trade as a surveyor in the roughest conditions. Jacky had every advantage wealth could offer, and Washington worried that wealth was turning the young man's head.

When the Washingtons sent Jacky to his boarding school in May 1768, he went in high style, with his personal slave and two horses, "to furnish him with the means of getting to Church," as Washington wrote to the headmaster, lest he get the wrong impression about the purpose of the horses. The letter suggests that the future commander in chief had had little success inculcating a sense of discipline and duty in his stepson. He was throwing up his hands, hoping that Boucher might succeed where he had failed. But Boucher had to be careful not to antagonize Jacky, and must never lose sight of who he was. The letter simultaneously asks for special attention, given the boy's wild temperament, and for special consideration, given his lofty status as a Custis. Washington offered Boucher ten to twelve pounds above the regular fee "to engage your peculiar care of, and a watchful eye to him. He is a promising boy—the last of his family—[and] will possess a very large Fortune; add to this my anxiety to make him fit for more useful purposes, than a horse Racer." Later he wrote to Boucher, "His mind [is] a good deal released from Study, & more than ever turned to Dogs Horses and Guns."[21] Boucher himself painted a troubling picture of Jack's temperament and feared for the young man's future. He wrote to Washington:

> The chief failings of his Character are that He is constitutionally somewhat too warm, indolent, & voluptuous. As yet these propensities are but in Embrio: Ere long, however, They will discover Themselves, & if not duly & carefully regulated, it is Easy to see to what They will lead. At best, He will soon lose all Relish for mental Excellence—He will unwillingly apply to any Improvemts either in Arts or Sciences. Sunk in unmanly Sloth, his Estate will [be] left to the Managemt of some worthless Overseer; & Himself soon be entangled in some matrimonial Adventure, in wc. as Passion will have much to say, it is not very likely Reason will be much listened to.[22]

When the moment arrived to choose a college for Jack, the natural choice was Virginia's own William and Mary, which had the great advantage of being close by, so Martha would not suffer the pain of separation from her son and Washington could keep an eye on him. But after making inquiries, Washington discovered that William and Mary was a virtual bedlam. When Washington vetoed it he referred vaguely to its being in a state of "Mismanagement," but an acquaintance was more specific when he wrote that he would never even think of sending his sons there because "so little attention is paid either to the learning or the morals of the boys." Given that Jacky displayed no tendency at all toward serious scholarship, it would seem that Washington's overriding concern in vetoing William and Mary was its moral atmosphere. Jack needed no encouragement to head down the wrong path in that regard.[23]

Washington's efforts to instill discipline in Jacky ran afoul of Martha. Jacky's son, G.W.P. Custis, wrote, "She was extremely indulgent to him, and she often pleaded in his behalf, when Washington found it necessary to exercise a wholesome restraint on him . . . the wayward boy was frequently away from his studies, engaged in fox-hunting and other amusements at Mount Vernon."[24]

Jacky could do no wrong in his mother's eyes, and Martha spoiled him. Washington wrung his hands over Martha's indulgence toward her son, but he understood its source. As a young mother Martha had lost two infants, her teenaged brother had died, her husband's adolescent half brother had died less than a day after developing a neck pain, and after just seven years of marriage her first husband had died with terrible suddenness. These losses haunted her for years, fastening on her an anxiety over separations, which she tried to overcome. On a two-week trip to George's relatives in Westmoreland County in 1762, she had decided to leave the then seven-year-old Jacky at home at Mount Vernon with the servants as a test—not for the child but for herself: "to see how well I could stay without him." Apparently it was the first time they had been apart, and the fortnight's separation became a nightmare of anxiety for her. Every time she heard a dog bark or any kind of noise she was certain it meant the arrival of a messenger from Mount Vernon with news that "he was sick or some accident had happened to him." She felt so fretful that she decided "I think it is impossable for me to leave him."[25]

Her anxiety for his health continued into his adolescence. On a visit home from school, Jacky apparently made the mistake of telling his mother that he enjoyed swimming. In his own youth, spent on the frontier, Washington had endured an unwilling plunge into icy water in midwinter and had spent a night in wet clothes without ill effect. Washington might have recalled that incident when Martha made known to him that she was terribly afraid of what might happen to Jack if he went swimming too often or too long. Whatever reassurances Washington could offer had no effect on Martha's anxieties. Knowing that direct instruction to Jack himself would be useless, Martha told Washington to make the matter the responsibility of Jack's schoolmaster. In a letter to Boucher, Washington dutifully included the directive to keep Jack out of the water, carefully pointing out that this restriction was his wife's idea, not his: "I have further to desire, at the request of Mrs. Washington, that you will restrain Jacky from going too frequently into the Water, or staying too long in it when there; as she is apprehensive of bad consequences from either." In the same letter Washington told Boucher to buy Jacky silver knee buckles, silver shoe buckles, and silver spurs. He put no limit on the cost.[26]

Martha's anxiety over her son's health, exaggerated as it was, grew not just from Martha's past losses but from a present travail. Patsy was suffering a mysterious illness that worsened as time went on. From the age of six she had endured agonizing "fits" that struck with sudden, terrible violence. She suffered from epilepsy, an ailment known and named at that time but not well understood. Washington's diary and account books are replete with entries for doctors' visits and medicines. The doctors prescribed a variety of potions—one containing arsenic—as well as dietary plans and admonitions to keep the child's body cool. She was given bland food and purges to make her vomit, and she also had to undergo periodic bloodletting, the universal cure, which did nothing for her ailment beyond adding to it another layer of pain and terror. Washington was deeply concerned, and made notations of Patsy's fits in the margins of his diary to keep track of their number and severity. In some desperation the Washingtons summoned to Mount Vernon in February 1769 a certain Joshua Evans, who must have been presented to them as some kind of wizard. He fitted Patsy with an iron "cramp ring" bearing a supposedly magical inscription that would ward off the fits—a belief that went back to the Middle Ages. On the November 1769 visit to Williamsburg, while Martha and Patsy were at Eltham with Anna Maria and Burwell Bassett, they received a visit from one of the most distinguished physicians in Virginia, Dr. John de Sequeyra. Born in London in 1712, Sequeyra came from a family of Sephardic Jewish physicians in England and had studied medicine at the University of Leiden. Sequeyra prescribed some medication that Washington procured in Williamsburg at Dr. William Pasteur's apothecary shop on Duke of Gloucester Street.[27]

The Washingtons tried to make Patsy's childhood and early adolescence as normal as possible. She studied with a dancing master and music tutor. Washington bought her a costly spinet and songbooks. Both parents lavished her with clothing—gloves, gauze caps, shoes of leather and satin, jewelry—as well as a "very handsome and fashionable saddle" and an exotic pet parrot. On this particular trip, Martha and Patsy went on a shopping spree in Williamsburg. They bought clothing together, and later Washington shopped by himself for Patsy. He picked out an ornamental comb.[28]

Though Patsy and Jack were not his own children, Washington held them in tender regard. He even gave serious consideration to a proposal from Jack's teacher which Washington must have regarded as the extremity of extravagance: to further Jack's education as a gentleman, Boucher proposed taking him on a grand tour of Europe, a year-long jaunt that Boucher thought would cost as much as £1,600. Washington put him off, making vague reference to Jack's plantations not being as profitable as all that, but he did not completely reject the idea, saying that he would take it up with knowledgeable friends in Williamsburg.

The Washingtons' concern for Jacky and his future grew more intense in 1773, when a sudden, heartbreaking loss made him the sole heir of the Custis family. In a letter Washington described what befell the family on a pleasant June afternoon at Mount Vernon: "[Patsy] rose from Dinner about four Oclock, in better health and spirits than she appeared to have been in for some time; soon after which she was seized with one of her usual Fits, & expird in it, in less than two Minutes without uttering a Word, a groan, or scarce a Sigh.—this Sudden and unexpected blow, I scarce need add has almost reduced my poor Wife to the lowest ebb of Misery."[29]

The day after his arrival in Williamsburg with Jack, Washington made the short stroll from Mrs. Campbell's lodging house down Duke of Gloucester Street to the capitol, where the burgesses convened their autumn session. In marked contrast to his later preeminence in American politics, Washington was never a leading figure in pre-Revolutionary Virginia. He was not part of the inner circle of leaders in the House.[30] He held no important committee posts and submitted only one important bill. Indeed, he barely spoke. One observer said that he was regarded as "too bashful and timid for an orator." Another wrote, "He is a modest man, but sensible, and speaks little—in action cool, like a bishop at his prayers." Thomas Jefferson recalled: "I served with General Washington in the legislature of Virginia before the Revolution. . . . I never heard [him] speak ten minutes at a time."[31]

Eloquence was never Washington's strong suit; he had a different way of working. There is a story about him and his friend George Mason that reveals Washington's method and how he could compensate for his deficiencies as an orator. When a disagreement arose in Fairfax County over where to build a new church, Mason and Washington found themselves on opposite sides of the question. Mason thought the new building should be built on the location of the old. According to a county history, he "pleaded that this was the church of their ancestors and should not be abandoned. It was reported that his eloquence upon this occasion was such that everyone was sure he would carry his point." But then Washington unfurled a survey he had drawn, showing the two proposed sites and the locations of every parishioner's house. Washington's survey defeated Mason's eloquence—the new church was built where Washington wanted it, which just happened to be closer to Mount Vernon than the old location.[32]

Washington had had his eye on a seat in the House of Burgesses from the time when he was in his early twenties. In 1755 he asked his brother Jack to sound out the constituents in Fairfax County about a possible race, but to do so "with an air of Indifference and unconcern." He decided the time was not right, nor was the place.[33] Three years later he decided to run not from his home county of Fairfax but from the western county of Frederick, where he owned land and where he was a well-known and respected figure because of his ongoing service with the militia defending the frontier.

An eighteenth-century Virginia election was very different from a modern secret ballot. In the first place, the vote was restricted to males who owned a certain minimum amount of property. In the 1758 election in Frederick County, 397 men were qualified to vote. The balloting was quite public: the voters gathered outside the courthouse, with the managers of the election sitting at a table. As the managers called out names, the eligible voters stepped forward in sight of all and called out, for all to hear, the names of the two candidates they wished to vote for. Each county elected two burgesses.

The most influential figures in this election were outsiders, like Washington himself. Friends from eastern Virginia who also owned property in Frederick made the journey to Winchester to win over votes for Washington. Leading the Washington delegation was no less a figure than Lord Fairfax, the proprietor, a man to whom all in the western part of Virginia had to show deference.* The law forbade candidates from entertaining voters with liquor, but dispensing drinks was an old custom. Washington decided to observe custom rather than law. His seconds handed out the drinks, dispensing 66 gallons of rum punch, 58 gallons of beer, 35 gallons of wine, plus hard cider and a bit of brandy.[34] In this, his first election, Washington won resoundingly with 309 votes out of 397 cast.

---

* Washington's brother-in-law, Fielding Lewis of Fredericksburg; Colonel William Fairfax; his son George William Fairfax; John Carlyle; and Dr. James Craik, Washington's lifelong, closest friend, appeared at the polling place. Washington needed all the assistance he could get because he could not personally be present for the balloting. He had requested leave from his military post, and even though he received permission to absent himself, he believed that circumstances required him to remain at his duties.

In his next election in Frederick, in 1761, Washington was nervous enough that he decided to circumvent a more serious election regulation than the liquor provision. In direct, willful violation of the law, Washington sent damaging information about an opponent to the county sheriff, who was in charge of the election and legally required to be impartial. An unscrupulous sheriff could tip the balance in a close election—he had the authority to disqualify voters; he alone determined when the balloting began and when it ended; and he would cast the deciding vote in the event of a tie.

When Washington sent the illegal material to the sheriff (the item itself has been lost), he wrote, "You may, if you think it expedient, communicate the contents to your Neighbours and Friends." He continued: "I hope . . . you will contribute your aid toward shutting him [Washington's opponent] out of the Public trust he is seeking." In his first election Washington had won when his supporters turned out not only in large numbers but very early in the balloting. In this election, which Washington feared might be closer, he told the sheriff to use his influence to get Washington's supporters called first, with the apparent intention of creating the impression of a groundswell. He wrote that if his "friends" and those of his running mate could be "hurried in at the first of the Poll it might be an advantage." Washington knew that seeking the sheriff's aid was illegal and that if word of the scheme got out it might cost him the election, so he counseled deception: "as Sheriff I know you cannot appear in this, nor would I . . . have you do any thing that can give so designing a Man as [my opponent] the least handle." There is wonderful irony in Washington denouncing his opponent as a "designing" man in a letter proposing an illegal election conspiracy. Just a few weeks later, when Washington was at home recuperating from an illness he had contracted on the campaign trail, he blandly told a visitor, "I deal little in politics."[35]

A class element entered into these campaigns. One of Washington's election strategists wrote him from Frederick that his opponent was proposing commercial schemes that he adjudged "strange & chimerical" but might nonetheless erode Washington's support because they "attracted the attention of the Plebeians, whose unstable

Minds are agitated by every Breath of Novelty, whims and nonsense." Washington's support, in contrast, came from a different class of voter. His friend wrote that he would feel better when "I was certain that the Leaders and all the Patrician Families remain firm in their resolution of continuing for you." Of course, the patricians were more important than the plebeians because more of them were allowed the vote. He won the 1761 election from Frederick and won in his home county of Fairfax in 1765, which he represented in the House of Burgesses continuously until the Revolution.[36]

The legislature that Washington joined was, in effect, "a tobacco planter's club," in the words of the Virginia historian Carl Bridenbaugh. "For over half a century 'gentlemen of the best families and fortunes' had been consciously coalescing into an exclusive ruling class based principally on the possession of great tracts of land."[37] Writing in 1950, Bridenbaugh addressed the mystery of patriotism's origins, and the origins of leadership, and decided that the plantation system had produced them:

> What was there about the Old Dominion that produced within the space of half a century a galaxy of statesmen who, for sagacity, ability, courage, political insight, and absence of provincialism, could challenge any other country or period of history to produce their equals? The answer, in all probability, may be discovered in the plantation way of life and in the system of government that was evolved to meet the needs of this society. . . . Early did they develop an awareness of their privileged status; early did they acquire the habit of command. They came into manhood prepared and expecting to rule; it was a birthright bred in their bones and nourished on plantation fare. . . . Ruling over their own acres was their first lesson in statesmanship; the plantation was their primer of politics.[38]

Bridenbaugh concluded that each of these masters had learned to rule from youth, "commencing with control over his personal servant as a little boy."[39] They were accustomed to ruling their plantations and their "people" as they saw fit. An English traveler who journeyed through Virginia and got to know a number of the great planters, including Washington, wrote: "they are haughty and jealous of their liberties, impatient of restraint, and can scarcely bear the thought of being controuled by any superior power."[40]

Though Bridenbaugh, very much a historian of the old school,* did not attempt to plumb the implications of his theory that the greatness of the Virginia founders arose from their practiced mastery over slaves, he had hit upon a provocative idea. Two decades later the Yale historian Edmund S. Morgan radically altered the view of the relationship between slavery and freedom in Virginia. In an address in 1972 to the Organization of American Historians, Morgan declared that slavery had paradoxically made American liberties and representative government possible. Had the Virginians not replaced an unruly class of white indentured servants with a thoroughly subjugated class of black slaves, they would never have considered creating a society based on individual liberties; it would have been too dangerous. It was slavery, he said, that "enabled Virginia to nourish representative government in a plantation society . . . [it was] slavery that made the Virginians dare to speak a political language that magnified the rights of freedmen."[41]

Morgan pointed out that with the influx in the 1600s of indentured servants—the indigent and the criminals whom England wished to be rid of—"Virginia thus acquired a social problem analogous to England's own [and] the colony began to deal with it as England had done, by restricting the liberties of those who did not have the proper badge of freedom, namely the property that government was supposed to protect." Thus in 1670 the colony limited voting to landholders and householders, and several years later the secretary of the colony complained to England of the "filth and scum" the mother country had sent to Virginia. At that time about a quarter of Virginia's freemen had no land and lived in near poverty as wage earners—or

---

* In his 1962 presidential address to the American Historical Association, he lamented that "many of the younger practitioners of our craft . . . are products of lower middle-class or foreign origins, and their emotions not infrequently get in the way of historical reconstructions."

thieves. The anxiety they engendered in the upper class made their numbers seem larger: Governor William Berkeley wrote that he ruled uneasily over a people of whom "six parts of seaven at least are Poore Endebted Discontented and Armed." That armed discontent erupted in Bacon's Rebellion in 1676, the first American revolt against royal authority, one that Morgan called "the largest popular uprising in the colonies before the American Revolution." Under Nathaniel Bacon, the rebels drove Berkeley from his capital at Jamestown, took control of the government, and then burned Jamestown. The rebellion broke apart when Bacon died of a fever.[42]

The great shift in England's emigration policy in the late seventeenth century had the unintended effect of making Virginia a safe cradle for notions of liberty. Morgan stated that the "decrease in the importation of indentured servants [brought] a decrease in the dangerous number of new freedmen who annually emerged seeking a place in society that they would be unable to achieve." The labor gap was filled with slaves, who "could be repressed by methods that would not have been considered reasonable, convenient, or even safe, if applied to Englishmen." Slaves had not even the hope of freedom, even for their children or their children's children; thus "slaves had none of the rising expectations that so often produce human discontent." Only when the ruling Virginians had eliminated the threat of a discontented white working class could they begin to entertain ideas of freedom. Morgan concluded, "The rights of Englishmen were preserved by destroying the rights of Africans." Moreover, the tobacco wealth created by the slaves bought American independence.[43]

The Virginia planters grew increasingly restive as Great Britain sought to impose tighter control over them in the 1760s with taxes and restrictive laws. Virginia's political fight with the crown had roots in the colony's financial plight. Poor tobacco harvests in the 1750s compelled the colony to pass a law altering the payments it made to its Anglican clergy. The clergy appealed over the heads of the Virginia legislature to England. A royal decree voided the law in 1760 along with many other laws that did not include the so-called suspending clause, which meant that final enactment was suspended until crown approval had been received from London. The colonists fumed that they were left unable to pass emergency laws of immediate need. Another dispute arose over the colony's attempt to issue paper money to pay the expenses of defense during the French and Indian War. English merchants wanted to be paid in sterling, but there was not enough of it in Virginia to pay both debts and defense costs. Naturally, the British merchants wanted no part of colonial paper. London's peremptory order to pay up in sterling caused Washington to remark that the requirement "will set the whole Country in Flames." He believed that London's refusal to approve the issuance of paper money put Virginians directly at risk—when Indians attacked settlements all along the Virginia frontier during the summer of 1763, Washington thought the defense was inadequate because the colony did not have enough money.[44]

After the war ended in 1763, the British government's annual military expenditure in North America was still as high as £350,000. And its annual revenue from royal customs duties was £1,800. This absurdly low figure was due in large measure to the adroitness of the American smuggling industry.[45] Word reached Virginia in May 1764 that in London Parliament was considering imposing taxes on the colonies to help pay the enormous debt of the war. Though Parliament had levied taxes on commercial transactions and the colonists had not objected to them, Parliament had never before imposed a general tax on the colonists. The power to set taxes had always been exercised locally, by the representatives of the colonists themselves in their legislatures. (In Virginia the local taxing power was delegated to the churches, which taxed believers and nonbelievers alike, at rates set by the church governing boards; as one historian notes sardonically, "the average Virginian knew at first hand about taxation without representation because of his annual experience with the local vestry.")

In the fall of 1764 the Virginia lawmakers received a letter from Massachusetts saying that passage of the new taxes was expected at almost any time. A committee of burgesses was formed to write letters to the king, to the House of Lords, and to the House of Commons protesting the taxes. The Virginians wrote that they "conceive it to be a fundamental principle of the British constitution, without which freedom can no where exist, that the people are not subject to any taxes but such as are laid on them by their own consent, or by those who are legally appointed to represent them." Taxation by Parliament, where they were not represented, "must necessarily establish this melancholy truth, that the inhabitants of the Colonies are slaves of Britons from whom they are descended."[46]

These men knew slavery when they saw it. They explicitly linked British actions with enslavement, recognizing in the government's actions the complex legal, social, and economic restraints they themselves had placed on African-Americans. Washington himself made this connection explicit: "The crisis is arrived when we must assert our rights or submit to every imposition that can be heaped on us till custom and use shall make us as tame and abject slaves as the blacks we rule over with such arbitrary sway."[47] By "arbitrary sway" he meant not overseers with whips but a heavy apparatus of laws and social customs that could turn a proud, independent man into a toady. The passage of the notorious Stamp Act of 1765, which required payment of a tax on every sheet of official paper and every newspaper, created jobs for a whole new class of colonial bureaucrats. Washington's friend George Mercer came back from a trip to England in October 1765 with a box of tax stamps, happy with his remunerative new job as the royal stamp man. He was surrounded by a threatening mob when he set foot in Williamsburg and was hanged in effigy. Mercer resigned his post the next day.[48]

The Stamp Act did not unduly alarm Washington, because he realized that so many planters and lawyers would defy it that the courts would be compelled to close; if lawyers refused to buy stamps to affix to their legal papers, no papers would be filed. The heaviest losers would be not Virginians but British merchants suing for debts. As Washington foresaw, the government revoked the Stamp Act when English merchants complained that it cost them colonial revenue.[49]

Washington's metamorphosis into a Revolutionary is a mystery. Then, as now, no one could quite tell how he made up his mind about something. One historian writes, "Many scholars have searched in vain for signs that Washington responded to the policies of the parent state on the basis of principle or ideology. . . . his reaction was less that of the ideologue than of the individualist."[50] Washington was stirred to action by passage of a new set of taxes, the Townshend duties of 1767. In response, nonimportation groups were organized throughout the colonies. A circular letter from Annapolis urging the "Gentlemen & Planters" to join the boycott reached Washington. He forwarded it in April 1769 to his friend George Mason with a stinging note:

> At a time when our lordly Masters in Great Britain will be satisfied with nothing less than the deprication of American freedom, it seems highly necessary that something shou'd be done to avert the stroke and maintain the liberty which we have derived from our Ancestors. . . . That no man shou'd scruple, or hesitate a moment to use a-ms [arms] in defence of so valuable a blessing, on which all the good and evil of life depends; is clearly my opinion; yet A-ms I wou'd beg leave to add, shou'd be the last resource.[51]

This was the first time a Virginian had suggested that force of arms would be needed to deter the "lordly Masters in Great Britain." Washington's thinking had an almost uncanny clairvoyance. At the very moment he was writing those words, a British warship was approaching the colony, with the new governor, Lord Botetourt, aboard, bearing secret orders to dispatch the warship to Boston to gather troops to occupy Virginia if it became unruly in its resistance to the taxes. Somehow, by some supernatural approximation, George Washington intuited this threat to his country across leagues of empty ocean.[52]

That May, Washington carried to Williamsburg a plan for a boycott, but Governor Botetourt dissolved the House of Burgesses before Washington could formally submit it. The burgesses thereupon gathered at Raleigh Tavern, where Washington proposed the plan, which was adopted. When Washington arrived in Williamsburg with his family for the November session, he and the other burgesses expected a harsh reception, but Governor Botetourt surprised them with a conciliatory opening speech. He expected, and he would urge, that Parliament would repeal all the taxes except for the trifling one on tea.

Washington had little interest in political theorizing, but intuitively grasped the connections between political power, money, and the debt he and the other planters were struggling under. Debt had political ramifications: it weakened the planters both economically and politically, making them a potential prey to tyranny. As another planter observed, financial weakness "leads us to a servile dependence upon power, and fits us for the chains prepared for us." By switching from growing tobacco to producing wheat, Washington had hoped to wriggle free of his dependence on the British market and reduce his debt. Washington was enraged when his merchant advised him in 1764 of the necessity of keeping up with his interest payments. He yearned for the day when he would be free of debt and "all further mention of it." But in the meantime, he wrote, "I did not expect that . . . so steady, and constant [a client] would be reminded in the Instant it was discovered how necessary it was for him to be expeditious in his payments." He concluded with an observation that suggests he felt debt to be as obnoxious a burden as an unjust law: "it is but an irksome thing to a free mind to be anyways hampered in Debt."[53]

An essayist in the Williamsburg newspaper upbraided the planters for their "luxury and idleness." Another writer declared that "*luxury* and *extravagance*" were "the certain forerunners of *indigence, dependance,* and *servility.*" In an exchange of letters in 1769 Washington and George Mason debated the merits of economizing. Mason wrote, "A Man may be as warm in a Coat that costs but Ten Shillings as in one that cost Ten Pounds." Washington agreed that Virginians were living far above their means, but in a society where appearances counted heavily in establishing a family's status, he knew it was essential for a gentleman to be seen living "genteely and hospitably." Imagining the thinking of a hypothetical debtor, Washington wrote, "Prudence dictated economy to him but his resolution was too weak to put it into practice. . . . How can I, *says he,* who have lived in such a manner change my method? I am ashamed to do it." In 1769 Washington noted that the newspapers carried reports of the ruin that debt had brought upon prominent families. "The public papers furnish but too many melancholy proofs" of the damage done by debts, "Estates daily selling for the discharge of Debts."[54]

That fall in Williamsburg Washington heard a proposal put before the burgesses that astonished and outraged the body. It came from one of the elder statesmen of the house, Richard Bland, an acknowledged expert on the rights of British subjects under constitutional law, and one of the men who was already framing the arguments for American liberty. As esteemed as he was after some twenty-seven years as a burgess, Bland found himself "denounced as an enemy of his country" for what he suggested.[55]

He proposed a law allowing masters to emancipate slaves at will. His proposal was seconded by an obscure, newly elected burgess from Albemarle County. No sooner had Bland articulated his idea than it was rejected utterly in a torrent of anger. But the idea *had* been put forth. Washington was probably as astonished as the rest of his colleagues, not just at the proposal but at the man who made it, who was one of Washington's stalwart political friends. He might have asked himself how one of their own could entertain such an idea.

When he heard the idea—Bland might even have sounded him out about the law privately before proposing it—Washington would have remembered the case of old John Custis and his black son, who was set free and almost inherited the wealth that, at that moment, Washington himself possessed. And if Washington and Bland did have a conversation about this emancipation scheme, he would have learned that the proposal was based on an idea so powerful that it was unanswerable; indeed, it was self-evident. Bland's proposal was derived from John Locke's theory of natural rights, the idea that "under the law of nature all men are born free." The burgess from Albemarle who seconded the proposal was Thomas Jefferson.[56]

By 1769 slaveholding was twisting the masters into ontological and epistemological knots. Slavery compelled contortions of lawmaking in order to have the regulations account for the undeniable fact that nature had erased the easy connection between being black and being enslaved. Jefferson wrote the emancipation bill, which he gave to his cousin Bland to submit, after an indentured servant named Thomas Howell had secretly come to him a few weeks earlier. Howell was on the run from his master's plantation and was desperately seeking a lawyer to represent him. His situation was precisely that of the Bowdens, the family of indentured servants who served the Washingtons. He had been indentured for thirty-one years because his mother had been born an indentured servant, and she was indentured because one of her parents had been mixed-race or black. Jefferson thought this state of affairs was "wicked." The likelihood is that young Howell, with one grandparent of color, appeared to be white or very nearly white, and he had been ensnared by laws that had been designed to punish racial mixing. Several months later, Jefferson was to take Howell's case to the highest court in Virginia and make the historic argument, "Under the law of nature, all men are born free, every one comes into the world with a right to his own person, which includes the liberty of moving and using it at his own will. This is what is called personal liberty, and is given him by the author of nature, because necessary for his own sustenance."[57]

Jefferson did not limit his efforts to Howell alone. As soon as he met Howell and learned of his predicament, he proposed the emancipation bill. He seems to have realized that the institution of slavery in Virginia had reached a deeply troubling new stage of its evolution. Slavery had existed for enough generations that the enslaved population included people who were very nearly, or actually, white. His law would give masters the power to free such people if they chose to do it. The irony, of course, is that later Jefferson himself would hold his own offspring in slavery. In all likelihood their skin was as white as his, since their mother, Sally Hemings, was three-fourths white (she was also the half sister of Jefferson's wife). The older and more experienced slaveholders in the House of Burgesses shuddered at the idea. The fury of the burgesses suggests that they knew the extreme danger of allowing any exceptions to slavery. The wall, once opened in a single place, might come tumbling down. That was why the idea was so dangerous, even though the proposed law gave no rights to slaves, only to masters. Masters would decide who would go free and who would remain bound, but the lawmakers could not allow such power to come into existence. Freedom, once loosed, was impossible to confine.

I had been on Williamsburg's main street for less than ten minutes when I heard someone talking about how much a slave was worth. The street was thronged with visitors on this spring day and I could not tell where the remark had come from. I was standing at the center of the town, near the courthouse on Duke of Gloucester Street. A town crier, sporting a tricorn hat and a bright red vest, stood on the courthouse steps, solemnly proclaiming from a document to a group of modern onlookers. He was reading the "newly passed" leash-and-collar law for colonial dogs. The authorities had decreed that pets must wear a collar displaying the initials of the owner, and no one could own more than two dogs. Next to the courthouse children took turns posing for pictures in the pillory. From the upper steps of the courthouse I could see a woman in a broad-brimmed straw hat addressing a large group proceeding toward Bruton Church.

The guide was talking about a slave woman named Secordia, the property of one of the leading men of the colony, Peyton Randolph. The guide said that one of the few things known about Secordia was her value, £10, when she was about fifty years old. Williamsburg's researchers thought this was a very low figure, the guide said, and were trying to figure out why a fifty-year-old woman was worth so little. A young voice suggested that Secordia might have been pregnant, which brought a burst of laughter from the women in the group.

We were standing in front of Bruton Church, where Secordia may have worshiped. The baptism of her daughter is recorded in its books. The guide took up the fragmentary story of this slave family.

"Secordia may in fact have been educated to some degree. Her child was. Her child was sent to the Bray School here in Williamsburg. It was a school run by a charitable group that was loosely associated with the Church of England. It was set up specifically to teach the children of slaves to read and to write so they could read the Bible and repeat their catechism. There was a very strong *servants should obey their masters* emphasis about the training."

Secordia's religious faith is a matter of some speculation among scholars. Did she truly believe in Christianity, or did she attend Bruton Church because Peyton Randolph required it? The baptism of her child might also have been a requirement. "That's just part of being a good master; you are to be the father to your household. Everything we know about him suggests he took that role very seriously." Randolph sent the children of a number of his slaves to the Bray School, and he required that slaves working closely with the family attend church. In the silence imposed by the lack of anything written by Secordia herself, scholars have wondered what she really believed, what she really wanted to do, and what she was compelled to do. Secordia's church attendance could be taken as a sign of a contented slave, but mastery could reach even to compelling religious worship.

As the church bell began tolling loudly—it was just noon—the guide posed a question to the group. The baptism records showed that some free black women also went to church here and had their children baptized. As free people they were under no obvious compulsion. Was their faith genuine?

"There are some things that would seem immediately distasteful. The hierarchy of that church vestry is exactly the same as the hierarchy at the county court and down the street at the capitol building. You can worship here, but are you ever going to be accepted as an equal? Certainly not. Can you think of any reason, if you were a free woman, why you might choose to have a child baptized here?"

"You would fit in with society better," someone suggested.

"All right—you'd get some ties to the society. You might need them. There's one other very significant thing."

"To record the birth?"

"It's the mother's condition that determines the child's condition. If the mother is a slave then the child is a slave. If the mother is free then the child is free. There is no piece of paper, no record in the courthouse. The only thing that proves a child is free is the knowledge of everybody else in the community, and part of that comes from going to church and being seen as a member of this community. The only written record that a child is free is the baptism record right here at Bruton Church."

Puzzled at this explanation, a visitor asked about the child's father. Wouldn't his status as a slave or free man have some bearing on the condition of his child? The guide repeated that a child's status always followed that of the mother. That brought her to the story of Peyton Randolph's slave named Moses.

"Moses had a long-term relationship—it could not be given legal status as a marriage—with a free white woman named Elizabeth Maloney, who was Irish. They had several children together. Everybody in town knew it. He was called into court a few times to make sure those children were supported. He had no real way to do it. We think Peyton Randolph may have actually provided some support for them, but Peyton Randolph did not own those children. But the suggestion in the court records, which are very scanty, is that Peyton Randolph actually protected this family. So a relationship with a master could go both ways."

A document from Bruton Church adds a layer of mystery to understanding George Washington's character as a master. In transcribing the registers of baptisms of slaves, the researchers found the names of twelve slaves belonging to Washington, baptized at Bruton Church in the 1760s. These slaves lived on Custis plantations that came under Washington's control. The notations are spare: "Baptised. . . . Roger son of Molly Belonging to Coll George Washington," on February 3, 1765. All the entries indicate infant baptisms except one, James Westover, listed among the "Grown Persons" baptized on June 7, 1767. Oddly, Westover does not appear in any listing of Washington or Custis slaves, and his use of a surname makes him unusual. It is possible that the Washingtons knew him only as "James" and had no idea he had a surname. It was rather common for enslaved people to have surnames that they kept private from the masters, who would have had little interest in a slave's surname anyway. A slave claiming a surname might have struck them as comical. The Bruton records provide genealogical information because the infants' mothers are named. The register shows, for example, that a slave mother named Daffney brought two children to the church for baptism, William in 1764 and Jenny in 1768.[58] But the baptismal register raises more questions about the Washingtons than it answers: out of the hundreds of Washington and Custis slaves, why were only twelve baptized? Were these favored slaves who were granted special permission by George or Martha for the sacrament, or did the mothers sneak away from their duties, surreptitiously taking their infants into town? Did religious faith make them more accepting of their lot as slaves or more restive?

On the morning I was in the old capital, two of Williamsburg's modern-day "slaves"—African-American interpreters portraying enslaved people—were about to debate that very question. I was walking along a side street when I saw two black men in eighteenth-century garb sitting in the shade of a broad oak tree. The tree was in an isolated spot, and its low-hanging branches provided not only shade but privacy. From the main street, some seventy-five yards away, it would have been hard for a master to see a manservant taking his ease there instead of running the master's errands. The two men were engaged in a lively conversation, with two white tourists listening earnestly. At first I thought this would be a good opportunity for a spontaneous interview with the interpreters, but I quickly realized that these two men were acting "in character," frozen in the 1770s in slavery.

They were portraying actual people of the 1770s—one was free, a carpenter and self-styled Baptist preacher named William Moses, and the other a slave named Will. Their conversation grew into a debate between the faith of the one and the nihilism of the other, sarcastically expressed on both sides. As I approached I heard Will expressing his envy of the preacher's freedom: "I need to be like you. I need to be able to walk like you and do like you do, you being free and all."

But the preacher was not very impressed with what he had in the way of freedom: "I guess there ain't nothing wrong with it. Depends on how you look to it. But I want real freedom"—the freedom to walk about and not have to answer interrogations about whether he was slave or free. They talked about sneaking onto a ship bound for England, where there was no slavery, but the preacher thought one "shouldn't have to run off to get freedom."

Part of the routine of Williamsburg's reenactors is that they try to engage their audience in a dialogue. The preacher turned to me and asked if I had ever been a stranger anywhere. I was so startled at being abruptly addressed by an eighteenth-century black man that I answered no.

"You never been nowhere where people don't know you?!"

"Yes, I go places where people don't know me."

"When you go there, sir, and don't nobody know you, do folks accost you and inquire of you whether you might be an indentured servant?"

"No."

"You ain't got to worry about nobody taking you up either?"

"No."

He turned back to the "slave." "That's what I want, Will. Freedom like that. If I want to go to Richmond, I would like to go without being concerned that somebody will come and take me up, turn me into a slave. Or inquire whether I am a slave or not. I want true freedom—come and go as I please."

Now he politely introduced himself to me and the other two listeners. "William Moses, carpenter and preacher, free to the town." He was registered at Bruton Church as "a free-born Negro."

Will mentioned that his master, Southall, had barred the preacher from his tavern because Southall thought the preacher was giving the slaves "ideas." Moses scoffed, "You think it's going to take the presence of a free Negro to get somebody thinking on freedom?" He also pointed out that you didn't have to be black to be labeled a troublemaker in Williamsburg. Did any of his listeners—there were a few more of us now—know James Ireland, "a Baptist preacher, like me?" Ireland was white but he was in jail at that moment for preaching without a license. "He was right out here in front of this courthouse and he wanted to commence preaching. T'ain't but one church, the old English church, Bruton Church," Moses said, so the authorities jailed the upstart Baptist.

Another character arrived under the tree, a young black woman in a white cap and flowing white blouse, bearing a wicker basket. She appeared to be on a round of errands. Her name was Judith, and she was well acquainted with the two men already under the tree. Her arrival brought a sarcastic outburst from Will.

Judith's husband was the black foreman at Carter's Grove, the plantation just outside of Williamsburg owned in the 1770s by Nathaniel Burwell. Will taunted her about abandoning her children, left at Carter's Grove while she tended her own master's house in town. She belonged not to Burwell but to another man, named Powell. Will also asked her if her husband had lashed any slaves lately. That was one of his tasks as foreman, to dole out punishments to his fellow slaves when his master ordered it. To compensate him for his distasteful duties, Burwell gave the foreman a cabin to himself, with a comfortable rope bed, an ample fireplace, and a wine gourd hanging from the ceiling. (I would later see this cabin at Carter's Grove.) Judith replied angrily that her husband didn't choose to be the foreman, Nathaniel Burwell ordered it.

Perhaps drawn by the sound of raised voices, more visitors had drifted into the shade beneath the tree. A crowd of some forty people listened intently as the slaves debated the conditions of their enslavement.

"A man can't be a real husband," Will said.

This remark enraged the preacher, who lit into Will in defense of Judith's husband.

"The only reason you can't be one, Will, is you choose not to be one. You ain't going to tell me he ain't being the best husband and father he can be to his children. He's doing the best he can to enjoy every minute he can with his wife and his children. You stop speaking against somebody else's happiness. If you don't want to be happy, go off and grumble and complain to yourself."

But Will sensed that he had struck a nerve, and he continued to probe it. "If Judith's children be sick down in the quarter, and her master Powell's children be sick here, whose children do you reckon she has to see first?"

"You know the answer to that question," the preacher snapped. "What's the purpose of asking it? You act like this is something she don't know."

The preacher spoke of marriage and children giving the slaves a "moment of daylight" when they didn't have to think about enslavement. "Do you want to stand in darkness?" he demanded of Will. "Then the master has won."

Will refused to yield to this message of human sweetness and moments of daylight. He suspected that it all came from the preacher's absurd faith. "You say we have to wait on the Lord."

"That's true. That's what you have to do. And I can tell you this: waiting on the Lord will be to your advantage. The Good Book says if you wait on the Lord, He'll renew your strength."

Feeling bold, I decided to test the preacher with questions. "Doesn't the Bible say that slavery is acceptable? Weren't there slaves in the Old Testament?"

"True words, sir, true words. The fancy britches down at Bruton Church stand there and read out the Good Book and tell negroes that"—here he orated contemptuously—"*slaves ought to serve their masters well if they want to receive their REWARD in Heaven.* In that same Good Book it says if you *do* have to serve, you ought not to work but six years. Then on the seventh year you're supposed to loose them. They call it a year of *Jubilee!*"

"When is that day coming?"

"Well, it's probably come and gone."

Like Will, a white onlooker grew impatient with the preacher's pieties. "The only action you take is you just keep praying to God," he said.

"Is there a greater action I can do, sir? Is there something that's got more strength in it than me praying to God?"

"Change the law."

"And I'm a burgess now and I can change the law?" Once more the preacher turned to Will. "Do you trust God to bring you through slavery?"

"I need a sign," Will scoffed. "Tell God I need my freedom."

From time to time historical fragments wash up from slavery that give the briefest glimpse of the mind of a slave. Such fragments are rare because literacy among slaves was rare. In searching for documents about the lives of Virginia slaves I came across a brief item discovered by accident by an American researcher in England reviewing colonial papers at the Lambeth Palace Library in London.[59] There, amidst documents sent to the Bishop of London from Jamaica, he found a letter from America, misfiled among the West Indian papers. It was a desperate appeal from a Virginia slave that somehow had been smuggled out of Virginia and sent to the bishop from Jamaica. The letter was written in secret. The slave had stolen the paper and made the ink himself. It bore one date at the top, August 4, and another at the bottom, September 8—the dates when the writer began and ended the letter. He had composed it in the few hours of time he had to himself on a series of Sundays.

> I am but a poore SLave that writt itt and has no other time butt Sunday and hardly that att Sumtimes. . . . wee your humbell and poore partishinners doo begg Sir your aid and assistancce in this one thing . . . that your honour will by the help of our [sovereign] Lord King George and the rest of the Rullers will Releese us out of this Cruell Bondegg [bondage] and this wee beg for Jesus Christs his Sake who has commanded us to seeke first the kingdom of god.

With garbled spelling, in sentences scrawled in haste with one eye over his shoulder in terror of discovery, the slave explained to the bishop that he belonged to a class of mixed-race people the bishop might never have heard of:

> there is in this Land of verJennia a Sort of people that is Calld mo-latters which are Baptised and brouaht up in the way of the Christian faith and followes the wayes and Rulles of the Chrch of England and sum of them has white fathars and sum white mothers and there is in

this Land a Law or act which keeps and makes them and there seed
SLaves forever—

And then he explained his own condition:

and here it is to bee notd that one brother is a SLave to another and
one Sister to an othe . . . and as for mee my selfe I am my <u>brothers</u>
SLave but my name is Secrett

That his master was his own brother did not ameliorate his enslavement, what he called "our Sevarity and Sorrowful Sarvice."

we are hard used up on Every account in the first place wee are in Ig-
nornce of our Salvation and in the next place wee are kept out of the
Church and matrimony is deenied us and to be plain they doo look
no more up on us then if wee ware dogs

The writer knew enough of the Bible to draw the bishop's attention to
the connection between the enslavement of the Jews in Egypt and the
enslavement of the Africans in America: "wee are commandded to
kepp holey the Sabbath day and wee doo hardly know when it comes
for our task mastrs are has hard with us as the Egypttions was with
the Chilldann of Issarall god be marciftl unto us." Like the Jews, the
American slaves were a captive people whom God could free.

The letter closes with a chilling postscript: "wee dare nott Subscribe
any mans name to this for feare of our masters for if they knew that
wee have Sent home to your honour wee should goo neare to Swing
upon the gallass [gallows] tree."

The Williamsburg tour guide wondered if Secordia actually believed what she was hearing in church—but this unknown slave surely
did, judging by his shock, as a Christian, at being a captive in this be-
nighted country. He yearned for divine justice, believing that if only
he could bring news of their plight to the highest official of the
church, then the slaves would be freed. Such cruelty and injustice
could not continue if godly people knew of it.

The interpreters at Williamsburg enacted one highly dramatic incident whose moral point was so clear that modern-day spectators, carried away by the emotion of the moment, actually tried to intervene and change history. A group of "slaves" gathered in secret, illegally, to discuss whether they should run away. As they argued among themselves a slave patrol, made up of three white interpreters bearing muskets, pushed the onlookers back and descended on the group. A visitor at one such enactment tried to organize resistance against the slave handlers. "There are only three of them and a hundred of us!" he yelled. The actors, white and black, had to break character to restrain him. In another enactment, a slave named Peter discussed with his wife whether he should run away to freedom by himself. The British were offering liberty to any slave who would join them in suppressing the American rebellion, he told her. Though Peter was clearly leaning toward the "wrong" side in the Revolution, his predicament deeply touched the children in one group of onlookers, who instinctively felt that freedom was more important than anything else. Groups of them formed a protective cordon around Peter, even following him around Williamsburg when he was out of character. One nine-year-old from Colorado asked his family to return to Williamsburg a year later because he specifically wanted to help Peter escape. At Peter's invitation the boy stepped into the drama, and together they decided to seek freedom. Asked why he was taking sides with a slave, the boy said, "Some people were doing wrong things and some people were doing right things, and I just picked the side of the people doing the right things."[60]

It has not been easy for Colonial Williamsburg to reach this juncture in its presentation of history. Williamsburg has reflected, and magnified, the many controversies sparked by changing perceptions of the country's racial past. The initial restoration at Williamsburg had its origins in 1924, when a professor of biblical literature from Williamsburg, the Reverend William Archer Rutherfoord Goodwin, gave a lecture before the Phi Beta Kappa Society in New York. Goodwin had previously been rector of the historic Bruton Parish Church and had raised the funds to have it restored. As he looked over his audience that night in New York, he noticed the famous profile of the philanthropist John D. Rockefeller, Jr. It was not an opportunity Goodwin would let slip. After the talk he invited Rockefeller to visit Williamsburg. Two years later Rockefeller visited the town with his wife. Williamsburg was then in a virtually ruined state, but Goodwin told the oil magnate that Williamsburg was worth saving and restoring.[61] Rockefeller agreed, and made Goodwin his confidential agent. With funds secretly provided by the philanthropist, Goodwin began buying up properties in Williamsburg, to the puzzlement of the citizens, who could not imagine what Goodwin intended to do with all those decrepit old buildings. Goodwin and Rockefeller communicated in coded telegrams. In one such communication authorizing the purchase of a building, Rockefeller wrote, "Authorize purchase of antique referred to in your long letter." It was signed "David's father." The astonishment of Williamsburg's citizens was complete when they found that the illustrious Rockefeller was the eminence behind the purchases.[62]

The vision shared by Rockefeller and Goodwin was a grand and worthy one:

> It is the purpose of our associates to make this favored city a national shrine . . . dedicated to the lives of the nation's builders. We will be the custodians of memorials to which the eyes of the world will be turned. We should return thanks that this place has been chosen as a shrine of history and of beauty. There will be windows built here, through which men may look down the vistas of the past.[63]

In 1932 the president of Colonial Williamsburg, Kenneth Chorley, said that the purpose of the restoration was celebratory: "to commemorate the history and success of the American Revolution" and to diffuse "healthful" information in regard to American history.[64] Historical interpretation was very closely linked to good citizenship.

At the very same time Colonial Williamsburg was being created, a political scientist, Charles Edward Merriam, articulated the usefulness of history and the crucial interplay of past and present in American life. His overriding concern was the use of history in molding citizens, a body politic that transcended time and place to achieve an almost mystical unity of Americanness—one people of one blood. Merriam promulgated his historical creed in his 1931 book *The Making of Citizens: A Comparative Study of Methods of Civic Training.*

> The underlying design is of course to set up a group of the living, the dead, and those who are yet unborn, a group of which the individual finds himself a part and of which he is in fact glad to count himself a member, and by virtue of that fact an individual of no mean importance in the world. All the great group victories he shares in; all the great men are his companions in the bonds of the group; all its sorrows are by construction his; all its hopes and dreams, realized and thwarted alike, are his. And thus he becomes although of humble status a great man, a member of a great group; and his humble life is thus tinged with a glory it might not otherwise ever hope to achieve. He is lifted beyond and above himself into higher worlds where he walks with all his great ancestors, one of an illustrious group whose blood is in his veins and whose domain and reputation he proudly bears.[65]

This manifesto, published in 1931, had its effect for decades. It was cited as late as 1977 in an influential guide for public historians, Freeman Tilden's *Interpreting Our Heritage.* Though specifically referring to work for the National Park System, Tilden's vision has been a guide for professionals at many other "living history" museums. It articulates broadly and deeply held beliefs about the kind of history Americans want: "My experience is that the groups of people who seek out interpretation in the areas of the National Park System are wonderfully well-mannered and pathetically eager for guidance toward the larger aspects of things that lead toward wisdom and toward the consolations that come from a sense of living in a natural world and a historic continuity that 'make sense.'" Tilden refers to the historical interpreters at "a precious monument of our wise and heroic ancestors" as the "middlemen of happiness." The purpose of park guides was to give visitors not just information but the opportunity to be "lifted up through wonder into joy."[66]

At Williamsburg, as at so many other historical sites, the yearning for a history that "makes sense" has collided with actual historical realities. Slavery wrecks the simple heroic narrative of the Founding. This narrative worked so long as slavery was depicted as part of the refinement and gentility of the eighteenth century. When the harsher aspects of slavery began to be presented we entered the era of the paradox, in which somehow slavery and the campaign for liberty coexisted. Because the founders were considered, a priori, good people, incapable of doing anything manifestly evil, it was surmised that they were blind to slavery's evil. It was deemed inappropriate to impose modern standards on them. But avoiding judgments requires a very careful selection of subject matter, in order to create a narrative that can make sense and that never collides with a moral puzzle. The yearning for pure narrative conquers any wish for an examination of difficult and vexing historical issues. Once we go beyond the state of paradox, which has often become a state of perpetual suspension of judgment, we enter a dangerous and, some would say, "unhealthful" realm of questioning. *Could* the founders have ended slavery then and there? Washington freed his slaves. He did not think emancipation was impossible. Why did the others not follow? Why not judge Washington's peers by Washington's standards?

Until recently the prevailing interpretation of the African-American experience presented in mainstream history texts could be remarkably contemptuous. Americans who went to college in the 1950s learned the basics of American history from a textbook written by Samuel Eliot Morison, of Harvard, and Henry Steele Commager, of Columbia, who wrote, "As for Sambo, whose wrongs moved the abolitionists to wrath and tears, there is some reason to believe that he suffered less than any other class in the South from its 'peculiar institution.'" Most slaves, they wrote, "were adequately fed, well cared for, and apparently happy. . . . Although brought to America by force, the incurably optimistic Negro soon became attached to the country, and devoted to his 'white folks.'"[67]

Colonial Williamsburg came into existence in the 1920s on a wave of nostalgia for the past, what one writer described as "the growing interest in America's past as a bulwark against unsettling change."[68] The South as a whole, with its beautiful architecture and rigid social order, became a historical refuge, a place of repose. Writing of the mansions on the South's old plantations, a photographer said in 1948, "seeing these houses . . . we shall be taken out of ourselves; out of our own era, with its organized madness."[69] The same atmosphere of escape suffused Williamsburg. A Virginia woman who served as a hostess at Colonial Williamsburg in the 1940s wrote, "It seems to be a kind of aristocracy just to live in Williamsburg where everything—stick and stone and chandelier and outhouse—is restored to the noble beauty of colonial days."[70] Visitors bristled at any suggestion that the founders were not perfect, she wrote. When a hostess mentioned that Jefferson had "made merry with his fair Belinda in the Apollo Room," a visitor became angry. "Do you mind telling me *why* you seek to Cast Tarnish on Thomas Jefferson? . . . One would think that in Williamsburg of *All* Places, the memories of our great National Heroes would be treated with Respect. Merrymaking in a Tavern? Indeed, I don't believe it. . . . And for the life of me I can't understand why you would say Such a thing."[71] Travel writers still look to Colonial Williamsburg for nostalgic trips through time.

Colonial Williamsburg at first presented the rosiest possible view of slavery, even though the Reverend Goodwin himself knew precisely what slavery had been like in the town. There was at least one former slave still alive in Williamsburg then, a woman named Eliza Baker, who was born in the town on July 2, 1845. Goodwin went to interview her personally. The transcript of his interview, still in the Williamsburg archives, is remarkable for its frankness.[72] In response to the question, "Tell us about your life, Eliza," she replied that her parents were slaves owned by Colonel Bassett. Her mother worked for the Galt family, and "I was hired out for general housework" to two successive families.

"When you were a little girl could you see your mother often?"

"No. To see my mother I would have to steal into the house where she was, hide in the cellar coal bin, just to speak to her when I got a chance. . . . If you was caught out after nine o'clock you would be whipped—given nine and thirty."

"Where was the whipping post?"

"The whipping post was in the bottom of the ravine back of the new Court House you-all built. There was a big cage there which they put you in before they whipped you. . . . After they had whipped you, you had to pay a dollar to get out of the cage. Free colored people, who didn't belong to nobody, they had to pay a dollar to get out of the cage. Anybody who belonged to anybody the owner would have to come down and get them out and pay the dollar. . . ."

"Was any education given to the colored people?"

"If they caught you with a book in your hand, they would whip you. . . ."

"Were the owners good to the slaves?"

"Some treated 'em right tough, and some right good. They made you do what they wanted you to do, and if you didn't do what they wanted you to, they put you in their pocket."

"What do you mean by 'put you in their pocket'?"

"That means the nigger trader would get you. Mr. Hansford was a nigger trader. He lived where Mr. Ball lives now."

"How did they use to sell slaves?"

"From the block on the Court House Green. I have heard many a crying-out on the block. The nigger trader would tell what the man could do. A good carpenter would sell for $400. A good cook and a good seamstress would sell high. The darker you were the more you would go for. A woman would go for $175 or $200. Little children, eight or ten years old, would go for $60 or $75."

"Who would sell them?"

"Mr. Moses Harrel would cry them out. 'Here they go!' he would cry. Hardly any parents would stand by to see their children sold. . . ."

"Who were the pretty girls around here when you were young?"

"Oh, there were so many belles and things around. They were *good-looking*. They should have been, for their families were selling us to make pocket change to send them to the Springs every summer and to school in the fall."

"Who lived at the Wythe House?"

"Different people lived there. George Washington, they say, lived there one time."

In 1940 a new African-American school in Williamsburg was funded largely through the generosity of the Rockefeller family. John D. Rockefeller, Jr., donated a thirty-acre site for the school; Mrs. Rockefeller sent a personal check for $50,000; and the Rockefeller family education fund sent an additional $35,000. But in the restored section of town, African-American history remained relentlessly benign and barely visible. As early as 1954 many visitors sensed that Williamsburg was telling only part of the story. A consultant who reviewed visitor comments wrote, "They want to see how really poor people lived, and slaves, and indentured servants. The absence of any evidence of lower-class life gives some visitors a feeling that either Williamsburg is ashamed of this aspect of colonial life . . . or simply negligent in giving the whole picture."[73]*

Although Colonial Williamsburg has long employed African-American interpreters, they did not actually interpret slavery itself until 1979, when six black interpreters were hired to portray slaves.[74] What they were enacting, most of all, was the humanity of the slaves. There was a double purpose to this endeavor. First, they were portraying the humanity of the slaves for modern white visitors, to let them know that slavery did not grind every vestige of humanity from the enslaved: slaves had families, they were husbands and wives and grandparents, they yearned for freedom; some actively resisted, with little success. And second, the interpreters were enacting what the masters would have seen and heard, to show that the humanity of the slaves was inescapably obvious.

* African-American visitors to Colonial Williamsburg were virtually nonexistent: they had no place to stay. Rockefeller himself wrote the text of the official explanation that was to be given to any blacks who sought a hotel room: "The management has thus far not found it practicable to provide for both colored and white guests. I am sorry we cannot accommodate you." Jewish travelers were also excluded from the Williamsburg Inn.

The interpreters want to establish in the minds of visitors the fact of an African-American presence at this cradle of American liberty, and they also want to portray the *character* of the African-American presence. In the archives at Colonial Williamsburg there is a letter written in 1936 by a group of African-Americans asking for some consideration of them and the character of the people they descended from: "We wish to let you know that, as Negro citizens we are interested in the Restoration Movement. . . . because colored people were among the earliest settlers in this area, we have helped to build up and to preserve the Nation and stand willing to sacrifice again and again." They knew that without their story the American narrative made no sense as a useful guide to public life, that the narrative would never make sense until it grappled with the most paradoxical, vexing, and painful questions.[75]

To find out what Washington would have seen and done when he was in Williamsburg, I looked in the town's newspapers, of which in the 1760s there were two, both called the *Virginia Gazette*. Their faded pages are preserved on microfilm—the originals are far too fragile to bear handling any longer. There are gaps in the holdings, but fortunately a run of papers had survived from the times when Washington visited Williamsburg. As I scanned the film from April 1769 my eye was caught by an unusually large headline, which read simply:

A SCHEME

A line of smaller type below revealed that this was an advertisement for a lottery. For the purchase of a ticket at £10, gamblers could buy a chance at winning one of the items detailed under the headline CONTENTS of PRIZES. There followed a long list of items in small type— so long it ran off the bottom of my screen—difficult to read in the blurred and faded microfilm.[76]

The first item on the list was a parcel of 1,800 acres "of good Land," with a forge and a "geared Grist-mill, both well fixed, and situate on a plentiful and constant Stream." The next five items were also parcels of land, almost 9,000 acres in total, featuring apple and peach orchards, groves of oaks that would yield planks and staves, and other lands "very fine for Corn and Tobacco." The sixth lot, however, was something quite different: "A Negro man named *Billy*, about 22 years old, an exceeding trusty good Forgeman, as well at the Finery as under the Hammer, and understands putting up his Fire; Also his wife named *Lucy*, a young Wench, who works exceeding well both in the House and Field." This couple was valued at £280.

The roster of prizes continued with *Joe*, 27, "a very trusty good Forgeman"; *Mingo*, about 24 years old; *Ralph*, about 22; *Isaac*, about 30; *Sam* and his wife, *Daphne*, "a very good hand at the Hoe, or in the House." I knew that slaves had been sold at auctions, but I had never heard of people being raffled. This was new.

I scrolled down to the bottom of the list to look for the name of the man offering these lots. At the bottom of the advertisement, a large line of type indicated that the sale was for the benefit of Bernard Moore. But just above his name, in a list of "Gentlemen" who were the managers of the lottery, I saw the name *George Washington*. Washington himself was raffling off slaves.*

I had seen a series of entries in Washington's diary during his Williamsburg stay that had seemed so trivial I hadn't paid attention to them. December 14: "Dined at Mrs. Campbells & spent part of the Evening in drawing Colo. Moores Lottery." December 15: "went to Southalls in the Evening to draw Colo. Moores Lottery." The next night it was ten o'clock before the lottery was finally completed.

Bernard Moore was deeply in debt to the Custis estate, from which he had borrowed £1,000, and the account had accumulated another £338 in interest. Washington, acting as guardian for his stepchildren, had organized the raffle along with other creditors. They could make more money with a lottery than with an auction because they could

---

* Four of the seven Virginians who went to the First Continental Congress were on the list of Bernard Moore's managers. They were rafflers of children.[77]

appeal to the sporting blood of Virginians. As one historian wrote, "it was determined to liquidate all of Moore's property by an elaborate lottery, for, while few had large sums of ready money, there were many who would gamble."[78]

The drawings took place in a tavern, amid the banging of dice boxes and tankards, and the inevitable bawdy songs. Fifty-five people were offered, in thirty-nine lots. The majority of prizes, twenty-one, consisted of single men. There were six families, and five lots of women with a child or children. The managers were well aware of the family connections among the people because the listing denoted "wife of," "daughter of," "children of."

The managers had broken up families at random, or according to some requirement I could not detect. But then a pattern emerged, one that made perfect sense within the universe of slavery. The best male workers, appraised at the highest values, got to keep their wives and children: it was a privilege of their "rank" in the hierarchy of slavery. Their high value gave them leverage, and the managers wanted to keep them docile. The less valuable families did not get to stay together.

One lot offered the prize of "A Negro Woman named *Kate,* and a young Child, *Judy.*" The next lot offered "A Negro Girl, *Aggy,* and Boy, *Nat,* Children of *Kate.*" Since this was to be a raffle, fate would decide if the same player won both lots. The odds were low, given that 1,840 tickets were offered for sale. In similar fashion another item offered, with stunning bluntness, "A fine breeding Woman named *Pat,* lame of one side, with Child, and her three Children, *Lat, Milley,* and *Charlotte.*" The next item offered "A fine Boy, *Phill,* son of *Patty,* about 14 years old." Another lot offered *Robin,* "a good Sawyer," and his wife, *Bella.* They would remain together, but the next item showed that they would lose their two daughters: "A Negro Girl named *Sukey,* about 12 years old, and another named *Betty,* about 7 years old, Children of *Robin* and *Bella.*"

Robin and Bella, like the other slave parents to be separated from their children, certainly did not know that their twelve- and seven-year-old daughters were about to be taken from them. If they knew, they would run, but none of them knew. They were on Moore's plantation, far from the candlelit tavern on Duke of Gloucester Street where the planters drew lots to divide them. The first sign they would have would be the one Martha Washington dreaded when she was apart from her Jacky—a barking dog, the sign of a stranger coming on the place.

The business of slaveholding required such transactions. In times of financial difficulty, the slaves paid the price for their masters' troubles. This sale and numerous others that took place around the colony had their origin in a financial scandal at the highest level of Virginia's government. In May 1766 executors began to settle the estate of John Robinson, the recently deceased treasurer of the colony, speaker of the House of Burgesses, and a close friend of Washington's. To their astonishment, the executors found that Robinson had embezzled more than £100,000 of public funds.[79] The scandal touched many of the most prominent people in Virginia, as Robinson had lent the stolen funds to other burgesses as well as members of the august Royal Council. His method was simple. Notes that the colony had redeemed had been turned over to Robinson, in his capacity as treasurer, for destruction. But instead of destroying the redeemed notes, which were still negotiable, he used some for his own purposes and lent some to others. The Robinson debt fiasco rippled through the Virginia economy. A number of leading men were implicated, including Bernard Moore, who had borrowed heavily from Robinson's embezzled funds as well as from the Custis estate. When it became clear that Moore could never repay his debts, his property was liquidated.[80] The 1769 raffle did not include the entirety of Moore's property; this sale was a stopgap, an attempt to hold off creditors while he reorganized his finances. He was unable to do so, and the rest of his slaves were sold in 1771, a sale in which Washington also participated. In modern terms, it was as if the collapse of a Wall Street brokerage, due to the malfeasance of its officers, had led to the sale of the children of the cleaning staff to pay the debts of corporate vice presidents.

Just before Washington made his November 1769 trip to Williamsburg, he had forced another sale of slaves.[81] A rascally acquaintance of his, John Posey, had run up large debts and Washington moved to foreclose. Washington attended the sale in person.

To be SOLD for ready money, at Rover's Delight in Fairfax county, on Monday the 23d inst.

A TRACT of valuable LAND in said county lying on Potowmack river, adjoining to the land on which the subscriber now keeps ferry, and very fit for farming. . . . At the same time and place, and upon the same terms, will likewise be sold, about twenty-five choice SLAVES, consisting of men, women, and children. . . . The money arising from the slaves to be paid into the hands of George Washington, Esq.

No biographer of Washington had ever mentioned his raffling of slaves, though Douglas Southall Freeman gives ample coverage to Bernard Moore's financial problems. Freeman had examined the lottery advertisement; he footnotes it. And yet he says nothing about its contents. Freeman is an encyclopedic biographer: few details escape his notice and his pen. But by omitting this transaction, leaving it in silence, he gives the impression that it never occurred. Later writers who based their work on Freeman might have believed that Washington himself never took part in such activities as raffling off black children and "wenches" for profit and perhaps amusement.[82]

When the sale of human beings is mentioned at all by some leading old-school historians and biographers, it is mentioned in a breezy fashion, as if slave sales were just another charming and antique aspect of a charming, antique period. In a lively passage intended to evoke for the reader the atmosphere of old Williamsburg, Jefferson's biographer Dumas Malone mentions the offices of the *Virginia Gazette*, noting that "people often went there to . . . advertise the sale of 'parcels of Virginia-born wenches,' or to offer to the horse-breeding public the services of stallions in their prime." By juxtaposing African-American "wenches" and horse breeding, Malone catches the mind-set of many eighteenth-century Virginia masters. He continues, imagining for the modern reader a stroll through Williamsburg that Jefferson might have taken: "Near the Capitol in the 1760s, as now, was the Public Gaol, and beyond the Capitol he could have come into still another world. Here was an open space known as the Exchange, where planters squared accounts with one another, consigned tobacco to factors and sea captains, and arranged to purchase Negro fellows or some of those likely wenches."[83]

I only had to spend a few days with the microfilm of the *Virginia Gazette* to see what an appalling business this was. The pages were studded with advertisements, stacked one on top of the other, for slaves.

To be SOLD . . . *for ready money*
Upwards of forty
FINE SLAVES
Most of them *Virginia* born

To be SOLD *at public auction*
About FOURTEEN very likely
NEGROES

To be SOLD *at public auction,*
by a decree of the General Court,
for ready money
SIX
SLAVES

Amid the profusion of auction announcements one stood out. In this chronicle of misery, this one item, with heart-stopping power, gave a glimpse of utter depravity:

THIRTY choice *VIRGINIA* born
SLAVES
consisting chiefly of boys and girls,
from 14 or 15 down to the ages of two or three years.
Credit will be given. . . .[84]

Behind this advertisement lay a story of monstrous horror. A trader had obviously gone from plantation to plantation, gathering up young teenagers and toddlers whom the masters felt they could do without. It was customary to have an elderly slave look after the smallest children while the mothers and fathers worked in the fields. The parents would have come back from their work at night to find their two-year-old gone forever. We can only imagine the terror of the children, taken suddenly by strangers, trussed and shoved into a wagon.

In the year before the Moore raffle, Washington had been in Williamsburg when there was an auction on the steps of the fabled Raleigh Tavern. The advertisement promised "choice" slaves—"MEN, WOMEN, BOYS, and GIRLS"—from another master, Armistead Lightfoot, tangled up in the Robinson debt fiasco. Washington could not have missed seeing it—it was a massive auction of some fifty people. Just a few months before the Lightfoot sale, Governor Fauquier had died; in his will he had laid down strict guidelines for the settlement of his estate. With clear concern for the family connections among his slaves, Fauquier specified that mothers and children were not to be separated, that the *slaves* were to be given the right *to choose their new masters*—and as an encouragement for buyers under these terms, Fauquier specified that the sales be made at below-market rates.[85] The example set by this foreigner had no effect on the practices of the Virginia planters.

Two centuries later the African-American interpreters at Colonial Williamsburg decided, as an educational presentation, to re-create an estate auction that would include, on a very small scale, the sale of slaves. In retrospect the decision was a naive one, because the staff was not prepared for the powerful emotions released by the enactment even though it gave only a faint inkling of the emotions that might have been unleashed at an actual auction when fifty slaves, not four, went on the block. The auction reenactment was carried out only once; it was never repeated because its cruelty was too much for both the black and white interpreters, though everyone knew it was merely a fiction. I watched the auction on a videotape made by news organizations—the event received international coverage—because I wanted to get some sense of what George Washington himself would have seen, perhaps even a sense of what he might have felt at such a sight. I did this because the first sign of Washington's very gradual change of heart regarding slavery was a sudden reluctance to break up families by sale. Something he had seen, something he had done, had stuck in his memory and become abhorrent to him. He began to see that the business of slaveholding required transactions so foul that he could no longer stomach them.

The auction reenactment took place on the steps of Wetherburn's Tavern. The street was jammed with television cameras and two thousand onlookers, some of whom had waited hours in front of the tavern to get a close-up view of the event. Two men were to be sold, and two young women. All the bidders were men, naturally, and just as naturally the prospect of males offering money to possess in total the person of a young woman was unsettling.

In keeping with the realism of the program, the interpreters first conducted a tedious mock sale of various items of property. The slave sale was part of an estate auction. Masters had died, and their property had to be liquidated to settle their debts. Along with land, cattle, horses, pots, pans, and pewter spoons, there were these people to be sold. So at the conclusion of the sale of the animals and inanimate property, a door opened and a woman was led out before the crowd. The auctioneer, in character, alluded to the fact that the bidders had already had the opportunity to examine the slave, so the bidding began. Also in keeping with historical realism, the bidders included a black man. Among Williamsburg's tiny free black population in the 1770s was a man named John Ashby, who had in fact been able to save his wife from slavery by buying her from her master. As "Ashby" called out a bid, a white bidder challenged his right to participate, but the officials in charge replied that Ashby had submitted the proper documents of credit. With Ashby determined to buy his wife, the bidding became brisk, but he managed to outbid the whites and secure his spouse.

Next came Billy, a burly man in a broad black hat and leather apron, bearing a tray of tools. He was a carpenter, a highly valued, skilled slave who, the auctioneer pointed out, could be rented at great advantage. Billy stood impassively, watched closely by an equally burly, flinty-eyed constable. He was sold from the estate of William Byrd III, an asset that went to pay off the card-table losses of this profligate gambler. The bidding ended at £75.

The auctioneer now announced Daniel and Lucy, house slaves, not mentioning a fact that would have been known to many if not all the bidders—Daniel and Lucy were married. Daniel was brought out first, resplendent in bright red and green livery and a tricorn hat. He too stood impassively as "Mr. Tayloe" won him.

Lucy was the final item. In an unplanned bit of realism, the woman playing Lucy was about eight months pregnant. The pregnancy made her so valuable that the man who had already bought her husband might not be able to afford her as well. Slave and auction advertisements often specified that a woman was pregnant, such as the notice for "a Negro woman, Charlotte, 18 years of age, big with her second child."[86]* Mr. Tayloe bid energetically for Daniel's wife, but he could not match the purse of a Mr. Nelson. To make the obvious point even more obvious for the onlookers, one interpreter playing a bidder called out "two for one!" Nelson won, and Lucy sobbed as she was led away.

The emotion was real, and the woman who played Lucy later said she could not enact such a thing again. To come to grips with the feelings they had stirred in themselves by the reenactment, the Williamsburg staff invited a historian who had studied the psychology of slavery to give a lecture to the staff. She said that in the collective memory of African-Americans, there were five areas that were "ultrasensitive," and Williamsburg had ventured into two of them: one was auctions and the other was separation of families. In the oral histories of black families these events continued to echo and inflict pain. Families rarely spoke of such matters except among themselves because the humiliation they felt, even with the passage of time, was so great.

When I was at work in Williamsburg, trying to get a sense of the

* Charlotte's seller was Patrick Henry.

events Washington experienced there, I was asked to consult with two researchers on a project to locate descendants of Carter's Grove slaves and to document their history. The master was Nathaniel Burwell, and the blacks from that plantation used the name Burrell, as it was pronounced. The African-American Burrell family had passed down an oral tradition that they were descended from a slave named Matilda whose five children were fathered by master Burwell. Such relationships were of course quite common, but very hard to authenticate. What struck me were two other fragments of oral history carried down by the generations. One was that the Burwell masters "sold off the dark slaves and kept the light slaves." If the white Burwells were having children with their slave women, the light slaves would have been their own offspring, whom they kept off the market. The other fragment of history involved Matilda herself. Far from venerating her as the matriarch of her family, the history asserted "she was very black and evil," and she hated light-skinned babies, the "yellow babies" born of a white father and a slave mother.

I thought that Matilda's hatred must have grown from having seen dark children being sold and yellow children being saved, and then I realized that *some of her own children*, born of the master, would have been yellow-skinned. She hated her own offspring, whose pale color lifted them above the fate of the dark ones, perhaps their own siblings. The masters had managed to infect the slaves with self-hatred. I remembered the question posed under the oak tree by the preacher to his bitter fellow slave: "Do you want to stand in darkness? Then the master has won." Matilda had been deformed by her hatred and stood in its darkness. It was so horrible to the others that they remembered it, and they remembered the cause of it: the masters "sold off the dark slaves and kept the light slaves."[87]

When Williamsburg, in our era, carried out its mock sale of slaves, they could not even approach the reality of the events Washington had seen and the emotions they had unleashed. From the descriptions George Washington wrote of his runaway slaves we know that Washington had stared deeply into their faces and tried to divine their thoughts. Did he look as deeply into the faces of the people he bought and sold at auction? Did he see terror and the horror of being separated from family? There is evidence that he did, an indication in the middle of a long letter written to him in 1775 by the manager of Mount Vernon. Washington had agreed to take possession of a slave in payment of a debt owed by a planter named Adams. The manager wrote of Adams, "he verily believe'd the Fellow woud Run away immediately, for he was so attachd to his Wife & children that he had repeatedly declared he had rather Die than leave them. . . . Adams said you promised if the [whole family] were [available for sale] you woud purchase them."[88]

In 1773, an overseer had used similar terms to convey to Washington the agony of slave mothers kept apart from their children. These separations, the overseer wrote, felt "like death to them." By 1775 Washington was unsettled and uneasy enough to buy a whole family he did not need rather than separate them. This was the first hint of the long transformation that culminated in Washington's decision to emancipate his slaves. Washington's later statement that he would refuse to sell people like "cattle in the market" has been taken as a sign of his benevolent character, a sign that a man such as Washington would never do such a thing. In fact, he had done it. But then he began to face what he had done, while all around him the buying and selling went on unabated. Thomas Jefferson observed that Washington's mind was "slow in operation, being little aided by invention or imagination, but sure in conclusion."[89] With the raffle of children in Williamsburg, Washington reached a moral nadir, and from that depth began a long moral transfiguration that concluded in the writing of his will—his indictment of the laws, the country, and the people that enacted events that, to him, had the feeling of death.

CHAPTER SIX

"So Sacred a War as This"

THERE ARE FEW AMERICAN MONUMENTS more stirring than the granite obelisk on Lexington Green in Massachusetts, the site of the first battle of the Revolutionary War. That marker, put up in 1799, just twenty-four years after the fighting, was the first memorial in honor of the Revolution's heroes. It was set in place by people who had lost fathers, husbands, and sons in the fatal events of April 19, 1775. In the gray dawn of that day, about seventy-seven Minute Men formed a line on the Green to face a task force of seven hundred British army regulars who had marched from Boston to confiscate weapons and powder the Americans had stockpiled. Alerted by Paul Revere the night before, the Minute Men had gathered to stop the British, and when the sun rose that morning, revealing an enemy that outnumbered them almost ten to one, the Minute Men heard their commander say, "Stand your ground. Don't fire unless fired upon. But if they mean to have a war, let it begin here." The war did begin there and then, as the ranks of British regulars opened fire on the Americans in "a continuous roar of musketry," as Paul Revere described it. Eight Americans died on the spot; another ten were wounded.

The monument memorializes that moment with unforgettable words:

SACRED TO LIBERTY &
THE RIGHTS OF MANKIND!!!
THE FREEDOM & INDEPENDENCE
OF AMERICA.
SEALED AND DEFENDED WITH THE
BLOOD OF HER SONS.

The obelisk carries the names of the men who died that morning: Robert Munroe, Jonas Parker, Samuel Hadley, Jonathan and Caleb Harrington, Isaac Muzzy, John Brown, and Azael Porter.

THE BLOOD OF THESE MARTYRS IN THE CAUSE OF GOD AND THEIR COUNTRY WAS THE CEMENT OF THE UNION OF THESE STATES. . . . RIGHTEOUS HEAVEN APPROVED THE SOLEMN APPEAL; VICTORY CROWNED THEIR ARMS, AND THE PEACE, LIBERTY, AND INDEPENDENCE OF THE UNITED STATES OF AMERICA WAS THEIR GLORIOUS REWARD.

One of the men who shed his blood on Lexington Green on April 19, Prince Easterbrooks, was wounded that morning but survived to fight another day. On the list of wounded printed up immediately after the battle and distributed as a broadside, he was described as "A Negro man." It was a surprise to me, a native of Massachusetts, to discover that a black man had fought on the sacred ground at Lexington Green. And when I first visited Lexington I had no idea that Massachusetts had slaves.[1]

Prince Easterbrooks was not an anomaly. George Washington won the Revolutionary War with an army that was more integrated than any American military force until the Vietnam War. It is difficult to arrive at a precise count of the black soldiers because in many records race is not recorded. In the 1960s the historian Benjamin Quarles, the first to study the black role in the Revolution systematically, estimated that about five thousand blacks served in the Continental Army.

More recently other historians calculated that the black presence in the army in 1778 (a year from which reliable records survive) ranged between a low of 6 percent and a high of 13 percent. At one point, at the end of the war, the figure was even higher.[2]

Documents and eyewitness accounts from the Revolution attest to a large number of blacks in arms. "You never see a regiment in which there are not negroes," wrote a foreign officer, "and there are well-built, strong, husky fellows among them."[3] The United States owed its liberty in significant measure to black troops. Here is the mystery of the era written in blood: in the face of the known heroism of these black troops, how is it that the Revolution preserved slavery? George Washington, the slaveholder who led the war for liberty, personifies that paradox.

The paradox was addressed by Richard Brookhiser in his book *Founding Father.* Quoting the contemptuous jibe of Samuel Johnson—"How is it that we hear the loudest *yelps* for liberty among the drivers of Negroes?"—Brookhiser notes that "the contrast between ideals and practice has amused the Revolution's enemies and embarrassed many of its friends for two hundred years." And he suggests that Washington "encompassed the contradictions the way that all men, including ourselves, encompass their contradictions: by not thinking of them."[4] This idea that the issue of liberty for slaves was beneath the concern of Washington and his peers, that it simply did not register on their conscience or consciousness, is widely held. There is also a general feeling that blacks did not and could not become free during the Revolution because whites as a group believed that blacks were an inferior race.

Samuel Johnson's derisive slap at the Revolution was echoed in more sober and eloquent terms by the friends of the Revolution. The Boston patriot James Otis, in a 1764 pamphlet, *Rights of the British Colonies,* read throughout the colonies, proclaimed:

> The Colonists are by the law of nature free born, as indeed all men are, white or black. . . . Does it follow that tis right to enslave a man because he is black? Will short curl'd hair like wool, instead of christian hair, as tis called by those whose hearts are as hard as the nether

millstone, help the argument? Can any logical inference in favour of slavery be drawn from a flat nose, a long or a short face?[5]

Abigail Adams grew up in a slaveholding family, yet in 1775, just before the outbreak of the fighting, she wrote to her husband, "I wish most sincerely there was not a single slave in the province; it always appeared a most iniquitous scheme to me [to] fight ourselves for what we are daily robbing and plundering from those who have as good a right to freedom as we have."[6] Washington's friend and mentor Landon Carter, at home on his plantation in Virginia, was stunned when he read the Declaration of Independence because he thought it meant that the slaves had to be freed; he read the document literally and could see no other interpretation of it.

Washington grappled with the contradiction of revolution and slavery from the first day he took command of the American forces in Massachusetts. He did not ignore the subject; indeed he could not. Fierce debate over the subject of slavery raged around him throughout the war and the years thereafter.

As early as 1774 he had predicted that if a war with Great Britain broke out, "more blood [would] be spilt [than] history has ever yet furnished instances of in the annals of North America."[7] In May of that year he traveled to Williamsburg for the regular meeting of the House of Burgesses, but this time the session had unusual urgency. Five months earlier tax protesters in Boston had dumped East India Company tea into the harbor, and the British government had responded with a draconian plan of four laws that became known in America as the Intolerable Acts. These laws closed the port of Boston until the tea was paid for, and abrogated key provisions of the charter of Massachusetts Bay Colony by giving the royal governor the authority to pack the Massachusetts courts and legislature with loyal supporters by appointment.[8] Furthermore, the Boston Port Act provided for enforcement of the harbor's closure by British warships.

In Williamsburg, Washington voted with the other burgesses for a resolution that called the closing of the port "a hostile invasion of

Boston." As a further, disguised protest, the burgesses named June 1, 1774, a day of "fasting, humiliation, and prayer to implore the divine interposition, for averting the heavy Calamity which threatens destruction to our Civil Rights, and the evils of Civil War; [and] to give us one heart and one Mind firmly to oppose, by all just and proper means, every injury to American Rights." Not mollified by the religious cloak thrown over the protest, Governor Dunmore abruptly dissolved the house.[9] The burgesses gathered in the Apollo Room at Raleigh Tavern and on May 27 issued the historic call for delegates from all the colonies to meet in a Continental Congress.

George Washington was elected one of Virginia's representatives, but at Philadelphia that fall he was appointed to neither of the two most important committees. The Virginians who commanded center stage were Peyton Randolph, elected president of the Continental Congress, and the towering orators Patrick Henry and Richard Henry Lee. Many observers—including British spies—assumed that if the colonists did resort to bloodshed they would turn leadership of an American army over to the fiery Charles Lee (Indians had aptly named him "boiling water"), a former British officer with wide military experience who was then settled in Virginia.[10]

For much of the month-and-a-half-long session Washington chose to remain quietly in the background, rarely speaking. He described his own role in the proceedings as "an attentive observer and witness." After hours he gathered with delegates from other regions for drinks, cards (he won seven pounds), and discussions. Recollections of Washington's military career during the French and Indian War circulated among the delegates; it was particularly remembered that in the aftermath of Braddock's disastrous defeat in the forest, Washington had saved the battered remnant of the British column from annihilation. One representative from Rhode Island, lost in admiration, wrote a bit of doggerel:

> . . . With manly gait
> His faithful steel suspended by his side
> Pass'd W-shi-gt-on along, Virginia's hero.

Word that he was rich (richer than he was in reality) added to his growing luster. John Adams reported that in a speech to the Virginia convention Washington had declared, "I will raise one thousand men, subsist them at my own expense, and march, myself at their head, for the relief of Boston." Though Washington never made such a statement, the story spread among New Englanders, who were of course much taken with the idea.[11]

Upon Washington's return to Mount Vernon, a number of Virginia's county militias elected him as their field officer. It was apparent that if war came, he would be called upon to be the supreme commander in Virginia.[12] An English traveler happened to observe the militia exercises, and thought that the 150 men under Washington's command made "a formidable appearance." Northern Virginia was in tumult, according to the traveler, who found "utmost confusion" in Alexandria, where patriot committees seized and read foreign mail, and were interrogating and intimidating tradesmen to stop the purchase of British goods. Some of those who refused to cooperate "have been tarred and feathered, others had their property burnt and destroyed by the populace."[13]

When news reached Virginia that shots had been fired at Lexington and Concord, Washington believed it was the start of the long-feared British campaign to enslave the Americans. He wrote to his close friend and neighbor George William Fairfax, a loyalist, to explain the position he had chosen:

> Before this Letter can reach you, you must, undoubtedly, have received an Account of the engagement in the Massachusetts Bay. . . . General Gage [the British commander] acknowledges, that the detachment . . . was sent out to destroy private property; or, in other Words, to destroy a Magazine which self-preservation obliged the Inhabitants to establish. . . . Unhappy it is . . . to reflect, that a Brother's Sword has been sheathed in a Brother's breast, and that, the once happy and peaceful plains of America are either to be drenched with Blood or Inhabited by Slaves. Sad alternative! But can a virtuous Man hesitate in his choice?[14]

Washington wrote the letter from Philadelphia, where he was attending the Second Continental Congress, convened to deal with the crisis in Massachusetts. He had set off from Mount Vernon in his carriage with his fellow delegate Richard Henry Lee. As they rolled north they met up with other Virginia delegates, and as the convoy of Virginians approached Philadelphia, five hundred horsemen came out to greet them. Farther on, a band and companies of foot soldiers joined in an enormous parade leading into Philadelphia.[15]

The imposing, six-foot-tall Washington strode into the sessions of the Congress wearing his Virginia militia uniform. He was the only delegate in uniform and it made an impression—perhaps exactly the impression Washington intended to make—during the deliberations to choose the commander in chief for the American forces already in the field in New England. Washington did not explicitly put himself forward as a candidate, but there can be little doubt that, fortunately for the American cause, his patriotism and his ambition lay behind his decision to appear before a deliberative body in martial array. He was not the only candidate. John Hancock of Massachusetts felt certain to be chosen. Most radical leaders endorsed "boiling water" Charles Lee, but his English pedigree made him suspect.

Washington had military experience, and he also possessed an air of gravity. One Connecticut delegate described him as "no harum-scarum, ranting, swearing fellow, but sober, steady, and calm." Washington was elected commander in chief on the first ballot; in his first official act he insisted that he would serve without pay. His expenses would be covered, nothing more. He left immediately for Massachusetts.[16]

In a farewell letter to Martha from Philadelphia he told her he expected to be home at Mount Vernon by autumn. (As it turned out, at Christmas he was still in Massachusetts, so Martha went to him.)[17] By winning a quick campaign, Washington hoped to compel the British government to negotiate a settlement of the colonists' grievances—independence was not yet a goal in the summer of 1775—and avoid the massive bloodshed he had feared and written about the previous year. His determination was absolute. "I can answer for but three things," he wrote to Burwell Bassett, his friend and Martha's brother-in-law, "a firm belief in the justice of our cause, close attention to the prosecution of it, and the strictest integrity." Yet the future remained uncertain. He continued to Bassett, "I am now embarked on a tempestuous ocean, from, whence, perhaps, no friendly harbor is to be found."[18]

Whatever shred of optimism Washington carried north with him vanished when he reached Cambridge in July. He had been told his army would number 20,000 men, but the rosters showed only 14,000 present and ready. He had ordered an inventory of the powder supply and was told there was more than enough; when the barrels were counted again an error was discovered—they had only ninety barrels, just a third of what had been claimed in the first report. The men had no tents; they were short of clothing and tools; no one had any idea how anything could be paid for. Altogether the situation was "exceedingly dangerous," he wrote; and within a few months Washington regretted having accepted command.[19]

Nor was the Virginian heartened by the class of manpower he found in Cambridge. The "embattled farmers" of New England did not particularly impress this Southern planter—"they are an exceeding dirty & nasty people"; and he found an "unaccountable kind of stupidity in the lower class of these people," a stupidity shared, he thought, by many of the Massachusetts officers.[20] One of Washington's aides later deplored "the principles of democracy [which] so universally prevail" and the "levelling spirit" that erased class boundaries.[21] The militia seemed likely to melt away when it felt like it. The commander in chief set about the task of assembling a strong and respectable regular army.

Washington had high standards for the type of soldier he wished to enlist. In 1754, during the skirmishes with the French and Indians along the Ohio River, he had complained because his soldiers—and he was referring to white men—consisted of "loose, Idle persons that are quite destitute of House and Home." The kind of army he wished to put in the field against the British would express the identity of its country. As the historian John Shy writes, "Washington and other . . . American leaders stressed a regular army . . . because they felt a need to be seen as cultivated, honorable, respectable men, not as savages leading other savages in a howling wilderness."[22]

Blacks did not figure in Washington's initial military calculations despite his desperate need for troops. He may have shared a view that was common among upper-class white Americans and Britons—slavery was a condition of dishonor and the presence of slaves would dishonor an army. Contemporary statements are quite explicit on this point. Even before Washington arrived, the Massachusetts Committee of Safety passed a resolution opposing the enlistment of slaves because their service would "be inconsistent with the principles that are to be supported, and reflect dishonor on this Colony." The presence of *blacks* did not present a problem to Massachusetts officials; however, the presence of *slaves* did bother them—the order did not exclude free blacks. A similar objection was also raised by one of Washington's generals, Philip Schuyler of New York, who said the slaves among his troops "disgrace our arms." He explained, "Is it consistent with the Sons of Freedom to trust their all to be defended by slaves?" The war shaped Schuyler's view of blacks; he became a champion of abolition and a founder of the New York Manumission Society in 1785.[23]

The use of slave troops had precedent in the colonies, but so scant that Washington might not have been aware of it. In 1715 South Carolina armed some four hundred slaves to fight alongside six hundred whites against the Yamasee Indians; but the colony did so with great trepidation. One white colonist warned of the grave and obvious danger—"our Slaves when arm'd might become our Masters." A slave uprising in that colony in 1739 proved the danger of allowing blacks access to arms. In the wake of that revolt, as John Shy writes, "Carolinians no longer dared arm Negroes; in fact, they hardly dared leave their plantations in time of emergency. . . . increasingly the South Carolina militia became an agency to control slaves, and less an effective means of defense." During the French and Indian War, Washington used slaves as laborers (their proper place, in his view) but not as soldiers; and at the height of that war Virginia devoted more resources to policing its internal slave population than to patrolling its frontier.[24]

Arming slaves would have profound implications for the psychology of slave and master. It was one thing to hand a favored "trusty" slave a musket so that he could hunt, with permission, on the master's land for the master's table, but it was quite another to hand a slave a musket so that he could go out and kill white men. The preservation of slavery required unremitting psychological degradation. As one Englishman remarked, arming slaves would "instruct them that they are men."[25]

What Washington saw when he arrived at Cambridge must have been shocking to him—blacks carrying guns and awaiting action. The New England army had blacks in its ranks for the simple reason that "virtually everyone went to war," as Shy observes.[26] Blacks were enlisted and accepted in Minute Man units. More blacks responded to Paul Revere's alarm. Blacks had taken part in the engagements at Lexington and Concord on April 19 and at Bunker Hill on June 17. One black man, Peter Salem, so distinguished himself at Bunker Hill that he was presented to Washington after the commander's arrival. An archetypal figure out of American lore, a sharpshooter, Salem had enlisted in a company of Minute Men from the town of Framingham. He saw action in the fighting around Lexington and Concord, where he became familiar with the figure of Major John Pitcairn, the officer of Royal Marines who led the British detachment at Lexington Green. At Bunker Hill, Pitcairn was leading a charge on the American defenses when Salem shot him. Salem's act won him the esteem of his comrades. The Boston historian Samuel Swett, writing in the 1820s, said that "a contribution was made in the army for Salem and he was presented to Washington as having slain Pitcairn." Salem's story is archetypal in other ways. He served throughout the war, he died in poverty, and his fame was slowly and deliberately extinguished. John Trumbull, "the painter of the Revolution," depicted Salem clutching a musket in his renowned historical canvas *The Battle of Bunker's Hill*. The historian William C. Nell, reviewing in 1855 the published engravings based on Trumbull's work that were produced for the popular market, noticed that in the older reproductions Salem "occupies a prominent position," but in the midcentury versions the black hero had disappeared from the scene.[27]*

---

* Trumbull observed the Bunker Hill battle from a distance and painted the scene seven years after the event. He served on Washington's staff as aide-de-camp in Cambridge in the summer of 1775. He knew the Boston topography intimately, having sketched the British defenses for Washington—an act which got him his appointment.

In a lecture in Cambridge in 1864, a local historian, Samuel Abbot Smith, told the story of another black Minute Man. Smith said that when the alarm went out that British regulars had fired on Americans at Lexington, a dozen "exempts"—men exempted from armed service on account of their age—turned out anyway, spontaneously formed a unit, and "chose for their leader David Lamson, a mulatto, who had served in the [French and Indian] war, a man of undoubted bravery and determination." They took up a position behind a wall of earth and stones and, thus concealed, awaited the arrival of the British column. When a British supply column trundled past on the other side of the wall, Lamson called out his order, and his men rose up with muskets leveled. The British tried to escape but the Minute Men fired, killing two of the British and wounding others.[28]

Thus in the first months of the war in Massachusetts, blacks had spontaneously joined the patriot cause; left to itself, the army had integrated spontaneously. Change was occurring on its own without a formal policy imposing or urging it. The natural movement was toward freedom. Washington and other leaders would have to act to stifle this movement.

The patriotic spirit of the black troops can be seen clearly in a postwar pension petition filed by one Jehu Grant, who served in the army for ten months. He said that the "songs of liberty . . . saluted my ear, thrilled through my heart." He described his decision to sign up:

I was then grown to manhood, in the full vigor and strength of life, and heard much about the cruel and arbitrary things done by the British. Their ships lay within a few miles of my master's house, which stood near the shore, and I was confident that my master traded with them, and I suffered much from fear that I should be sent aboard a ship of war. This I disliked. But when I saw liberty poles and the people all engaged for the support of freedom, I could not but like and be pleased with such things (God forgive me if I sinned in so feeling). And living on the borders of Rhode Island, where whole companies of colored people enlisted, it added to my fears and dread of being sold to the British. These considerations induced me to enlist into the American army, where I served faithful about ten months, when my master found and took me home.[29]

Southern slaveholders recognized that the New England army was setting precedents that might later bind them. Hearing that blacks were serving in Massachusetts, Edward Rutledge of South Carolina stood before the Continental Congress in September 1775 to demand that all black men, whether slave or free, be immediately expelled from the armed forces. Other Southerners joined Rutledge in his attempt to thwart integration before it got out of control. A diarist wrote that this demand, though "strongly supported by many of the Southern delegates," failed to carry because it was "powerfully opposed." Here was an early instance in the national debate over race where Southern sectional prejudices tried to override the Northerners' preferences and discount the service record of blacks.[30]

In Cambridge Washington began to lay the groundwork for removing blacks from the army. In a report to the president of the Continental Congress, John Hancock, Washington wrote, "From the Number of Boys, Deserters, & Negroes which have been listed in the Troops of this Province, I entertain some Doubts whether the Number required can be raised here." Though Washington did not seem to think that he could make use of blacks, he thought the British could, so he must have had some inkling that they might make decent soldiers. At his first council of war, held a week after his arrival in Cambridge, the first question he posed to his assembled officers was the enemy's strength. He inquired as to the number of "Troops formerly & lately arrived . . . the Tories who may take Arms, such Sailors as may be spared from the Fleet & the Negroes." He clearly viewed the blacks in Boston as likely enemies.[31]

Washington was putting in place a national policy for blacks in the military. He was establishing precedents. Soon his headquarters issued general orders forbidding the enlistment of "any deserter from the Ministerial army, nor any stroller, negro, or vagabond." This order could have resulted partly from Washington's assumption that any black wandering about was probably a runaway. There was no claim that blacks who had already fought were incompetent, inferior, or in any way unable to discharge the duties of a soldier, nor is there mention in Washington's papers of any complaint from the white soldiers and officers who had served with the blacks at Lexington, Concord, Bunker Hill, or in the camp at Cambridge over the summer. There is no record of a popular outcry against the black presence, no record of fights or disciplinary problems caused by racial integration. The common white New England soldier seems to have accepted blacks. The objections to the black presence came not from the rank and file but from the highest levels of policy makers and politicians. Had there been problems, Washington certainly would have been made aware of them and would have cited them in his correspondence to Congress as grounds for an exclusion policy.[32]

Samuel Swett, the Massachusetts historian, laid the blame on outsiders: "Many northern blacks were excellent soldiers but southern troops would not brook an equality with whites." But Swett was not entirely accurate. Northern generals joined with Washington in limiting the number of blacks in the army. At a council of war in October, Washington and seven other generals considered the question, "Whether it will be adviseable to re-inlist any Negroes in the new Army—or whether there be a Distinction between such as are Slaves & those who are free?" The decision of the officers was "Agreed unanimously to reject all Slaves, & by a great Majority to reject Negroes altogether."[33]

Accordingly, in November 1775 Washington issued a general order excluding all blacks, whether free or slave: "Neither Negroes, Boys unable to bare Arms, nor old men unfit to endure the fatigues of the campaign, are to be inlisted." The language of this order was deliberately vague with respect to old white men and boys. To simplify matters, Washington could have established a hard-and-fast age requirement; but he knew that some teenaged boys were capable of bearing arms while some were not, and that some fifty-year-old men could endure a campaign while others could not. The order seems directed against recruiters who might have been inclined to sign up youths and oldsters in need of food and lodging at the army's expense. Once enlisted, an elderly idler might enjoy the hospitality of the army for months before it was discovered that he could not walk more than a mile. The only blanket exclusion was laid down on the basis of color.[34]

The effect of Washington's orders on the actual practices of his recruiters is not clear. Revolutionary pension records contain the petition of a black man who signed up and served in Washington's army without any apparent problem during the very period when Washington had banned blacks. The soldier, Jacob Francis, was a recently freed man from New Jersey who had settled in Salem, Massachusetts. In his petition for a pension he stated, "About the last of October, I enlisted as a soldier in the United States service for one year." In his account of his time with Washington's army he does not mention being harassed in any way. Indeed, Francis left a firsthand account of his encounter with Major General Israel Putnam of Connecticut, one of the officers involved in the vote to exclude blacks from the army. (It is not known how he voted, because individual votes at the October council of war were not recorded.) Putnam made no disparaging remarks to him. The account is a rare sample of Revolutionary War humor.

I recollect General Putnam more particularly from a circumstance that occurred when the troops were engaged in throwing up a breastwork at Lechmere Point across the river, opposite Boston, between that and Cambridge. The men were at work digging, about five hundred on the fatigue at once. I was at work among them. They were divided into small squads of eight or ten together and a noncommissioned officer to oversee them. General Putnam came riding along in uniform as an officer to look at the work. They had dug up a pretty large stone which lay on the side of the ditch. The general spoke to the corporal who was standing looking at the men at work and said to him, "My lad, throw that stone up on the middle of the breastwork."

The corporal, touching his hat with his hand, said to the general, "Sir, I am a corporal."

"Oh," said the general, "I ask your pardon, sir," and immediately got off his horse and took up the stone and threw it up on the breast-work himself and then mounted his horse and rode on, giving directions, etc.[35]

Francis was not drummed out for being black. His major complaint was that the U.S. government still owed him back pay.

Unbeknownst to Washington, his November 12 general order barring blacks was trumped by the British. On November 7, in Virginia, Governor Dunmore had issued a proclamation inviting slaves to join the king's cause and thereby become free. About eight hundred Virginia slaves quickly rallied to Dunmore, forming the "Ethiopian Regiment." Just as quickly, they were defeated by patriot forces in the Battle of Great Bridge.[36]

Dunmore's proclamation seemed to confirm the darkest of Southern fears. Washington wrote to Richard Henry Lee, a fellow Virginian, "If that Man [Dunmore] is not crushed before spring, he will become the most formidable Enemy America has—his strength will Increase as a Snow ball by Rolling." Washington said that Dunmore was motivated by a "Resentment" that would result in "the total destruction" of Virginia. James Madison had written in 1774 that if war did break out "I am afraid an Insurrection among the slaves may & will be promoted [by the British]." But if slaveholders expected to be murdered in their beds by loyalist slaves, they were wrong. There was no general uprising by the slaves, nor did Dunmore's Ethiopians pose a genuine military threat, because Dunmore had to abandon Virginia. But when the British returned in force to Virginia in 1781, Thomas Jefferson estimated that 30,000 slaves—men, women, and children—fled their masters for freedom with the British.[37]

Washington received personal notification of Dunmore's edict from his cousin Lund Washington, who was managing Mount Vernon for him. On December 3, 1775, Lund wrote, "Our Dunmore has at length Publishd his much dreaded proclamation. . . . What effect it will have upon those sort of people [the slaves and indentured servants] I cannot tell." Lund went on to say that he would have no worry about the slaves escaping, but the white indentured servants on the place might try to escape. One of the servants had told him, "there is not a man of them, but woud leave us, if they believe'd they coud make there Escape. . . . Liberty is sweet." He may have thought that the blacks would hold themselves back from running because of what he called their "Slavish" character. But Lund was wrong. As soon as the opportunity presented itself, a group of Mount Vernon slaves left on a British warship.[38]

Despite Dunmore's gambit Washington remained adamant. He would not recruit slaves. But he did reverse part of his earlier order and gave instructions to allow free blacks to reenlist. His general orders issued December 30, 1775, stated, "As the General is informed, that Numbers of Free Negroes are desirous of inlisting, he gives leave to recruiting Officers, to entertain them, and promises to lay the matter before the Congress, who he doubts not will approve of it."[39]

The next day Washington wrote to John Hancock explaining his reversal. He cited grassroots opinion as grounds for his change of mind: black soldiers had come to headquarters to complain that they were "very much dissatisfied at being discarded." Washington added that if the Continental Army did not take them, the British would. Congress gave Washington the permission he asked for, authorizing the reenlistment of free blacks "who have served faithfully in the army at Cambridge . . . but no others."[40]*

With his order of December 30, for the first time in his life Washington had responded in a fair way to an appeal from free blacks. The consummate man of procedure had "made it a rule" not to recruit blacks, but then he reversed himself because the men were dissatisfied. He was acting contrary to official local practice. In January 1776

---

* This act of Congress had unintended consequences after the Revolution because, once loosed, liberty is hard to contain. A Connecticut judge ruled in 1784 that the state's slaveholders could not reenslave men who had served in the army: "As none but freemen could by the legislation of Congress be enlisted into the Continental Army— the consent of said master to such enlistment in judgment of law amounts to a manumission."[41]

Massachusetts passed a militia act excluding blacks, even freemen, from service; later in the year New Hampshire barred blacks from its army.[42]

If gaining advantage over the British in the recruitment of blacks had been Washington's main reason for the reversal, he would have pushed for accepting slaves, who were far more numerous in New England than free blacks. But there were two insuperable obstacles to admitting slaves: the slaves' status was considered to dishonor the free men fighting in the Revolutionary cause; and their principal status was as property, and Washington the slave master would have never tampered with the property of another master. Yet his order had removed race as the defining element; he had managed to see free blacks as being different from black slaves. Though he told Hancock that he feared free blacks would join the British, that is unlikely to have been his main reason for the reversal, since there were not enough free blacks around to tip the military scale. It seems that their personal appeals had moved him, that the humanity of these free black people made itself apparent to him.

There may have been another factor at work as well. At the moment when Washington was considering the change in policy, he was contacted by a most unlikely person—a black poet who sent him verses extolling "freedom's cause."

A few weeks before Christmas in 1775 Washington received a letter at his headquarters in Cambridge that had been wending its way through the colonial and military postal systems for several weeks.

To His Excellency
George Washington

Sir,
I have taken the freedom to address your Excellency in the enclosed poem, and entreat your acceptance, though I am not insensible of its inaccuracies. Your being appointed by the Grand Continental Congress to be Generalissimo of the armies of North America, together with the fame of your virtues, excite sensations not easy to suppress.

Your generosity, therefore, I presume, will pardon the attempt. Wishing your Excellency all possible success in the great cause you are so generously engaged in. I am,

Your Excellency's most obedient humble servant,
Phillis Wheatley[43]

For George Washington, December 1775 was a month of startling revelations: black men demanding a place in his army; a black woman sending him a poem. Just five months earlier Washington had numbered all of Boston's blacks among his potential enemies; then came this tribute from a black Bostonian:

> *Celestial choir! enthron'd in realms of light,*
> *Columbia's scenes of glorious toils I write.*
> *While freedom's cause her anxious breast alarms,*
> *She flashes dreadful in refulgent arms.*
> *See mother earth her offspring's fate bemoan,*
> *And nations gaze at scenes before unknown!*
> *See the bright beams of heaven's revolving light*
> *Involved in sorrows and veil of night!*
>
> *The goddess comes, she moves divinely fair,*
> *Olive and laurel bind her golden hair:*
> *Wherever shines this native of the skies,*
> *Unnumber'd charms and recent graces rise.*
>
> *Muse! bow propitious while my pen relates*
> *How pour her armies through a thousand gates,*
> *As when Eolus heaven's fair face deforms,*
> *Enwrapp'd in tempest and a night of storms;*
> *Astonish'd ocean feels the wild uproar,*
> *The refluent surges beat the sounding shore;*
> *Or thick as leaves in Autumn's golden reign,*
> *Such, and so many, moves the warrior's train.*

In bright array they seek the work of war,
Where high unfurl'd the ensign waves in air.
Shall I to Washington their praise recite?
Enough thou know'st them in the fields of fight.
Thee, first in peace and honours,—we demand
The grace and glory of thy martial band.
Fam'd for thy valour, for thy virtues more,
Hear every tongue thy guardian aid implore!

One century scarce perform'd its destined round,
When Gallic powers Columbia's fury found;
And so may you, whoever dares disgrace
The land of freedom's heaven-defended race!
Fix'd are the eyes of nations on the scales,
For in their hopes Columbia's arm prevails.
Anon Britannia droops the pensive head,
While round increase the rising hills of dead.
Ah! cruel blindness to Columbia's state!
Lament thy thirst of boundless power too late.

Proceed, great chief, with virtue on thy side,
Thy ev'ry action let the goddess guide.
A crown, a mansion, and a throne that shine,
With gold unfading, WASHINGTON! be thine.[44]

The poem strikes the modern eye and ear as mannered and antique, but its classical allusions and heroic cadences struck home with George Washington. Wheatley wrote of him in the diction of his beloved play *Cato*. The first editor of Washington's papers, Jared Sparks, writing in the 1830s, was familiar with the literary taste of Washington's time, and he was impressed by the quality of the poetry: "The classical allusions are numerous, and imply a wide compass of reading, a correct judgment, good taste, and a tenacious memory."[45]

Writing with the fullest sympathy for Washington and with a deep familiarity with his frame of mind, Sparks suggested that Wheatley's works might have jolted Washington into a deeper understanding of the humanity of the black people: "it cannot be doubted, that they exhibit the most favorable evidence on record, of the capacity of the African . . . intellect for improvement."

Today we can sense only the tiniest aftershock of the tremor this poem would have set off in the mind of a slaveholder. Washington was highly impressed and moved by it. To an aide, Joseph Reed, he wrote, "With a view of doing justice to her great poetical Genius, I had a great Mind to publish the Poem, but not knowing whether it might not be considered rather as a mark of my own vanity than as a Compliment to her I laid it aside."[46]

Poets do not write tributes to world leaders today, but in Wheatley's time it was a standard literary convention. David Humphreys, a Yale-educated Connecticut poet and officer in the Continental Army, composed a similar tribute to the chief, which was circulated among high-ranking officers. When the poem made its way finally to Washington's desk he hired Humphreys as an aide; the two became close friends, and after the war Humphreys wrote the first biography of Washington.

After receiving Wheatley's poem, Washington did the unthinkable. He invited the black poet to his headquarters and temporary home in Cambridge. He wanted to meet this extraordinary woman whose talent he so admired. At that time Phillis Wheatley was the most famous black person in America; indeed she was the *only* famous black person in America. She was the first black, the first slave, and only the third American woman to have a book of poems published. Her second published poem, an elegy on the death of a noted preacher, had brought her fame in the Northeast and abroad; it was published as a broadside in Boston, Newport, New York, and Philadelphia, and was included in an anthology published in Great Britain. After a collection of her work was published in London, she sailed to Great Britain in an eighteenth-century version of an author's book tour. Benjamin Franklin paid a call on her in London.

Now General Washington himself invited her to his quarters. (It is known today as the Longfellow House, because it was eventually home to the acclaimed nineteenth-century poet.) What must the frail asthmatic young woman have thought as she ascended the stairs of the stately Georgian mansion in Cambridge, a mansion built on the profits from trade in rum and molasses—and slaves—in the West Indies? Its Tory owner had fled, as had his neighbors, so that the houses along this stretch of Brattle Street were known as Tory Row. The aristocrat from Virginia—surrounded by his well-born aides-de-camp, his wife, Martha (who had arrived from the South in her coach manned by slaves in scarlet and white livery), and five house slaves—felt at home amid the spacious house with its carved woodwork and windows that commanded a view of the Charles River.

What must he have thought as he greeted Phillis Wheatley, the African whose verses extolling freedom had moved him so profoundly? Details of the encounter are not known. Washington's records indicate only that he invited Wheatley, not that she actually visited. There are brief accounts of her visit in two books by Benson Lossing, who may have gotten his information from Martha's grandson. Lossing stated that Wheatley spent half an hour with the Washingtons and the general's officers, from all of whom "she received marked attention." Driven by curiosity, Washington would certainly have asked about her past.

Wheatley's path to literary fame was a most extraordinary one. In 1761 Susanna Wheatley, the wife of a wealthy Boston tailor and merchant, went down to the docks to shop for a household slave among the newly arrived captives from Africa. The Wheatleys already owned several household slaves, but these servants were getting on in years, and the foresighted Susanna went looking for a young one she could properly train and prepare to take on household duties for many years to come. The ship *Phillis* had just docked. Among the human cargo being displayed on the wharf she saw several "robust, healthy females," but her eye was drawn to a wretched, "poor, naked child" covered only by a piece of filthy carpet. Susanna judged her to be but six or seven years old because the child still had her baby teeth. Deeply touched by this tiny bundle of misery, Wheatley bought her, took the child home, and nursed her back to health. The family named her Phillis after the ship that had brought her from Africa.

As a member of the Wheatley family wrote in a later memoir, "She soon gave indications of uncommon intelligence, and was frequently seen endeavoring to make letters upon the wall with a piece of chalk or charcoal."[47] Susanna's teenage daughter Mary took it upon herself to teach Phillis to read and write. The child proved such a brilliant pupil that she "astonished" Mary. Soon she was learning Latin. By age nine she was acting occasionally as secretary to Mary's brother, Nathaniel, who dictated letters to her. The family realized that a person of such intelligence, though a slave, should not be condemned to a life of menial household chores. The other Wheatley slaves lived in the carriage house; young Phillis lived in the white family's own dwelling.

Wheatley began writing poetry just four years after she arrived in Boston, and gained wide attention in the colonies in 1770, when she was about seventeen, for her "Elegiac Poem" marking the death of the evangelist George Whitefield. Three years later a collection of her poems was published in London, *Poems on Various Subjects, Religious and Moral,* which went through two other British editions and at least seven American editions. But before publication could take place, Wheatley had to undergo questioning by a committee of Boston's loftiest political figures to prove that it was she, and not someone else, who had actually written the works that had been appearing under her name in the newspapers.[48]

Her publisher commissioned a portrait of the author for the collection. It shows a slender, attractive young woman seated at a writing table. Quill pen in hand, poised over a sheet of paper, Wheatley appears lost in thought, but her erect posture and the force of her creative gaze convey strength and certainty of purpose. The engraving for the book was based on an original sketch done by a black artist from Boston, who captured the ambiguous stature of a poet, on the cusp of fame, who was also "Negro Servant to Mr. John Wheatley," as the portrait's caption dutifully notes. Wheatley had to play a careful game, well aware that she occupied a truly unique position. She had been passing through impenetrable social barriers. When she visited the home of a white family, the servants noted "it was the first time they ever carried tea to a colored woman." For a woman raised as a slave, the experience of breaking barriers was disconcerting and painful. A member of the white Wheatley family wrote, "Whenever she was invited to the houses of individuals of wealth and distinction, (which frequently happened,) she always declined the seat offered her at their board, and, requesting that a side-table might be laid for her, dined modestly apart from the rest of the company."[49]

Her diffidence emerges in a poem she wrote when she was fourteen. Entitled "On Being Brought from Africa to America," the work has become notorious as an apology for slavery from the pen of a slave. One scholar called it "the most reviled poem in African American literature" because of the sentiments of its opening line, though the balance of the poem appeals for racial understanding:

> *Twas mercy brought me from my Pagan land,*
> *Taught my benighted soul to understand*
> *That there's a God, that there's a Saviour too:*
> *Once I redemption neither sought nor knew.*
> *Some view our sable race with scornful eye,*
> *"Their colour is a diabolic die,"*
> *Remember, Christians, Negros, black as Cain,*
> *May be refin'd, and join th' angelic train.*[50]

Yet beneath the diffidence and well-polished modesty lay anger, which emerged in a signed letter of February 1774 published in two Boston newspapers: "In every human Breast, God has implanted a Principle, which we call Love of Freedom; it is impatient of Oppression, and pants for Deliverance." Referring to slaveholders as "our Modern Egyptians. . . . those whose Avarice impels them to countenance and help forward the Calamities of their Fellow Creatures," Wheatley implied that some divine retribution might strike them: "God grant Deliverance in his own way and Time. . . . This I desire not for their Hurt, but to convince them of the strange Absurdity of their Conduct whose Words and Actions are so diametrically opposite." She concluded by saying, "it does not require the Penetration of a Philosopher" to choose between "oppressive Power" and "the Cry for Liberty."[51]

The author of such a passionate, eloquent, and angry diatribe against the slaveholders could not have written an effusive tribute to a slaveholding general without a motive deeper than flattery. Given that the author was black—what an oddity to him!—Washington would have been inclined to see the poem as a specifically black statement. One modern critic speculated that the "we" in "we demand / The grace and glory of thy martial band" referred to black Americans. More striking is the emphasis in Wheatley's poem on the epic size of the American army—as thick as golden autumn leaves, so vast that it pours through a thousand gates. With her pointed reference to America as the land of freedom, she may have been making a disguised appeal for Washington to admit her fellow blacks into his army.[52]

There is no doubt that Washington was deeply impressed by what he read, for he tossed aside the conventions of social contact between a master and a black and wrote Wheatley a letter remarkable for its graciousness, given that he had never done such a thing before. He addressed the letter to "Miss Phillis." Nothing could have induced him to address a black woman by her last name—a convention reserved for whites—but at least he added a courteous title.

Cambridge, February 28, 1776.

Miss Phillis:
Your favour of the 26th of October did not reach my hands 'till the middle of December. Time enough, you will say, to have given an answer ere this. Granted. But a variety of important occurrences, continually interposing to distract the mind and withdraw the attention, I hope will apologize for the delay, and plead my excuse for the seeming, but not real, neglect.

I thank you most sincerely for your polite notice of me, in the elegant Lines you enclosed; and however undeserving I may be of such encomium and panegyrick, the style and manner exhibit a striking proof of your great poetical Talents. In honour of which, and as a tribute justly due to you, I would have published the Poem, had I not been apprehensive, that, while I only meant to give the World this new instance of your genius, I might have incurred the imputation of Vanity. This and nothing else, determined me not to give it place in the public Prints.

If you should ever come to Cambridge, or near Head Quarters, I shall be happy to see a person so favoured by the Muses, and to whom Nature has been so liberal and beneficent in her dispensations. I am, with great Respect, Your obedt humble servant,

G. Washington[53]

We should compare Washington's openness with the dripping contempt that another slave master directed at Phillis Wheatley. Thomas Jefferson was outraged at the enthusiastic acclaim for the Boston poet, and it particularly bothered him that sophisticated foreign readers found much to admire. Voltaire referred to her "very good English verse"; and the naval hero John Paul Jones sent some of his own poetical writings to "the celebrated Phillis the African favorite of the Nine [Muses] and Apollo."[54] Jefferson felt he had to snuff the groundswell of esteem:

Misery is often the parent of the most affecting touches in poetry. Among the blacks is misery enough, God knows, but not poetry. Love is the peculiar *oestrum* [inspiration] of the poet. Their love is ardent, but it kindles the senses only, not the imagination. Religion, indeed, has produced a Phyllis Whately; but it could not produce a poet. The compositions published under her name are below the dignity of criticism.[55]

His low regard for Wheatley sprang from a deeper contempt. He explicitly linked Wheatley's supposed artistic shortcomings to her race: "I advance it, therefore, as a suspicion only, that the blacks, whether originally a distinct race, or made distinct by time and circumstances, are inferior to the whites in the endowments both of body and mind."

If Washington had shared Jefferson's racial views, he would never have met Wheatley and he would never have caused her poem to be published. For Washington to entertain a black person at his headquarters shows how far he had come in a very short time. Such a meeting would have been unthinkable in Virginia; he would have opened himself to the scorn of his peers.

Wheatley's most powerful message was her mere presence. At the time when the commander was mulling the status of black men in "freedom's land," a free black woman gained an audience, and presented herself as an emblem of racial conciliation. Washington's meeting with Wheatley and his decision to admit blacks to his army reveal his dawning awareness of something. The historian Walter Mazyck expresses it succinctly: "One may pity a helpless individual or group but never respect such persons. However, when they first show signs of independent thought and action, at that moment respect is born."[56] It is hard to credit "the North" for the change in Washington, for Northerners held slaves and some of them resisted enlisting blacks as stoutly as any Southerner. Boston's reigning patriot, John Hancock, had household slaves. Rather, one must credit Northern blacks for the general's newfound tendency, as tentative as it was, to put aside the customs of mastery and follow humane instincts. Their demeanor, spirit, and patriotism apparently touched him.

Washington did arrange to have the poem published, through his aide Joseph Reed, in *Pennsylvania Magazine* in April 1776. It also circulated on Washington's home ground, as published in Williamsburg's *Virginia Gazette*. Thus in public print the name of the chief was linked with that of "the famous Phillis Wheatley, the African Poetess."[57]

Washington drove the British from Boston in March 1776. His victory was a bloodless one. By placing artillery in a commanding position atop Dorchester Heights, a brilliant tactical coup, he made the British position untenable and compelled their evacuation. Ordered by the

The earliest known portrait of George Washington, painted from life by Charles Willson Peale in 1772 when Washington was forty. (Courtesy of the Washington/Custis/Lee Collection, Washington and Lee University, Lexington, Virginia)

(opposite page, top) An engraving of the Washington family—George Washington Parke Custis, George, Eleanor Parke Custis, and Martha—based on a painting by Edward Savage done in stages between 1789 and 1796. The slave wearing Washington livery may be William Lee, though the identification is uncertain: Lee's hair was said to have turned white before the time of this portrait. (Courtesy of the Mount Vernon Ladies' Association)

Martha Washington (top), 1776, and her children Martha (Patsy) Parke Custis (left) and John (Jacky) Parke Custis (right), c. 1771, in miniature watercolors on ivory by Charles Willson Peale. (Courtesy of the Mount Vernon Ladies' Association)

An 1804 engraving of the eastern façade of Mount Vernon, overlooking the Potomac, with the piazza where Washington read his newspapers every afternoon. (Courtesy of the Mount Vernon Ladies' Association)

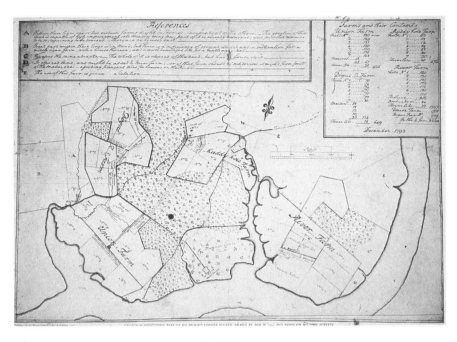

(above) Washington's survey of the five farms that made up the Mount Vernon plantation, drawn in 1793. (Courtesy of the Henry E. Huntington Library, San Marino, California)

(left) Mount Vernon's Greenhouse, designed by Washington (as reconstructed in the late twentieth century); the wings were built to house slaves. (Courtesy of the Mount Vernon Ladies' Association)

(opposite page, bottom) Virginia slaves at work under the supervision of an overseer, in a 1798 watercolor by Benjamin Henry Latrobe.
(Courtesy of the Maryland Historical Society, Baltimore)

Interior of the Greenhouse barracks, a speculative 1960s reconstruction that may be far cozier than the original. (Photograph by Robert C. Lautman, courtesy of the Mount Vernon Ladies' Association)

WILLIAMSBURG: Printed by WILLIAM RIND, at the NEW PRINTING-OFFICE, on the Main Street. All Persons may be supplied with this GAZETTE at 12/6 per Year. ADVERTISEMENTS of a moderate Length are inserted for 3/. the First Week, and 2/. each Time after: And long ones in Proportion.

Hand Set and Printed at the Printing and Post Office in Williamsburg, Virginia, 1986.

Washington's advertisement in a Maryland Gazette *of 1761 seeking the return of four runaway slaves.* (Courtesy of the George Washington Papers)

Virginia Gazette *advertisement for "A Scheme of a Lottery," November 1769, in which Washington and others raffled off a debtor's slaves in Williamsburg.* (Courtesy of the Colonial Williamsburg Foundation)

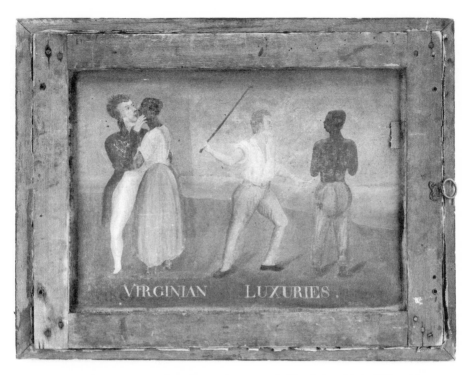

One master beats a man as another embraces a slave woman in this painting with the chilling caption *"Virginian Luxuries," by an unknown artist.* (Courtesy of Abby Aldrich Rockefeller Folk Art Museum, Colonial Williamsburg Foundation, Williamsburg, Virginia)

Washington holds the Declaration of Independence while a slave holds the general's horse in a 1780 engraving by Noël Le Mire. (Courtesy of the Mount Vernon Ladies' Association)

Publifhed according to Act of Parliament, Septr 1. 1773 by Arch^d Bell,
Bookfeller N° 8 near the Saracens Head Aldgate.

The poet Phillis Wheatley, whose literary tribute to Washington during the Revolution deeply impressed the general, as she appeared in the frontispiece of her 1773 collection, Poems on Various Subjects, Religious and Moral. (Courtesy of the Library of Congress)

(below) With a well-aimed pistol shot, the young slave William Ball saves the life of Washington's cousin and helps secure an American victory in the Battle of Cowpens, an episode celebrated in this 1845 painting by William Ranney, which hangs in the South Carolina State House. (Photograph by Sam Holland)

A watercolor of American soldiers at Yorktown done by a French officer, Jean-Baptiste-Antoine DeVerger, includes a black infantryman of the First Rhode Island Regiment. This is the only known contemporary rendering of a black soldier in the Continental Army. (Courtesy of Anne S. K. Brown Military Collection, Brown University Library)

Portrait of a black Revolutionary War sailor by an unknown artist. (Collection of Alexander A. McBurney, M.D.)

Washington's aide-de-camp John Laurens, author of a plan to free slaves who fought for the American cause, in a miniature watercolor on ivory by Charles Willson Peale, 1780. (Courtesy of the Gibbes Museum of Art/Carolina Art Association, on loan from a private collection)

The spy James Armistead, who provided critical intelligence about British troop movements to Lafayette during the Yorktown campaign but was nevertheless retained in slavery after the Revolution. (Courtesy of the Valentine Richmond History Center)

William Costin, the Washingtons' mixed-race grandson/nephew by Jacky Custis and Martha's half sister Ann Dandridge, in a portrait by Charles Fenderich made when Costin was employed as a porter by the Bank of Washington. (Courtesy of the Library of Congress)

West Ford, said by some to be the son of George Washington and a slave named Venus, in an undated portrait passed down in Washington's family and donated to Mount Vernon in 1985. (Courtesy of the Mount Vernon Ladies' Association)

Census of the Mount Vernon slaves compiled by Washington in 1799 as he prepared his will. The "dower" slaves belonged to the Custis estate. (Courtesy of the Mount Vernon Ladies' Association)

Washington's nephew Bushrod Washington, who inherited Mount Vernon, in a 1783 portrait by Henry Benbridge. (Courtesy of the Mount Vernon Ladies' Association)

An ambrotype from the 1850s or 1860s showing a former Mount Vernon slave named Tom, who escaped from the Peter family (heirs of the Washingtons) about the time of the Civil War. (Courtesy of the Mount Vernon Ladies' Association)

A portrait attributed to Gilbert Stuart that may depict Washington's esteemed chef Hercules, who fled the presidential household in Philadelphia in 1797. (Courtesy of Museo Thyssen-Bornemisza, Madrid)

"—but I did not want to go, and
I jumped out of the window."

Designed and Published by J. Torrey, Jun. Pa.

Washington grew to detest the selling of slaves because of the anguish it caused. This nineteenth-century engraving depicts a woman who jumped from a window after being sold. (Courtesy of the Library of Congress)

APOTHEOSIS OF WASHINGTON

The popular engraving Apotheosis of Washington *symbolized the nation's reverence for Washington and the profound grief at his sudden death in 1799.* (Courtesy of the Mount Vernon Ladies' Association)

Continental Congress to protect New York from British invasion, he proceeded south with his army, which was integrated then and would remain so throughout the war.

The commander needed his black troops because white enlistment was precarious. As one historian has observed, "The popular enthusiasm of 1775 began to give out rapidly in 1776 and became hardly visible by 1777." To alleviate a critical shortage of sailors in September 1778, Benedict Arnold (then still loyal to the American cause) proposed to make an offer of freedom to slaves who were already at work as merchant seamen on American vessels. He outlined a plan "to engage in the marine service of the united states about 5 or 6 hundred black and Mulatto Slaves who are employed as mariners in coasting vessels, by giving to them the pay and privileges of American Seamen, and assuring them of their freedom after the war, or three years Service." But such proposals had to run the political gauntlet. A New Jersey official advanced a plan in August 1776 for a black unit to serve as a home guard, declaring that "neither the Hue of their Complexion nor the Blood of Africk have any Connection with Cowardice." But John Adams, then a representative of Massachusetts in the Continental Congress, protested that some Southerners would not stand for it: "Your Negro Battalion will never do. S[outh] Carolina would run out of their Wits at the least Hint of such a Measure." Adams was always concerned over the potential Southern response to the use of black troops or emancipation proposals. He was relieved when the Massachusetts legislature tabled a proposal in 1777 to abolish slavery in the state. "The Bill for freeing the Negroes, I hope will sleep for a Time," he wrote. "We have causes enough of Jealousy, Discord and Division, and this Bill will certainly add to the Number."[58]

Some objections to black troops came from within the army. When Washington's army arrived in New York in the summer of 1776, a Pennsylvania officer noted that Colonel John Glover's regiment from Marblehead, Massachusetts, included "a number of negroes," and "to persons unaccustomed to such associations," the presence of blacks and whites together "had a disagreeable, degrading effect."[59] This was the opinion of an outsider who judged by appearances and by his own prejudices. If there was something disagreeable about blacks and whites serving together in the Marblehead regiment, it was not apparent in their performance in New York.

Glover's men were sailors. He had raised his unit from among the hard-bitten seamen of the North Shore of Massachusetts. There were a thousand of them. Ordered south in the wake of the main army, the regiment reached New York on August 28 in the midst of an appalling military disaster. A British fleet of four hundred warships and transports disembarked 32,000 troops, against which Washington could offer 20,000 Continentals, many of them young and untried in battle. In his first experience of combat commanding large numbers of men, he committed the error of dividing his forces between Manhattan and Brooklyn; he also failed to gather intelligence and to send out mounted patrols that would have warned him of British movements. The British outflanked him in Brooklyn: in a single day of fighting they inflicted more than a thousand casualties and drove the Americans into defensive lines near Brooklyn Heights. On the night of August 27, 1776, the Continental Army, and the American cause, appeared doomed to extinction. Only a heavy rainstorm prevented the British from immediately moving in to annihilate the rebels—and annihilation it would have been, for the British were already killing American prisoners. A British historian wrote, "Nine thousand disheartened soldiers, the last hope of their country, were penned up, with the sea behind them and a triumphant enemy in front, shelterless and famished on a square mile of open ground swept by a fierce and cold northeasterly gale."[60]

After two days of holding this position under a driving rain, awaiting the inevitable attack, Washington was persuaded that a withdrawal across the East River was the army's only hope. Glover's men had arrived on the night of August 28 and had gone immediately into the defensive lines; now they were called out to save Washington's army. The regiment, with its "number of negroes," performed a miracle on the night of August 30, evacuating the entire army to Manhattan. The evacuation was covered, but also made more hazardous, by a dense fog. The historian David McCullough writes: "How it was all managed is almost beyond imagination. Every conceivable kind of small craft was employed, manned by Massachusetts men—soldiers from the ranks but sailors and fishermen by trade—from Marblehead and Salem. . . . It can be said that the fate of the American army was in their hands."[61]

Glover's regiment carried out this "Dunkirk of the American Revolution," as McCullough calls it, without losing a single man. Among the last to leave was the commander in chief. An eyewitness wrote, "I think I saw General Washington on the ferry stairs when I stepped into one of the last boats." Through that long night Washington had witnessed personally the skill and courage of the black sailors of Massachusetts, who rescued his army.[62]

Glover's sailors, white and black, saved the American cause another time. It was they who ferried Washington and his army across the Delaware River to make the surprise attack on the Hessian barracks at Trenton on Christmas night, 1776. The famous patriotic painting by Emmanuel Leutze, *Washington Crossing the Delaware*, depicts Washington with a black soldier at his side—his name was Prince Whipple, and he was the slave of a New Hampshire officer.

It would be gratifying to be able to relate a story of Washington's life being saved in battle by a slave, but such a thing never happened as far as anyone knows. We shall have to settle for the true story of Washington's cousin, Lieutenant Colonel William Washington, commanding cavalry at the Battle of Cowpens in 1781. Outnumbered, surrounded by British dragoons, Washington was about to be hacked to pieces when a slave boy, a waiter, leaped on a horse with pistol in hand, took aim, and shot the dragoon nearest his commander, saving the life of William Washington. Like the crossing of the Delaware, this exploit is memorialized in a painting. And like the crossings of the East River and the Delaware, this battle was a crucial turning point of the war. By saving William Washington's life, that slave ensured the success of the colonel's cavalry charge against Banastre Tarleton's dragoons. The American victory at Cowpens, bloody, bitterly fought, and won against great odds, blunted the British campaign to consolidate its conquest of the South.[63]

There were blacks in Washington's army at Valley Forge during the winter of 1777–78, leaving their bloody footprints in the snow. Indeed, Valley Forge deserves a place in the history of emancipation, for it was here that Washington made a crucial decision to integrate his army further. In this, the nadir of the Revolution, as white patriotism waned, Washington looked to black men to fill the gap. In the camp at Valley Forge on January 2, 1778, Brigadier General James Mitchell Varnum of Rhode Island sent Washington a note asking permission to raise black troops from his home state: "It is imagined that a Batalion of Negroes can be easily raised there. Should that Measure be adopted, or recruits obtained on any other Principle, the Service will be advanced." Washington gave his immediate approval. He authorized the dispatch of two officers to Rhode Island to carry out the recruitment and sent a letter to the Rhode Island governor requesting "that you will give the Officers employed in this business all the assistance in your power."[64]

In the following month the Rhode Island General Assembly passed an act stating that "history affords us frequent Precedents of the *wisest*, the *freest*, and *bravest* nations having liberated their Slaves, and inlisted them as Soldiers to fight in Defence of their Country." The act granted permission to "every able-bodied Negro, Mulatto or Indian man slave" to enlist and become free—"upon his passing muster, he is absolutely made free, and entitled to all the wages, bounties, and encouragements given by Congress to any soldier enlisting." About 250 men thereupon joined the First Rhode Island Regiment. The regiment fought a brave rear-guard action in the Battle of Rhode Island the following August, three times repulsing attacks from Hessian units, the mercenaries hired from Germany by King George III. Nearly thirty thousand Germans served in Britain's royal forces in America.[65]

Today, espousing the moral and political values of the twenty-first century, we can look back and see the cruel irony of slavery being preserved despite the brave service of many black Americans in the Revolutionary War. Ironies of this sort multiply in any study of slavery, and we cannot fully understand the eighteenth-century realities by assessing George Washington according to our lights. To assess his actions, and to approach a judgment of them, require us to look carefully at the realities of Washington's own time.

Many people today believe that an emancipation of the slaves at the time of the Revolution was impossible because the decision makers then, the elite of white society and politics, firmly held the idea that blacks were an inferior species of humanity. This modern view arises from the writings of Thomas Jefferson, whose thoughts on the subject of black inferiority have been taken to reflect the general thinking of his time. In 1781 and 1782 Jefferson wrote a long survey of Virginia's government, economy, geography, and society at the request of a French diplomat in Philadelphia. He intended it for private circulation among France's *philosophes*; but the appearance of a pirated edition in France led Jefferson to have it published in Paris in 1785 as *Notes on the State of Virginia*.[66]

In *Notes* Jefferson railed against slavery as "a hideous evil" and predicted that it might bring a calamity on the United States, but he also laid out his racial theories. The Jefferson scholar John Chester Miller writes that Jefferson tentatively advanced the hypothesis that blacks "were superior to whites in music and equal to them in courage, memory, adventurousness and the moral sense but inferior to Caucasians in reasoning powers, forethought, poetry and imagination." In a letter of 1807 Jefferson broadened his views with a statement that blacks were "as inferior to the rest of mankind as the mule is to the horse, and as made to carry burthens."

Perhaps Jefferson's most damaging statements were made on the subject of sex. He wrote in *Notes* that black men lusted for sexual relations with white women because they were more attractive than black women, just as orangutans in the jungle lust for "the black women over those of his own species." Miller speculates that Jefferson's statement was actually based on a theory that "in pursuing white women blacks were trying to raise themselves in the scale of creation." The implication that blacks were close kin to the orangutan, Miller writes, "was unmistakable and devastating." He continues, "Jefferson helped to inaugurate the historical tendency in America to invest racial prejudice with the gloss of pseudoscientific verification it acquired in the nineteenth century." Jefferson's belief in his own racial theorizing must be questioned now that DNA testing has shown that he kept his own kin (either his children or his brother's, depending on one's interpretation) in slavery at Monticello; he lived in a condition of deep denial. Writing before the DNA discovery, Miller sees self-rationalization in Jefferson's racial theories: "it is obvious that the idea of the innate racial inferiority of blacks afforded Jefferson some alleviation to the harrowing sense of guilt which beset him."[67]

Whatever his deeper motivations might have been, Jefferson promulgated the notion that blacks were a lower species. If that belief had been widely held in his time, then it would be a rather simple matter to explain the perpetuation of slavery by the American revolutionaries: they did not know any better. These theories of Jefferson's about race have been remembered and endlessly cited, but Washington's record has not. Jefferson's ideas grew on the plantation; Washington's policies were tested in the camps and on the battlefield. Washington's writings as a military commander show no evidence that he believed blacks to be an inferior species. At the start of the war this Southern plantation master wanted no blacks in his army, but he changed. Under his leadership, the Continental Army became integrated. The war was a powerful solvent; it eroded even the adamant foundations of slavery. By their valor and by their ubiquity in arms, the black soldiers forced themselves into the consciousness of their officers in an entirely new way. Men of high station, bred to believe in their own superiority, began to realize that the ideas they had about the capabilities of slaves were based not on facts but on prejudice, a prejudice advanced by whites who had an economic interest in preserving slavery. In Congress and in the camps, there was talk that the time had come to give slaves freedom if they would serve. The movement toward emancipation became so powerful that the leaders of that time, including influential officers in Washington's headquarters, could see the outlines of a new order taking shape. One declared plainly that the Continental Army was creating "a foundation for the Abolition of Slavery in America."[68]

The success of the Rhode Island Regiment had a far-reaching effect. When General Washington dictated his letter to the Rhode Island governor endorsing Varnum's plans to recruit blacks, the staff officer who took the dictation was Colonel John Laurens, a twenty-three-year-old South Carolinian. The members of the general's immediate staff—"my military family," as Washington referred to them—were hand-picked from the country's finest families, and young Laurens was no exception. The artist Charles Willson Peale captured the twenty-six-year-old John Laurens in a miniature watercolor painted on ivory. Though clad in his army uniform, Laurens's half smile softens the image. He has a rather full face, a prominent nose and dark eyebrows; his eyes engage the viewer in a gentle yet forceful stare.

The scion of a very wealthy family, Laurens also boasted a superb political pedigree. His father, Henry, was president of the Continental Congress from November 1777 to December 1778, and an ardent admirer of George Washington. At one of the dark moments of the war, Henry Laurens said of the general that "his virtues are the only present props of our Cause."[69] Later, the elder Laurens was one of the American representatives at the Treaty of Paris negotiations, along with Benjamin Franklin, John Jay, and John Adams. In 1782 John Singleton Copley painted him as president of the Continental Congress. With his ruffled cuffs, velvet knee breeches and waistcoat, silver-buckled shoes, and curled powdered wig, he looks as formal and stuffy as the heavy drapes behind him. He sits uncomfortably in his straight-backed chair, taking no pleasure in it. One foot is awkwardly placed atop an ottoman, an arm tensely planted on a table covered with official documents. He appears to be all business—dour, humorless, thin-lipped, and a bit jowly, with a rather full nose—a man clearly accustomed to money and power.

The Laurens men, father and son, came from the highest tier of the country's financial elite. At the outbreak of the Revolution, Henry was one of the wealthiest individuals in America. His son had been educated in England and Geneva. They owned plantations in both South Carolina and Georgia, but the real source of their immense wealth was slave trading. As a young man Henry Laurens, the son of a saddler, had joined a Charleston trading company and built it into the biggest slave-trading operation in the North American colonies. In his career he imported between 7,000 and 8,000 Africans and traded many thousands more on the domestic market in South Carolina.[70]

When Washington set in motion the Rhode Island plan, which led to the emancipation of several hundred blacks, John Laurens immediately contacted his father, and the two of them began a scheme to respond to the success of the Rhode Island arrangement. Given the origin of their wealth, one might expect that the Laurenses would have conspired to undermine it before it spread to other states. In fact, the slave trader and his son were laying out a plan for emancipation.

The young Laurens stood ready to make the personal sacrifice that was necessary. He asked his father to turn over to him some able-bodied slaves "instead of leaving me a fortune." He was ready to give up all the slaves that formed the foundation of his future wealth, but that issue did not concern John Laurens at the moment. The moment had come to take a radical step in the Revolutionary War: "I am tired of the Languor with which so sacred a War as this, is carried on."[71]

John Laurens saw "a twofold good" in his plan. In the first place, he hoped his slaves would be augmented by others, enough to form a substantial, formidable new fighting force: "A well chosen body of 5,000 black men, properly officer'd to act as light troops . . . might give us decisive success in the next campaign." In the second place, Laurens believed that military service to the United States could be an intermediate and temporary status, a step on the road to full freedom. Enlistment "would advance those who are unjustly deprived of the Rights of Mankind to a State which would be a proper Gradation between abject Slavery and perfect Liberty." The men would remain slaves while they served, and would receive their freedom at the conclusion of the war. As a student in Europe, Laurens had read the works of John Locke, whose philosophy of innate human liberty underpinned the thinking of many American revolutionaries. He believed that blacks had the same inherent qualities and rights as free whites; their enslavement was unnatural. Service in war would reveal their natural capacities, which had been obscured but not erased by enslavement: "I am tempted to believe that this trampled people have so much human left in them, as to be capable of aspiring to the rights of men by noble exertions."[72]

Laurens's plan grew from a disillusionment with slavery that had been simmering in him for two years. In April 1776, a year after the outbreak of the fighting, Laurens articulated the paradox that lay under the Revolution: "I think we Americans . . . cannot contend with *a good Grace*, for Liberty, until we shall have enfranchised our Slaves." Americans could not reconcile "our spirited Assertions of the Rights of Mankind [with] the galling abject Slavery of our negroes." In August, his father replied, "I abhor Slavery . . . in former days there was no combatting the prejudices of Men supported by Interest, the day I hope is approaching when from principles of gratitude as well [as] justice every Man will strive to be foremost in shewing his readiness to comply with the Golden Rule." Weighing against their efforts were "great powers . . . the Laws & Customs of my Country," and "avarice." Thus, despite his abhorrence of slavery, he realized that with any movement toward abolition it was "necessary to proceed with caution." He was determined to find some mechanism to free his slaves, and he expected that his son would concur, though it would deprive him of a large part of his inheritance. John wrote back that he agreed completely, but that an emancipation would have to take place by "shades and degrees."[73]

The winter at Valley Forge made young Laurens realize that the time had come for the process of "shades and degrees" to begin. Desperate for soldiers, Washington had approved the Rhode Island plan, and that was going to lead to the emancipation of Northern slaves. Would Washington lend his support to a plan that would involve Southern slaves? He did. John reported to his father that General Washington believed that "blacks in the southern parts of the continent offer a resource to us that should not be neglected." Washington immediately approved Laurens's plan, stating only that he was sorry for the owner who would lose property.[74]

Then, just as the plan seemed to be gaining momentum, Henry Laurens began to have doubts that slaves would fight as long as they remained slaves. He proposed that the men should be freed immediately and unconditionally, and *then* given the choice, as free men, to serve or not to serve: "set them at full liberty—& then address them in the language of a recruiting officer [as you would] to any other free men." In that circumstance, however, Henry thought that the majority of the blacks, like many of the whites, would choose to stay home with their families rather than risk death in battle. Then he raised a further objection. Having sounded out his fellow delegates to the Continental Congress about the idea, he concluded gloomily, in a letter to John in February 1778, that "I will undertake to say there is not a Man in America of your opinion." He added that if his son dared to make his proposal public, "you would not have heard the last jeer till the end of your life." The idealist son could not move the father, a practical politician. Despite Henry Laurens's misgivings about slavery, he was not yet prepared to see his son exposed to public ridicule. John's original plan had the virtue of simplicity, a simplicity born of intense idealism. His father concluded, after several weeks of exchanging letters with his son, that such a landmark undertaking could not be launched by one individual or even a few, but could only proceed after "mature deliberation by the Collective Wisdom of States." Frustrated at his father's resistance, John Laurens shelved his plan in March 1778.[75]

Just a year later the situation had changed completely. In December 1778 a British fleet landed an amphibious force on the Georgia coast and quickly captured Savannah, reclaiming Georgia by this one stroke. Southern loyalists flocked to the king's cause, and the produce of Georgia's farms went to the British, who were now in position to threaten the Carolinas and, eventually, Virginia. Within months, rumors flew that the British were offering a deal: if they could keep Georgia and South Carolina, they would accept the independence of the other eleven colonies.[76]

John Laurens revived his plan to raise a regiment of blacks. He wrote to his father saying that if South Carolina did not receive outside support in the form of reinforcements from the Continental Army, only a black regiment could save it from the "impending Calamity." He renewed his pledge to give up his slave property to establish the black corps—"I would chearfully sacrifice the largest portion of my future expectations to its success."[77]

John Laurens had needed no prodding to revive his enthusiasm for the plan. He had fought in two engagements during the previous year—the battles of Monmouth in June and Rhode Island in August 1778—at which black troops had fought bravely. Proof that blacks could and would fight for the American cause was in hand. Laurens had also gained the support of a powerful ally at Washington's headquarters, Alexander Hamilton, then another of Washington's close aides. In 1774 Hamilton had left King's College in New York after the Boston Tea Party to join a radical group. He served as an artillery officer in the New York campaign, impressing Washington so much that he appointed Hamilton to his personal staff with the rank of lieutenant colonel. Hamilton and Laurens became close friends, and they were united also in their personal devotion to George Washington. So deep was Laurens's esteem for his chief that in December 1778 he fought a duel, with Hamilton as his second, against General Charles "boiling water" Lee, who had made remarks questioning Washington's character. (His challenge to Lee stated, "I am informed that in contempt of decency and truth you have publickly abused General Washington in the grossest terms. The relation in which I stand to him forbids me to pass such conduct unnoticed." The duel ended when Lee was slightly wounded and the seconds persuaded the duelists that the honor of both had been satisfied.)[78]

Laurens and Hamilton spent many days at Washington's headquarters refining the plan to recruit slaves. Hamilton lent direct support in the form of a passionate letter of March 14, 1779, to the new president of the Continental Congress, John Jay, delivered personally by John Laurens. The letter deserves to be quoted at length; it systematically demolishes objections to freeing and arming slaves, and it expresses ideas hashed out at headquarters, within earshot of the commander himself, if not in actual conversations with him.

Col Laurens, who will have the honor of delivering you this letter, is on his way to South Carolina, on a project, which I think, in the present situation of affairs there, is a very good one and deserves every kind of support and encouragement. This is to raise two three or four batalions of negroes; with the assistance of the government of that state, by contributions from the owners in proportion to the number they possess. It appears to me, that an expedient of this kind, in the present state of Southern affairs, is the most rational, that can be adopted, and promises very important advantages. Indeed, I hardly see how a sufficient force can be collected in that quarter without it; and the enemy's operations there are growing infinitely serious and formidable. I have not the least doubt, that the negroes will make very excellent soldiers. . . . I frequently hear it objected to the scheme of embodying negroes that they are too stupid to make soldiers. This is so far from appearing to me a valid objection that I think their want of cultivation (for their natural faculties are probably as good as ours) joined to that habit of subordination which they acquire from a life of servitude, will make them sooner bec[o]me soldiers than our White inhabitants. Let officers be men of sense and sentiment, and the nearer the soldiers approach to machines perhaps the better.

I foresee that this project will have to combat much opposition from prejudice and self-interest. The contempt we have been taught to entertain for the blacks, makes us fancy many things that are founded neither in reason nor experience; and an unwillingness to part with property of so valuable a kind will furnish a thousand arguments to show the impracticability or pernicious tendency of a scheme which requires such a sacrifice. But it should be considered, that if we do not make use of them in this way, the enemy probably will; and that the best way to counteract the temptations they will hold out will be to offer them ourselves. An essential part of the plan is to give them their freedom with their muskets. This will secure their fidelity, animate their courage, and I believe will have a good influence upon those who remain, by opening a door to their emancipation. This circumstance, I confess, has no small weight in inducing me to wish the success of the project; for the dictates of humanity and true policy equally interest me in favour of this unfortunate class of men.[79]

With his home ground facing grave danger, Henry Laurens dropped all his previous objections to raising a black corps. Now he saw the enlistment of black troops as vital to the defense of South Carolina. With mingled optimism and desperation, on March 16 Laurens sent an urgent request to General Washington to throw support behind the most ambitious plan yet to free slaves for the cause:

> the Country is greatly distressed, and will be more so, unless further reinforcements are sent to its relief. had we Arms for 3000 such black Men, as I could select in Carolina I should have no doubt of success in driving the British out of Georgia and subduing East Florida before the end of July.[80]

Given that Washington had supported the Rhode Island plan, and had encouraged John Laurens to embark on his campaign of raising black troops in the South, Henry Laurens clearly expected to receive a ringing endorsement from the commander in chief, which he could use to overawe any opponents. Instead, on March 20 Washington sent a stunning rebuff:

> The policy of our arming Slaves is, in my opinion, a moot point, unless the enemy set the example; for should we begin to form Battalions of them, I have not the smallest doubt (if the War is to be prosecuted) of their following us in it, and justifying the measure upon our own ground; the upshot then must be, who can arm fastest, and where are our Arms? besides, I am not clear that a discrimination will not render Slavery more irksome to those who remain in it; most of the good and evil things of this life are judged of by comparison; and I fear a comparison in this case will be productive of much discontent in those who are held in servitude; but as this is a subject that has never employed much of my thoughts, these are no more than the first crude Ideas that have struck me upon the occasion.[81]

This is one of the most puzzling letters Washington ever wrote, because so little of it is true. First, the enemy had already "set the ex-

ample" of arming slaves more than three years earlier, when Governor
Dunmore invited Virginia's slaves to obtain their freedom by joining
the British cause. Washington himself had written in 1778, in a letter
to a Congressional committee, "The enemy have set every engine at
work, against us, and have actually called savages and even our own
slaves to their assistance." Second, the subject of enlisting slaves, despite Washington's denial, had indeed occupied his thoughts: in 1775
he wrote general orders about it and discussed the question in coun-
cils of war; in January 1778 he endorsed the Rhode Island plan for recruiting slaves as well as John Laurens's initial efforts to form a South
Carolina slave battalion. The British could not have failed to notice
the seven hundred American blacks who fought in Washington's
army at the Battle of Monmouth.[82]

Washington's greatest fear about the Laurenses' plan was not that
it was premature or inappropriate or that it would fail, but that it
would succeed. By withholding his support, Washington was trying
to derail a scheme that would be "productive of much discontent"
among slaves remaining in bondage, including his own. At the moment, the Laurenses' plan aimed at South Carolina and Georgia, but
Virginia would be next. Just days later, Congress would formally call
on Virginia to raise troops; if white recruits could not be found in sufficient numbers, Congress might extend the emancipation plan to
Washington's home ground. A letter of February 24, 1779, from the
general to his manager, Lund Washington, reveals that when Henry
Laurens was appealing to him for help in recruiting and freeing slaves,
Washington was considering a massive sale of slaves.

> The advantages resulting from the sale of my negroes, I have very lit-
> tle doubt of; because, as I observed in my last, if we should ultimately
> prove unsuccessful (of which I am under no apprehension unless it
> falls on us as a punishment for our want of public, & indeed private
> virtue) it would be a matter of very little consequences to me,
> whether my property is in negroes, or loan office certificates. . . . the
> only points therefore for me to consider, are, first, whether it would

be most to my interest, in case of a fortunate determination of the present contest, to have negroes, and the Crops they will make; or the sum they will now fetch and the interest of the money. And, secondly, the critical moment to make this sale.[83]

The letter suggests that Washington withheld his support from the South Carolina plan because he feared the consequences for his own slave property. If the existence of free black battalions turned out to be "irksome" to Washington's slaves, they would demand their freedom, too. He was "revolving" in his mind not only the price of slaves but the uncertain consequences of setting some slaves free while trying to keep the others in bondage. Preserving slavery in the midst of the Revolution—indeed, laying plans for selling his slaves—might be a moral crime so severe it called for providential punishment: defeat by the British, which Henry Laurens had told him would occur without black troops. The choice seemed plain: enlist the black battalion and win the war, or cling to the slave system and face the heightened prospect of defeat. In the middle of this letter to Lund, he speaks in an aside of a divine retribution that might befall the Revolution for its moral failings—the "punishment" that would befall the rebels "for our want of public, & indeed private virtue." There seems little doubt, given the context, that the moral failing Washington had in his mind was slavery.

His letter to Lund makes it plain that the humanity of the slaves was not in question. Washington already was refusing to separate families by sale, but he continued to think of slaves as property, property that would be the financial foundation of his life after the war, if he could win it. And if he were to sell this property, he needed to calculate the optimum time for such a sale:

With respect to the first point (if a negro man will sell at, or near one thousand pounds, and women and children in proportion) I have not the smallest doubt on which side the balance, placed in the scale of interest, will preponderate: My scruples arise from a reluctance in offering these people at public vendue, and on account of the uncertainty of timeing the sale well. In the first case, if these poor wretches are to be held in a state of slavery, I do not see that a change of masters will render it more irksome, provided husband and wife, and Parents and children are not seperated from each other, which is not my intentions to do.

In the Mount Vernon archives, the historian Fritz Hirschfeld found two unpublished letters revealing that at the moment when the success of the Laurens plan hung in the balance, Washington felt caught between financial considerations and his conscience. The letters were written by Lund Washington on the subject of selling slaves. The general had made it clear to Lund that he wished "to get quit of negroes" but had set impossible conditions. In April 1778 Lund wrote, "with regard to sell[in]g the Negroes . . . you have put it out of my power, by saying you would not sell them without their Consent." He then described how he had been on the verge of selling a woman named Bett who had apparently given him some trouble: "her Mother appeared to be so uneasy about it, and Bett herself made such promises of amendment, that I could not Force her to go with the Man." Another woman about to be handed over to a buyer "was so alarmed at the thoughts of being sold that the man could not get her to speak a Word of English, therefore he believed she cou'd not speak." Lund concluded, "unless I was to make a Publick Sale of those Negroes & pay no regard to their being Willing or not, I see no probability of sell[in]g them—but this is a matter that may be fixd upon you." In September Lund wrote, with obvious irritation, "you say again you wish to get quit of negroes . . . tell me in plain terms, whether I should sell your negroes at Publick sale or not, & how many of them & indeed who."[84]

Virtually paralyzed, Washington grappled with his conscience, hoping to be able to sell slaves in a manner he could justify to himself. (Jefferson solved this problem by the simple expedient of selling slaves from a distant plantation, where he would not have to see the sale.) The only morally acceptable solution he could imagine at that time was a sale or barter by which whole families would be transferred intact. (As it turned out, Lund sold nine slaves in January 1779, including the two women he mentioned, perhaps without Washington's knowledge.) Having witnessed the breakup of families in the past, Washington vowed never again to do such a thing himself; and yet the slaves represented one of his most valuable assets, so he resisted a recruitment plan that might lead to the loss of his property, despite compelling military necessity.

A moment when radical change might have been possible thus passed. The window had opened at Valley Forge, when Washington was in desperate need of black men for the American cause. He had felt the presence of the revolutionary moment and sensed it melting away. Washington's view of human nature was pragmatic—and pessimistic. And in his role of mentor Washington wrote to young John Laurens, the passionate idealist, his gloomy assessment of the reason emancipation would fail: the moment for such a sacrifice was gone. He fastened no blame on the blacks, did not claim that they were inferior or unworthy, but passed his judgment on the character of the country, and may very well have been speaking of himself and his own imperfection:

> That Spirit of Freedom which at the commencement of this contest would have gladly sacrificed every thing to the attainment of its object has long since subsided, and every selfish Passion has taken its place—it is not the public but the private Interest which influences the generality of Mankind nor can the Americans any longer boast an exception.

Despite Washington's refusal of support, John and Henry Laurens persevered. On the surface their scheme was an enlistment plan, but everyone, especially Washington, recognized the implications. Emancipation, which had been heretofore an incidental side effect of black enlistment, was gaining momentum as a goal in itself. The enlistment of slaves in the heart of plantation country would have far greater impact than the enlistment of blacks in Massachusetts and Rhode Island. The slave masters knew that freedom, once loosed, could not be readily contained and that slavery could not long coexist with it.

Yet some Southern leaders were so desperate to raise troops that they were now willing to tolerate emancipation. John Laurens had powerful Southern allies when he presented his proposal to the Continental Congress—William Henry Drayton, who represented South Carolina in the Congress, and Daniel Huger, the governor's envoy. Thus, on March 29, 1779, the Continental Congress unanimously passed a resolution, which one might call the first Emancipation Proclamation:

> Resolved, That it be recommended to the states of South Carolina and Georgia, if they shall think the same expedient, to take measures immediately for raising three thousand able bodied negroes.

> Resolved, That congress will make provision for paying the proprietors of such negroes as shall be inlisted for the service of the United States during the war, a full compensation for the property at a rate not exceeding one thousand dollars for each active able bodied negro man of standard size, not exceeding thirty five years of age, who shall be so inlisted and pass muster.

> That no pay or bounty be allowed to the said negroes, but that they be cloathed and subsisted at the expence of the United States.

> That every negro who shall well and faithfully serve as a soldier to the end of the present war, and shall then return his arms, *be emancipated* and receive the sum of fifty dollars.[85]

A biographer of John Laurens wrote, "Few delegates in Congress failed to recognize the revolutionary implications of the resolution." William Whipple, a delegate from New Hampshire, said the plan would "produce the Emancipation of a number of those wretches and lay a foundation for the Abolition of Slavery in America." No one envisioned an immediate, general emancipation, but the Continental Congress had unanimously taken a step on the path toward a gradual one.[86]

John Laurens headed to South Carolina to push his plan, which required the consent of the South Carolina and Georgia legislatures. Hamilton wanted to join him, but Washington refused to allow Hamilton to leave his staff post. In May 1779, in the lower house of the South Carolina Assembly, the Laurens proposal "was received with horror by the planters, who figured to themselves terrible consequences."[87] One member of the upper house of the South Carolina Assembly was so outraged by the Laurens plan that he set forth a proposal to secede from the American war effort. The plan was voted down. It was of course highly ironic that a proposal to arm and free slaves be considered by an assembly of slaveholders, but such was the composition of every Southern government.

It is tempting to ask what would have happened if Washington had thrown his support behind the Laurens plan. Would his prestige have cowed the planters into submission? Military necessity demanded the recruitment of black battalions. There were no other men available. But the planters regarded the preservation of slavery as the bedrock of their postwar society and economy. If the United States had won independence but put slavery on the road to extinction, then they would have lost the war. The planters were prepared to see their region fall to the British before they would arm three thousand slaves. Independence had to be accompanied by the preservation of slavery. If preserving slavery prolonged the war—so be it.

When a British fleet landed an invasion force near Charleston, South Carolina, in 1780, and proceeded slowly to prepare its siege, Laurens wrote to Washington from the threatened city. He was bitter about the haughty blindness of his fellow citizens: "the Carolinians as usual have been superior to foresight and precaution. The delay of the enemy produced no other effect than to increase their supineness, and finally to produce a disbelief of the enemys intentions." Several days later, with the siege under way, he wrote to another correspondent that the number of men at his disposal was "far too few for defending works of nearly three miles in circumference, especially considering many of them to be citizens, and unaccustomed to the fatigues of a besieged garrison, and many of the Continental troops half naked."[88]

As a direct result of the failure to form a black legion to defend South Carolina, Charleston fell to the British. Much of it was reduced to rubble by British bombardment; John Laurens was captured and the American side suffered some of the heaviest casualties of the war. But slavery remained intact. In an eerie portent of the Civil War, as Philip S. Foner writes, "when the British threatened them with the expropriation of their slaves unless they took an oath of allegiance to George III, the majority of South Carolina planters, including prominent former leaders of the Revolution, foreswore their allegiance to the Patriot cause and solemnly pledged loyalty to the British crown."[89]

John Laurens did not give up. Released in an exchange of prisoners, he gained a seat in the South Carolina Assembly and pressed his plan again. To Alexander Hamilton he wrote that he would not cease his efforts "while there remains the smallest hope of success." This time he had a powerful ally in the person of General Nathanael Greene, the commander hand-picked by Washington. "What a Herculean task we have," Greene wrote in 1781, "to contend with a formidable enemy with a handful of men." At the Battle of Rhode Island in 1778, Greene had fought alongside black troops, and he could not understand why South Carolina neglected this resource. To the governor Greene tartly observed that "the natural strength of this country in point of numbers seems to consist much more in the blacks than in the whites." But South Carolina did find a way to make use of its slaves. In 1792 the legislature passed a law by which white recruits were lured into South Carolina's service by the promise of payment in slaves confiscated from loyalists.[90*]

Greene warned South Carolina officials that if peace were sud-

---

* Both South Carolina and Georgia raised money by taking slaves from Tories and selling them. The historian Benjamin Quarles has written that the Southern war effort was financed in large measure by the sale of blacks.

denly declared with Great Britain remaining in possession of lands actually occupied by her troops, South Carolina would lose the city of Charleston, which was still in British hands. But black regiments could expel the British and forestall that possibility. The situation was so dire that Laurens was beginning to garner support. One delegate wrote in February 1782: "We have had another hard Battle on the Subject of arming the Blacks. . . . About 12 or 15 were for it & about 100 against it. . . . But I do assure you I was very much alarmed on the Occasion. I was repeatedly told that a large party [of supporters] was made & I believe it was; but upon a fair full Argument, people in general returned to their Senses, & the business ended."

In a letter to Washington in May 1782, Laurens attributed the final demise of his plan to "the howlings of a triple-headed monster in which Prejudice Avarice & Pusillanimity were united." Nathanael Greene's analysis, less colorful but more revealing, was that the plan failed "from an apprehension of the consequences." One South Carolinian foresaw that the Laurens plan would inevitably lead to a general emancipation after the war, which would bring about the ultimate horror of the Southerner: "whites & blacks inter-married."[91] For many slaveholders, the union of a white woman and a black man was indeed the ultimate horror. When Jefferson worked on revising Virginia's slave codes in the late 1770s, he proposed a law that would have required exile from the state for a white woman who had a black man's child; if she had insisted on remaining in her homeland, she would have been outlawed, meaning she could have been beaten or killed with legal immunity for the perpetrators. Thus Jefferson would have authorized the legal lynching of such women.

The failure of emancipation to take root during the war is one of the great *What ifs* of the Revolution. Another is: What if blacks had not fought for the American cause? What if a slave had not saved Colonel William Washington's life, with the result that his cavalry charge dissolved and the Battle of Cowpens had become a British victory? As the historian Thomas Fleming speculates, both North and South Carolina might well have gone over to the British. What if

Glover's regiment of Massachusetts sailors had not had the man-power to complete the evacuation of Washington's army before the fog lifted in New York—and Washington himself, waiting for the last boat, had been captured?

In reading Washington's wartime letters I came across a thoroughly mundane note of February 1776 from the headquarters in Cambridge to his kinsman Burwell Bassett in Virginia. "Few things of impor-tance have occurred here of late," he wrote, while sending along some routine military information (which surprised me; surely it was a se-curity lapse) as well as greetings from Mrs. Washington, who was with him. But there was an arresting aside. Washington thanked Bas-sett for looking after his lands in the distant Ohio country, and con-tinued, "in the worst event, they will serve for an Asylum." Here was his plan of what he would do in the event of a military catastrophe. He would not surrender to British justice, for surely he would be drawn and quartered as a traitor, but would go to ground out west. In such an event he could not bring his family, of course, because he would be a hunted man. He knew every foot of that terrain, having surveyed it and fought on it. One wonders if he had in mind some hollow in the hills or a cave he had found, isolated, suitable for a crude habitation, defensible by a small band of men, and with a way out. He had to know that such an asylum would not be safe for long, that in-evitably he would have to disappear farther west. The letter showed that, though ever resolute, George Washington knew also that he could lose, that the stupendous force arrayed against him might one day annihilate his army. Certainly he would wish to be in the thick of the fighting on such a day, but he might not be, and might find him-self cut off with a handful of staffers from "my military family." Here in this letter was a slight note of dread and, perhaps, a coded mes-sage—in "the worst event," if you hear nothing of my whereabouts, you will know where to look.[92]

In keeping with Washington's contradictory nature, the hallmarks of his generalship were caution and boldness. His primary purpose in the war was to keep the American army intact until luck brought him the moment when he could strike a heavy blow against the British. In reply to demands from Congress that he engage the British in a major battle that would decide the outcome of the war at once, Washington wrote, "we should on all occasions avoid a general action or put anything to the risk, unless compelled by necessity, into which we ought never to be drawn." His aim, he said, was to "protract the war" until the British wearied of it. On the other hand, as the historian John Ferling writes, "there was a gambler's audacity to Washington's makeup, a willingness to run great risks by attempting bold strokes." The nighttime crossing of the Delaware to attack Trenton was one such stroke; and when Washington had the British cooped up in Boston, he considered launching a major assault to end the war quickly, but he thought better of it.[93] Nevertheless, another hallmark of Washington's command, which derived from his essential character, was iron discipline, which informed his acts and military thinking, from camp life to strategy. On a day-to-day basis, Washington's personal adherence to discipline inspired his staff with devotion to duty and to the commander himself. One of his officers, James McHenry, wrote to a family member in 1778:

> I cannot say that the fatigues of our late march [have] been of any disservice to my constitution—in sleeping in the open fields—under trees exposed to the night air and all changes of the weather I only followed the example of our General. . . . When I joined his Excellency's suite I gave up soft beds—undisturbed repose—and habits of ease and indulgence which reign in some departments—for a single blanket—the hard floor—or the softer sod of the fields—early rising and almost perpetual duty. These habitudes however I prefer to those of idleness and inactivity—they are more consistent with the profession of the soldier and repetition has now made them agreeable. This however is descriptive of all the General's family.[94]

On the highest plane, discipline governed Washington's conduct of the war. Irksome as the Congress was in its delays, meddlings, and failures, Washington never wavered from the principle that the civilian government controls the state's military forces. And in strategic matters, Washington brushed aside urgings from his erstwhile competitor for the post of commander, General Charles "boiling water" Lee, that the army fundamentally alter its methods to bring the war to a swifter conclusion. Lee thought as a general; Washington thought in terms of a military, political, and social totality larger and more lasting than a theater of war.

Early in 1778 Lee proposed to Congress, where he found strong supporters, and to Washington that the army adopt the tactics of guerrilla war. As John Shy writes:

> He sought a war that would use the new light-infantry tactics already in vogue among the military avant-garde of Europe, the same tactics the free men at Lexington and Concord had instinctively employed. [But] to Washington—a practical man not given to theorizing—this was all madness. He never seriously considered resorting to a war of guerrilla bands drawn from the militia. . . . A strategy of that kind would change the war for independence into a genuine civil war with all its grisly attendants—ambush, reprisal, counter-reprisal. It would tear the fabric of American life to pieces. It might even undermine the political process, and throw power to a junta.[95]

In Washington's mind a disciplined path, though slow and arduous, offered the only acceptable route to victory, for to throw discipline aside invites chaos, and risks winning a victory that is hollow because it lacks honor, and tenuous because it leaves wanton destruction and bitterness in its wake.

Washington needed every ounce of personal discipline and resolve to endure the string of defeats the war dealt him. After driving the British from Boston in March 1776, he suffered the disastrous defeat in New York in June, barely managing to escape with his army into New Jersey. He won bold, morale-boosting victories at Trenton on December 26 and Princeton on January 3; but in September 1777 he was thoroughly beaten at the Battle of Brandywine, a loss that allowed the British to occupy Philadelphia, forcing Congress to flee to a temporary capital at York, Pennsylvania. Even Washington's admiring biographer Freeman concludes that the general conducted the Brandywine operations "as if he had been in a daze."

But just twenty-three days later, on October 4, Washington led eight thousand Continentals and three thousand militia in a surprise attack on nine thousand British regulars camped at Germantown, then a separate settlement but now a northern part of Philadelphia. Certain that the Americans could not launch another major attack so soon after their defeat at Brandywine, the British had taken only minimal precautions. Washington decided upon a highly complex plan requiring coordinated maneuvers of different columns. The assault, launched at sunup, was enveloped in thick morning fog that initially aided the Americans; Washington was about to give the order to push onward into Philadelphia. But then the American units began to collide in the fog and fire on each other. A stunned Washington watched as an imminent American victory dissolved into panic.

Even in defeat Washington seemed to possess an almost mystical good luck. Far from being demoralized, the men felt that they could have won had it not been for the fog. An officer said, "They are now in high spirits and appear to wish ardently for another engagement." More important, Washington's pluck and determination echoed loudly across the Atlantic. Flexner writes: "In Europe, it seemed almost inconceivable that an untrained rabble would attack a mighty regular army so effectively and so soon after they had been defeated. . . . The French foreign minister, Vergennes, when discussing a possible alliance with American commissioners, stated that 'nothing struck him so much' as the Battle of Germantown." Such an army, Vergennes said, could do anything.[96]

The other major factor in the deliberations in France was the American victory in October at Saratoga, New York, where General Horatio Gates captured a large British army under General John "Gentleman Johnny" Burgoyne, wrecking the British strategy to split New England from the rest of the rebels along the axis of the Hudson

River. American messengers raced to Boston, where a dispatch was sent by a fast ship to France. The note was handed to the envoy to France, Benjamin Franklin, on December 4. News of Burgoyne's surrender electrified the French capital, and within days the French informed Franklin that they would join the Americans in an alliance against Great Britain. Congress ratified two treaties with France on May 4, 1778. In one of these documents France recognized the independence of the American colonies.

Washington took his tattered army of ten thousand into winter quarters at Valley Forge, Pennsylvania, in December 1777. Over the next six months perhaps as many as 2,500 soldiers died of starvation and exposure. The ragged clothes of the dead were reclaimed and reissued to the living. In the comfort of Philadelphia the British fed themselves on the bounty of Pennsylvania's farms, purchased with hard cash. Much of the blame for the suffering at Valley Forge has to be fastened on Quartermaster General Thomas Mifflin, whom Washington eventually replaced with the more energetic Nathanael Greene. Yet despite the privations, the high spirit of the army remained intact. The military historian Mark M. Boatner writes: "Washington was never faced with the expected mutiny or mass desertions. Much of this can be attributed to the faith Washington's officers and men had in his leadership."[97]

Against all odds, Washington's army emerged from Valley Forge stronger than it had been in December. In January at Valley Forge he gave his approval to General Varnum's plan to recruit black troops in Rhode Island. General Greene got the men fed, clothed, and equipped (though erratic supplies and pay would bedevil the Americans for the rest of the war). Washington's circle of officers had been enhanced the previous summer by the unexpected arrival of a young French aristocrat (he was nineteen), the Marquis de Lafayette, burning with admiration for the American cause and eager to lead troops. He acquitted himself so well at the Battle of Brandywine, where he was wounded, that Congress gave him command of a division of Virginia troops, at Washington's recommendation. Also, the harsh, profanity-laden ministrations of a Prussian drill master, Friedrich Wilhelm Augustus von Steuben, absolutely transformed the army. Descending on Valley Forge in February, he won Washington's approval to train the troops in classical European battlefield techniques. One authority called his program "perhaps the most remarkable achievement in rapid military training in the history of the world." In large measure Steuben's training allowed Washington to pull victory from defeat at the Battle of Monmouth, New Jersey, which took place in June 1778, just after the army left Valley Forge.[98]

The Battle of Monmouth was the last major engagement in the North, as the British shifted their attentions to the South, where for a long while everything went in their favor. The fall of Savannah in December 1778 brought Georgia under British control, a hold that was strengthened by the failure of a combined American and French counterattack in October 1779. After the capture of Charleston in May 1780, the British had a secure base for their 8,300-man force, under Lord Cornwallis, which maintained control of a 15,000-square-mile region with the aid of local loyalists. Without consulting Washington, Congress dispatched the hero of Saratoga, General Gates, to dislodge the British, but Gates met with disaster at the Battle of Camden in August 1780. A chastened Congress now asked Washington whom to send, and he unhesitatingly picked Nathanael Greene, with Steuben as second in command.

In March 1781 Greene managed to repeat a Battle of Bunker Hill in North Carolina at Guilford Court House, near the Virginia border southwest of modern Danville, when his militia and Continentals inflicted savage casualties on Cornwallis's 2,000-man force. North Carolina sharpshooters fired two volleys at the approaching enemy line and, as a British officer reported, "one half of the Highlanders dropped on that spot." Royal Welsh Fusiliers dutifully followed, though they could plainly see the Americans, forty yards ahead, "taking aim with the nicest precision." When the fighting became hand-to-hand and the enemies merged, Cornwallis reached for the devil's tool: over the protests of his officers he ordered grapeshot fired into the mob, killing his own men as well as enemies. Greene called out to retreat and the Americans melted away. Cornwallis held the field, but the size of his losses—a fourth of his command—compelled him to retreat to the coast. "I never saw such fighting," he said, "since God made me."⁹⁹

Frustrated at his failure to bring Greene to heel, Cornwallis decided, in defiance of orders, to march north into Virginia. There he joined other British commanders, including the traitor Benedict Arnold, who had been busily laying waste in a series of devastating raids, some of them mere plundering expeditions. One raiding party very nearly captured Thomas Jefferson at Monticello. In January 1781 Washington dispatched a force under Lafayette to bring some relief to Virginia.¹⁰⁰

By May, after six years of fighting, an American victory seemed not only uncertain but unlikely, by Washington's own estimate. At the army's encampment in White Plains, New York, he began to keep a wartime journal in which he set down "our prospects." The words that leap from the page are "bewildered and gloomy." He enumerated the woes that beset him: "Instead of having Magazines filled with provisions, we have a scanty pittance. . . . Instead of having our Arsenals well supplied with Military Stores, they are poorly provided, and the Workmen all leaving them." As for "Field equipage," all he had were the promises of the several states to deliver something at some unspecified time. His greatest lack was men: "Instead of having the regiments compleated . . . scarce any State in the Union has, at this hour, an eighth part of its quota in the field and little prospect, that I can see, of ever getting more than half."¹⁰¹

Washington's situation changed utterly in August when he received two pieces of news. From Virginia Lafayette reported that Cornwallis had given up seeking a battle on the open field and had withdrawn to Yorktown on the York River, which empties into Chesapeake Bay. The other dispatch informed him that a French fleet was heading toward the Chesapeake. This unexpected combination of circumstances presented a unique but fleeting opportunity to change the course of the war. Washington put aside plans to dislodge the enemy from New York City, ordered feints and diversions to persuade the British he was remaining in New York, and commenced a fast march south.

The men with Washington represented the hard core of devotion to the cause and to their commander. An astonishing number of them were black. In July 1781 Washington's camp was visited by an officer serving on the staff of the French allies. The officer, Baron Ludwig von Closen, surveyed the American army and wrote in his journal: "A quarter of them were negroes, merry, confident, and sturdy." Indeed, in the judgment of that officer, the blacks were among the finest soldiers Washington had: "three-quarters of the Rhode Island regiment consists of negroes, and that regiment is the most neatly dressed, the best under arms, and the most precise in its maneuvers."[102]

Two historians, Sidney Kaplan and Emma Nogrady Kaplan, wrote a book published in 1989 entitled *The Black Presence in the Era of the American Revolution*. The title rightly suggests that Americans had to be informed that there *was* a black presence in the founding moment. Blacks had been so systematically overlooked or deliberately erased from the history texts that average Americans found it hard to imagine that blacks had played any role at all in creating the country. Worse, they might tend to have a naive faith in the history they learned as children, and question any attempts to tamper with an image of the past that they believed served the country well. If blacks were actually important during the Revolution, then why did we not know about it earlier?

I put that question to a historian, Robert Selig, whose reply was that there were so many black soldiers in the Revolutionary army that their presence had ceased to be remarkable to contemporary observers and therefore was underreported. Washington did not comment on the large number of black men in his army at White Plains because by 1781 he was used to seeing them in the uniform of the Continental Army. But when an outsider, Baron von Closen, visited the camp he was struck by the fact that one of four Continental soldiers was black. Closen had no political agenda to advance, he had no reason to lie or exaggerate, and he wrote down his observations privately. We also learn of the black presence through the complaints of those who didn't like it. In this fashion the once obscure facts of history reemerge.

In the judgment of the outsider Closen, the finest regiment in Washington's command, "the best under arms . . . the most precise in its maneuvers," happened to be 75 percent black. This observation would be nothing more than an intriguing footnote except that this Rhode Island unit, mostly black, would be hand-picked by Washington and Lafayette to carry out the most important assignment of the climactic battle of the Revolution—the assault that ended the war.

On its march to Yorktown, Washington's army of 2,000 Continentals and 4,500 French troops crossed the Hudson River on August 21, passed through Philadelphia on September 2, and by September 26 reached Williamsburg, where Lafayette was waiting with another 3,000 French soldiers put ashore by the fleet. Altogether Washington would have 17,600 men against about 8,300 British, Germans, and loyalists. When Cornwallis withdrew behind formidable defensive works, Washington settled in for a methodical siege. Time would seem to favor the Americans, but they received information that a British relief fleet had set sail from New York. While French and American artillery pounded Yorktown, troops dug a series of trenches that inched closer and closer to the British fortifications. To protect the diggers, Steuben organized a system of sentries to shout warnings of British artillery fire. On October 9 Lafayette was about to give the order for a battery to fire when he asked Thomas Nelson, a resident of Yorktown, to suggest a target. A militia commander and signer of the Declaration of Independence, Nelson pointed out his own house, the finest left standing, and said in all likelihood that's where Cornwallis would be. The barrage struck the house but it survived, with the marks of the bombardment visible today.

On October 14, General Washington realized that the moment had come when the entire war could be determined in a single bold coup. He had identified two points in the British defenses that held the key to the British position. These points were the heavily fortified

Redoubts 9 and 10—formidable strongholds consisting of earthen mounds surrounded by moats and ringed by rows of sharpened stakes. French and American artillery had pounded these strongholds, but still the British held on. Victory could not be won without the capture of the redoubts, which could only be taken by storm. To carry out this assignment Washington selected the elite units of his army, including the First Rhode Island Regiment. The attack had to be carried out with stealth and under extraordinary conditions at night.

To preserve secrecy the selected units—two detachments with four hundred men in each—camped apart from the main army on the day preceding the attack. Late in the day, in a sign of the supreme importance of the mission, Washington himself appeared in their camp and addressed the men, something he had only rarely done during the war. The officer who commanded the Rhode Island men, Captain Stephen Olney, recalled later that Washington's remarks were brief. He told them "to act the part of firm and brave soldiers"; the success of the American enterprise depended on the capture of the redoubts. It was a moment of great emotion and of great fear; as Olney listened to his commander address the troops, "I thought then, that his Excellency's knees rather shook, but I have since doubted whether it was not mine." After Washington concluded his remarks, "the column marched in silence . . . many, no doubt thinking that less than one quarter of a mile would finish the journey of life with them."[103]

French units were assigned to attack Redoubt 9; American troops were assigned Redoubt 10. They were commanded, ironically, by Alexander Hamilton and John Laurens: this action would either vindicate their faith in the black troops or end in their humiliation. Olney's Rhode Islanders took the position of honor in the vanguard of the column that would attack the front of Redoubt 10. Washington looked on as the soldiers filed off silently into the darkness, enduring the agony of the commander who can only watch and wait. Because the attack depended on surprise, Washington had issued an extraordinary order: lest an accidental shot give away the surprise, the men were forbidden initially to load their weapons. They were ordered to fight hand-to-hand, with bayonets. As Freeman describes the scene (without any mention of the presence of black troops), "Washington and the other Generals might almost have held their breath as they waited for the discovery of the attack." The commander was banking on the discipline of his troops; the slightest sound, carried in the night air, could give away the operation. Abruptly, the silence was shattered. As Freeman writes, "the jaw of every waiting officer must have set as there rolled swiftly down from the North the sound of the fire of the guard . . . the sharp bark of small arms came from the redoubt the Americans were assaulting."[104]

The American column had crept to the edge of the fortification, the ring of sharpened tree trunks called the abatis, when they were spotted by the defenders, who "fired a full body of musketry." With surprise lost, the Americans let out a loud "Huzzah!" and charged. Some men hacked away at the abatis with axes while others looked for gaps made by the artillery bombardment. About a dozen Rhode Islanders squeezed through the abatis, climbed over the earthen wall supporting it, and tumbled into a ditch. Olney rolled in after them and called out, "in a tone as if there was no danger—Captain Olney's company, form here!" In an instant he felt the stabs of British bayonets in his hand, leg, and abdomen. Two of his men hastily loaded their muskets and fired into the British defenders, saving Olney from further harm. All along the line the British were firing madly into the darkness and hurling grenades. One American sergeant thought the column was being wiped out: he could see his men falling everywhere he looked; then, as if in a dream, they rose again. The sergeant realized the men had not been shot but, in the darkness, had fallen into shell holes. Someone called out, "Rush on, boys! The fort's ours!" The Americans clambered up the side of the redoubt. Hamilton ordered a soldier to kneel and jumped from the man's back into the redoubt. After ten minutes of hand-to-hand fighting, the British surrendered. Lafayette appeared and sent a jaunty message to the French officer leading the other attack, "I am in my redoubt. Where are you?"[105]

The next day Washington himself, elated by the victory at York-town, visited his men in the captured fort. In frustration British snipers were pecking away at their lost redoubts, and an occasional artillery round landed nearby, but Washington ignored the danger to savor the triumph. "Washington could not conceal his enthusiasm over the success of these brilliant feats," writes the historian Henry Johnston, "and in General Orders he praised the troops unstintingly." No mention was made of the fact that the Rhode Island contingent was mostly black—it was no longer extraordinary to see black men in arms. To preserve a shred of British honor, Lord Cornwallis ordered one more pro forma attack on the American lines, but the capture of the redoubts had sealed the fate of his army. After brief negotiations, the British and Hessians, some of them in tears, filed silently out of their fortifications and stacked their arms as drummers beat out a solemn march.[106]

Every victory has its price. In the wake of such a grand triumph no one wished to dwell on the cost in human lives. Paintings of the Yorktown victory show its undeniable glory and give no hint of the scene of horror beyond the lines of fluttering banners and crisply uniformed officers. Once again, a foreigner noted it, Private Georg Daniel Flohr of the Royal Deux-Ponts. Walking over the now calm battlefield, he wrote of seeing "all over the place and wherever you looked—corpses—lying about that had not been buried." He took note of who these people were: "the larger part of these were *Mohren*"—Moors, Negroes. Blacks had fought on both sides, with the Americans and the French, with the British and the Hessians; and, as Flohr observed, blacks had paid the highest cost in defeat and victory.[107]

The heaps of dead also represented a betrayal by the British. They had promised freedom to any slave who would join them, and in the panic of the final days of siege, as food ran short and disease swept the trenches, Cornwallis had issued a brutal order. A Hessian officer wrote:

> I would just as soon forget to record a cruel happening. On the same day of the enemy assault, we drove back to the enemy all our black friends. . . . We had used them to good advantage and set them free, and now, with fear and trembling, they had to face the reward of their cruel masters. Last night I had to make a sneak patrol, during which I came across a great number of these unfortunates. In their hunger

these unhappy people would have soon devoured what I had; and since they lay between two fires, they had to be driven on by force. This harsh act had to be carried out, however, because of the scarcity of provisions; but we should have thought more about their deliverance at this time.

A Virginian who was present wrote that "an immense number of Negroes" died "in the most miserable Manner."[108]

Many of these men were suffering from smallpox. An epidemic had broken out, but there is evidence that the British had deliberately infected some blacks with the disease and expelled them toward the American lines to spread the contagion. An American soldier wrote, "During the siege we saw in the woods herds of Negroes which Lord Cornwallis . . . in love and pity to them, had turned adrift, with no other recompense for their confidence in his humanity than the smallpox for their bounty and starvation and death for their wages."[109]

During the war many Virginia slaves had served in the army as substitutes for their masters. Their number is not known, but there were enough of these veterans around to prick the conscience of the Virginia legislature after the war. They had served with the promise of emancipation, but once independence was won, with their assistance, their masters managed to forget their promises and returned the men to slavery. The Assembly passed a bill denouncing masters who "contrary to principles of justice and to their own solemn promise" had kept such men enslaved. By blanket decree, it emancipated these men and ordered the attorney general to represent any black claimants. But the black veterans fell afoul of a loophole: though entitled to end their enslavement, they could not begin legal proceedings on their own because they were still slaves. The legislature itself, moved by a sense of justice, freed some men by statute; the total of these emancipations was eight.[110]

The success of Washington's rebellion against tyranny fed hopes for freedom among Virginia slaves for many years. About two decades after the Revolution a Richmond slave named Gabriel Prosser launched a revolt to obtain freedom with as much courage, but with as much chance of success, as the men at the Alamo. This doomed crusade, led by a messianic blacksmith, remains one of the most poignant episodes in our history. The revolt was betrayed by one of the conspirators; twenty-seven men were rounded up and condemned to hang. Given the chance to speak his last words as he stood facing the noose, one of the condemned men declared: "I have nothing more to offer than what General Washington would have had to offer, had he been taken by the British and put to trial. I have adventured my life in endeavoring to obtain the liberty of my countrymen, and am a willing sacrifice in their cause."[111]

CHAPTER SEVEN

A Different Destiny

OWARD THE END OF THE WAR in September 1781, as the American army was racing south to bag Cornwallis, an episode of the greatest poignance occurred. Riding the fastest horse he could find, Washington abruptly left his army behind him in Maryland. Like Odysseus "yearning to see . . . but the smoke leap upwards from his own land . . . craving for his wife and for his homeward path," Washington galloped the sixty miles from Baltimore to Mount Vernon in a single day. The most powerful man on the continent sped through the countryside alone except for one trusted aide, David Humphreys. It had been more than six years since the hero had seen his home, though the image of it had never left him. "How many Lambs have you had this Spring?" he had written to his manager just a few months earlier. "How many Colts are you like to have? are you going to repair the pavement of the Piazza? is anything done with . . . the Well at the edge of the Hill in front of the House?" In the depths of war nothing had given him more comfort than the image of Mount Vernon. "An account of these things," he wrote to Lund Washington, "would be satisfactory to me and infinitely amusing in the recital." As he reined up in front of the mansion Washington laid eyes on four grandchildren for the first time, the offspring of Martha's son, Jacky Custis. The youngest, still a babe in arms, had been named for the general—George Washington Parke Custis.[1]

The hero's homecoming to Mount Vernon was but a brief interlude. Just hours behind him galloped his staff and the French high command, all of whom descended on Mount Vernon to plan the Yorktown campaign. After three seemingly magical days at home, Washington headed south to the final battle, and would not see Mount Vernon again for two more years.

Washington's brief visit to Mount Vernon included a scene that signifies the ambiguities of trying to comprehend slavery. In addition to his relatives, the large throng of other onlookers who turned out en masse to greet Washington included the Mount Vernon slaves. Humphreys, who witnessed the scene, later recorded it in a poem:

> *Return'd from war, I saw them round him press,*
> *And all their speechless glee by artless signs express.*[2]

One might be tempted to try to puncture this Currier & Ives vision of the slave master returning to gleeful tributes from his slaves, except that it probably happened as Humphreys described it. (He was no apologist for slavery—he called it in a preceding line "that foul stain of manhood.") There are other accounts of other slaves greeting their returning masters with apparent joy. But it is impossible to know precisely what the "artless signs" really expressed, especially since a number of Washington's slaves had unambiguously expressed their feelings about slavery by running away to the British.

Among the blacks captured with the British at Yorktown were two people who had once belonged to George Washington. They were among seventeen slaves who had fled Mount Vernon in early 1781 when the British warship *Savage* dropped anchor in the Potomac and demanded supplies from Washington's manager. Washington was able to recover the two at Yorktown and return them to slavery at Mount Vernon because of a clause in the articles of Cornwallis's surrender permitting the repatriation of captured slaves. He recovered several others at Philadelphia, but a few more managed to reach British lines in New York where, for a time at least, they were beyond Washington's reach.[3]

Another black man who was returned to slavery at Yorktown was

James Armistead, despite the fact that he had rendered distinguished and dangerous service to the American cause. In the weeks leading up to the Battle of Yorktown, when Lafayette was shadowing Cornwallis's army in Virginia and wondering what the British were planning, Armistead volunteered to join Lafayette's network of spies. He entered the British camp at Portsmouth, Virginia, probably posing as a runaway. He wangled a job, perhaps as a forager, that allowed him to move back and forth across the British lines. Lafayette used him as a courier for written instructions to other spies in the network—documents, Lafayette said, "of the most secret and important kind; the possession of which if discovered on him would most certainly have endangered [his] life." Lafayette also had Armistead feed false information to the British that the Americans had been reinforced. Impressed with Armistead's apparent ability to collect intelligence, the British hired him as a spy, making him one of the earliest double agents in American history. Lafayette reported Armistead's findings directly to Washington. On July 31 Lafayette wrote: "a correspondent of mine servant to Lord Cornwallis writes on the 26th July at Portsmouth, and says [the British] are still in town but expected to move." He revealed that his agent was boldly trying to steal documents from Cornwallis's headquarters but had been unsuccessful: "his Lordship is so shy of his papers that my honest friend says he cannot get at them." On August 25 Lafayette wrote to Washington that, through Armistead, "I hear that they begin fortifying at York."[4]

Armistead had joined Lafayette's spy service with the assumption that he would be made free, but that was not the case. His master, William Armistead, reclaimed him after the war. (Washington might actually have met James and William Armistead before the war, for William had business dealings with the Custis estate.) Three years after the Yorktown victory, James Armistead managed to get a meeting with Lafayette, who was more than a little surprised to hear that this loyal agent of the Revolution remained a slave. He immediately wrote out a letter of recommendation that James could use to campaign for his freedom:

This is to certify that the Bearer by the name of James has done Essential Services to me while I had the Honour to Command in this State. . . . He properly acquitted himself . . . and appears to me entitled to every reward his Situation can admit of.

Lafayette[5]

It was another two years before Armistead received his freedom, when by special act of the Virginia House of Delegates and Senate, his petition for freedom was unanimously approved by both houses. Armistead became free in January 1787. Thereupon, in tribute to his patron and protector, he took the surname Lafayette. He bought some land next to that of his former master; tax records show that he owned three slaves, who may have been members of his family. The white and black Lafayettes met again in 1824 when the French hero made a final triumphal tour of the United States, a tour that naturally included Yorktown. Riding in a carriage through a crowd of well-wishers, the marquis recognized his old comrade in the throng despite the passage of years. He ordered the carriage to halt, and stepped out to embrace his black friend.[6]

Washington's victory at Yorktown did not officially end the war. After the battle, Washington returned to his headquarters at Tappan, twenty-five miles up the Hudson River from New York City, which was still in British possession. Sporadic fighting continued while American and British negotiators in Paris hammered out a treaty. Slavery was not an issue in the negotiations until the very last minute, through an odd series of events. Protocol required that Lord Cornwallis, taken prisoner at Yorktown, had to be exchanged for an American captive of equal rank. For this role, fate produced Henry Laurens. (In the sporadic raids and counterraids between British and American forces that occurred after the Battle of Yorktown, young John Laurens was killed in a particularly foolish and notably futile engagement.) Henry had been captured at sea in 1779 on a voyage to Europe, and the British had held him in the Tower of London for almost two years. While awaiting an exchange, he was bailed out of prison by a British friend, Richard Oswald, his old partner in the international slave trade. Laurens had sold Oswald's slave consignments in South Carolina for a 10 percent commission. Now Laurens was swapped for Cornwallis and given his freedom.[7]

Since Laurens, former president of the Continental Congress, was in Europe when treaty negotiations were under way, Congress sent him instructions to join the negotiators. He then carried out one of the most abrupt turnabouts of policy one could imagine: this former advocate of liberating slaves inserted a clause in the treaty that compelled the British to hand over any slaves who had taken refuge with them, though the British had promised freedom to those refugees. Laurens inserted the clause at the very last minute—the working copy in the Foreign Office files shows the passage written above another line and linked with a caret—but he easily secured the approval of his fellow American negotiators and their British counterparts.

John Jay, one of the American treaty negotiators, later acknowledged: "By this agreement, Britain bound herself to do great wrong to these Slaves." But in his account of the negotiations, John Adams described the eleventh-hour maneuvering over the slaves approvingly: "Mr. Laurens said there ought to be a stipulation that the British troops carry off no negroes or other American property. We all agreed. . . . the article which he caused to be inserted at the very last . . . which would most probably in the multiplicity and hurry of affairs have escaped us, was worth a longer journey, if that had been all."[8]

The terms of this provisional treaty were published in New York City in March 1783; when the formal treaty was signed on September 3, 1783, the Laurens clause remained as written. The British officer responsible for enforcing the treaty during the evacuation from New York was General Sir Guy Carleton, a man with an exceptionally high sense of honor, whose "public character," one historian observes, "was very similar to that of the revered George Washington." And now Sir Guy and General Washington sparred, face-to-face, over the fate of the refugee slaves, including some of Washington's own.[9]

Instructed to treat the refugees with the most "honorable" care, General Carleton obeyed scrupulously. He issued a public order that the terms of the treaty be "STRICTLY attended to and COMPLIED with," and sent a request to Congress for observers to ensure American satisfaction. In addition to the official observers, however, slave owners and gangs of hired slave catchers came to New York to round up as many escaped slaves as they could find. To the rage of the slave catchers, Carleton decreed that he would evacuate people who had been in the British camp for at least a year; this group numbered thousands of former slaves. To the protests that he was stealing slaves guaranteed to their masters by the treaty, Carleton replied that the blacks were no longer slaves, since they had become free the moment they crossed into British lines. In his interpretation the treaty did not cover these refugees because they were no longer property. In his view, a series of British military commanders had made promises of freedom to any slaves who joined them, and Carleton was bound by honor to respect those promises.[10]

In April 1783 Carleton ordered his officials to begin issuing documents of protection to the blacks that, when displayed, compelled a slave catcher to give way or face arrest by British forces. After all, the city was still a British zone, under British military authority. One former slave recalled, "Each of us received a certificate . . . which dispelled all our fears, and filled us with joy and gratitude."

> This is to certify to all Concerned that the bearer hereof, a Negro, named _____, Aged ____, and formerly the property of _____, appears to have come within the British Lines, under the Sanction, and Claims the Privilege of the Proclamation respecting Negroes, heretofore issued for their Protection. . . .
>
> By order of the Commandant.[11]

Thirteen Virginia slave owners who traveled to New York to seize three hundred of their escaped people were told by a British officer that "no slaves were to be given up" who possessed a certificate. Two

Virginia slave owners appealed directly to General Washington to do something. Washington replied, "Several of my own are with the Enemy but I scarce ever bestowed a thought on them; they have so many doors through which they can escape from New York, that scarce any thing but an inclination to return . . . will restore many." Judging by this remark, he was at first resigned to losing the slaves who had reached British lines in New York—his own and those of other planters. But soon the Virginians pressured him into requesting a parley with Carleton at the American headquarters in Tappan, New York. Carleton sailed up the Hudson in the frigate *Perseverance* for the meeting on May 3, 1783.[12]

Washington apparently expected that a summit conference between the two top commanders would settle this nettlesome issue quickly and to the satisfaction of the planters. Speaking "without animation & in a low tone," he raised the issue of the "preservation of property . . . especially the Negroes." But his equanimity was broken when Carleton informed him that many of the blacks had already been embarked. A British observer noticed that "Mr. Washington appeared to be startled—already imbarked says he." Given the rank of his interlocutor, Washington could not indulge in any displays of temper, but he went on to "express his Surprize" that the treaty had been violated. To this, according to the eyewitness, "Sir Guy then observed, that no Interpretation could be put upon the Articles inconsistent with prior [promises] binding the National Honor which must be kept with all Colours." Carleton continued lecturing Washington on the subject of honor. Notwithstanding any clause in the treaty, Carleton declared, in his view the British government could not have meant to breach "their Faith to the Negroes who came into the British lines." Finally, he upbraided Washington for even suggesting that a crown official would consent to a "notorious breach of the public faith towards people of any complection"—an imputation that Carleton said he regarded as hostile. When Washington continued to protest, Carleton said that the slave owners could apply for compensation, but he would never hand over the people. Perhaps weary of debating the matter with Washington, the British general evaded another meeting the following day by claiming illness. Washington knew he was beaten. He wrote to one of the Virginians who had complained to him, "the Slaves which have absconded from their Masters will never be restored to them."[13]

On legal grounds, Washington may have been justified. Commenting privately on the negotiations, a New York judge (and loyalist), Thomas Jones, agreed with Washington that the Laurens clause in the treaty was binding, but on moral grounds he excoriated the British treaty negotiators who had yielded on this point and had "thought the sacrifice of 2,000 negroes . . . a mere bagatelle." He believed that Carleton had undone the negotiators' moral error and redeemed British honor. "Sir Guy . . . possessed the honour of a soldier, the religion of a Christian, and the virtues of humanity. . . . He shuddered at the article that gave up the blacks, and at once resolved to apply a substitute." The very highest authorities in Britain sided with Carleton. Lord North called Carleton's stand "an Act of Justice" that did not violate the treaty. King George III himself, "in the fullest and most ample Manner," expressed "His Royal Approbation."[14]

The documents suggest that British officers and officials were genuinely baffled by Washington's insistence on recovering the slaves in person rather than accepting cash compensation for them. The British did not grasp a fundamental point of plantation economics: the value of slaves lay not only in their productivity but in their fertility. Cash payments for lost laborers would not compensate the planters for the loss of future offspring. The planters were banking on the future generations. The historian Ellen Wilson, who has examined the British state papers on these negotiations, came across a torrid denunciation of the American commander. A memorandum stated that in the conference with Carleton, Washington had demanded the return of the slaves "with all the Grossness and Ferocity of a Captain of Banditti." The British could understand the American position that the slaves had been property, but they could not comprehend Washington's position that the slaves' value trumped the slaves' humanity.

The British actually feared that some slaves would kill themselves and their families rather than return to slavery.[15]*

As British troops departed American soil from Savannah, Charleston, and New York in 1783, some 13,000–14,000 blacks left with them. Not all were free. White loyalists who owned slaves were allowed to take their slaves with them, some British officers held slaves, and some American blacks who had joined the British for freedom were sold into slavery in the West Indies and East Florida. A small number of American blacks departed for Europe as free people with Hessian units in which they had served. Examining German military records, the historian Robert Selig found that "on the eve of departure for Europe, the Hessians discharged some two dozen black men who wanted to stay in America. About 30 soldiers plus an unknown number of officer servants not on regimental rosters, some with their wives and children, crossed the Atlantic for Cassel, where they arrived in late 1783."[16]

In some instances the free blacks were given the option of choosing their destination—England, Nova Scotia, Jamaica, or other destinations where a British ship might be able to take them (though free blacks who went to England later faced discrimination, unemployment, and poverty). Many chose to go to Africa. Whatever their destination, the freed people were desperate to leave rather than return to slavery and the mercies of their former owners. In Charleston, as time and available berths ran out, panic set in. When it became apparent that the evacuation of all refugees could not be completed by the time the last ships had to leave, the British posted troops on the wharves to beat back refugees with cutlasses and bayonets. The most desperate dove into the water and clung to the sides of departing British long-

---

* As president, Washington continued to press for the return of the slaves until 1790. In 1798 the United States and Britain agreed to financial compensation instead, but no final settlement was reached and the issued simmered until 1812, when the mere rumor of the possibility of war caused hopes to soar among some Virginia slaves for a return of the British. A group of slaves in the Virginia interior actually laid plans for an elaborate uprising to coincide with the expected British invasion.

boats. One eyewitness wrote, "to prevent this dangerous practice the fingers of some of them were chopped off."[17]

As the result of Carleton's resistance to Washington, the name of Washington and the spirit of the American Revolution reached Africa. One escaped slave who had taken refuge in New York was a certain Henry Washington from Mount Vernon. When Carleton's officials put him on the list for evacuation in the "Register of Negroes," he stated his age as forty-three and said that he had fled Mount Vernon in 1776, much earlier than 1781 with the slaves on the *Savage*. Under Carleton's policy Henry Washington took a British ship to Nova Scotia (as did two other former Mount Vernon slaves, a man and a woman) and from there continued to Sierra Leone, where he planned to begin a farm making use of the scientific farming techniques he had learned at Mount Vernon. In 1800 Washington was among several hundred settlers who rose up in a brief rebellion against white rule there. The precipitating issue was one familiar from the American Revolution: taxes. The settlers were required by the Sierra Leone Company, which ran the colony for the British government, to pay taxes, or quitrents, for the use of their land; the land itself remained the property of the company. The settlers formed a provisional government and wrote up a set of laws, which they nailed to the office door of a company administrator. The company responded by sending a corps of recently arrived Jamaican blacks against the rebels. In the trials that followed the defeat of the rebellion, Henry Washington was among the rebels sentenced to banishment to another location in Sierra Leone, where he became one of the two leaders of a new settlement.[18]

It became the honor of the Marquis de Lafayette to inform George Washington that a preliminary treaty of peace had been signed on January 20, 1783. Lafayette was in Cadiz, Spain, when news of the signing reached him. Overcome with joy (and apparently unaware of the Laurens clause), Lafayette arranged for the fastest French ship available, the aptly named *Triumph*, to carry the news to Congress, and particularly to George Washington. In his letter to Washington, dated February 5, he wrote, "I rejoice at the blessings of a peace where our noble ends have been secured." He recalled the travail they endured together at Valley Forge and said that he intended to revisit America in the near future.[19]

In Lafayette's mind, history had arrived at a peculiar, perhaps unique moment. Lafayette saw that the birth of American independence marked the birth of a new age in world history. He declared that the creation of the United States "has begun, for the civilized world, the era of a new and of the only true social order founded on the inalienable rights of man." He gave much of the credit to "our beloved matchless Washington." At that moment, historical planets were aligned but would not long remain so: in the same letter he proposed to begin emancipating America's slaves. He did not envision freeing all the slaves at once, which would be too ambitious an undertaking; rather, he envisioned a small start but one that would be powerfully symbolic and persuasive. He proposed to Washington that the general begin freeing *his* slaves.

> Now, my dear General, that you are going to enjoy some ease and quiet, permit me to propose a plan to you, which might become greatly beneficial to the black part of mankind. Let us unite in purchasing a small estate, where we may try the experiment to free the negroes, and use them only as tenants. *Such an example as yours might render it a general practice*; and if we succeed in America, I will cheerfully devote a part of my time to render the method fashionable in the West Indies. If it be a wild scheme, I had rather be mad this way, than to be thought wise in the other task. [Emphasis added]

Of all the officers who fought by Washington's side in the Revolution, Lafayette was probably the man closest to him. (Lafayette had personally underwritten the American war effort in the amount of some $1 million.) Washington always spoke of him with affection, and Lafayette regarded Washington with profound admiration. Their relationship was one of father and son. Twenty-five years older than

Lafayette, Washington was childless, and the Frenchman had lost his father when he was an adolescent. Lafayette alluded to this bond in a letter to Washington written during the French Revolution: "Give me leave, my dear General, to present you with a picture of the Bastille, just as it looked a few days after I ordered its demolition, with the main key of the fortress of despotism. It is a tribute which I owe as a son to my adoptive father—as an aide-de-camp to my general—as a missionary of liberty to its patriarch."[20]*

With his intimate emotional connection to Washington, Lafayette detected in his friend enough signs of doubt over slavery that he was able to propose the plan. He obviously thought that Washington would be amenable to the idea; he also might have thought that, left on his own, Washington might not embark on such a scheme at that time, but might proceed if a partner offered to share some of the expense. The offer suggests Lafayette's grasp of Washington's thinking, as the letter combines practicality, some slight flattery, and idealism. He proposed to help underwrite the emancipation by joining in the purchase of the necessary land. His allusion to Washington's unique status as an exemplar has the tone of flattery but was a statement of fact. And Lafayette defused any objection that such "a wild scheme" was doomed to failure by pledging his personal reputation: if people thought him mad because he strove to free slaves, so be it. Personal honor was an intangible but no less real asset: Lafayette was implicitly challenging potential detractors to assault his personal honor. He also seemed to be saying to his former commander: let us once more be comrades in idealism.

Lafayette never reconciled himself to the contradiction between American liberty and American slavery. He said, "I would never have drawn my sword in the cause of America, if I could have conceived that thereby I was founding a land of slavery." He wrote to John Adams: "In the cause of my black brethren, I feel myself warmly interested, and most decidedly side, so far as respects them, against the

---

* The key to the Bastille remains on display at Mount Vernon to this day, enclosed in a crystal case in the stair hall.

white part of mankind. Whatever be the complexion of the enslaved, it does not, in my opinion, alter the complexion of the crime which the enslaver commits—a crime much blacker than any African face." The very idea that slaves were still being transported on ships flying the American flag in 1786 appalled Lafayette, for whom the symbols of freedom had profound resonance: "It is to me a matter of great anxiety and concern, to find that this trade is sometimes perpetrated under the flag of liberty, our dear and noble stripes, to which virtue and glory have been constant standard-bearers."[21]

During Lafayette's famous tour of America in 1824, the city of Savannah banned all blacks from attending the parades in the visitor's honor, but Lafayette made a point of paying a public call on a slave who had served in the Revolution. In New Orleans he met with a group of black veterans and greeted each of them personally. He said to them, "I have often during the War of Independence seen African blood shed with honor in our ranks for the cause of the United States."[22]

Very tentatively, and very vaguely, Washington accepted Lafayette's suggestion for an emancipation—at least he seemed to agree to consider it—but he put off any immediate action. He wrote in April 1783:

> The scheme, my dear Marqs. which you propose as a precedent, to encourage the emancipation of the black people of this Country from that state of Bondage in wch. they are held, is a striking evidence of the benevolence of your Heart. I shall be happy to join you in so laudable a work; but will defer going into a detail of the business, 'till I have the pleasure of seeing you.[23]

The following year, 1784, Lafayette visited Mount Vernon, where he and Washington continued their discussion about the experiment. As a houseguest present at the time recalled the conversation: "[Washington] wished to get rid of [his] Negroes, & the Marquis wisht that an end might be put to the slavery of all of them." But despite his desire to be "rid of" his slaves, Washington was not yet ready to take steps to liberate them. Lafayette, however, actually purchased a plantation in Cayenne, on the coast of French Guiana, to begin his experiment of gradually preparing slaves for emancipation. About a year after the conversation at Mount Vernon, he told his lawyer to buy land there, with the provision that the seller must not "sell or exchange any black" living on the land. Perhaps hoping to prod his reluctant friend into action, Lafayette wrote to Washington several months later to advise him that he was embarking on his emancipation plan: "I Have purchased for Hundred and twenty-five thousand French livres a plantation in the Colony of Cayenne and am going to free my Negroes in order to make that Experiment which you know is My Hobby Horse."[24]

Washington was effusive in his praise for Lafayette's endeavor but evaded taking action himself. He wrote from Mount Vernon in May 1786:

> The benevolence of your heart . . . is so conspicuous upon all occasions, that I never wonder at any fresh proofs of it; but your late purchase of an estate in the colony of Cayenne, with a view of emancipating the slaves on it, is a generous and noble proof of your humanity. Would to God a like Spirit would diffuse itself generally into the minds of the people of this country; but I despair of seeing it. Some petitions were presented to the Assembly, at its last Session, for the abolition of slavery, but they could scarcely obtain a reading. To set them afloat at once would, I really believe, be productive of much inconvenience and mischief; but by degrees it certainly might, and assuredly ought to be effected; and that too by Legislative authority.[25]

Lafayette never sent Washington a detailed account of what happened at the Cayenne plantation, La Belle Gabrielle, but if he had, the general would have seen that Lafayette's plan took into account his reservations about setting slaves "afloat" without adequate preparation. Lafayette agreed that people who had been enslaved and freed abruptly could not be expected to function successfully. The blacks at Cayenne were not freed immediately but were paid for their work and given some education. The experiment lasted only a few years—when Lafayette was imprisoned in 1792 by the Austrians, his property was confiscated and sold by the French Revolutionary government.[26]

The retirement Washington so deeply yearned for did not last long. By 1786 the new United States was in a crisis over the weakness of the federal government as established under the Articles of Confederation agreed to in November 1777 and ratified in 1781. While the Revolutionary War was still going on, Jefferson had worried about the future stability of the United States, writing in 1781, "from the conclusion of this war we shall be going down hill." Two years later he feared that conflicts among the states could invite foreign intervention, writing to Edmund Randolph, "I know no danger so dreadful and so probable as that of internal contests. . . . The states will go to war with each other in defiance of Congress; one will call in France to her assistance and another Gr. Britain, and so we shall have all the wars of Europe brought to our own doors." In fact Europe stood at the American door: British troops remained in the United States in defiance of the Treaty of Paris and Spain continued to control the Mississippi. Abroad the new nation was humiliated when Barbary pirates kidnapped thousands of Americans and held them for ransom. Washington said that America's weakness had made it a laughingstock: "What a triumph for the advocates of despotism to find that we are incapable of governing ourselves, and that systems founded on the basis of equal liberty are merely ideal and fallacious!"[27]

Washington was among those who believed that only a radical restructuring of government could save the Revolution from failure, that a strong central government was essential. "Things cannot go on in the same train forever," he remarked. There were dangers from all levels of society. He took note that "respectable characters speak of a monarchical form of government without horror," but he was equally concerned when a group of impoverished Massachusetts farmers, under the leadership of the veteran soldier Daniel Shays, rose up in armed protest against taxes. To Washington it seemed "we are fast verging to anarchy and confusion." He was elected to lead the Virginia delegation to a convention in Philadelphia to revise the Articles. On the day of his departure from Mount Vernon in May 1787 he suffered a sudden, racking headache, which one biographer, John Ferling, takes as a sign of "a severe case of raw nerves."[28]

Washington's arrival in Philadelphia on May 14 was triumphal. "Yesterday His Excellency General WASHINGTON arrived here," reported the *Pennsylvania Packet*. "He was met at some distance and escorted into the city by the troops of horse, and saluted at his entrance by the artillery. The joy of the people on the coming of this great and good man was shown by their acclamation and the ringing of bells."[29]

Washington was elected to preside over the convention, occupying, both literally and figuratively, an august position. The historian Max Farrand describes Washington as almost a godlike figure:

> He sat on a raised platform; in a large, carved, high-backed chair, from which his commanding figure and dignified bearing exerted a potent influence on the assembly; an influence enhanced by the formal courtesy and stately intercourse of the times. Washington was the great man of his day and the members not only respected and admired him; some of them were actually afraid of him. When he rose to his feet he was almost the Commander-in-Chief again. There is evidence to show that his support or disapproval was at times a decisive factor in the deliberations of the Convention.[30]

As president of the convention Washington was not allowed to take part in the debates, which were recorded by James Madison. His influence on the constitutional provisions that emerged can only be a matter of speculation. In describing the general's view of the convention, Ferling notes his pragmatic mode of thinking about politics:

Washington always thought of political activists in terms of the interests they represented, and his correspondence is studded with references to the "financial interest," the "mercantile interests," the "local interest," the "interested views of desperate characters," the "minor part," and the "better kind of people." . . . With such an outlook he would have had far less difficulty than have some historians in seeing this Convention as an assemblage of various interest groups intent on altering the national charter in such a way as to protect and further their own factional considerations.

But there was one striking challenge to a total focus on "interests"; it came during the debate on slavery.[31]

The question of allowing the continued importation of slaves immediately brought the moral and ethical underpinnings of the slave system into the light. Luther Martin of Maryland declared that the importation of slaves "was inconsistent with the principles of the Revolution, and dishonorable to the American character." John Rutledge of South Carolina replied, "Religion and humanity had nothing to do with this question. Interest alone is the governing principle with nations. The true question at present is whether the Southern states shall or shall not be parties to the Union." It was in the financial interest of the Northern states to allow an increase in Southern slaves, he pointed out: "If the Northern states consult their interest, they will not oppose the increase of slaves, which will increase the commodities of which they will become the carriers."[32]

Oliver Ellsworth of Connecticut agreed: "Let every state import what it pleases. The morality or wisdom of slavery are considerations belonging to the states themselves. What enriches a part enriches the whole, and the states are the best judges of their particular interest." Charles Cotesworth Pinckney of South Carolina repeated his colleague's threat that his state would never accept the Constitution if it prohibited the slave trade, because "South Carolina and Georgia cannot do without slaves." He raised the possibility that, someday, "South Carolina may perhaps, by degrees," eliminate the slave trade. This prospect appealed to Roger Sherman of Connecticut, who observed "that the abolition of slavery seemed to be going on in the United States, and that the good sense of the several states would probably by degrees complete it." He thought the slave trade should be left alone. His Connecticut colleague Ellsworth agreed: "Let us not intermeddle." He, too, believed that slavery was waning anyway, and predicted, "As population increases, poor laborers will be so plenty as to render slaves useless. Slavery, in time, will not be a speck in our country."[33]

Pinckney rose to clarify his earlier remark that South Carolina might someday cease to import slaves. He "thought himself bound to declare candidly, that he did not think South Carolina would stop her importations of slaves, in any short time; but only stop them occasionally." And Rutledge bluntly threatened, "If the Convention thinks that North Carolina, South Carolina, and Georgia, will ever agree to the plan, unless their right to import slaves be untouched, the expectation is vain. The people of those States will never be such fools, as to give up so important an interest."

The southernmost states, South Carolina and Georgia, remained intransigent because their markets had the greatest appetite for the slave trade. Philip Morgan writes: "Virginia had been weaning itself gradually of African supplies in the last years of the colonial era. The process was essentially complete by the onset of the Revolution. Suffering no great wartime loss of black labor, Virginia never again imported Africans. In South Carolina, by contrast, the Revolution interrupted a veritable orgy of African slave-trading." He cites the observation of a Georgian in 1784, the "Negro business . . . is to the Trade of this Country, as the Soul to the Body."[34]

Pennsylvania delegate Gouverneur Morris observed that a compromise was needed if the Southern states would not yield on slavery: "These things may form a bargain among the Northern and Southern States." Despite their protestations about the immorality of slavery, New Englanders were happy to compromise on the issue. Joseph Ellis writes that a "secret deal" broke the deadlock over slavery: "The bargain entailed an exchange of votes whereby New England agreed to back an extension of the slave trade for twenty years in return for support from the Deep South for making the federal regulation of commerce a mere majority vote in the Congress rather than a super-majority of two-thirds." The Washington scholar Dorothy Twohig enumerates the concessions extracted by the slave states in exchange for their support of the Constitution:

> The three-fifths clause gave them extra representation in Con-gress, the electoral college gave their votes for president more po-tency than the votes from the north, the prohibition on export taxes favored the products of slave labor; the slave trade clause guaranteed their right to import new slaves for at least twenty years; the fugitive slave clause gave slave owners the right to repossess runaway slaves in free states; in the event of a slave rebellion the domestic violence clause promised the states federal aid.[35]

So a bargain was struck. The slave trade was allowed to continue, and the word "slavery" was never mentioned in the Constitution. The delegates genuinely feared that disagreements over slavery and other issues would cause the states, as Ellsworth remarked, to "fly into a va-riety of shapes and directions, and most probably into several confed-erations, —and not without bloodshed." They handed the problem to the future. Interestingly, those with the least direct experience of slav-ery were the ones who clung to the hope, or illusion, that the institu-tion was waning. The Southerners knew they would never give it up.[36]

In the midst of the debate, in a moment of uncanny prescience, one of the Virginians predicted that bloodshed was not being avoided but merely delayed. Washington's friend and neighbor George Mason de-nounced "this infernal traffic" and derided the idea that slavery was dying by degrees: "The Western people are already calling out for slaves for their new lands, and will fill that country with slaves, if they can be got through South Carolina and Georgia." He tallied the evils slavery brought on a country: "Slavery discourages arts and manufac-tures. The poor despise labor when performed by slaves. They prevent the immigration of whites, who really enrich and strengthen a coun-try. They produce the most pernicious effect on manners. Every mas-ter of slaves is born a petty tyrant." In tones of thunder, he voiced a prediction that Washington himself was to make years later, though not so forcefully. Slaves "bring the judgment of Heaven on a country," Mason warned. "As nations cannot be rewarded or punished in the next world, they must be in this. By an inevitable chain of causes and effects, Providence punishes national sins by national calamities."[37]

Throughout this debate Washington sat listening wrapped in his *ex officio* silence. When delegates denounced the immorality of slavery, he heard echoes of the points Lafayette had already raised with him directly in their correspondence the previous year. If he really had expected that Lafayette's benevolent spirit might "diffuse itself generally into the minds of the people of this country," the debate crushed that hope, along with the dream that an emancipation "by degrees" might be effected "by Legislative authority." What Washington really thought or felt about the debates cannot be clearly known, but in his letter to Lafayette a year earlier he had expressed how his thinking on the subject of leadership was evolving. Forward-thinking individuals had to wait for the thinking of the people to catch up to theirs; otherwise a democratic government could not succeed. At the same time, the forward-thinker had to be prepared to suffer for his ideals. The implication is that Washington was not prepared just yet to suffer in the cause of emancipation:

> It is one of the evils of democratical governments that the people, not always seeing & frequently mislead, must often feel before they can act right—but then evils of this nature seldom fail to work their own cure. It is to be lamented, nevertheless, that the remedies are so slow, & that those, who may wish to apply them seasonably are not attended to before they suffer in person, in interest & in reputation.[38]

The preeminent issue was the preservation of the union. In a letter two years before the convention Washington declared, "I confess to you candidly that I can foresee no evil greater than disunion." He could see that mere discussion of slavery tended to divide the new nation dangerously. He saw the apparent intransigence of South Carolina and Georgia. With his personal knowledge of slavery and slaveholders, it is doubtful that he shared the impression that slavery was withering away.[39]

Fritz Hirschfeld writes, "Whatever Washington may have thought of the slavery issues being debated and decided at the federal convention, it is interesting to note that the proslavery views that found their way into the Constitution were (coincidentally or not) those most compatible with Washington's own values and beliefs." And he cites the interpretation of the historian John Hope Franklin: "The fathers of the Constitution were dedicated to the proposition that 'government should rest upon the dominion of property.' For the Southern fathers this meant slaves."[40]

Washington set his seal on the bargains in the Constitution in his official "Letter of the President of the Federal Convention" to the president of Congress, transmitting the Constitution. He stated that the single most important objective was guaranteeing the continuation of the Union: "In all our deliberations on this subject we kept steadily in our view, that which appears to us the greatest interest of every true American, the consolidation of our Union, in which is involved our prosperity, felicity, safety, perhaps our national existence." He acknowledged that this focus led to compromises: "This important consideration, seriously and deeply impressed on our minds, led each state in the Convention to be less rigid on points of inferior magnitude, than might have been otherwise expected." The Constitution was, he said, "the result of a spirit of amity, and of that mutual deference and concession" which might not meet "the full and entire approbation of every state." The Constitution enshrined slavery.[41]

Another critical moment in history had passed. The founders who believed that slavery would wither away were wrong. The compromise on slavery has made the American endeavor vulnerable to the charge of moral blindness, and to the charge that the United States was corrupt at its creation. The historian Joseph Ellis sums up the frustration of modern scholars who study the Constitutional debates, saying that slavery was "the tragic and perhaps intractable problem that even the revolutionary generation, with all its extraordinary talent, could neither solve nor face." Among Americans today there is probably a consensus that it is futile to criticize the founders at this distance in time for acting as they did: the political system was at an impasse over slavery; economic interests and racial prejudice precluded even a gradual emancipation plan. Certainly there were dissenters, such as the Quakers, but they were in the minority. The greatness of the Constitution, created in "the miracle at Philadelphia" (a paraphrase of Washington's words), overshadows its weakness on this issue, despite the horrific consequences for ensuing generations of enslaved people and for the country as a whole.[42]

The compromise over slavery implicitly contained a moral judgment: if the founders, including Washington, were able to agree on such a compromise, then to them slavery was morally acceptable. Nineteen slave owners attended the Constitutional Convention. Knowing full well the cruelties of slavery, they insisted on preserving it, and Washington acquiesced. Jefferson said of Washington: "His integrity was most pure, his justice the most inflexible I have ever known, no motives of interest or consanguinity, of friendship or hatred, being able to bias his decision. He was indeed, in every sense of the word, a wise, a good and a great man." When Washington set his seal on the bargain over slavery, he could not but have had in mind the system he himself imposed at Mount Vernon and his own lifelong experience as a master.[43]

And so, it seemed, the issue of slavery was settled and the course of our history set. But not long after Washington put his seal on the Constitution and its great compromise, his own spirit of "deference and concession" began to crack. He began to speak, in private, of his "regret" over slavery. But, more important, Washington seems to have believed he had found a way around the political impasse over slavery. As Lafayette had proposed to him, his example, his prestige, could be the sword that cut the Gordian knot. He laid a plan, in secret, to free his slaves.

Having presided over the framing of the Constitution, Washington returned to Mount Vernon, deeply yearning for permanent retirement from public life. But soon, inevitably, a clamor arose for him to become the first president of the newly constituted nation. The office, after all, had been tailored for him specifically. As Pierce Butler of South Carolina said, the delegates at the Constitutional Convention had "cast their eyes toward General Washington as President and shaped their ideas of the powers to be given to a President, by their opinions of his virtue."[44]

Washington's close friend, former comrade in arms, and biographer, David Humphreys, was at Mount Vernon in late 1788 and early 1789. Humphreys recorded their intimate conversations as the general agonized over the decision to accept or reject the presidency. His notebook contains a startling statement of Washington's:

> The unfortunate condition of the persons, whose labour in part I employed, has been the only unavoidable subject of regret. To make the Adults among them as easy & as comfortable in their circumstances as their actual state of ignorance & improvidence would admit; & to lay a foundation to prepare the rising generation for a destiny different from that in which they were born; afforded some satisfaction to my mind, & could not I hoped be displeasing to the justice of the Creator.[45]

The more I studied these remarks the more curious they became. The statement bears a striking resemblance to the emancipation clause in Washington's will written ten years later, alluding to care for the elderly (the "Adults") and to training or education for slave children. But more curiously, the passage is written in the past tense, describing thoughts or actions that had already taken place. In broad outline, the Humphreys statement sounds like comments on an emancipation that had already occurred. But Washington in 1789 was not training children and certainly none of his slaves were "comfortable in their circumstances." It seemed to make no sense until I examined a photocopy of Humphreys's original notebook. This fragment was composed amid public statements Humphreys was drafting for Washington prior to his assuming the presidency. Indeed, a draft of Washington's acceptance of the presidency appears just a few pages before the remark on slavery. Very likely, this passage about slavery was not just a private expression of regret, but the draft of a public statement in which Washington intended to announce that he had freed some of his slaves before taking office.[46]

The effect of such an act would have been profound. As the first president, Washington was well aware that his every public act set a precedent. (He later remarked in a private letter, "The eyes of Argus are upon me.") If Washington had done such a thing, it would have established the precedent that a slaveholding chief executive would emancipate his slaves before taking office. This way of approaching the issue bypassed the political process altogether; after all, the nation had just ratified a Constitution that approved slavery, so what hope was there for an emancipation bill? Washington would do what Lafayette had urged—lead the country by personal example.

As vague as the statement was, I thought I could detect in it some of Washington's specific intentions. He said he had made the "Adults . . . easy & . . . comfortable." Certainly, he could not have been referring to people of working age but only to the elderly, those past labor. The old slaves would remain at Mount Vernon, supported by Washington—but they would be free, so presumably they could leave if they wished. The children would become free upon reaching their majority, after they had received some rudimentary education and training. The working adults would remain slaves; they would not be cast loose to fend for themselves. But when they reached the end of their working lives they would be freed. This scheme eliminated the most obvious objection to emancipation—that the slaves were not ready for such a step—and it was astonishingly similar to the plan Washington wrote out in detail in his will ten years later.

As I first considered this interpretation, it seemed somewhat far-fetched. Perhaps, I thought, I was reading too much into this document. Washington could not possibly have considered such a radical step in 1789. But then I came across *yet another* emancipation that Washington planned while he was actually in office. In 1794 he wrote to his private secretary, Tobias Lear, asking him to look for a buyer for his land in western Virginia. He told Lear that he wished to consolidate his farming operations, but in a passage of the letter that Washington marked *Private,* he declared: "I have another motive which makes me earnestly wish for the accomplishment of these things, it is indeed more powerful than all the rest. namely to liberate a certain species of property which I possess, very repugnantly to my own feelings."[47]

This is the same man who had blithely written, during the Revolution, "The advantages resulting from the sale of my negroes, I have very little doubt of; . . . the only points therefore for me to consider, are . . . the sum they will now fetch and the interest of the money." Fifteen years later Washington had changed utterly. He was now planning to yield up his most valuable remaining asset, his western lands, the wherewithal for his retirement, to finance the emancipation of his Mount Vernon slaves. This was the thinking not of a benevolent master but of a man sickened by slavery, willing to sacrifice his own substance to end it. And he was going to do it publicly, as a sitting president. Slavery was incompatible with holding the highest office. He could see *a different destiny.* With that phrase Washington overturned a pillar of the slave system: the belief that blacks were destined by nature and by law to be slaves for life, and their children likewise, and their children's children. There is a vision in that statement, an understanding that the generation that would see freedom was already alive.[48]

Washington's plan contradicted one of the most important conditions for emancipation he had laid down to Lafayette a few years earlier, that it be effected "by Legislative authority." He had now given up waiting for a general emancipation by legislative authority and was prepared to begin freeing his own people. Another striking, mysterious aspect of the Lear letter was that Washington kept it secret. At his instruction, the private portion of the letter was omitted from the official record of his correspondence, and survives only in the original of the letter.

During the Revolution Washington had witnessed the heroism and patriotism of the black troops, yet this had not been enough to persuade him to begin freeing his slaves. There was no evidence in the following decade of a sudden and massive improvement in the character of the slaves that would have convinced Washington that they were "ready." In fact he told David Humphreys that his slaves were ignorant and improvident. Nor is there evidence for a sudden and unusual deterioration in the slaves' condition or the atmosphere of slavery itself at that time. Washington's stated reason for wishing to free his slaves in 1794 was not a sudden belief in their readiness for freedom or the urgency of it, but his conviction that slavery was "repugnant." What, then, suddenly made slavery so repugnant to him?

I had begun my research on Washington with a fundamental error. I had assumed that his decision to free his slaves had come rather abruptly in the last months of his life, out of a sense of remorse that gripped him as he approached death. But his remark about slavery to Humphreys, and the plan he outlined to Lear to sell his land to finance an emancipation, showed that he had already decided upon an emancipation as early as 1789, ten years before his death. He had experienced a moral epiphany. The hallmark of his plans for emancipation was that they were drawn up in secret, even the final one in his last will. He kept his ideas secret most of all from his own family. The only explanation for this secrecy is that he knew they would oppose him if they found out what he was doing before he could actually carry out his plans. His isolation was complete.

Washington might have believed that the United States would begin to do away with slavery in 1808, when Article 1, Section 9 of the Constitution called for an end to the importation of slaves. That clause, part of the great compromise over slavery, was challenged in the first session of Congress, during Washington's first term as president. In February 1790 a Quaker group presented petitions, soon endorsed by Benjamin Franklin, that Congress consider an immediate end to the importation of slaves and debate ways of beginning a gradual emancipation. The petitions reopened the whole question of slavery, which the South had considered closed until 1808. In his superb account of the ensuing uproar in *Founding Brothers,* Joseph Ellis demonstrates how "virtually every argument that southern defenders of slavery would mount during the next seventy years of the national controversy, right up to the eve of the Civil War, came gushing forth" during this debate. (Ellis might have added that these arguments continue to echo right up to *this* day.) The Southerners proclaimed that slavery was "a necessary evil," that they could not till their fields without slaves—"rice cannot be brought to market without these people." One asked, "What is to be done with the slaves when freed?" and cited Jefferson's remark that "deep rooted prejudices" would forever prevent whites and blacks from getting along peacefully—evidence that *Notes on the State of Virginia* had already become a philosophical pillar of the proslavery platform. Another asked if the Quakers would mind "giving their daughters to negro sons, and receiving the negro daughters for their sons."[49]

The Quaker petitions backfired. Rather than vote upon some loosening of slavery's hold on the country, Congress tightened it. Led by James Madison, the House of Representatives passed a resolution that enlarged the protection offered to slavery. The Constitution had protected the slave trade until 1808; the resolution stated that "The Congress have no authority to interfere in the emancipation of slaves, or in the treatment of them within any of the States." Madison himself said it was unconstitutional "to attempt to manumit them at any time." Slavery was, apparently, made permanent.[50]

The only recorded comments made by the President during the debate were private ones in letters to a Custis in-law, Dr. David Stuart. On March 28 he wrote, "The memorial of the Quakers (and a very mal-apropos one it was) has at length been put to sleep, and will scarcely awake before the year 1808." He followed this with another remark in June: "The introductions of the Memorial respecting Slavery, was to be sure, not only an illjudged piece of business, but occasioned a great waste of time. The final decision thereon, however, was as favourable as the proprietors of that species of property could have expected considering the great dereliction to Slavery in a large part of this Union." These comments show that Washington felt the need to prevaricate when speaking to his relatives on the subject of slavery. He did not say that the Quakers were wrong, but only that their approach was ill-timed. Their attempt had confirmed what he already suspected, that a legislative plan for an emancipation was a political impossibility. And yet Washington had already told Humphreys of his regret over slavery, and the plan that he outlined to Lear indicates that the obstacles to emancipation raised by other Southerners did not seem insuperable to him at all.[51]

He had a solution to the labor problem and the problem of what to do with the slaves once they were free: free them, then hire them right back. Before Washington wrote to Lear about his intention to free his slaves, he wrote to an Englishman, Arthur Young, asking his help in finding English farmers willing to emigrate to Virginia and rent Washington's farms. There was an ample supply of workers, he said. "Many of the Negroes, male and female, might be hired by the year as labourers."[52]

Washington was thinking about the various feasibilities for emancipation outside the political process while it became ever clearer that waiting for a political solution was hopeless. His peers, indeed his own family, were driven wild by the mere suggestion of the slaves' emancipation. His seemingly dismissive remarks about the Quakers were calculated to soothe the wrath of his relative, David Stuart, who wrote two letters to Washington bellowing about the damage Congress was doing simply by debating the issue. His letters show the intensity of the pressure Washington was under from his fellow Virginians and from his own family. The Stuart letters also show that the Southern defense of slavery in the Congressional debate was a tissue of rationalizations. His complaints to the president did not mention either loss of labor or racial mixing. Washington's peers in Virginia had a substantial investment in slaves, and Stuart was enraged that the debate was driving down market prices for them.

> The late transactions of Congress have soured the Publick mind to a great degree. . . . With respect to the slave business, I am informed . . . that great advantage has been taken of it . . . by many who wished to purchase slaves [by] circulating a report that Congress were about to pass an act for their general emancipation. This occasioned such an alarm that many were sold for the merest trifle. That

the sellers were of course much enraged at Congress taking up a sub-ject which they were precluded by the Constitution from meddling with for the present, and thus [causing] the alarm [that] induced them to sell. As the people in that part of the country were before much opposed to the Government it may naturally be supposed that this circumstance has embittered them much more against it.[53]

The South had monetized slaves; they were portable wealth. As the inheritor of slaves, Washington knew this—he knew it when he raf-fled slaves to collect a debt in 1769 and when he wrote of "The advan-tages . . . from the sale of my negroes" in 1779—but the scale of the transactions was growing larger. He made a well-known statement in 1794 against the sale of slaves as if they were animals, a statement that has been taken as a sign of Washington's high-mindedness. In fact it was an angry blast at a relative who had blithely asked his advice on the slaves' market value. The relative, Alexander Spotswood, was planning to move his family from Virginia to Kentucky, and he asked Washington airily, "Would you advise carrying many negroes? . . . I think in that country they must be of much value, and will increase fast." Washington replied to his kinsman, with restraint, that he had no idea "what you can sell for here, and buy at there." But later in the letter he let his anger come through: "I am principled agt. selling ne-gros, as you would do cattle in the market."[54]

David Humphreys said of Washington, "He loved truth, he sought it unceasingly & he endeavoured to regulate all his actions by that standard." In the last decade of his life Washington grasped some truth about slavery that was eluding everyone around him. Slavery had evolved into a system that his sense of justice could no longer tol-erate. For all its superficial benevolence, the slave regime cloaked crimes that Washington could no longer stomach. The transcripts of public debates contain only part of the truth of Washington's struggle with slavery. The rest, perhaps the most important part, played out in private, in secret, among families.[55]

CHAPTER EIGHT

"A Sort of Shadowy Life"

*S*OMETIME IN THE 1920S, the eminent Richmond newspaper editor Virginius Dabney came across a gravestone that inspired him to write about a shadowy, little-understood aspect of Southern life.[1] As a Virginian with very deep roots in the Old Dominion (witness his name), Dabney was well equipped to address the mystery posed by the marker about the peculiar nature of the emotional ties on old plantations:

> There was, in fact, in many instances a feeling of profound attachment between master and slave in the Old South, a feeling which transcended racial barriers and frequently lasted until death intervened. This is beautifully exemplified in the following inscription, placed over the grave of a faithful Negro by the southern family he had served:

> JOHN:
> A FAITHFUL SERVANT
> AND TRUE FRIEND:
> KINDLY AND CONSIDERATE:
> LOYAL AND AFFECTIONATE:
> THE FAMILY HE SERVED
> HONORS HIM IN DEATH:
> BUT IN LIFE, THEY GAVE HIM LOVE:
> FOR HE WAS ONE OF THEM

Dabney addressed the question raised by the last line of the epitaph, which fairly quivers with ambiguity. What could the masters have meant by that oblique statement that this slave "was one of them"? Did it mean only that they loved him as if he were a brother despite his color and status? Or did they intend this perpetual token of their esteem to be taken literally?

In the Old South the family was the unit about which much of the life of the section revolved. Since most planters lived in comparative isolation, often miles from the nearest habitation and usually a great distance from anything remotely resembling a city, the family circle occupied a place which it could not have occupied under different conditions.

In summer the head of the household and his wife and children whiled away many a long hour together on the verandah or under the trees which almost invariably surrounded the home, while during the winter months they gathered in close communion about the family fireside. Unfortunately, however, this idyllic picture was in many instances seriously marred by the fact that while the planter was rearing a large brood of children in the "big house," he was rearing another brood of mulattoes in the slave quarters.

Northern abolitionists frequently adverted to the clandestine relationships on Southern plantations between white men and black women. If these relationships were not as widespread as unfriendly critics contended, there was a firmer basis for charges of miscegenation than for the accusations of cruelty which were hurled at the heads of the planters. . . .

It was astonishing for the editor of the *Richmond Times-Dispatch* to put such an acknowledgment into print. The example he chose, a mute gravestone, spoke eloquently of the evasions slavery compelled. This white family buried a brother who had been their slave, their "faithful servant." In life they had all enacted a masquerade, but death required, at last, some truth. In a region that publicly proclaimed strict boundaries between races, very, very few plantation families admitted that in fact they lived along a misty borderland of races. By necessity, plantation masters and mistresses became geniuses at the art of concealment. Slavery abrogated humane customs and compelled varieties of relationships and emotions that we can only guess at. Many things could not be spoken of—secret children, ambiguous legacies, shadow families. The history of slavery is in large part the history of families; and the recovery of that history has become today, most powerfully, the work of white and black families trying to piece together their history and understand themselves.

The Southern diarist Mary Chesnut composed a famous cry of anguish over the ubiquity of the sexual exploitation of slave women and over the fabric of lies that cloaked it:

> God forgive us, but ours is a monstrous system, a wrong and iniquity. Like the patriarchs of old, our men live all in one house with their wives and their concubines; and the mulattoes one sees in every family partly resemble the white children. Any lady is ready to tell you who is the father of all the mulatto children in everybody's household but her own. Those, she seems to think, drop from the clouds. . . . A magnate who runs a hideous black harem with its consequences under the same roof with his lovely white wife, and his beautiful and accomplished daughters? He holds his head as high and poses as a model of all human virtues to these poor women whom God and laws have given him.[2]

Letters from a Virginia plantation in the 1840s reveal the anguish such liaisons caused within a household and the secrecy with which they were cloaked. Mary B. Carter, mistress of Shirley Plantation, wrote to her minister asking if she should sell a slave woman for committing adultery. In response, the Reverend Okeson wrote: "By the permission of God slavery exists. . . . He chose that you should be born in Virginia—that you should grow up under the peculiar influences of slavery . . . *be what you are*; . . . *suffer* and *do* whatever may be peculiar to your position. In all these things it is your duty . . . to cheerfully acquiesce in the will of God." The minister admitted that as the mistress of slaves she had *"peculiar trials* as well as *peculiar privileges,"* but it was her job to advance *"the salvation* of the *souls of your negroes."* It was thus her duty to keep the offending slave woman on the plantation. Mrs. Carter mulled over this dogmatic declaration, but her suffering was so great that she wrote to the minister again, seeking further advice and, in the process, revealed the identity of the man with whom the slave was committing adultery. Accepting the dictate that she could not banish the woman, she had another question: Could she then divorce her husband? The minister wrote back that she most certainly could not.[3]

An atmosphere of denial still lingers over racial mingling because white plantation families hardly ever wrote down anything that explicitly admitted to such indiscretions by their own men. In the absence of clear documentation, and in the silence that settled over the subject with the passage of time, later generations of white families could plausibly deny that their forebears had indulged in such activities.

Washington's biographers, by and large uninterested in slavery, never bothered to look very deeply for any suggestion that their subject had any relationship with slaves beyond ownership; but Washington did have kin among the slaves (it would be unusual if he hadn't). Martha's half sister, Ann Dandridge, lived at Mount Vernon. Exactly what Ann did at the mansion is not known, but she probably joined the circle of seamstresses that sat in the parlor with the mistress every day, fashioning shirts and mittens and anything else the household needed. Martha's sewing circle was described by a visitor, who limned an atmosphere of tranquil yet industrious domesticity: "Then we repaired to the old lady's room, which is . . . nicely fixed for all sorts of work—on one side sits the chamber maid with her knitting[,] on the other a little colored pet, learning to sew, an old, decent woman with her table and shears cutting out the negroes winter clothes, while the good old lady directs them all, incessantly knitting herself."[4] Despite the condescension in the phrase "little colored pet," the account captures the snugness of domestic life at Mount Vernon, the intimate bonds between the mistress and the house servants. It also captures the sense of slavery's eternity, the perpetuation of servitude over the generations. On one side Martha has "an old, decent woman" cutting out cloth; at her other side a "little colored pet." The one was probably grandmother to the other. The mother of the pet could probably have been found in the kitchen.

The family knew who Ann Dandridge was, but to visitors she was just another mixed-race attendant, the special favorite of the mistress, a "child of the plantation" brought from the old Dandridge place. Maintaining slavery generation after generation meant keeping up these fictions. In this manner slavery absorbed its moral transgressions, kept them secret, and made them part of the outwardly charming fabric of the plantation scene. But that is the system Washington wished to uproot. Sustaining the system, with its veneer of gentility and benevolence, meant maintaining the conditions under which "opulent" gentlemen, exercising their traditional habit of command, might continue to father children with the servant women. And that is what happened to Ann Dandridge.

The correspondence files at Mount Vernon bulge with letters from people whose family lore maintains that they have some connection to Washington: my great-great-grandfather was his aide-de-camp, or a pallbearer at his funeral; Washington was godfather to my grandmother's grandmother; and so on. The connection is often tangential, but any link to the great man is precious. The letters are often full of confidence. They state the facts with certainty and seek only a stamp of authenticity from the Mount Vernon experts. It is the task of Mount Vernon's staff patiently to review the evidence. They take these queries seriously, partly out of respect for the average citizen's reverence for Washington, and partly because they know that important new information can emerge from the most unlikely sources.[5]

A very common query involves a hallowed family heirloom, passed down for generations. The sword/pistol/lock of hair was positively identified by great-grandfather as having been owned or at least touched by George or Martha Washington, and then given to the family. Sometimes the letter writer insists that the item had actually been used by the Washingtons at Mount Vernon. In nearly every case a curator writes back to say that at some point in the past a mistake was made, that the object in question could not possibly have come from Mount Vernon.

In going through old correspondence files I came across a letter of this sort from a woman in California. I quickly skimmed it and put it aside, but on second thought I went back and looked more closely. The letter came from a woman named Marcia Carter in 1981: "I have in my possession a China tea set, Williamsburg design, taken from Mt. Vernon in 1802 to Washington, D.C. The persons who took the tea set were forebears on my father's side. . . . My mother, who is deceased, left me the information on all the antiques I've acquired."[6] Mrs. Carter enclosed a snapshot of a four-piece porcelain set with a handwritten description. The file no longer contained the snapshot, which had apparently been returned to Mrs. Carter without being copied; but the description was there: "China Tea Set—175 years old as of 1977. Williamsburg design—Old English—brought by William Custis Costin & wife, Philadelphia Judge to Washington, D.C. immediately after the death of Martha Dandridge Custis Washington, in 1802, from Mt. Vernon, Virginia."

This letter echoed the tone and substance of many others: I have a hoary old piece from Mount Vernon—can you authenticate it for me? Like other correspondents, Mrs. Carter based her statement on her family's oral history: "my mother . . . left me the information." But this letter was more specific than most and included the intriguing information that Carter's forebear was a relative of Martha—her ancestor's middle name was Custis. No "William Custis Costin" appears in the Custis family tree, however.

The file held Mount Vernon's reply to the query, written by a curator, who offered the answer most common in these situations: the set was probably not from Mount Vernon. She thought that in its form and decoration the set was too late to have been owned by the Washingtons, but she held out some hope. If Mrs. Carter would send more information about her ancestor, then the staff could check the list of purchasers at the Mount Vernon estate auction held after Martha's death in 1802. Perhaps her ancestor had bought the set.

Mrs. Carter responded by sending two documents, a handwritten family tree and an excerpt from a book, both of which revealed something her first letter had not mentioned: her family was black. She may have withheld that information from her first letter on the assumption that Mount Vernon would dismiss her query out of hand if it came from the descendant of a slave. Not only was she claiming to own something from Mount Vernon, she was also claiming kin to the Custis, Dandridge, and Washington families. And her documents also indicated that the mother of her ancestor William Custis Costin was Ann Dandridge.[7]

Mrs. Carter sent an account of William Costin's lineage from a nineteenth-century book entitled *History of the Negro Race in America From 1619 to 1880,* by George W. Williams, who apparently obtained his information from the 1871 Congressional report that first revealed the Costin-Dandridge connection. Williams wrote:

> William Costin's mother, Ann Dandridge, was the daughter of a half-breed (Indian and Colored), her grandfather being a Cherokee chief, and her reputed father was the father of Martha Dandridge, afterward Mrs. Custis, who, in 1759, was married to General Washington.

Like the author of the Congressional report, Williams was uncertain of the identity of William Costin's father, writing that his "reputed father was white, and belonged to a prominent family in Virginia." But Mrs. Carter's handwritten family tree, which traced her genealogy back eight generations, identified the father as a "Custis." The first name of the Custis was not included, but Martha's son Jacky was the only male Custis living at Mount Vernon at the time. If this family tree is accurate, it reveals that George and Martha Washington had a grandchild among the servants at Mount Vernon. (A portrait of William Costin is among the illustrations in this book.)

As intriguing and as compelling as it might appear, a family tree based on oral history is a slim reed upon which to base historical statements, and historians are often forced by lack of additional evidence to dismiss such stories as apocryphal. However, a document in the Virginia Historical Society archives substantiates Mrs. Carter's oral history. The document was written in the 1860s by Elizabeth Van Lew, one of the most famous and most successful spies of the Civil War, an agent of the Union in Richmond. As a reward for her courageous service to the Union cause, Van Lew was made postmistress of Richmond, where she integrated the postal service and did all she could to promote the rights of African-Americans. She also sought to tear away the veil of hypocrisy that she believed had covered antebellum race relations. She had many friends in political circles in Washington, D.C. For reasons that remain unclear, Van Lew composed a private dossier about William Costin's daughter Harriet. This document, not previously published, was found among Van Lew's papers after her death:[8]

> Harriet Park Costin
> Great grand daughter of Mrs. General Washington— Mrs. Washington's son Jno. Park Custis was her grandfather and her grand mother was half sister to Mrs. W. being named Ann Dandridge— . . . The mother of Ann Dandridge was an Indian squaw of the Pamunkey tribe below Richmond— her father was also Mrs. Washington's father.

Van Lew states that Martha's son Jacky and Ann Dandridge were the parents of William Costin. In the rest of the "dossier" Van Lew notes the Costins' connections to people of the highest social and political rank in the country, including the man soon to be lionized as the greatest hero of the Confederacy—Robert E. Lee. He was married to Mary Custis, the great-granddaughter of Martha Washington. Mary's grandfather was Jacky Custis, and her father was George Washington Parke Custis. William Costin and George Washington Parke Custis were half brothers, the sons of Jacky Custis.* "Wash" Custis built Ar-

---

* Van Lew had inside information about the family. Referring to the blood tie between Harriet Costin and Mary Lee, Van Lew wrote, "Mrs. Lee knowing this, when her father . . . died, had his coffin opened for Harriet and her sister when she would permit no one else to see him." A check written by Custis to his half brother, framed with a portrait of Custis, can be seen in the upstairs hall of Tudor Place, the house of Custis's sister.

lington House, the mansion overlooking the Potomac where in 1861 Lee made his fateful decision to side with Virginia rather than accept Lincoln's offer to command federal forces that would soon enter the Southern states. During the war the government seized Arlington and converted its grounds into Arlington National Cemetery.

Van Lew concluded her dossier with a physical description of Harriet: "Harriet is rather a dark mulatto of medium size—with a strong trace of the indian yet in the countenance— Her hand is delicate in form and movement— She is very neat in figure and dress, unaffectedly ladylike and sensible. . . . She is a representative of three distinct races—"

The genealogy recorded by Van Lew had a troubling corollary: the child of Jacky Custis and Ann Dandridge was born of incest. Ann was the half sister of Jacky's mother. It is difficult to believe that Jacky was not aware of his blood tie with Ann Dandridge. Certainly Ann knew it: her descendants knew her ancestry in detail, and they could only have learned it from her. This young master was breaking an ancient taboo that knows no racial distinction, but all things, without exception, were permitted a master.

Jacky Custis is not an appealing figure. Aware from his youth that he would possess an enormous fortune, he did little to acquire the education or discipline one needed to manage such an inheritance. He repeatedly exasperated Washington with his laziness and indifference to the code of rules that Washington himself had internalized as a young man. He was so vain that he could boast, unselfconsciously, of his pride in his vanity. In 1773 he wrote from King's College in New York that there was "as much Distinction made between me, & the other Students as can be expected"—as if Washington would be delighted to hear such news. One wonders if this was a self-imposed fantasy, since King's College (later Columbia) had many other wealthy scions on its roster. Despite the homage paid him as a Custis and against the wishes of George and Martha, he left college to get married.[9]

Though he was the adopted son of the commander in chief of the Continental Army, Jacky Custis sat out the Revolution at home, tending his plantation business disastrously. He was incompetent with money, and to his incompetence he added an amazing lack of scruples. He tried to cheat Washington himself, his own stepfather, in a livestock deal. Years of coddling by his mother made him utterly self-absorbed. In August 1776 when Washington was on his way to New York at the head of an army, Jacky brusquely wrote that the general must take care of his overdue bills from college; a creditor in New York was pressing him. In another letter to his stepfather, Jacky expressed his annoyance that soldiers were allowed to vote: "In several counties it has been determined contrary to an express order of convention, that every man who bears arms is entitled to vote. This, in my opinion, is a dangerous procedure, and tends to introduce anarchy and confusion as much as anything I know."[10]

Jacky got a brief taste of army life in 1776, when he accompanied his mother on her journey to Cambridge. According to the historian Benson Lossing, Washington made him a messenger: "Young Custis was attached to the military family of Washington while in Cambridge, and was sometimes employed in carrying messages, by a flag, between the belligerent commanders." Custis met a young British officer who gave him a sprig of weeping willow cut from a tree near Alexander Pope's villa at Twickenham, "carefully preserved in a case of oiled silk." Jacky carried it back to Virginia and planted it.[11]

Young Custis enjoyed that brief taste of martial glory, and sought another when the opportunity presented itself, with tragic results. When Washington suddenly galloped up the road to Mount Vernon in 1781, announcing that he was off to catch Cornwallis at Yorktown, Jacky begged to join him. He had missed the war but could savor the victory. In the American camp at Yorktown Custis contracted typhoid fever. He was carried from Yorktown to the Bassett plantation at Eltham and died there, in his mother's presence. Jacky left a widow, Eleanor Calvert Custis, and four small children. To ease her grief, Martha brought the two youngest children, Nelly and George Washington Parke Custis, known in the family as "Wash," to Mount Vernon and raised them as her own. Eleanor kept the two oldest at Abingdon (where Reagan National Airport now stands). In 1783 she married Dr. David Stuart of Alexandria.[12]

Ann Dandridge bore Jacky's child, William, around 1780. She was a woman of highly ambiguous status—legally a slave though not acknowledged as such on any record at Mount Vernon.* After giving birth to William, she apparently married a slave named Costin and had four daughters by him between 1788 and 1795, all of them nieces of Martha Washington, and all of them becoming at birth slaves-for-life of the Custis estate.

Jacky's son William had a different fate, however. He was legally regarded as free even though his mother was a slave—an inexplicable exception to the law that makes sense only if one posits that Martha simply wanted it so. Some four decades earlier, her father-in-law John Custis had gone before his cronies on the Royal Council and told them, *Make my black son free,* and they did it because John Custis wanted it so. She may have made it known among her heirs that she wished her grandson, William Costin, to be regarded as free; as for the more distantly related offspring, they would be slaves.

Slavery, by its nature, was an engine of concealment and deception, and there was a great deal to hide. Martha found it natural to keep some of her relatives enslaved. The plantation was her realm, where she made the law and where, she imagined, her people would be treated well in perpetuity. They could desire nothing more. A Virginia law of 1782 authorized private manumission, but it would have been politically impossible for the Washingtons to initiate the required legal process on William's behalf: they would have publicized the fact that they had black kin. Washington could not fairly be blamed for the sins of his adopted son, but his reputation would have been sullied merely by the association.

Once George and Martha Washington were both dead, a relative freed Ann and her family. No publicity ensued, though the procedure was transacted in Washington, D.C., with one of the witnesses being William Thornton, architect of the U.S. Capitol. The manumission

---

* Similarly, Washington brought a slave named George to Mount Vernon from his mother's plantation whose name is also not mentioned in the records. Perhaps he died soon after arriving at Mount Vernon; perhaps he became disabled and Washington felt justified in not listing him on the annual "tithables" list of taxable slaves.

was carried out by Thomas Law, an Englishman who had married Jacky's daughter Eliza in 1796. After Martha's death in 1802 Law almost immediately emancipated Ann. Five years later he emancipated Ann's children, as well as William Costin's wife, Philadelphia "Delphy" Costin, and their children.[13]

Thomas Law was unusually sensitive to the plight of mixed-race people, and his story sheds some light on Washington's racial thinking. He had amassed a fortune as an official of the East India Company, and in India, in the custom of young British colonials, he had taken an Indian mistress, by whom he had three sons. His work in India complete, Law settled in Washington, D.C. (then known as the Federal City), in 1795 as a kind of racial exile. One son came with him; another joined them in 1803. He knew that his mixed-race sons would not be accepted in British society, but he believed—quixotically but correctly, as it turned out—that they might be accepted in the American South. He wrote in a letter of 1829 to a relative in England: "by coming to America one object was to settle my natural children where a variety of climate reconciles differences of complexion, & where there are not such strong prejudices." Law's sons attended Harvard and Yale.[14]

In the Federal City Law met the lovely if somewhat unstable Eliza Custis. He wrote in 1832, "I caught her fancy on my first arrival in America. She was a beautiful young woman with a fine personality & . . . related to Genl. Washington. I told her of . . . my having three natural children, she wrote that she would be a mother to them . . . & Genl. Washington approved of the match." When Law met Washington, he did not hide his son from the general, whose eye surely discerned that the young man was not a pure Anglo-Saxon. Law was a frequent guest at Mount Vernon; his son John—now a kinsman of Washington by marriage—dined there as well.[15*]

In 1985 Mount Vernon received a large packet of manuscripts and artifacts from a descendant of the white Washington family. Among the

---

* It was Thomas Law who introduced Washington in 1798 to the Polish traveler Julian Ursyn Niemcewicz, who visited Mount Vernon with Law.

artifacts was a pencil sketch, in an elaborate wooden frame, of a very handsome young man of the early nineteenth century. The head-and-shoulders portrait depicted a man in his twenties, dressed in the garb of a country gentleman—wide-lapeled coat and a cravat knotted around his neck. The ornate frame suggested that the man in the portrait had been an esteemed figure in the Washington family, and indeed, along with the gift of manuscripts there came a scrap of oral history. The donor remarked upon the "great affection" felt by her great aunt toward this man. Though the portrait unquestionably depicted a white man, he was unquestionably a black man, because he had been born a slave. His name was West Ford. He was set free in the early 1800s; he lived much of his adult life at Mount Vernon; he was given a substantial bequest of land adjacent to Mount Vernon; and he died there in 1863.[16]

West Ford is never mentioned in George Washington's papers. But in 1999 his name became permanently linked with Washington's because Ford's descendants made a highly publicized claim that Ford's father was George Washington. The claim was not a new one—it had appeared in print at least as early as 1940—but mainstream scholars either were unaware of it or regarded it as not worth mentioning. The assertion gained fresh currency, and tremendous impact, because it came immediately after the "scandal" that engulfed the reputation of Thomas Jefferson in 1998, when DNA testing proved that a slave family from Monticello had a blood tie to Jefferson. After evaluating the DNA findings and other historical evidence, including oral history, officials at Monticello held a press conference to announce that they believed that Jefferson was "most likely" the father of children borne by his slave Sally Hemings.[17]

For more than a century the descendants of Sally Hemings had persistently claimed that Jefferson had been the father of her children, and just as persistently mainstream white historians had derided the claim. Twentieth-century science had vindicated African-American oral history and had shown that generations of mainstream white scholars had been wrong. Suddenly, the apparent certainty of scholars on questions relating to the founders and slavery seemed shaky. The discovery of a single new document, or the performing of one scientific test, could overturn decades of academic scholarship.

Many people refused to accept the judgment of Monticello's historians and officials, and denounced the finding as an example of political correctness run amok. I happened to overhear a conversation between two tourists in the Monticello bookstore right after the announcement—white women in their forties who had apparently driven some distance to visit Jefferson's home, and happened to arrive on the morning of the momentous press conference. One of them dismissed the brouhaha succinctly: "he's just been on the pedestal too long and they think it's time to knock him off." To much of the public, "revisionist" historians were acting like special prosecutors, ransacking the historical record for evidence to bring down a president in order to make a political point: Jefferson was "the oppressor" and Hemings "the victim." These categories could then be used to advance a present-day political agenda that affirmed the perpetual victim status of African-Americans.

The discovery of the Jefferson-Hemings link seemed to lend credence to the claim of West Ford's family that Washington had fathered Ford. The headline in a July 1999 *New York Times* article about West Ford made the connection explicit: "After Jefferson, a Question About Washington and a Young Slave." The public link with Hemings entangled the West Ford story in the Jefferson political wrangle. Some conservative observers, feeling that they had "lost" Jefferson, circled the wagons around George Washington. Without examining the historical documents themselves, some observers attacked Ford's descendants and the journalists who reported their claims. One wrote that the *New York Times* "is willing to adopt standards even shoddier than those of the most reckless tabloids in writing stories that smear our Founding Fathers."[18]

A large amount of documentation about West Ford survives. In addition to the portrait of him that the white Washington family had kept and then sent to Mount Vernon, another was published in *Harper's*

New Monthly Magazine in 1859. The journalist Benson J. Lossing visited Mount Vernon and spoke with West Ford while the latter was making a plow. He described Ford as "an old mulatto" and "a very intelligent man." On the following day Lossing returned to make a sketch of Ford, who turned up not in work clothes but wearing a satin vest and a silk cravat. He wanted to wear his best clothes, he told Lossing, because "artists make colored folks look bad enough anyhow." Ford told the journalist that he had lived at Mount Vernon for fifty-seven years and would remain there as long as the Washingtons owned the place, though he owned his own farm nearby.[19]

A clerk in the nearby town of Alexandria wrote a description of West Ford in 1831 in the county's register of free blacks: "a yellow man about forty seven years of age five feet eight and a half inches high pleasant countenance, wrinkle resembling a scar on the left cheek, a scar on the left corner of the upper lip." Ford brought with him his two children so that they could be registered as free people: "Daniel with a scar in his forehead about fourteen years of age the other a Girl about eleven years of age, the children of Priscilla Ford a free woman."[20]*

The oral history of West Ford was eventually published in several different places. In a 1937 interview in the *Illinois State Register,* his grandson George W. Ford told a reporter that "his grandfather frequently went when a lad, as a personal attendant, with General Washington when he attended church in the more immediate neighborhood of Mount Vernon, Polick [Pohick] Church." He did not say that West Ford was the son of George Washington, but his granddaughters later claimed that the family had held back from making the paternity claim out of fear of reprisals.[21]

The paternity claim was first made in print in a 1940 *Pittsburgh*

---

* The clerk made no reference to the existence of a marriage between West and Priscilla Ford and was careful to specify that Daniel and the unnamed girl were "the children of Priscilla Ford a free woman." The legal status of children followed that of their mother. The clerk did not write that West Ford was the father of the children, only that "West Ford has with him two children." Their relationship to him was legally irrelevant.

Courier newspaper article stating that West Ford was "known as a negro son of George Washington." The article juxtaposed portraits of West Ford and George Washington to show their resemblance. The author of the article, J. A. Rogers, also wrote a book in 1942 entitled *Sex and Race in the New World,* in which he wrote, "In the District of Columbia is a Negro family, which claims descent from Washington." Rogers may have been in contact with descendants of Ford but did not specifically say so.[22]

In 1977 the *Washington Post* published an article about the finding of the long-lost Fairfax County register of freed slaves, a discovery, made by the county historian Donald Sweig in the attic of the county courthouse, that caused tremendous excitement among the region's historians and particularly among African-American researchers. The register was of special value to West Ford's descendants because it contained the physical description of him mentioned earlier, and it offered the first documentary proof that their ancestor had been owned and freed by Hannah Washington, George Washington's sister-in-law. The descendants assumed that their West Ford was the "West" emancipated by Hannah in her will, although they had not been able to prove the connection. The *Post* reporter interviewed West Ford's great-great-great-granddaughter Judith Saunders Burton, a resident of Gum Springs, the African-American community in Fairfax County founded by West Ford, though the article did not quote her directly.

> The register provides no information to reinforce some historians' speculation that Ford was the son of George Washington . . . Mrs. Burton thinks historians have tended to gloss over the possibility in an excessive display of deference to the first President. She said that both West Ford and his mother, Venus, are buried in the graveyard at Mount Vernon where Washington was originally interred.[23]

Judith Burton recounted the oral history of her family in her 1986 doctoral dissertation. Her grandmother, Catherine C. Ford Saunders, the great-granddaughter of West Ford, "often told the story of West

Ford riding everywhere in the wagon with George Washington." Burton's father had "stated that George Washington carried West Ford to Christ Church with him and that a pew was provided for West." But, she added, "no documented evidence has been found to verify these oral history claims." She summarized the family traditions: "West Ford was treated as a family member by the Washingtons. He owned his own home, while others of his race lived in slave quarters. He attended church with the Washingtons, went game hunting with them, and traveled in their company. According to the Ford family's oral history, West Ford's children were educated in the estate schoolhouse along with the Washington children." She pointed out that since Virginia's "Black Laws" of 1831 made the education of black children illegal, the Washingtons would have been defying the law by teaching Ford's children. Ford occupied a "prestigious position" at Mount Vernon, serving not only as a carpenter and wheelwright but also as the foreman of the estate's servants.[24]

If the descendants of West Ford had not come forward with their family's story, Ford would have remained an obscure, probably forgotten figure. Or his story might have been used, as so many similar stories have, as yet another poignant vignette from slavery time that sums up the closeness of masters and faithful servants, the bond of loyalty and responsibility they felt toward each other. Indeed, on the surface, the story is the epitome of the Southern benevolence tale. A poignant subtext emerges in the dreamlike fragments of memory it contains: *he took me to church, he took me hunting, we went riding together.* It is a pastiche of memories of a happy childhood, of the things a child, made to wear the mask of denial, might remember of his lost father.

Judith Burton was unaware that she had distant relatives in other parts of the country who had been told similar stories by their elders. But in 1985, after another newspaper article had appeared referring to her alleged connection to George Washington, she was contacted by two women from Colorado—Linda Bryant and Janet Allen, granddaughters of George Ford, the descendant who had given the 1937 interview to the *Illinois State Register*.[25]

Following the Jefferson-Hemings DNA announcement in 1998,

Bryant and Allen went to the press in Colorado with their story. The *Rocky Mountain News* published an article on November 12, 1998, headlined "Aurorans take cue from Jefferson study, hope to prove Washington link." The article said, "Two black sisters who claim an ancestral link to George Washington have asked for help from researchers who used DNA testing to determine Thomas Jefferson fathered a child by a slave. Janet Allen and Linda Bryant believe their great-great-great-great-grandfather, West Ford, was Washington's illegitimate son." The reporter quoted Linda Bryant: "We want our legacy for our children and our children's children in American history besides slavery. . . . We are looking to proclaim our heritage." To see if a DNA study of Washington and Ford descendants was feasible, they contacted Dr. Eugene Foster, the retired pathology professor from the University of Virginia who had conducted the Jefferson-Hemings research. The potential for a Washington discovery on a scale of the Jefferson revelation attracted the attention of the national media. In 1999 and 2000 the story was covered in the *New York Times*, the *Chicago Tribune*, the CBS *Morning Show*, and the PBS program *Frontline*.[26]

To the *New York Times* reporter, Judith Burton stated, "My grandmother used to tell us all the time when we were very young that West Ford was the son of George Washington. . . . His mother was Venus. Venus was the daughter of Jenny who was the servant to Hannah Washington, George Washington's sister-in-law." Linda Bryant added a detail that had been passed down in her branch of the family: "We were told she [Venus] was his personal sleep partner and that when it was obvious she was pregnant he no longer slept with her. . . . When she was asked who fathered her child, she replied George Washington was the father."

The Ford descendants could not cite firm documentation for Washington's paternity. No contemporary record yet found states the name of West Ford's father, a documentary gap that is not at all unusual. Masters and mistresses of plantations seldom recorded the names of the fathers of slaves because they had no reason to do so. The legal status of a child was determined by the legal status of the mother: if the mother was a free woman, then the child was free; if the mother was a slave, then the child was also a slave for life. The race, legal status, and individual identity of a slave's father were all irrelevant under the law and were, by and large, irrelevant to the masters. The law did not recognize marriages among slaves, so there are no official records of slave marriages except some scattered registers made after the Civil War.* By law, Virginia counties began to keep death records for slaves in 1853, but there are no systematic official records of births among slaves.

Historians of slavery look for anomalies, and West Ford's life presents a number of them. The most striking anomaly was his emancipation, a rare occurrence that indicates that the slave was of particular concern to the owners. Every emancipation leads to the question: why?

George Washington did not free and could not have freed West Ford because he never owned him; nor did he own Ford's mother, Venus. They were slaves of George's brother John Augustine Washington and his wife, Hannah Bushrod Washington. Their plantation, Bushfield, was on the Northern Neck in Westmoreland County, about ninety-five miles by road from Mount Vernon. George Washington was very close to his brother John, who had managed Mount Vernon while George Washington was fighting in the French and Indian War; John's two daughters, Mildred and Jenny, were born at Mount Vernon. When John faced financial problems in the 1780s George was unable to help but wrote to George Mason asking him, as a personal favor, to make a loan to John Augustine, which he would guarantee. And Washington was fond of his nephews Corbin and Bushrod. He helped Corbin find work and advised Bushrod when he was starting out on a career as a lawyer. Corbin died at the age of thirty-four in 1799, leaving a widow and children; Bushrod was appointed an associate justice of the U.S. Supreme Court by President John Adams in 1798. Washington chose Bushrod to be an executor of

* West and Priscilla Ford were both freed people, and they were able to get married at a Presbyterian church in Alexandria and have their marriage recorded in county records. Nevertheless, when Ford registered his children as free blacks the clerk noted their mother's status, not their father's.

his will and to inherit Mount Vernon itself; the justice lived there until his death in 1829.[27]

West Ford was freed by the last will and testament of Hannah Washington, who died about 1801. Hannah freed no one else—evidence that she had no strong objection to slavery itself—and in freeing him she did not mention any faithful service or meritorious act by which Ford had earned his freedom. Nor did Hannah's husband and sons free any slaves. West Ford was obviously a very special case.

The second striking anomaly about Ford is that thanks to the Washington family, he became a landowner. Bushrod bequeathed him 160 acres of land adjacent to Mount Vernon. The gift of land to West Ford was a large one, and it conferred upon him financial security, some status, and a large measure of independence. Land instantly conferred identity to a free black. Bushrod's bequest ensured that Ford and his family would not live at the whims of white employers.[28]

In 1833 Ford sold the land he had inherited and bought 214 acres at a place called Gum Spring Farm. Gum Springs, which got its name from a well-known spring that gushed from the base of a gum tree, is two miles north of Mount Vernon. The tract had bordered Muddy Hole Farm, one of the five farms that made up Washington's Mount Vernon estate. Washington referred to the spring in his diaries. In the 1840s Ford's daughter and her husband moved onto the place and helped Ford make it into a successful operation, raising corn, oats, and potatoes. By 1860 Ford was the second richest free black in Fairfax County. His farm became the nucleus of an African-American community that thrived there in the nineteenth century, and remnants of that community still survive today.[29]

The favors shown West Ford by Hannah and Bushrod would seem to indicate that if he had been the son of a white Washington, his father was a member of John Augustine's immediate family. Indeed, one oral history states that Bushrod was the father, while the other is emphatic that the father was George Washington. A peculiarity of this latter history is that it was passed down in two different lines of his descendants, an aspect that caught the attention of Mount Vernon's historian, Mary Thompson. She told the *New York Times* reporter, "It is very interesting that the tradition came down in two branches of the family, separated for over 100 years."

Discovering the identity of West Ford's father hinges, of course, on finding the details of his birth, and no record of his date of birth exists. His first known appearance in a document is on a 1786 tax list of slaves under age sixteen (and thus not yet taxable) owned by John Augustine Washington. He is listed simply as "West" and his age is not given. The birth dates of slaves can sometimes be conclusively established from plantation records—payments to midwives, tax records, accounts of the distribution of blankets to newborns, or other notations in a plantation ledger. Ages recorded during a slave's adulthood are notoriously unreliable—errors of five or ten years are not uncommon. When West Ford was an adult his age was written down several times in several different contexts, and the resulting birth dates range between 1784 and 1787. The most reliable indicator of West Ford's birth date is a statement in the will of Hannah Washington. When she freed Ford, Hannah described him as "a lad called West, son of Venus, who was born before my husband's will was made and not therein mentioned."[30]

John Augustine wrote his will on June 22, 1784. After his death it was duly copied into the Westmoreland County ledger of deeds and wills by a county clerk on July 31, 1787. (That version was published in a 1944 book, *The Washingtons and Their Homes,* by John W. Wayland.) As Hannah stated, her husband made no mention of West Ford in his will, though he did mention Ford's mother. If West Ford was born before this will was made in June 1784, then he was conceived in October 1783 or earlier; and George Washington could not possibly be the father because he was up North commanding the Continental Army until December 1783.[31]*

That would certainly seem to close the case, except that there is a serious problem in the dating of John Augustine's will. He wrote his will in June 1784, but he added a codicil in November 1785. Specialists

---

* No one has even suggested that Ford was conceived during General Washington's campaign in Virginia in 1781.

have debated the question of dating the will back and forth: Should they follow the date of the "first" will or of the codicil? It had seemed to me that the evidence pointed to the first option, but then I discovered, to my surprise, that no one (including officials at Mount Vernon and West Ford's descendants) had ever seen the original texts of either document. Everyone had read the version published in the Wayland book in 1944. When I finally looked at the will and codicil exactly as they were written down by the clerks in the official record—the handwritten ledger of Westmoreland County Deeds and Wills—an entirely new interpretation emerged, as well as something about the psychology of the Washingtons as they contended over the fate of West Ford. It was fascinating to see, in the last testaments of John Augustine and his wife, the clash of the Virginia obsessions about money, race, and bloodlines.[32]

William Faulkner's story "The Bear" describes how two cousins from a Southern family open up the old plantation ledger books and find things they do not wish to find. They find, in their own forebears' handwriting, the record of buying and selling people, of the births and the deaths, and they find hints of their blood link to the slaves. As they scrutinize "the yellowed pages and the brown thin ink," the names they found "took substance and even a sort of shadowy life with their passions and complexities too as page followed page and year year; all there, not only the general and condoned injustice and its slow amortization but the specific tragedy which had not been condoned and could never be amortized."[33]

West Ford took on substance in this old Westmoreland ledger, which hinted at passions and complexities under the placid surface of dispassionate legal language. The Washington wills recorded a struggle over the fate of West Ford. I tried to unravel the psychology of that struggle to gain a clue to Ford's identity. He was, supposedly, just a slave, but the documents revealed he was much more than that to the Washingtons.

John Augustine was the brother who was closest to George, and yet they had vastly different attitudes toward slaves. John Augustine was indifferent to the blacks. In his will he directed his executors to sell as many "negroes" as they thought necessary to pay his debts and fund the legacies he bequeathed his daughters. He made no provision for keeping families together. The slaves were merely human capital to be converted by sale into £1,600 specie, "to be raised as soon as possible after my death by my Executors and put to interest of good landed security." He doled out slave children as if they were baubles: "I give to my Grandaughter Ann Aylett Washington a Negro Girl between the age of six and ten years old." Ann could pick any child she liked. He bestowed the same largesse on his daughter: "I also give my daughter Mildred a Negro Girl." She, too, could have her pick of the black children.[34]

This will was exactly the kind of document that the slaves feared most—an open-ended warrant for their sale and dispersal. Two-thirds of John Augustine's 130 slaves were subject to this threat immediately upon his death: they were bequeathed to his sons Bushrod and Corbin, who were free to dispose of their inheritance as they pleased. The other third was safe from sale for as long as Hannah lived. John Augustine wrote, "I bequeath to my beloved Wife Hannah Washington during her natural life, the use of one third of all the Negroes I am possessed of." Hannah's portion was a "lifeboat" on which he reserved a few spaces for the household slaves his widow would need. He specified that among the forty-odd slaves apportioned to her "are to be included my waiting man Jerry, his wife suck, my Semstres Jenny, and her daughter Venus." At Hannah's death, they would be divided up among the heirs and once again threatened with sale.

It was striking to see the level of control John Augustine wished to maintain over his slaves even after his death, for he left little to the discretion of his wife. He could have allowed her the power to choose her own household slaves, but he did not. He gave Hannah use of these enslaved people only during her lifetime; she would have no control of their disposition after her death. Apparently, Hannah was not satisfied.

A year and a half later, in November 1785, John Augustine took out the will and revised it. The only substantial changes he made to the document concerned the slaves he was allotting to Hannah. John Augustine added Billy—Jenny's husband and Venus's father—to the "lifeboat." This nuclear family would remain intact under Hannah's care. Hannah was also given power to control their fates after her own death. John Augustine wrote a clause between the lines of his original will stating, "Billy, Jenny & Venus I impower my Wife to devise to such of my Children by her as she pleases."

John Augustine's will was a very carefully constructed financial blueprint for the distribution of assets. All the beneficiaries knew in advance what they would get, so they could plan accordingly. But a clause in the will indicates that Hannah, at her sole discretion, could completely overturn this carefully crafted arrangement. In effect, she wielded veto power over the entire will. She had tremendous leverage and used it to get at least some of what she wanted. The omission of the "devise" clause from the first will could hardly have been an oversight, and its later addition undoubtedly resulted from a negotiation (a fight?) between John Augustine and Hannah. The law allowed Hannah to claim a greater portion than her husband had allotted her. He knew this and had to negotiate with her to keep her happy lest she void the will after his death: "The above Legacys are intended in lieu of her dower in my Estate with which Legacys I hope my said wife will be satisfyed as she is entitled besides to all the lands her Father left her, but if she should never the less claim her right of dower in my Estate then the above Legacys to be void." So as a condition of consenting to the will, Hannah won crucial concessions: three slaves were placed in her care and guaranteed safety from sale. She could bequeath them as a group, whereas the rest of her life-use slaves were subject to dispersal at her death. We can only conclude that she interceded with her husband to rescue this family of slaves from possible sale.

West Ford was not included in this favored group, yet he would later emerge as the most important of all the slaves. His mother and his grandparents were specified to be saved. Why not West Ford? It seems that John Augustine was determined to see West Ford consigned to the generality of slaves liable to sale. Hannah may have pleaded West Ford's case to him but her pleas were unavailing, which is why West Ford was never mentioned (even obliquely, as "increase"). Her will indicates that she took ownership of West Ford very soon after her husband's death—it was obviously something she wanted to do but could not during her husband's lifetime.

Hannah bided her time and got what she wanted when her husband was gone. West Ford might have been sold off as a common field hand if John Augustine had his way, and no one might ever have known of his existence. But Hannah Washington had different plans for West Ford. In her will, written in 1800, she singled him out for manumission:

> a lad called West, son of Venus, who was born before my husband's will was made and not therein mentioned, I offered to buy him of my dear sons Bushrod and Corbin Washington, but they generously refused to sell him but presented the boy to me as a gift it is my most earnest wish and desire this lad West may be as soon as possible inoculated for the small pox, after which to be bound to a good tradesman until the age of 21 years, after which he is to be free the rest of his life. . . .[35]

Immediately preceding these instructions, Hannah made provision for the rest of West Ford's family—the favored few who had been specifically mentioned in the "devise" clause of John Augustine's codicil:

> my dear husband left me in his will the following slaves to dispose of as I chose at my death provided I gave them to our own children . . . —Billey who is dead . . . his wife Jenny their daughter venus who has brought a daughter since called Bettey, these three slaves I give my beloved grandson Richard Henry Lee Washington.

Richard was the son of Corbin Washington, who had died in 1799. Technically, she was violating the stipulation that the slaves go to one of John Augustine's children.

When referring to "his will," Hannah obviously meant John Augustine's revised document, for it was only in that version that Billey was placed under her care and that she gained the right to decide the eventual fate of West Ford's family. To her, the revised will was *the* will. All of this may seem a small matter, but changing the date of West Ford's birth casts a different light on the possibility of George Washington having sired the child.

John Augustine's original will—the actual document in his own handwriting—unexpectedly surfaced in the Mount Vernon archives in September 2003. The manner in which he shoehorned additions into the document confirmed my suspicion that he made his crucial changes in November 1785—compelling reason to date West Ford's birth to November 1785 or earlier.

Given a birth date of November 1785 or earlier, West Ford's conception had to take place in February 1785 or earlier. Washington's diary for 1784 is missing (or he never kept one) except for a journal of a trip he made to see his western Virginia lands in September and early October of that year. His highly detailed diary resumes in January 1785. The slave Venus lived at Bushfield, some ninety-five miles away from Mount Vernon. Washington's papers prove with almost total certainty that he did not visit Bushfield in 1784 or early 1785.[36]

This seemed, once more, to close the West Ford case and to prove that George Washington could not possibly have been involved. But then I found a document that changed everything. I had not been looking in the right place. It had not occurred to me that a document from several months *later* than February might reveal the whereabouts of Washington and Venus at that time, and that it would reveal that they were indeed together—and not at Bushfield but at Mount Vernon. John Augustine wrote his brother George a letter on July 17, 1785, mentioning two visits to Mount Vernon by Hannah *and her maid.* I had overlooked the significance of this apparently trivial letter because John Augustine did not specify the dates of the visits and did not mention Venus by name.[37]

Previous to my setting off to Mt. Vernon and Alexandria the last time I was up, a great Coat of yours that you had been kind enough to lend my son Corbin when he was last at your House, and a book that my Wifes maid the time before the last that she was there had put up supposing it to be her Mistreses, as she had one in the Chariott to read on the road, was carefully sowed up in a bundle and deliver'd to me, but I forgot both and brought them back, this is the first safe opportunity by Mr. Carters Vessel that has since offered to send them.

Hannah and her maid had to have visited Mount Vernon in the fall or early winter of 1784. The approximate date of their visit is established by Corbin's travels: the mention of the overcoat indicates that Corbin's visit took place at a time of year when the weather can abruptly turn cold because he came without a coat and borrowed one. Washington's diary for January 1785 onward does not record this visit, so Corbin must have come to Mount Vernon in the autumn of 1784, when the diaries are missing. Hannah's visit with her maid would date to the same time. (Corbin also visited Mount Vernon in July 1784, his first visit in more than a decade. If Hannah's visit with Venus had occurred before July, Corbin would have returned the book then. And he would not have borrowed an overcoat in July.) John Augustine did not name the maid who came with Hannah, but, as evidenced by Hannah's will, Venus was the house servant closest to her and the one most likely to travel with her mistress on such a rare, pleasurable journey.

It had seemed impossible that Washington had even been near Venus when West Ford was conceived; now it seemed not only possible but likely. The question of West Ford's paternity became one of character, not circumstance.[38]

The stories of Venus and Ann Dandridge take us into a dimension of slavery so loathsome that masters and slaves alike kept it hidden. But the sexual abuse of black women by masters pervaded the plantation world. Among some men of the upper class in Virginia, having sex with slave women was a sport. A few years ago Colonial Williamsburg received a portrait of an unknown Virginia aristocrat of the early nineteenth century. When the curators removed the frame they found on the reverse of the canvas a painted scene of a gentleman kissing a young female slave while another white man beat a male slave with a stick. The title of the scene read "Virginian Luxuries."[39] This genteel bit of soft pornography makes light of the revolting violence against black women and men that some aristocrats practiced and others countenanced. Word of the easy availability of victims spread north. Yankee visitors expected to indulge in this mode of recreation as a matter of routine, even at Mount Vernon. An officer who stayed with Washington in 1784 wrote in disappointment: "Will you believe it, I have not humped a single mulatto since I am here." It is distasteful merely to mention such things, but we must gain some idea of what Washington meant when he said that slavery had become *repugnant.*

Because of my experience researching plantation genealogies, a number of families, both white and black, have asked me for advice and help in tracing ancestors whose origins had vanished into a tangle of mixed-race relationships that had been kept secret. The people who shared their stories with me had no prestige to gain, no scores to settle, no reporters calling them; they merely sought the facts of their ancestry. The desire to find the truth after a century or more of concealment is what drove their private research.

One oral history given to me conveyed the brutality of these encounters and the shame that resulted for the women.

The story we were told by our aunt was that our grandmother Jenny's mother (a young woman) lived on a plantation owned by a Mr. Williams. Mr. Williams would steal the young woman (my great-grandmother) away from her parents and away from the eyes of his wife and children up at the big house, until he got her pregnant. I was given the impression that this was not a love affair, but she and her parents were afraid [of] Mr. Williams and this thing went on. My grandmother, Jenny, was ashamed of the circumstances of her birth and would never talk about her childhood except to say that she was a lonely only child and she lived with her mother and grandparents.*

A former slave from Virginia gave a graphic account of how these encounters took place:

> Did de dirty suckers associate wid slave wimmen? . . . Lord chile, dat wuz common. Marsters an' overseers use to make slaves dat wuz wid deir husbands git up, do as dey say. Send husbands out on de farm. . . . Den he gits in bed wid slave himself. Some women would fight an[d] tussel. Others would be 'umble—feared of dat beatin'. What we saw, couldn't do nothing 'bout it. My blood is bilin' now [at the] thoughts of dem times. Ef dey told dey husbands he wuz powerless. . . . When babies came dey ain't exknowledge 'em. Treat dat baby like 'tothers—nuthing to him. Mother feard to tell 'cause she know'd what she'd git. Dat wuz de concealed part.[40]

The masters possessed absolute power over the slaves, and absolute power corrupts absolutely. In the plantation world there were few restraints on what the masters could do, and evil expanded to fill the opportunities available to it. From the start the masters could extract the maximum amount of labor for the minimum expenditure in food, clothing, and housing. The slaves were property, and the law allowed any form of property to be disposed of as the owner saw fit. Those masters who were so inclined could rape the women whenever they wished. Children were raffled off. No law prevented it, so it was done, and the slaves, both men and women, were powerless to resist any wish of the master. If the masters chose, they could tacitly acknowledge their illicit offspring; if they chose not to, they could send them to the fields, or keep them in favored positions such as seamstress or valet, or sell them. They did such things because, swollen with power, they could do anything.

The question is what Washington thought of such behavior. The

---

* I have changed the names in this account.

general, of all people, knew the corruption inherent in holding power; he spoke of "opulent" Virginians made "imperious and dissipated from the habit of commanding slaves and living in a measure without control." That last fragment of his thought—*without control*—must have made him shudder. He was surrounded by planters who had lost control. He himself did not want to hire out his extra slaves because he knew they would be mistreated.[41]

Washington's obsession with self-control argues against his being West Ford's father. He was fanatically concerned with his reputation and took the greatest care never to do anything that would bring dishonor upon himself. He wrote in 1788: "I have studiously avoided, as much as was in my power, to give any cause for ill-natured or impertinent comments on my conduct: and I should be very unhappy to have anything done . . . which should give occasion for one officious tongue to use my name with indelicacy. For I wish most devoutly to glide silently and unnoticed through the remainder of life."[42]

The letter from John Augustine shows that Hannah Washington and Venus likely made at least one and perhaps two visits to Mount Vernon in the autumn of 1784. They might have arrived in early October just when Washington had returned from a five-week trek through the Virginia outback. He returned to find Martha sick and confined to her bed. If Venus arrived at that moment, the opportunity for an encounter was there. If he did father West Ford, his encounter with Venus would have been a momentary, impulsive lapse of discipline. But impulsive lapses of discipline were exactly what he guarded against. He possessed tremendous self-control; he lived by a set of rules he carried around in his head, and the first rule was, *There are no exceptions to the rules.* Given the opportunity for a sexual encounter with a slave woman, he would most likely have turned away because the risk of discovery and "impertinent comment" would have been great. Of course, a similar argument was used by generations of scholars who insisted that Thomas Jefferson could not possibly have had children with a slave. We will probably never be certain one way or the other. DNA testing can prove only that West Ford was a member of Washington's family, not that he was or was not George Washington's son. A number of historians have argued that it is unlikely that Washington fathered a child with a slave because he may have been sterile. Martha gave birth to four children before her marriage to Washington and was apparently never pregnant afterward; she may have suffered from secondary infertility. Some have suggested that Washington's teenaged case of smallpox, or his bout with genitourinary tuberculosis, might have rendered him sterile; but smallpox is not linked to sterility, and an accurate diagnosis is impossible.

Evidence that George Washington was not Ford's father is contained in the oral history itself. The stories that Washington took West Ford riding and to church are plausible, but only if Ford was *not* his son. Washington would not have paraded evidence of an indiscretion around the county, although one of his relatives did not have such qualms.

Most of the evidence points to the sons of John Augustine or to John Augustine himself. But would Hannah have so persistently protected her husband's illicit child? Probably not. It is more plausible that she would have been very protective of the offspring of one of her sons. The Ford descendants' oral history that Venus's relationship with West Ford's father stopped abruptly may have had a basis in fact: John Augustine could have noticed her pregnancy, discovered who the father was, and angrily ordered his son to cease the affair. But the possibility remains that George Washington could have been West Ford's father.

A blood tie to the masters was no guarantee of benevolent treatment. West Ford gained freedom not because he was the son of a Washington but because he had a staunch patron in Hannah Washington. Had matters been left to John Augustine, he might have been sold off. And Hannah had to ensure his emancipation by including it in her will, giving it the force of law. She did not risk leaving his fate up to her sons.

The fragmentary accounts of excursions that George Washington supposedly took with West Ford fascinated Mount Vernon's historian, Mary Thompson. She thought that this part of the oral history might indeed be true, and pored through the records to see if there had been any opportunity for such jaunts. She noted that in January

1789 Bushrod Washington visited Mount Vernon with his family for several days. She speculated that West Ford, then four or five years old, was among the entourage of servants. He might well have ridden in a procession of carriages that wound its way through the countryside to church services. It would have been an experience the child could never forget—a visit with the great general himself! On such a visit, George Washington would have gazed upon the face of a slave who looked like him.[43]

The existence of illegitimate mixed-race children was part of the fabric of Washington's world. The sight of yet another near-white servant, this little lad called West bustling about the mansion house to fetch this or carry that or go tell the general the tea is served—this should not have ruffled the general at all, unless he looked the boy in the face and was seized by a sudden, icy revelation—*This child is a Washington.* Perhaps it is not a mere coincidence that Bushrod's January 1789 visit occurred at the same time that Washington declared to David Humphreys his regret over slavery and confided his plan for an emancipation, and his intention that the children of slaves should have "a destiny different from that in which they were born."

CHAPTER NINE

The Great Escape

$\mathcal{I}$N AN ALMOST COMICALLY UNDERSTATED FASHION, a new epoch in American history was ushered into being on April 14, 1789, at Mount Vernon. At about noon a lone rider appeared before the mansion. It was Charles Thomson, secretary of Congress, bearing the announcement of George Washington's election, by unanimous vote of the Electoral College, to the presidency of the United States. Then fifty-seven years old, Washington had expected this news yet dreaded it as well. Since his return to Mount Vernon after the Revolution, he had yearned to enjoy his retirement as a "private citizen on the banks of the Potomac . . . under the shadow of my own vine and fig tree."[1]

Washington invited Thomson into the mansion's cavernous new dining room. The two men stood facing each other as the visitor read aloud the official notification of the election, a letter from Senator John Langdon of New Hampshire, president pro-tempore of the Senate:

> Sir, I have the honor to transmit to Your Excellency the information of your unanimous election to the Office of President of the United States of America. Suffer me, sir, to indulge the hope, that so auspicious a mark of public confidence will meet your approbation, and be considered as a sure pledge of the affection and support you are to expect from a free and enlightened people.[2]

Washington did not look forward to facing "the 10,000 embarrass-ments, perplexities & trouble to which I must again be exposed in the evening of a life, already consumed in public cares." And he hated the idea of leaving his beloved Mount Vernon. "My movements to the chair of government," he wrote privately to a friend, "will be accom-panied by feelings not unlike those of a culprit, who is going to the place of his execution." But being a man of discipline and duty, as well as an ardent nationalist, Washington accepted the will of the nation. He knew he was the logical—in fact, the only choice; without him, the country might splinter into factions. His personal aura, and the elaborate mythology that had grown up around him as a military leader, helped validate this new political experiment. Since 1776 Washington had been called "the Father of the Country." In a popu-lar toast of the day, Americans raised their glasses to Washington, "the man who unites all hearts." In short order, his mass-produced image would appear everywhere—on lockets and plates, silverware and coins, prints and bric-a-brac.[3]

Not wanting to delay the machinery of government, Washington departed immediately for New York, the first capital. En route, he en-countered a rapturous public. In Philadelphia some twenty thou-sand—out of a population of twenty-eight thousand—lined the streets to cheer him on. He arrived at the foot of Manhattan, having been transported across the harbor on a ceremonial barge propelled by thir-teen oarsmen. Cheers followed him as he walked to his rented house.[4]

Martha remained behind for several weeks to make the necessary preparations for transporting the household to the North. She chose seven slaves to accompany them, who were to form the core of the presidential household staff. The president's valet, William Lee, had already gone north with Washington. Martha chose sixteen-year-old Ona Judge as her attendant. Ona's brother Austin came along as one of the waiters, along with a slave named Christopher. Giles and Paris rounded out the small staff.

Martha's nephew Robert Lewis made the journey as well. He left an account of the departure from Mount Vernon:

After an early dinner and making all necessary arrangements in which we were greatly retarded it brought us to 3 o'clock in the afternoon when we left Mt. V. The servants of the house and a number of field Negroes made their appearance to take leave of their mistress; —numbers of these wretches were most affected, and my aunt equally so.[5]

The slaves were "most affected" because they were bidding adieu to their relatives. And Martha was distressed to leave Mount Vernon once more for the tumult of public life. Her every move would be watched by a public anxious to see what tone the Washingtons would set for the presidency. Would they impose a royalist atmosphere on the republic, with elaborate court rituals? That was the official life the Washingtons had known in Williamsburg.

The Washingtons seemed completely at ease about bringing slaves to the new capital of a free and enlightened people. To them, life without slaves would have seemed impossible. The closeness they felt for their slaves formed a cocoon of fidelity, trust, and familiarity. Having their slaves around was a psychological bulwark; they were accustomed to giving instructions to people who obeyed instinctively, without question. Transporting the slave system intact to New York City was perfectly natural to them. As she traveled north, Martha made no attempt to hide the fact that she was bringing the president's slaves. An observer on the road wrote:

> Preceded by a Servant about ½ mile ahead, and two young Gentlemen on Horseback, Just before them, a mulato girl behind the carriage and a Negro man Servant on Horseback behind, this was her Suite, small attendance for the Lady of the President of the United States.[6]

The mulatto girl behind the carriage was Ona Judge, Martha's personal attendant.* She was an accomplished seamstress, though soon

---

* In 1800 Ona's sister Philadelphia Judge married William Costin, Martha's mixed-race grandson.

her duties as Martha's attendant gave her little time for needlework. At the Cherry Street house of the President in New York, Ona was responsible for the care of Martha's clothes and hair. She coiffed Martha's hair every morning and helped her dress for the arduous social life the presidency imposed. Martha had chosen Judge not only for her skills but for her appearance. She was young, well-groomed, and light-skinned—exactly the traits needed in a young woman who would accompany the first lady on all her social and official visits. Washington himself was also eager that his slaves make a good impression. With his mania for detail, he gave instructions on the proper manner for grooming hair: "get him a strong horn comb and direct him to keep his head well combed, that the hair, or wool may grow long."[7]

Judge's work obviously pleased the first lady, because when the capital was transferred from New York to Philadelphia in November 1790 Ona continued as Martha's maid in waiting. In contrast, the New York household's cooks, a white woman and her daughter, did not make the trip. Washington didn't like them: "the dirty figures of Mrs. Lewis and her daughter will not be a pleasant sight . . . in our new habitation." The Mount Vernon staff supplied a replacement: from the plantation the Washingtons summoned their slave cook Hercules, who erased the memory of the filthy Lewises with his dashing good looks, high-style clothing, and superb culinary skills. Washington was delighted, remarking that he gloried in the cleanliness and "nicety" of the kitchen Hercules ran. Young "Wash" Custis, who also lived in the president's house, wrote that when Hercules gave an order "his underlings flew in all directions." So skilled was the cook that the Washingtons made him a deal: he could sell the leftovers from the presidential kitchen and keep the proceeds. Hercules spent this income on fine clothes, which certainly suited the wishes of his owners, who were always concerned with the appearance of their staff. They also allowed Hercules to bring his son up from Mount Vernon as an assistant cook.[8]

The demands of presidential life on the Washingtons and their staff were enormous. To augment the small staff of slaves, the Wash-

ingtons hired white servants and purchased additional white indentured servants. Their household records show that during the
Philadelphia years they employed more than ninety different people
at one time or another. At the end of his second term, Washington
apparently let some white indentured servants go before their contracts were up, not wishing to bring them to Mount Vernon or to sell
their contracts. The biographer James Thomas Flexner came across a
document relating to this release of the servants and thought, incorrectly, that it referred to slaves. He writes that Washington "quietly"
emancipated some slaves when he was leaving Philadelphia, but the
Washingtons did not free any slaves at that time. The opposite is the
case: Washington was deeply concerned with hanging on to his slaves
in a city with a thriving free black community in which runaways
could disappear. The city boasted a relatively prosperous community
of free blacks because the presence of the federal government increased demand for domestic help and services.[9]

The president's anxiety about his and Martha's slaves became acute
in the spring of 1791. Transferring the capital from New York to
Philadelphia had created a delicate legal problem for him because
Pennsylvania had passed a law by which slaves brought into the state
became free after six months of residence. Most of the household's
slaves belonged to the Custis estate, but Washington was responsible
for them. If they had become free, he would have had to compensate
the Custis heirs. He thought he might be technically exempt from the
law because he did not regard himself and his household as residents
of Pennsylvania; but to be on the safe side he instructed his secretary
to shuttle slaves back and forth from Philadelphia to Virginia so that
they would not achieve the six months' residency. This action, one is
sorry to say, involves perhaps the only documented incident of George
Washington's telling a lie. Not only did Washington concoct a scheme
to evade the law, he also instructed his secretary to lie about it. He
wrote to Tobias Lear, "I wish to have it accomplished under pretext
that may deceive both them [the slaves] and the Public." The full text
of his letter reveals the depth of his anxiety and the extent of his
deception:

in case it shall be found that any of my Slaves may, or any for them shall attempt their freedom at the expiration of six months, it is my wish and desire that you would send the whole, or such part of them as Mrs. Washington may not chuse to keep, home, for although I do not think they would be benefitted by the change, yet the idea of freedom might be too great a temptation for them to resist. At any rate it might, if they conceived they had a right to it, make them insolent in a State of Slavery. As all except Hercules and Paris are dower negroes, it behoves me to prevent the emancipation of them, otherwise I shall not only lose the use of them, but may have them to pay for. If upon taking good advise it is found expedient to send them back to Virginia, I wish to have it accomplished under pretext that may deceive both them and the Public; and none I think would so effectually do this, as Mrs. Washington coming to Virginia next month . . . if she can accomplish it by any convenient and agreeable means, with the assistance of the Stage Horses &c. This would naturally bring her maid and Austin, and Hercules under the idea of coming home to Cook . . . I request that these Sentiments and this advise may be known to none but yourself and Mrs. Washington.[10]

Washington vastly underestimated the intelligence of the slaves. They saw right through the deception. Given that the slaves were in daily contact with free blacks and whites, information about the emancipation law came readily to hand. Some weeks after the president wrote his letter to Lear telling him to keep the plan in deep secrecy, Lear wrote to him that Hercules knew all about it:

I mentioned that Hercules was to go on to Mount Vernon. . . . When he was about to go, somebody, I presume, insinuated to him that the motive for sending him home . . . was to prevent his taking the advantage of a six months residence in this place. When he was possessed of this idea he appeared to be extremely unhappy and although he made not the least objection to going, yet, he said he was mortified to the last degree to think that a suspicion could be entertained of his fidelity or attachment to you, and so much did the poor fellows feelings appear to be touched that it left no doubt of his sincerity, and to shew him that there were no apprehensions of that kind entertained of him, Mrs. Washington told him he should not go at that time, but might remain till the expiration of six months and then go home to prepare for your arrival there.[11]

One deception begat another: Hercules may have been setting his masters up with his protestations of fealty. A few years later he disappeared without a trace during a return trip to Mount Vernon. Before absconding, Hercules may have sat for a portrait by Gilbert Stuart. A portrait attributed to Stuart and entitled *Cook of George Washington* hangs in a Spanish museum. It shows a handsome, very self-possessed dark-skinned man in a cook's white outfit and toque. He looks every inch the culinary tyrant who could send underlings flying. The portrait offers a clue to why the Washingtons did not bring this superlative chef along with them in the first place—he was too dark. A man who looked too African would not have set the proper tone for the president's household; but several months of having the "dirty" white Lewises in the kitchen led Washington to rethink his priorities.

The president intuitively grasped the importance of setting the right tone. He understood the strong element of theater that pervaded leadership: to be a powerful leader, one had to appear powerful. His striking physique and daunting manner lent him a personal gravity he used to great effect. Always mindful of the civilities he had been schooled in as a youth and at Williamsburg, he tempered and framed his authority in formality and ceremony, while always avoiding the royalist ostentation of old Williamsburg. Any hint of monarchy would have undermined the new republican government. Washington realized that he was creating a whole new etiquette that presidents would follow thenceforth—it was one of his burdens. "Many things which appear of little importance of themselves at the beginning may have great & durable consequences from their having been established at the commencement of a new general government," he wrote in May 1789, a month into the presidency. One of the first questions Congress tackled was how Washington should be referred to. John

Adams's preference for "His Exalted High Mightiness" was shelved in favor of "President of the United States." Senator Oliver Ellsworth of Connecticut complained that even fire companies and cricket clubs had presidents, but it was just that kind of democratic tone that helped set this government apart from Old World monarchies.[12]

Washington conducted himself with a quiet dignity, and even his household furnishings reflected a modest good taste. Table ornaments for the presidential household were purchased in Paris by Gouverneur Morris, who wrote to Washington extolling the "noble Simplicity" of the items. "I think it of great importance to fix the taste of our Country properly," he continued. "It is therefore my Wish that every Thing about you should be substantially good and majestically plain. . . ."[13]

For the task of forging a strong and effective central government, the president called upon an extraordinary number of qualified men as administrators. He was an astute judge of character and fortunate in being able to make use of the best minds of the Revolutionary generation. Having been commander of the Continental Army, Washington's range of acquaintances was unrivaled. Since he was held in such awe he did not fear surrounding himself with strong-willed egotists. Beneath his efforts to create an effective governmental apparatus lay a deeper ambition. In a letter to Patrick Henry he wrote that he wanted to establish "an American character" that was distinct from European models, marked by independence and personal freedom.[14]

Washington's ownership of slaves made him vulnerable to charges of hypocrisy from political enemies. A pamphleteer, not daring to sign his own name to an attack on the president, printed up a diatribe by a fictitious Vermonter in 1796: "Would to God! You had retired to a private station four years ago." He derided "the great champion of American Freedom" for holding "the HUMAN SPECIES IN SLAVERY."[15]

A vaguely phrased clause in the Constitution provided for the return of escaped slaves. Though the word "slavery" never appears in the Constitution (the euphemism employed was "The Migration or Importation of such Persons as any of the States now existing shall think proper to admit"), the existing institution was recognized legally. In addition, one of the Constitutional Convention delegates from South

Carolina—the strident Major Pierce Butler, a former British officer who had married into a prestigious slaveholding family—had been adamant that owners should have some legal recourse if their slaves escaped to free states. Butler's resolution (which, again, avoided the unseemly words "slave" or "slavery") was unanimously adopted as Section 2 of Article IV: "No Person held to Service or Labour in one State, under the Laws thereof, escaping into another, shall, in Consequence of any Law or Regulation therein, be discharged from such Service or Labour, but shall be delivered up on Claim of the Party of whom such Service or Labour may be due."[16]

In February 1793 President Washington signed the Fugitive Slave Act, which addressed the weakness of the Constitutional clause by setting out a precise mechanism for reclaiming escaped slaves. A slave owner, or his agent, was legally able to seize a runaway and bring him before a judge (either a federal, state, or local magistrate) in the place where he was captured. Upon proof of ownership, which was based on oral testimony or a certified affidavit, the judge would issue a document permitting the slave's return. Anyone interfering with this process would be fined $500; in addition, he or she could be sued by the owner. By this law slaves who had escaped were fair game for slave catchers who tracked down fugitives for a price. The law was, coincidentally, a serious breach of the concept of states' rights—states without slavery were compelled to yield to the conflicting property laws of slave states and to accept federal intrusion in the enforcement of those laws.[17]

The regime in the presidential mansion represented slavery at its most benign. Washington occasionally barked in rage at his slaves, but he barked at his white servants as well, and even the highest government officials shrank from him when they sensed his temper rising. There is no record of it, but it is inconceivable that anyone was ever whipped at the Philadelphia Executive Mansion, a practice that was still going on at Mount Vernon at that time. The slaves were well treated, well fed, well clothed—and Ona, Austin, and Hercules went by themselves to the theater!

The mere existence of slavery in the Executive Mansion under the first president remains a matter of great sensitivity. In Philadelphia today, the building that houses the Liberty Bell stands adjacent to the site of Washington's residence, the last parts of which were torn down in 1951. A new visitors' center for the Liberty Bell was planned in 2002 with its entrance on the spot where Washington housed his slaves. A historian, Edward Lawler, Jr., discovered that visitors would step on the very spot where slaves lived in order to view the Liberty Bell—a nineteenth-century symbol of abolition. An official National Park Service text describing the president's house omitted mention of the slave quarters, since the notion of slavery did not mix well with a modern celebration of early American virtues. To protests from historians and African-American leaders, the Park Service replied that since slaves may have shared quarters with indentured servants, they thought it best to refer only to a "servants' quarter." But in 2003 the Park Service relented: a new design includes an outline in stones of Washington's house and the slave quarters, and an exhibit about the first president and slavery.[18]

Despite their benevolent treatment in the Executive Mansion, the slaves were still slaves, and they grew restive even under a relatively light hand. The slave Paris, just a teenager, exasperated Washington by his disobedience and was sent back to Mount Vernon. Hercules' son, Richmond, was also sent back when he was caught stealing money; Washington speculated that Richmond may have been trying to get money for a joint escape with his father. Another slave, Christopher, who knew how to read and write, was caught in an escape attempt at Mount Vernon when a note to his wife about an escape plan was discovered. All these people were among the most highly favored slaves in the Washington household.

Slave masters always worried that allowing slaves to mix with free blacks would give them the notion to escape. In the South the problem was not acute because escape was difficult in a slave society. Slaves might become insubordinate or insolent from contact with free blacks, but the incidence of actual escapes was low. Runaways had to feed themselves by stealing, which was risky; they also had trouble procuring a change of clothes. Runaway ads in newspapers often noted the clothes that slaves were last seen wearing. They had so few items of clothing that masters knew every shirt and pair of breeches a slave possessed. In the North the situation was the opposite; though slavery existed, runaways would find sympathy in the predominantly free society and support not only from free blacks but also from whites. Though escape was still difficult because slave catchers always kept an eye on stagecoaches and the docks, slaves could find temporary shelter in dozens of places until the hue and cry died down. Philadelphia's large number of Quakers and relatively well-off free blacks gave birth to a well-developed underground, committed to abolition.

Like many masters and mistresses, the Washingtons mistook obedience for loyalty. Though Martha had a natural mistrust of most slaves, she had perfect confidence in the personal devotion of the slaves who made up her intimate circle. Perhaps assuming that Ona Judge would be delighted at the news, Martha told her that she would be bequeathed to one of her granddaughters, whom Martha loved but Ona Judge despised. Martha's remark made clear to Judge that an emancipation would not be forthcoming at her mistress's death. It is unlikely that the slaves had any inkling of George Washington's earlier plans for their emancipation, but there is evidence they assumed that there was a chance they would be freed at the deaths of their master and mistress. Once Martha let slip that a division of slaves had already been laid out, however, Ona Judge knew that her fate was sealed: "I knew that if I went back to Virginia, I never should get my liberty." New generations of Custis mistresses and masters awaited her. Judge decided to escape.

When the Washingtons told their staff that they would be returning to Mount Vernon in the spring of 1796, Ona began to put a scheme in place. Her getaway was well planned. She did not run impulsively with just the clothes on her back and no money. She packed her things, which did not arouse suspicion because the entire household was packing up. On her errands in Philadelphia, Judge had formed friendships among other African-Americans, probably including a number of free blacks.[19] She planned to take refuge among these friends. Judge had help in carrying out the riskiest part of her escape, either from another Washington slave or from an outsider. It was hard enough to leave the house without notice, but doubly difficult to do so while carrying baggage. She said that someone carried "my things" out of the Executive Mansion for her. She then waited for dinner, and while the Washingtons were intent upon their meal she walked out the door. This all had to be carefully coordinated because if someone had noticed that her bags were missing it would have raised suspicion.

Sometime in May 1796, Judge vanished into the Philadelphia underground. Where she went is not known, as she never identified her helpers in the city, nor is it known precisely how long she remained in hiding there. In May or June she emerged from her hideout and made her way to the docks for the second great crisis of her escape. She could not risk tarrying about lest she be recognized. Perhaps at night, perhaps just moments before the sloop weighed anchor, she boarded the *Nancy,* bound for Portsmouth, New Hampshire. Captain John Bowles plied the route between New Hampshire and Philadelphia every month.[20] The historian Evelyn Gerson, who spent ten years researching the life of Ona Judge, speculated that she may have chosen the *Nancy* because Bowles may have been known to be sympathetic to runaway slaves: "most likely this intelligence flowed through the free-black community from some of Bowles' own sailors." At that time many of the hands aboard American ships were "Black Jacks," African-American seamen.

The sight of Philadelphia slipping into the distance must have thrilled Ona. After a voyage of four or five days the *Nancy* docked at Portsmouth, and she disembarked a not-quite-free woman. She had escaped the Washingtons, but she had not escaped slavery. The institution was still legal in New Hampshire; worse, the Fugitive Slave Law allowed the Washingtons, if they wished, to dispatch a slave catcher in pursuit of her and to enlist local and state authorities to arrest her. Her best hope was to slip into anonymity. Despite the dangers, she was breathing free air; her escape had been a success; and the Washingtons had no idea where she was—no idea, that is, until one day, walking down a street in Portsmouth, she heard a voice call out, "*Oney!* Where in the world have you come from?"[21]

Through ignorance or carelessness, or perhaps overconfidence, Judge had come to the hometown of the Langdons, close friends of the president and Mrs. Washington. The voice calling out on the street was that of the Langdons' daughter Elizabeth, a frequent visitor to the Executive Mansion, an intimate of Martha's granddaughter Nelly Custis Lewis, who had seen Judge many times in the company of the Washingtons. Elizabeth looked up and down the street to catch sight of Mrs. Washington.

Judge kept her wits. There was no point now in lying about her escape, but she lied about her route to shield the people who had helped her, including Captain Bowles. ("I never told his name till after he died . . . lest they should punish him for bringing me away.")[22] To the question of where she had come from, Ona replied, "Come from New York, missis."

Langdon could not comprehend how servant and mistress had become separated, but the truth quickly emerged in the course of this strange conversation.

"But why did you come away—how can Mrs. Washington do without you?"

"Run away, misses."

"Run away! And from such an excellent place! Why, what could induce you? You had a room to yourself, and only light nice work to do, and every indulgence—"

"Yes—I know—but I wanted to be free, misses; wanted to learn to read and write—"

Thanks to this chance encounter, the Washingtons found out where Ona was. The president brought the matter up at the highest level of the government. After a cabinet meeting called to address a diplomatic crisis with France, Washington pulled aside his Secretary of the Treasury, Oliver Wolcott, and informed him that he had a very delicate personal problem that required the secretary's attention, but one he could not speak of in detail in an official capacity. The following day he sent a letter to Wolcott asking him, as a favor, to write to his subordinate, the customs collector at the port of Portsmouth, to recover the slave.

The next morning he wrote to Wolcott, in a letter marked *Private*:

> Enclosed is the name, and description of the Girl I mentioned to you last night. She has been the particular attendant on Mrs. Washington since she was ten years old; and was handy and useful to her being perfect Mistress of her needle. . . .
>
> I would thank you for writing to the Collector of [Portsmouth], and him for his endeavours to recover, and send her back: What will be the best method to effect it, is difficult for me to say. . . . To seize, and put her on board a Vessel bound immediately to this place, or to Alexandria which I should like better, seems at first view, to be the safest and leas[t] expensive. But if she is discovered, the Collector, I am persuaded, will pursue such measures as to him shall appear best, to effect those ends; and the cost shall be re-embursed and with thanks besides.
>
> I am sorry to give you, or any one else trouble on such a trifling occasion, but the ingratitude of the girl, who was brought up and treated more like a child than a Servant (and Mrs. Washington's desire to recover her) ought not to escape with impunity if it can be avoided.[23]

Everything about this was illegal. The president had set the machinery of the federal government in motion to recover private property. The Fugitive Slave Act, which Washington had signed, required the slave owner or the owner's representative to appear before a federal or state magistrate and provide evidence of ownership before attempting to transport a fugitive slave to another state. The property was not even his: Ona Judge was a dower slave, the property of the Custis estate. It was Martha who had set all this in motion. The president made noises that this affair was "trifling," but it sounds as if Martha was enraged at the disloyalty of the young woman. In another context Martha had complained of the habitual ingratitude of slaves: "the Blacks are so bad in thair nature that they have not the least gratatude for the kindness that may be shewed to them." She expected her slaves to love her, an illusion her husband did not share. Ona's flight punctured that illusion, dealt a financial blow to the Custis estate, and threw into disarray Martha's plans for dividing it. Ona had been pledged to a Custis heir; now that Ona was gone, the heir would have to be offered a replacement.[24]

At the end of the Revolution Washington had been philosophical about the loss of slaves who had reached British lines in New York. He negotiated with Carleton only under pressure. Now he was being pressured again, this time by his own wife. Politically and legally, Washington's position was extremely delicate. He wished to do nothing to stir up the abolitionists, but in her zeal to recover the lost property, Martha was either blinded to the political realities her husband had to grapple with or indifferent to them. He had to talk her out of advertising for Ona's recapture. She apparently did not see the damage it would do to his reputation if the president of the United States took out an ad offering a reward for the capture of a slave. To placate her, he set in motion this secret effort by federal agents to shanghai Ona Judge.

Secretary Wolcott immediately forwarded the president's request to his collector in Portsmouth, who leaped into action. The collector was Joseph Whipple, brother of a signer of the Declaration of Independence. His brother's slave, Prince Whipple, had crossed the Delaware with Washington during the fateful attack on Trenton.

Well aware of the sensitivity of the matter, Whipple replied to his superior without alluding to specifics, "I shall with great pleasure execute the Presidents wishes in the matter. . . . I have just ascertained the fact that the person mentioned is in this town." Whipple mentioned finding only one person, but Washington had hinted darkly that Judge was in the thrall of an unnamed "Seducer" who had enticed her away from Philadelphia. He had warned Wolcott to act cautiously: "If enquiries are made openly, her Seducer (for she is simple and inoffensive herself) would take the alarm, and adopt instant measures (if he is not tired of her) to secrete or remove her."[25]

Whipple took up the scheme with alacrity, concocting a cover story under which he would make contact with the fugitive. Pretending that he wished to hire her for his own family, he planned to hustle her onto a ship. But something in her demeanor caused him to lay aside his plan for a moment. He was struck by her appearance and character. Instead of diligently carrying out his orders, which emanated directly from the commander in chief, he made the mistake of engaging Ona Judge in a personal conversation. Whipple found himself in the awkward position of believing her version of events, a version that directly contradicted the president's. Even more awkward, he had to explain himself to his superior:

> Having discovered her place of residence, I engaged a passage for her in a Vessel preparing to sail for Philadelphia avoiding to give alarm by calling on her until the Vessel was ready, —I then caused her to be sent for as if to be employed in my family—After a cautious examination it appeared to me that she had not been decoyed away as had been apprehended, but that a thirst for compleat freedom . . . had been her only motive for absconding.[26]

From the safety of her asylum, Ona Judge became emboldened enough to attempt something she had never dreamed of while in slavery. She tried to strike a bargain with George Washington. Perhaps Whipple persuaded her to make the offer, but it seems that she missed her home and family and was willing to return to slavery, temporarily, if she could be assured of becoming free later on, which would allow her to spend her life in Virginia as a free person. She and Whipple phrased the bargain gently, with a preamble calculated to smooth the ruffled feathers of her owners:

> she expressed great affection & reverence for her Master & Mistress, and without hesitation declared her willingness to return & to serve with fidelity during the lives of the President & his Lady if she could be freed on their decease, should she outlive them; but that she should rather suffer death than return to Slavery & [be] liable to be sold or given to any other persons. —Finding this to be her disposi-

tion & conceiving it would be a pleasing circumstance to both the President & his lady should she go back without compulsion, I prevailed to her to confide in my obtaining for her the freedom she so earnestly wished for[27]

Whipple told Wolcott that Ona Judge had actually agreed to return to Mount Vernon on the assumption that Washington would accept the deal but that her friends in Portsmouth had quickly talked her out of it. They may have thought she was out of her mind to trade away the freedom she had already obtained. Whipple wrote, "many Slaves from the Southern States have come to Massachusetts & some to New Hampshire, either of which States they consider as an asylum; the popular opinion here in favor of universal freedom has rendered it difficult to get them back to their masters."[28]

He expressed his "great regret" that he had not recovered Judge. Perhaps not expecting that his letter to Wolcott would be handed directly to the president, he also undertook to suggest that perhaps the president might consider actually obeying the law in this matter:

> In the present case if the President's servant continues inflexible & will not return voluntarily, which at present there is no prospect of, I conceive it would be the legal & most effectual mode of proceeding that a direction should come from an Officer of the President's Household to the Attorney of the United States in New Hampshire & that he adopt such measures for returning her to her master as are authorized by the Constitution of the United States.[29]

Washington did not receive Whipple's letter for several weeks, but when he did read it he wrote a blistering reply. He berated Whipple for even suggesting that a master might negotiate with a slave:

> I regret that the attempt you made to restore the Girl (Oney Judge as she called herself while with us, and who, without the least provocation absconded from her Mistress) should have been attended with so little Success. To enter into such a compromise with *her*, as she

suggested to *you*, is totally inadmissable, for reasons that must strike at first view: for however well disposed I might be to a gradual abolition, or even to an entire emancipation of that description of People (if the latter was in itself practicable at this moment) it would neither be politic or just to reward unfaithfulness with a premature preference; and thereby discontent before hand the minds of all her fellow-servants who by their steady attachments are far more deserving than herself of favor.[30]

In no uncertain terms he blasted Whipple for bungling the deception that would have gotten Judge on a ship; he had *warned* them that Judge was a slippery character: "I was apprehensive (and so informed Mr. Wolcott) that if she had any previous notice more than could be avoided of an attempt to send her back, that she would contrive to elude it." And he was incensed that Whipple refused to believe the story about the "Seducer" and gave more credence to what a slave said than to what the president told him to believe: "Whatever she may have asserted to the contrary, there is no doubt in this family of her being seduced, and enticed off by a Frenchman, who was either really, or pretendedly deranged, and under that guise, used to frequent the family; and has never been seen here since [the] girl decamped."[31]

The seducer was a phantom. Ona later said she had the help of "colored people" in Philadelphia and mentioned no other accomplice, though one could argue she was merely protecting her own reputation. However, none of the whites she encountered in New Hampshire made any mention of a Frenchman traveling with her or of any companion at all; she hid the identity of Captain Bowles to protect him, and if she had been traveling with a Frenchman, Bowles would have had nothing to fear, because he could plausibly say that he had given legal passage to a male traveler who had a servant with him. Whipple stated plainly that "she had not been decoyed away." In a matter of hours after receiving his first instructions, Whipple had been able to track her down and identify her place of residence. If his network of sources enabled him almost instantly to uncover the hiding place of an obscure servant girl who was intent on not being discovered, his sources certainly could have rooted out a traveling Frenchman. But Whipple found no trace of the mysterious seducer.[32]

Gerson found that the story of the French seducer resembled the plot of a best-selling melodramatic novel of the time, *Charlotte Temple*, by Susanna Rowson, a well-known actress of the Philadelphia stage. As described by Gerson, *Charlotte Temple* "chronicles the life of a 15-year-old English girl named Charlotte, who encouraged by her scheming French governess, . . . decides to leave the protection of her devoted parents to elope with a British soldier named Montraville. Shortly after their arrival in America, Montraville impregnates the protagonist and then discards her for another woman." It is doubtful that the president had the time or the interest to read steamy novels, but someone in his family may have been familiar with the plot of *Charlotte Temple* and fed Washington the details he put into his letters. Washington never said that he saw the deranged Frenchman with his own eyes; he relied upon what "the family" told him. It was not he but "the family" that had no doubt about the Frenchman's existence. He did not by nature assert as fact something he could not personally vouch for.[33]

The source of this fictional Frenchman was probably Martha, just as she was the prime instigator of the campaign to get Ona Judge back. Washington repeatedly stated this; he, however, may have been inclined to let Ona Judge go. Recapturing her also might entail a nightmare of political turmoil, but Martha insisted.

The Frenchman was a very convenient fiction because the president worried that recovering Judge would be complicated by a certain highly uncomfortable possibility: he heard that Ona might be pregnant. At the end of his first letter to Whipple, Washington confided this fear: "it is not unlikely that she may . . . be in a state of pregnancy." Dragging an expectant mother, against her will, onto a ship bound for the slave states would arouse a hurricane of protest in the North, so the president was taking an enormous political risk to placate his wife. The scandal might be lessened if the Washingtons could

put out the story that Judge was the victim of a half-mad French seducer, but they actually suspected something worse. If Ona was indeed pregnant, the father, the actual "Seducer," might have been a
member of Martha's family. Around the same time that Judge disappeared abruptly from Philadelphia, the president's secretary also vanished. He was Bartholomew "Bat" Dandridge, Jr., Martha's nephew.
The dual disappearances sparked rumors about an affair between
Dandridge and Judge, rumors that reached the ear of John Adams in
Massachusetts. He wrote in his diary in July: "Anecdotes of Dandridge, and Mrs. W's Negro Woman. Both disappeared—never heard
of—know not where they are."[34]

The Washingtons were not sure what to think but apparently had
reason to believe the rumors might actually be true. They tried to find
not only Ona but the missing nephew. The president's inquiries finally reached Bat, who had gone to ground in Virginia. He wrote an
explanatory letter to Washington in May, saying that he had headed
to the country to rest his nerves. The president's reply to this letter is
lost, but Washington must have raised the question of a possible illicit
romance because on June 1, Dandridge wrote to him from the Green-
brier resort: "My quitting [your service] was not from any unworthy
motives." The Washingtons may not have believed Bat, who was
demonstrably erratic; months after receiving his denial of any "unworthy motive" they remained convinced that Ona had been seduced
in Philadelphia and would by then be noticeably pregnant. They
needed a cover story.[35]

Pregnant or not, Ona Judge had to be recovered. The president instructed his subordinate to use "compulsory means" but to act in secret—"I do not mean . . . that such violent measures should be used as
would excite a mob or a riot . . . or even uneasy Sensations in the
Minds of well disposed Citizens." If there was no chance of handling
the matter quietly, he told Whipple, "I would forego her Services altogether." He emphasized the need for speed and deception, and implied once more that the person behind this operation was not he but
his wife: "The less is said beforehand, and the more celerity is used in

the act of shipping her when an opportunity presents, the better chance Mrs. Washington (who is desirous of receiving her again) will have to be gratified."[36]

It is one thing to have the president angry with you, but it is worse to make an enemy of the president's wife. Apparently, word of Martha's personal involvement in the case reached Whipple, perhaps through the Langdons, since the hapless civil servant apologized profusely to Mrs. Washington in his response to the president, emphasizing that her suffering had become his: "I sincerely lament the ill success of my endeavours to restore your Lady her servant on the request of Mr Wolcott—It had indeed become a subject of Anxiety to me on an Idea that her services were very valuable to her mistress and not readily to be replaced."[37]

Having made his apologies, Whipple went on to say, in the gentlest terms, that he would do what he could but that the president should not expect a quick resolution. Stating that "a Servant (in her employment especially) returning voluntarily [is] of infinitely more value in the estimation of her employer than one taken forceably like a felon to punishment," Whipple promised that he would dispatch Judge to Virginia "if it be practicable without the consequences which you except—that of exciting a riot or a mob—or creating uneasy sensations in the minds of well disposed Citizens." Unfortunately, he continued, "At present there is no Vessel bound for Alexandria or Philadelphia."[38]

Whipple also conveyed a startling bit of news. Judge was getting married. "I have deferred answering your letter some days to find out the present retreat of the Girl and yesterday discovered that she was lodged at a Free-Negro's—that she is published for marriage agreeable to our laws in such cases to a Mulatto."[39] Had Judge been pregnant from an encounter six months earlier in Philadelphia it would have been obvious by then, but Whipple made no mention of it. He did not even bring up the story of the deranged French seducer.

So eager was Whipple to prove his loyalty and efficiency that he ordered a court officer to delay the paperwork for Ona's marriage.

Whipple wanted Judge to remain unencumbered, for if she had a legal husband, a free man, her extraction would be greatly complicated. Undeterred, and adept at evading the machinations of the authorities, Ona simply took out a license in a neighboring jurisdiction. She and John Staines, a sailor, were married in January 1797 by the same clergyman who had married Washington's private secretary Tobias Lear. Later that year, or in 1798, Ona gave birth to a daughter.

The marriage of Ona Judge would seem to bring her story to a happy ending. Washington's biographers have written that the president and his wife resigned themselves to Ona's loss, but that was not the case. A Washington letter that was not published until 1999 reveals that Martha's anger over Ona Judge did not subside and that she talked her husband into launching another effort to retrieve her.

In July 1799, Martha's nephew, Burwell Bassett, Jr., came to Mount Vernon for dinner and mentioned that he would soon be making a trip to Portsmouth. About two weeks later, Washington wrote to Bassett and outlined the story. He said that Ona Judge had once expressed a willingness to return and asked Bassett to try to bring her back. Washington stressed in his letter that he was not promising Judge freedom. He also indicated he was no longer willing to use coercion or force: "I do not however wish you to undertake anything . . . unpleasant or troublesome," but if Bassett could bring about Judge's return "by easy . . . & proper means . . . it would be a pleasing circumstance to your Aunt."[40]

Burwell Bassett suddenly turned up at Ona Judge's house in the fall of 1799 like an apparition out of a nightmare. Her husband was away at sea; she was alone with her baby, and completely vulnerable if the Southerner chose to invoke the Fugitive Slave Law and summon the authorities. But the Virginian was all unctuousness: if Ona would come back she would be forgiven for her flight and she would be free. Ona replied to him: "I am free now and choose to remain so." Her response seemed to satisfy Bassett, who left as swiftly as he had come.

Bassett was staying at the home of Senator John Langdon, whose daughter Elizabeth had first stumbled across Ona and alerted the

Washingtons. The president had stayed with the Langdons during his northern tour of the states in November 1789, and Langdon had dined with Washington in New York in January 1790. (At that dinner or on another social occasion, Langdon may have seen Ona in the company of the first lady.) That evening in Portsmouth, Bassett revealed to the senator that his plan had a second part: in the event Ona refused to return willingly, he had "orders to bring her and her infant child by force."

Here the story takes a dramatic turn. By the inflexible law of slavery, Ona's child, though born in New Hampshire, was a slave because her mother was still legally a slave. Despite his long friendship with the Washingtons, Senator Langdon was appalled. While Bassett was dining, Langdon slipped away and sent a message to Ona that she was in grave danger and must flee immediately with her child. For the second time, Ona Judge escaped slavery. She hastily packed up a few necessities, scurried from her house, and hired a wagon and driver to take her eight miles inland to the town of Greenland, where she hid in the home of a free black family named Warner. Bassett departed for Virginia without his quarry.[41]

Bassett had disobeyed Washington's specific instructions on several counts. He lied to Ona Judge when he said that Washington had promised emancipation if she returned, and also in telling Langdon that he had "orders to bring her and her infant child by force." It is difficult to conceive that Bassett would defy the explicit instructions of George Washington—unless he had received different instructions from his aunt.

Just a few weeks before Washington dispatched Bassett on this mission to recover Ona Judge, he had written the will providing for the emancipation of his own slaves. This is not one of those curious, charmingly ironic "contradictions" that we can write off to the paradox of slavery. In the Ona Judge affair George Washington was acting against his own solemnly stated will. The fact that he would try to recover, on his wife's behalf, a woman who had been in freedom for more than three years and who had married a free man, shows how sharply divided George and Martha had become on the subject of slavery.

Ona Judge made a significant remark to Whipple. She told him that she would rather suffer death than return to slavery and be *liable to be sold*. It would seem that Judge was mistaken, because she had to know that Washington was firmly set against selling slaves. But Judge had a network of connections that could rapidly bring news from the South, and in the spring before she fled she obviously had received word of events that were not set down in Washington's records. At the time of Ona's escape, the recent marriage of a Custis heir had set in motion the legal transfer of the assets of the Custis estate from one generation to the next. On the Custis plantations and at Mount Vernon, slaves were being counted up and some of them moved off, never to be seen again.

CHAPTER TEN

Mrs. Peter's Patrimony

$\mathcal{T}$HE POSTPONEMENT OF A MEETING in Washington, D.C., left me unexpectedly with a free day in the capital, and I took advantage of the opportunity to visit a place far down on my list of research items. Martha Washington's granddaughter Martha Custis, and her husband, Thomas Peter, built a mansion in Georgetown called Tudor Place. Remarkably, it remained in the Peter family, as a private home, for six generations spanning 180 years. It was opened to the public as a museum in 1988. I am a devotee of old houses, especially those that have come down with their furnishings intact, for such places are time capsules—it is a cliché but it is true. That powerful sense of being in direct contact with the past was captured in remarks written in 1969 by the last occupant of Tudor Place, Armistead Peter III:

> As I sit here in the library at Tudor Place, surrounded by so much that is dear to me, I cannot help wondering whether I can convey to readers of future generations the sense of the values that seemed so obvious and elementary to my own. Stated simply, I shall try to breathe life into the meaning and the value of a permanent home as a basic influence for good, and a necessary accompaniment of a stable society.[1]

The house has a close connection with George Washington. With an $8,000 bequest from Washington's will, Martha Peter purchased an entire city block, some eight acres of land in Georgetown Heights, an oasis of civilization above the mud-filled streets of the rough new capital and the mists rising off the Potomac. Washington's old comrade in arms, the Marquis de Lafayette, was feted at Tudor Place on his triumphant tour through the country in 1824. He warmly greeted Martha's granddaughter, whom he remembered fondly as a child at Mount Vernon, and gave her an engraving of himself as a gift; it still hangs at Tudor Place. Martha Washington bequeathed to her granddaughter an engraving of General Washington and a writing desk from Mount Vernon. The house contains other exceptionally precious relics—camp stools the general used during the Revolutionary War and a chest of drawers said to have been in the room where he died. When the curators first inventoried the items in the house, they had some seventy trunks of possessions to sort through. One of them held, as a director described it, "a bit of brown something carefully labeled as George and Martha Washington's soap."[2]

Tudor Place is one of William Thornton's most inspired designs. The centerpiece of the house is a circular domed "temple," or portico, a design that harkens back to Roman temples from antiquity. The new republic looked to ancient models for inspiration, and Thornton was among a small group of architects who espoused and helped develop a post-Revolutionary neoclassical style. Thornton combined his architectural genius with a deep humanitarian bent. A Quaker born in the West Indies, he witnessed firsthand the brutality of slavery. In 1804, more than a decade before Tudor Place was completed, he published a pamphlet in which he advocated freeing the slaves. Thornton freed his own slaves in his will; they were to be emancipated on the death of his wife.[3]

The brochure for Tudor Place noted that its archives has thousands of letters and documents of the Custis-Peter family. I inquired if any of these items had information about Washington or Custis slaves, and I was sent a copy of Thomas Peter's account book. His marriage to Martha Custis, like any marriage of that time, was partly a business transaction, and the business of plantation families always involved slaves. Upon her marriage Martha Custis received her "patrimony" from the Custis estate, an inheritance that included sixty-one slaves. A wife's property immediately came under the control of her husband, so Thomas Peter carefully enumerated his wife's patrimony in the first pages of his account book for 1796 as "Stock / To Sundries being [part] of Mrs. Peter's Patrimony / To Wit . . ." Thereafter he listed the sixty-one slaves she had brought to the marriage, filling three pages, and following the list he wrote in "10 Horses old & young / 70 Head of Cattle / 43 Head of Sheep / 46 [Head] of Hoggs." I had seen so many of these lists that it no longer startled me to see humans listed as "Stock" along with the farm animals.[4]

Peter's list was an unusually careful one. Each slave had his or her value written beside the name, which was common practice, but Peter also listed the ages of the people. And I noticed that he listed the slaves by families, which was rather unusual. It was easy to discern groups of children by their ages; above each cluster of children Peter listed adults, clearly the parents. He had come into control of twelve families. At least six, and possibly seven, were headed by two parents. Peter Twine and his wife Elly had four children; Michael and Molly—no last name given—had half a dozen children, ranging from six-month-old Polly to eleven-year-old Rose. Esther, twenty-six years old, came with three children, Bob, Squire, and Elijah. Three women were shown as "invalids" and given no value. A seven-year-old boy was written down as "insane," perhaps meaning feeble-minded; he still had a value of £30 in Virginia currency. The most valuable slave by far was a thirty-five-year-old blacksmith named Peter, assessed at £150. Some of the names are ones listed also in the records George Washington kept of the Custis estate accounts. The family with the last name Twine turns up in several places. Because the others were all listed only by first names, it is very difficult to trace them reliably.[5]

The following pages of the account book settled into a tedious pattern. Thomas Peter developed real estate in Georgetown, so there were payments for planking and bricks, bills for hauling dirt, payments on bank loans. The names of other Washington and Custis associates and family members turn up—Tobias Lear, Thomas Law, and Dr. David Stuart. Among all these mundane transactions I came to a day in May 1796 where he wrote down "Negroes Sold": Betty and her nine-year-old daughter, Jinny, and the infant, Mike, went for £90; Esther and her three children went for £130. This was precisely what George Washington had sworn never to do, to sell people in the market as if they were cattle. No sooner had his granddaughter come into her patrimony than her husband started selling the people. This was the accepted custom.

The true extent of the horror did not emerge until I began to compare the sales with the family lists. Peter was breaking up the families. He sold Arbour and Polly for £65; to another buyer he sold Darky and John for £75. This was a single family of three generations. Peter Twine and wife Elly were sold with two of their children, but the master kept the other two daughters—at least I thought so, until I looked farther into the pages of this book and the master's method became clearer.

Thomas Peter had held back Twine's two daughters because he was separating out the young girls for sale by themselves. He sold Dinah Twine, age twelve, and her sister Lyddia, age four, in November. He sold eleven-year-old Rose and eight-year-old Susan. In one transaction he sold four girls age eleven to thirteen. He did not record the buyers, just the prices. We can only imagine the blind terror of a four-year-old standing on the auction block, and we need not strain to imagine the nature of the market for thirteen-year-old girls. One could throw a cloak over this and say they were destined to be house servants, but so were Venus and Ann Dandridge. That Thomas Peter knew exactly what he was doing is evidenced by the fact that he systematically separated the girls from their families. The girls and their parents were sold at different times to avoid unpleasantness for the master. In these transactions one can see the precise point where the pursuit of happiness became corrupt.

Looking through the book again I found that the first of these sales took place in February 1796. News of it would easily have reached the slaves in the president's house in Philadelphia by May, when Ona Judge vanished. She had been told she was destined for a Custis heir, and she was not willing to test the kindness of that family. If Judge knew she was "liable to be sold" then Washington knew it as well.

The president apparently knew in advance of Thomas Peter's intention to sell slaves, was disgusted at the prospect, and tried in vain to stop the sales. Once the sales had actually begun he tried to get some of the Custis slaves back from Peter, but more important, he laid out his most ambitious plan yet to free all the Mount Vernon slaves, both his own and the slaves controlled by Martha's family. On paper this would seem legally and financially impossible, but Washington attempted it. In the fall of 1795 he opened negotiations with one of the Custis heirs, Dr. David Stuart, who had married the widow of Jacky Custis. Once again he acted in secret. He said he feared the political repercussions that would result from a president's emancipating slaves, and it seems that he also wanted to have a complete plan, including financing, in place before he approached all the Custis heirs with his idea. The tone of the negotiation was all business. Washington was acting out of principle, but he seems to have realized that it was useless to debate justice and morality with such people; you have to pay them.[6]

The first clue to this secret plan is in a letter Washington wrote from the Executive Mansion to his Mount Vernon manager, William Pearce, on January 27, 1796. He had heard that a neighboring plantation had been divided into small tenements for rent and wanted Pearce to find out the precise terms of the leases. Then came a very curious request: he asked Pearce to send him right away a list of all the marriages among the Custis estate's slaves at Mount Vernon: "Let me know who of the Dower Negros that are grown, have husbands and wives, and who those husbands and wives are. That is, whether these connections are, one Dower Negro with another Dower Negro; whether they are with other Negros on the Estate; or whether with the Neighbouring Negros." It was striking that he made this inquiry about slave families in the same breath with a discussion of land rental, and that he withheld his reasons: "I will let you know shortly the object I have in view."[7]

Pearce did as he was asked. Washington followed up with another request, writing on February 7: "Your letter came . . . with the list of Dower Negros which are taken exactly as I wished. I now wish you would forward to me a list of all the remaining Negros on the Estate." Along with the dower list, Pearce also sent him a newspaper advertisement, placed at Washington's request, offering his western lands for rent or sale. The details of Washington's plan are unclear, but one can infer that he intended the income from the land sale to provide some of the financing for the emancipation. Other funds would have to come from the Custis heirs, which was the tricky part.

On that same day, the president wrote to David Stuart to get the scheme moving immediately. In a letter marked *Private* he said, "You will perceive by the enclosed Advertisement, that I am making an essay to accomplish what I communicated to you in confidence when I was last in Virginia." Washington's repeated allusion to secrecy is remarkable. Because the plan had already been discussed in conversations at Mount Vernon (his previous visit home had been in October or November 1795), the letter contains only references to it: he mentions "the renting of my farms," says that the plan will take more than a year to put in place, and that it has two parts.

The kernel of the plan emerges not in Washington's letter but in Stuart's reply: the emancipation of the Custis slaves would be financed by hiring out the slaves to Stuart on the old Custis plantation on Virginia's Eastern Shore. They would be legally manumitted later. Washington also envisioned hiring out people to farmers who settled on his western lands—farmers he hoped to attract from England—though elsewhere he stated a reluctance to hire out his people to strangers lest they be abused. Stuart expressed misgivings. After recounting financial difficulties he was already facing, he wrote, "How far it will be prudent [for me] to encounter an additional, and even reasonable sum for the hire of those you speak of, I cannot determine at present—[even] at a low rate."

Washington and Stuart agreed that one of the most troubling aspects of the plan required the separation of families. The dower slaves would be immediately removed a great distance from Mount Vernon, leaving family members behind. Washington was loath to do this, but his plan was a rescue operation for the slaves themselves; eventually they would be reunited when he put in place the second part of his plan—the emancipation of his own slaves. Why could he not do this immediately? The answer was politics. He dreaded the repercussions of a sitting president freeing his slaves, writing to Stuart that "reasons of a political, indeed of imperious nature" forced him to delay the emancipation of his own slaves.

Washington was concerned with political implications because in the weeks when he was trying to put this plan in place he was simultaneously embroiled in one of the worst crises of his presidency, a crisis that he said was driving the Constitution "to the brink of a precipice." Led by Washington's fellow Virginian James Madison, Southern Congressmen of the Republican Party were attempting to deny funding to Jay's Treaty with Great Britain, which bound American debtors—mainly Southerners, including Washington himself—to honor their prewar liabilities to British creditors, and did not include compensation for slaves carried off by the British after the war. Washington hesitated to take any action, even a private one, that would further inflame the Southern Republicans against him and his Federalist allies.[8]

But Washington was also facing an urgent crisis in his family. Thomas Peter was already selling slaves. Washington wrote to Stuart that he suspected Peter had taken too many slaves from Mount Vernon and he wanted them back: "if a mistake has happened the sooner it is rectified the better." A new generation of masters and mistresses was taking control of the Custis estate; the great division of dower slaves was already under way, compelled by the marriages of the Custis children. Young Martha had married Thomas Peter in 1795. Eliza would soon marry Thomas Law, an upcoming event discussed in the letters. The youngest daughter, Nelly, would not be too far behind (she was to marry Washington's nephew Lawrence Lewis in 1799). The youngest of Jacky's children, G.W.P. "Wash" Custis, would inherit most of the dower slaves remaining at Mount Vernon upon Martha's death. The resulting division of slave families would be permanent and would put the people at risk of sale.

One wonders if Washington was led to his plan partly out of concern for the character of Wash Custis. Wash paid little attention to his studies—evincing a sloth that had presaged the disastrous plantation management of his father—and also showed troubling signs of having inherited Jacky's less desirable personal qualities. Washington wrote: "From his infancy, I have discovered an almost unconquerable disposition to indolence in every thing that did not tend to his amusements." In his time, Wash Custis was to follow in the path of his forebears by fathering children with his slaves.[9]

The president's plan was to put a halt to the division of slaves by the heirs, and possibly even reclaim some of the Peter slaves before they, too, were sold. To proceed with his plan, he told Stuart he would need the approval of "all who are interested." The financial aspects seem fantastic, but Washington had studied the numbers and thought he could do it. With his astonishing capacity for detail, he had already figured out that subdividing lands for rental would require building many new fences to accommodate the renters' livestock. When Pearce raised this issue Washington brushed it aside: "I am sensible that by dividing my farms into small tenements, I add very much to the consumption of my Timber, (and perhaps of the fuel) until hedges sufficient against every thing but Hogs, could be raised (which of quick growing wood might soon be done)." He had considered every aspect of the scheme meticulously.[10]

The emancipation never took place, and the reasons for its failure are unclear. Washington did not succeed in renting or selling his western lands, but that was only a part of the problem. Politics certainly were involved but only regarding the president's own slaves. The scheme mainly rested on persuading the Custis heirs to relinquish ownership of their slaves while retaining them as free laborers. David Stuart and Thomas Peter, the husbands of Custis heirs, were the only beneficiaries of the estate who had actually taken possession of land and slaves. Young Wash had by far the largest prospective interest. In Washington's last will, the vehemence of the language regarding the slaves proves his deep mistrust of the Custis heirs, with whose "pretenses" and "evasions" he was apparently familiar. One name conspicuously absent from the correspondence with Stuart is Martha's. There is no indication that Washington had his wife's aid in persuading the heirs—her family—to join in a venture based not on self-interest but on principles of human justice.

Because Washington was secretive by nature, his motivations are difficult to unravel. His exchange of letters with David Stuart in 1796 demonstrates a commitment to emancipation, but it is unclear whether his main motive was private, political, or a mixture of the two. A private emancipation by the president would have had political repercussions, which either restrained Washington or formed part of his plan. Washington had kept silent when the Quakers presented their emancipation petition to Congress in 1790, a proposal that would have accomplished what he long maintained he was looking for: a legislative plan for emancipation. He may have held himself back from the debate partly because he did not like the kind of allies it would have given him—he could not see himself making common cause with Quakers and others he regarded as fringe elements or "desperate characters." In the public realm he liked to move with comrades of his own class. To counteract the widespread, occasionally violent protests against the Jay Treaty, Washington was able to call upon a network of Federalist party loyalists. Through intermediaries he orchestrated a grassroots campaign to sway public opinion in what was the country's first exercise in "hidden-hand" presidential tactics. He may have envisioned a private emancipation at Mount Vernon as the beginning of another such campaign to move public opinion. To speculate along such lines may seem quixotic, except that the documents prove that Washington twice considered an emancipation during his presidency, that he was aware of the political implications, and that he tried to move forward with his plan anyway. It is possible that the political repercussions were not the obstacle but the goal, and that the plan failed because Washington looked around him for allies and even in his own family could find none.

CHAPTER ELEVEN

"The Justice of the Creator"

*G*RANDPA IS VERY WELL, and much pleased at being once more *Farmer Washington.*" Thus did Washington's granddaughter Nelly report to a friend the return of Washington from the presidency to his beloved Mount Vernon in March 1797. He said that the world he had left behind seemed to him "little more than vanity and vexation."[1] He eagerly resumed the familiar, comforting, yet rigorous routine of farm life, which a visitor described:

> He gets up at five o'clock in the morning, reads or writes until 7. He breakfasts on tea and cakes made from maize; because of his teeth he makes slices spread with butter and honey. He then immediately goes on horseback to see the work in the fields; sometimes in the middle of the fields he holds a council of war with Mr. Anderson [his manager]. He returns at two o'clock, dresses, goes to dinner. If there are guests, he loves to chat after dinner with a glass of Madeira in his hand. After dinner he diligently reads the newspapers, of which he receives about ten of different kinds. He answers letters, etc. Tea at 7 o'clock; he chats until nine, and then he goes to bed.[2]

The visitor who recorded this routine was the Polish nobleman Julian Niemcewicz, who met Washington in Georgetown in May 1798. Thomas Law brought Niemcewicz to evening tea at the home of

Thomas and Martha Peter, in the Georgetown house they occupied before they built Tudor Place.[3] His meeting with the hero left Niemcewicz tongue-tied:

> I saw him through the window and I recognized him immediately. One can guess how my heart was beating; I was going to see the man for whom, since my youth, I had had such a great respect, such a man as my unhappy fatherland lacked for its own salvation. . . . He held out his hand to me and shook mine. We went into the parlor; I sat down beside him; I was moved, speechless. I had not eyes enough to look on him. His is a majestic figure in which dignity and gentleness are united. The portraits that we have of him in Europe do not resemble him much. He is nearly six feet tall, square set, and very strongly built; aquiline nose, blue eyes, the mouth and especially the lower jaw sunken, a good head of hair. . . . He wore a coat of deep nut brown, black stockings, waistcoat, and breeches of satin of the same color.

Though Washington was renowned for his aloofness, he recognized the befuddlement of the foreign guest and plunged into some small talk.

"How long are you in this country?"

"Eight months."

"How do you like it?"

"I am happy, Sir, to see in America those blessings which I was so ardently wishing for in my own country. To you, Sir, are the Americans indebted for them."

"I wished always your country well and that with all my heart."

The arrival of Eliza Custis Law and her toddler broke the ice. The general swept the child up in his arms and handed her a sweet. He set the girl down and began to chat about farming, "a favorite subject of the General." It was a congenial evening. Niemcewicz basked in the presence of the young Custis women, "the most beautiful women one could see." Mrs. Peter played the harpsichord. They had tea and the general told jokes. Washington and the Pole got on so well that

Niemcewicz returned the next day as well. Washington was in an expansive mood; when the talk turned to housing projects to accommodate the new government, he told another joke: "They spoke of the offices that were going to be built for the departments [and] discussed at length the difficulty that there would be to finish enough houses to lodge the members. Gen. Washington said . . . 'Oh well, they can camp out. The Representatives in the first line, the Senate in the second, the president with all his suite in the middle.'" Later on Niemcewicz played billiards with the general, who then begged the favor of entertaining him at Mount Vernon.

The meeting of the nobleman and the general was fortunate for history, for Niemcewicz recorded in his diary some of the sharpest observations we have about Mount Vernon's master and his slaves. As Niemcewicz ambled about the region with apparent aimlessness, "possessing nothing and condemned to the life of a vagabond," as he said of himself, he wrote down all that he encountered with a keen eye and ear, and a sense of humor. After a day of misadventures he and two French companions trudged into Georgetown tired and famished: "We ate dinner table d'hote and paid in our capacity as foreigners double the normal price."[4]

Niemcewicz also possessed a moral sense that compelled him to question the obvious contradictions in this new republic.

We went this morning to roam about the Capitol. It was eleven o'clock. No one was at work; they had gone to drink *grog*. This is what they do twice a day, as well as dinner and breakfast. . . . The Negroes alone work. I have seen them in large numbers, and I was very glad that these poor unfortunates earned eight to ten dollars per week. My joy was not long lived: I am told that they were not working for themselves; their masters hire them out and retain all the money for themselves. What humanity! What a country of liberty.[5]

Before visiting Mount Vernon, Niemcewicz set out for a tour of the Virginia countryside with his French companions: "We passed along the fields where ten Negroes, men and women, were scratching at the soil and driving in little sticks. . . . Their emaciated and black skeletons were covered with shreds of rags, bare legs."[6] Eager to speak with the slaves, and not knowing the custom of the country, Niemcewicz and his companions tied up their horses and jumped a hedge to get into the field. The slaves told the visitors they were planting maize, and demonstrated how they scratched into the soil and planted a few grains. Their curiosity satisfied, the foreigners turned to leave when they heard "a furious voice" cry out, "Stop! Stop!"

We returned and saw two men armed with guns, running all out of breath and very anxiously towards the Negro with whom we had just spoken and asking him what we had wanted and what we had said to him. Right in the middle of these interrogations we approached. "What were you looking for here? What did you want with my Negroes?" he asked us in an agitated and frightened voice. We told him we were foreigners, that we were curious to see a tobacco plantation. . . . "I beg of you a thousand pardons . . . I thought that you had come to corrupt and seduce my Negroes." What more wretched existence is there than that of a man who lives in continual anxiety of seeing his unfortunates carried away; whom he knows to be discontented with him and whom he does not cease however, to torment. We left. We saw at the side of the road a few miserable cabins, dwellings of the Blacks.

A few days later Niemcewicz went to Mount Vernon with Thomas Law. Washington often grumbled about the horde of unwanted visitors that descended willy-nilly on Mount Vernon, but he was delighted to see Niemcewicz, who was made so comfortable that he remained for twelve days, remarking in his diary, "I was not as a stranger but a member of the family."[7] He passed long hours in discussions with Washington:

I have often heard the general reproached for his reserve and his taciturnity. It is true that he is somewhat reserved in speech, but he does not avoid entering into conversation when one furnishes him with a subject. . . . At the table after the departure of the ladies, or else in the evening seated under the portico, he often talked with me for hours at a time. His favorite subject is agriculture, but he answered with kindness all questions that I put him on the Revolution, the armies, etc. He has a prodigious memory.

Martha charmed him as well, and Niemcewicz wrote glowingly of her in his diary. "Mrs. Washington is one of the most estimable persons that one could know, good, sweet, and extremely polite. She loves to talk and talks very well about times past. She told me she remembered the time when there was only one single carriage in all of Virginia. Ladies invited to entertainment arrived on horseback."

The general took his visitor for a tour of his fields, and Niemcewicz went down to the river to watch the slaves fish for herring. If he ever discussed slavery with his host, Niemcewicz did not record it; that sensitive topic probably did not come up. But Washington's manager, James Anderson, spoke freely on the subject. He told Niemcewicz that Mount Vernon had three hundred slaves, but only one hundred were actually able to work. "They work all week," Niemcewicz wrote, "not having a single day for themselves except holidays. One sees by that that the condition of our peasants [in Poland] is infinitely happier." Anderson told him that "the mulattoes are ordinarily chosen for servants," and explained that the law of Virginia made slaves of the children of slave women, even if the father was white. Another foreign visitor to Mount Vernon wrote, "The general's house servants are mulattoes, some of whom have kinky hair still but skin as light as ours. I noticed one small boy whose hair and skin were so like our own that if I had not been told, I should never have suspected his ancestry. He is nevertheless a slave for the rest of his life."[8]

Either from his own observation or from what Anderson told him, Niemcewicz wrote, "General Washington treats his slaves far more humanely than do his fellow citizens of Virginia. Most of these gentlemen give to their Blacks only bread, water and blows." The Pole's assessment is contradicted by the observation of another foreign visitor, Richard Parkinson, an English farmer who considered leasing some of the Mount Vernon land a few months after Niemcewicz was there. In an account of his time in Virginia he wrote: "The management of negroes was a great obstacle. . . . they will not do without harsh treatment. Only take General Washington as an example: I have not the least reason to think it was his desire, but the necessity of the case: but it was the sense of all his neighbours that he treated them with more severity than any other man." Parkinson said he was "amazed" at how sharply Washington spoke when giving orders to slaves: "He spoke as differently as if he had been quite another man, or had been in anger."[9]

Contradictions such as these multiply in the record of slavery at Mount Vernon. Washington tried to put a stop to the excesses of overseers who treated the slaves as "brute beasts," but he also used these overseers as a threat to his house servants: if they misbehaved they would be exiled to the "several Plantations."[10] He did not treat all his slaves alike; some were "deserving," some were "worthless" (and therefore got less from him in the way of clothing). He instructed his manager in 1795: "the better sort of linnen to be given to the grown people, and the most deserving; whilst the more indifferent sort is served to the younger ones and worthless." He could be quite blunt in his assessments: in 1795 he wrote, "The death of Paris is a loss, that of Jupiter the reverse." Washington recognized competence when he saw it, writing of the "smart young negro man who acts as an Assistant in the mill." His mulatto overseer Davy did a reasonably good job, and for another assignment he suggested "the children of Daphne at the river farm [who] are among the best disposed negros I have."[11]

Niemcewicz saw evidence that the slaves at Mount Vernon were reasonably contented: "Either from habit, or from natural humor disposed to gaiety, I have never seen the Blacks sad. Last Sunday there were about thirty divided into two groups and playing at prisoner's base. There were jumps and gambols as if they had rested all week. I noticed that all spoke very good English." Yet he also saw the conditions in which Washington's slaves lived when Anderson and Law took him to the slave quarter on an outlying farm:

We entered one of the huts of the Blacks, for one cannot call them by the name of houses. They are more miserable than the most miserable of the cottages of our peasants. The husband and wife sleep on a mean pallet, the children on the ground; a very bad fireplace, some utensils for cooking, but in the middle of this poverty some cups and a teapot. A boy of 15 was lying on the ground, sick, and in terrible convulsions. The General had sent to Alexandria to fetch a doctor. A very small garden planted with vegetables was close by, with five or six hens, each one leading 10 to 15 chickens. It is the only comfort that is permitted them; for they may not keep either ducks, geese, or pigs. They sell the poultry in Alexandria and procure for themselves a few amenities.

From Washington's own description, a slave house might be so insubstantial that, in order to move it, the slaves could just pick it up and put it on a cart, and they might not even need the cart. A black overseer's house was so flimsy Washington's manager feared a strong wind might knock it over and kill the overseer's family. In one letter Washington referred to the slaves' houses as "coverings," implying that they offered but the bare minimum of shelter, and he admitted that white people would not live in them. His cousin and manager, Lund, thought of the slaves' houses as the benchmark of squalor: in describing to Washington the poor workmanship of some new chimneys in the mansion, Lund wrote in 1775, "they really smoke'd so Bad that the wall lookd as bad as any negro Quarter. . . ."[12] It might seem to be a contradiction that Washington kept his slaves in such miserable conditions while planning to free them. But in Washington's view, society was hierarchical: there would always be people at the bottom, laborers both white and black whose lot was a harsh one. Washington accepted the notion that a laborer's life would be hard, but he rejected the idea that the laborer should be enslaved.

Near the end of his visit, Niemcewicz saw the arrival, in grand style, of the Washingtons' granddaughter Eleanor, the widow of Jacky Custis, and her second husband, Dr. David Stuart. They thundered up the drive in a coach and four, with a pair of slaves on horseback and two black postilions clinging to the rear of the carriage. Niemcewicz had a long talk with Stuart about slavery, in which Stuart expounded on the inferiority of the black race, "which will never mix in the society of Whites."

Not mentioning that two years earlier Washington had tried to carry out a massive emancipation, Stuart mouthed the usual self-justifications that slave owners kept ready for outsiders: "He told me: no one knows better than the Virginians the cruelty, inconvenience and the little advantage of having Blacks. Their support costs a great deal; their work is worth little if they are not whipped; the [overseer] costs a great deal and steals into the bargain. We would all agree to free these people; but how to do it with such a great number?" The masters had one set of facts for outsiders and another among themselves. Stuart told Niemcewicz that "this unfortunate black color has made such a sharp distinction between the two races. It will always make them a separate caste." To Washington, his fellow slaveholder, Stuart had said the exact opposite: "the only thing to be regretted is, that they are not of the same colour with ourselves—But time which applies a remedy to all things, will no doubt soon find one for this."[13]

Niemcewicz captured more in his diary than he realized. His conversation with Dr. Stuart reveals the stubbornness that Washington had to battle in his own family, and it shows his isolation. Washington had looked hard for a way to free his slaves, yet Stuart was braying that it was impossible. Washington despised the selling of human beings, yet Thomas Peter was busy at it. Washington's own family had no qualms at all about the slave market. His brother John Augustine called for the sale of slaves in his will. His nephew Corbin wrote in his will of 1799:

as it is not uncommon for Negroes to become disobedient to their Mistresses after the Death of their Masters to prevent any inconvenience on this head I do hereby give my said dear Wife full powers & authority to sell & dispose of any of them so offending in her Opinion, and Vest the money arising therefrom in Other Negroes, or such other Property as She may consider most beneficial to herself and Children.[14]

After Washington's death, Bushrod, irritated by repeated escapes, sold fifty of his slaves from Mount Vernon to the Deep South traders. Thus Washington lived among an extended family and in a society that compelled him to silence and, when pressed, prevarication. In 1798 he made an eloquent little speech on slavery to a visiting Englishman—all of it false but for the last line.

A black coming at this moment, with a jug of spring water, I could not repress a smile, which the General at once interpreted. "This may seem a contradiction, but I think you must perceive that it is neither a crime nor an absurdity. When we profess, as our fundamental principle, that liberty is the inalienable right of every man, we do not include madman or idiots; liberty in their hands would become a scourge. Till the mind of the slave has been educated to perceive what are the obligations of a state of freedom, and not confound a man's with a brute's, the gift would insure its abuse. We might as well be asked to pull down our old warehouses before trade has increased to demand enlarged new ones. Both houses and slaves were bequeathed to us by Europeans, and time alone can change them; an event, sir, which, you may believe me, no man desires more heartily than I do. Not only do I pray for it, on the score of human dignity, but I can clearly foresee that nothing but the rooting out of slavery can perpetuate the existence of our union, by consolidating it in a common bond of principle."[15]

His remarks to the visitor seemed to defend the indefinite continuation of slavery; yet at the same time he admitted that its perpetuation threatened the nation. For years he had been plotting emancipation, and just a few months later he wrote the will that set his people free.

For the man who lived by the maxim "I have made it a rule . . . ,"

Washington displayed surprising vacillation when slavery was involved. On no other issue was he so vulnerable to pressure. During the Revolution he first forbade blacks to be soldiers, because that was what his officers seemed to want and that was the prejudice he brought from the South, but then he accepted them after a direct appeal from the blacks themselves. He first supported the Laurens plan for emancipation, then backed away. At the end of the war he thought the slaves who had reached British lines were gone forever, but when pressured by other planters he tried to force General Carleton, unsuccessfully, to yield up the escaped slaves. When he outlined his emancipation plan to Lear he said to keep it secret (in a break with procedure, a copy of that letter was not kept at Mount Vernon). He told Humphreys that slavery was his great regret, but that regret never appeared in his letters to his family (with the exception of the remarkable blast at Spotswood over selling slaves "as if they were cattle"). When he assured David Stuart that the Quaker emancipation proposal had been put to sleep, he did not acknowledge that he had been considering a private emancipation himself. He sensed his isolation on this issue, especially within his own family. When Washington wrote to his nephew Lawrence Lewis in 1799 to tell him what land he was getting in his will, he did not tell Lewis that he would not be getting slaves as well. One month after he had written his will, Washington wrote to another relative of the problem of surplus labor at Mount Vernon but said nothing of his plan to liberate the slaves. He was keeping his emancipation a secret. This pattern of concealment can only mean that Washington expected fierce opposition if he revealed his plan in advance—opposition he might not be able to overcome.[16]

Washington's decision to write his will seems to have been made abruptly in July 1799. The nineteenth-century journalist Benson Lossing, an intimate of the Custis family, printed the letter from Martha describing the dream Washington had about his impending death, the dream that set him to writing his will. The original of this letter has not been found, and the legitimacy of it has been questioned. But the core of the story has the ring of truth. Interestingly, Washington formulated his secret 1794 emancipation plan at another moment when he thought he was dying—he had disfiguring skin lesions which he took, incorrectly, to be cancerous. It makes sense that an intimation of death in 1799 would have impelled him to put his final emancipation plan on paper before it was too late.[17]

Washington knew all too well that Mount Vernon was overstocked with laborers. Anderson told Niemcewicz that only one hundred out of three hundred slaves actually worked. Washington himself thought there were twice as many slaves as the plantation actually needed. He also knew all too well what his heirs would do with the surplus: they would sell them. Washington himself owned only 123 of Mount Vernon's 316 slaves; forty others were rented; the rest were the property of the Custis estate and would go to the Custis heirs after Martha's death. Washington could free his own people but he could not touch the dower slaves. He acknowledged this difficulty in the will:

> Upon the decease of my wife, it is my Will & desire that all the Slaves which I hold in my *own right*, shall receive their freedom. To emancipate them during her life, would, tho' earnestly wished by me, be attended with such insuperable difficulties on account of their intermixture by Marriages with the dower Negroes, as to excite the most painful sensations, if not disagreeable consequences from the latter, while both descriptions are in the occupancy of the same Proprietor; it not being in my power, under the tenure by which the Dower Negroes are held, to manumit them.

By delaying his slaves' emancipation until Martha's death, he did not solve the problem of breaking up the slaves' families but merely put it off, which would have been evident to Martha. He foresaw "most painful sensations" and "disagreeable consequences" if this breakup of families were allowed to happen. This was a tacit appeal to Martha and the Custis heirs to join him in emancipating their slaves along with his. Unlike Hannah and John Augustine Washington, who had clearly discussed the fine points of John Augustine's will, George and

Martha Washington were not even speaking to each other about slavery by the end of their lives together. He had to appeal to her humanity from the grave.

> And whereas among those who will recieve freedom according to this devise, there may be some, who from old age or bodily infirmities, and others who on account of their infancy, that will be unable to support themselves; it is my Will and desire that all who come under the first & second description shall be comfortably cloathed & fed by my heirs while they live. . . .

Washington's stipulation that the old and the infirm be cared for until death would seem unnecessary; the plantation lore passed down to us holds that masters always cared for the old slaves. But that was not the case. Thomas Peter tried to sell off a sixty-year-old Custis slave, but found no takers. A decade after Washington died, his cousins at Blenheim similarly tried to rid themselves of an old couple, also finding no takers. Washington knew the magnanimity of the masters was uncertain. If they could pick up a few dollars for an aged, unwanted attendant, no scruple would restrain them; the prohibition against this had to be written into the will. Washington specified that "a regular and permanent fund be established for their support so long as there are subjects requiring it; not trusting to the uncertain provision to be made by individuals."

The clause that followed was perhaps the most extraordinary:

> [the children who] have no parents living, or if living are unable, or unwilling to provide for them, shall be bound by the Court until they shall arrive at the age of twenty five years; and in cases where no record can be produced, whereby their ages can be ascertained, the judgment of the Court, upon its own view of the subject, shall be adequate and final. The Negros thus bound, are (by their Masters or Mistresses) to be taught to read & write; and to be brought up to some useful occupation, agreeably to the Laws of the Commonwealth of Virginia, providing for the support of Orphan[s] and other poor Children.

Education for slaves—the very thought of it was revolutionary. With this clause Washington overturned generations of prejudice. Washington was not a racist: he did not believe that the slaves were inherently inferior people; he believed that the apparent deficiencies in African-Americans were the result of their enslavement, and that with education and the opportunity to find work they could prosper as free people.

His next clause may have been addressed directly to Thomas Peter:

> and I do hereby expressly forbid the Sale, or transportation out of the said Commonwealth, of any Slave I may die possessed of, under any pretence whatsoever. And I do moreover most pointedly, and most solemnly enjoin it upon my Executors hereafter named, or the Survivors of them, to see that *this* clause respecting Slaves, and every part thereof be religiously fulfilled at the Epoch at which it is directed to take place; without evasion, neglect or delay . . .

The vehemence of Washington's language suggests that he trusted none of his heirs and executors. The order for an emancipation should have been clear and sufficient in itself; but Washington did not think so. He expected evasions and pretenses. There is an extraordinary element in this clause as well. Virtually every emancipation plan proposed in Washington's time included forced exile for the freed slaves to Africa or the West Indies. Washington insisted that no one be exiled; the slaves had a right to live on American soil.

The final portion of the emancipation clause recognized the service of one particular slave:

> And to my Mulatto man William (calling himself William Lee) I give immediate freedom; or if he should prefer it (on account of the accidents which have befallen him, and which have rendered him incapable of walking or of any active employment) to remain in the situation he now is, it shall be optional in him to do so: In either case however, I allow him an annuity of thirty dollars during his natural life, which shall be independent of the victuals and cloaths he has been accustomed to receive, if he chuses the last alternative; but in

full, with his freedom, if he prefers the first; & this I give him as a testimony of my sense of his attachment to me, and for his faithful services during the Revolutionary War.

As faithful as William Lee had been to him for more than thirty
years, Washington did not reveal in other records that he had ever
grown especially close to him. Washington looked after Lee when he
was injured; gave him permission to bring his wife, whom Washington disliked, to Mount Vernon (though she may never have come;
there is no record of her); and granted Lee immediate freedom. But
there is no account of their conversing or sharing any intimate moment.
Washington did not love this slave, and when he set him free he acted
not out of sentiment but out of a sense of justice that extended to all
the slaves, including those who had malingered or stolen from him or
tried to escape. He did not free only a favored few, as other masters and
mistresses occasionally did. His sense of justice knew no exceptions.

Washington lived just five more months after writing his will. In December 1799 a sudden snowstorm blew in while he was on his daily
rounds inspecting his farming operations. That night he awakened
with a sore throat, his air passage so swollen that he struggled to
breathe. Doctors rushed to his bedside and applied, at Washington's
insistence, the standard treatment of the time, bleeding; he was probably suffering an acute infection. His death was slow and painful, tanta-
mount to a slow strangulation, but he endured the agony with immense
stoicism. Throughout his ordeal he was cared for by slaves—Molly,
Charlotte, Christopher Sheels, and Caroline Branham. He had one final decision to make, the nature of which is not known. He asked
Martha to bring him the wills he had written—not one, but two. He
glanced at the papers and asked her to burn one of them, which was
done. What clauses it contained, no one knows. He died on the night
of December 14, a Saturday, between ten and eleven o'clock.[18]
    After her husband died, Martha moved to a small bedroom on the
third floor. "Wash" Custis took another room on that floor to keep her
company, but there is some thought that she became a bit of a recluse.

Perhaps at her husband's request, she burned all of their decades of personal correspondence.[19]

Washington's emancipation clause had an unintended effect. Martha began to fear that his slaves would kill her to hasten the day of their freedom. Her grandson "Wash" Custis wrote, "The slaves were left to be emancipated at the death of Mrs. Washington; but it was found necessary (for *prudential* reasons) to give them their freedom in one year after the general's decease." Accordingly, on New Year's Day 1801, Washington's slaves were all set free. Martha died on May 22, 1802, then possessing only one slave in her own name. Two months before her death Martha added a codicil to her will about this slave: "I give to my grandson George Washington Parke Custis my mulatto man Elish—that I bought of mr Butler Washington . . . to him and his [heirs] forever."* The example George Washington set was not followed even in his own household; there were no exceptions even for a single soul. The Custis estate passed intact to Martha's heirs, augmented by Elish.[20]

In the end George Washington did precisely what he had said was impossible: he freed his slaves all at once, not by imperceptible degrees. Earlier he had insisted that an emancipation could only be done with the sanction of law, but he had lost faith that the political process could solve the problem of slavery. The interests opposed to emancipation were too strong and held too many seats.

Washington's will was a blueprint for a future that did not come to pass. He implicitly declared that slaves had a right to freedom, to education, to productive work. He believed that the African-Americans had a rightful place in the United States. The contrast with Thomas Jefferson is illuminating. Speaking of the impossibility of emancipation, Jefferson wrote, "We have the wolf by the ear: and we can neither hold him, nor safely let him go. Justice is in one scale, and self-preservation in the other." Washington did not dither over making fine metaphors; he simply freed his people.[21]

---

* Elish is a mystery, as is Butler Washington, about whom almost nothing is known.

Washington may have believed that, given his immense prestige, his will would have some lasting influence on the debate over slavery. But Jefferson's vision of America's racial future won out over Washington's. Jefferson wrote:

> It will probably be asked, Why not retain and incorporate the blacks into the state, and thus save the expense of supplying, by importation of white settlers, the vacancies they will leave? Deep rooted prejudices entertained by the whites; ten thousand recollections, by the blacks, of the injuries they have sustained; new provocations; the real distinctions which nature has made; and many other circumstances, will divide us into parties, and produce convulsions, which will probably never end but in the extermination of the one or the other race. —To these objections, which are political, may be added others, which are physical and moral.[22]

Jefferson was wrong about the blacks, whose history since Emancipation has consistently been one of forgiveness, not revenge. Yet Jefferson was correct about the "deep rooted prejudices entertained by the whites," as evidenced by subsequent events during Reconstruction and into the twentieth century.

The tragedy, for the nation, is that Washington did not act upon his convictions during his lifetime. Had he freed his slaves in 1794 or in 1796, while in office, the effect might have been profound. He would have set the precedent that the chief executive cannot hold slaves. When the question of slavery arose at the Constitutional Convention and later in Congress, South Carolina and Georgia were always adamant in their opposition to any emancipation plan, no matter how long it might have played out nor how the costs might have been defrayed. Those states threatened secession. As Joseph Ellis has pointed out, "perhaps, as some historians have argued, South Carolina and Georgia were bluffing. But the most salient historical fact cannot be avoided: No one stepped forward to call their bluff." Washington, the practiced Williamsburg gambler, was the man who could have called the bluff. Jefferson himself said that Washington was "the one man who outweighs them all in influence over the people."[23]

The biographer James Thomas Flexner argues that Washington supported Alexander Hamilton's plan to promote manufacturing because it would move the United States away from slavery. And it is clear that Washington could see the deleterious effects of the slave system. He wrote in 1796 to a British correspondent, "The present prices of lands in Pennsylvania are higher than they are in Maryland and Virginia, although they are not of superior quality; (among other reasons) because there are laws [in Pennsylvania] for the gradual abolition of slavery, which neither of the two States above mentioned have at present, but which nothing is more certain than they must have, and at a period not remote."[24]

Washington seems to have believed that a gradual emancipation would not have caused an insuperable labor problem. By the 1790s sharecropping was a long-established labor system; it was not born after the Civil War. It may seem fanciful to speculate from the distance of two centuries that sharecropping might have been a viable alternative to slavery in the 1790s, but evidently that is what Washington himself had in mind. Washington had white tenant farmers; in his youth, most white males on the Northern Neck were sharecroppers. David Stuart's February 1796 letter to Washington discusses in detail a sharecropping plan for the freed Mount Vernon slaves—even Stuart did not find the idea to be fantastic.

A gradual emancipation that turned slaves into free sharecroppers would have largely preserved the labor pool, but it would have deranged the financial planning of the elite, who had become dependent on slaves for portable, bequeathable, disposable capital. Land in Virginia was losing its value, having been ruined by tobacco; but slaves held their value, and increased in value if sent to the Piedmont or farther west. No one knew this better than Washington's relatives, such as his cousin Spotswood, who wrote to Washington about moving slaves to Kentucky to sell them in a higher market. Spotswood's scheme marked a rising trend. After studying the prices of slaves in Washington's era and later, Winthrop Jordan found that as slavery's profits declined in Virginia, "superfluous slaves could be transferred to regions where they would no longer be superfluous, to Kentucky or . . . to the southward." As early as 1793 "great numbers" of slaves, wrote a contemporary observer, were being transported from Virginia. Jordan writes: "by the turn of the century American slavery had taken on new dimensions."[25]

Though only a tiny minority of men and women in the United States were slaveholders, they controlled public policy over slavery. The figures from Washington's own county in Virginia, Fairfax, show that slaveholding was the domain of the very few. In 1782 only 7 percent of Fairfax residents owned slaves—and yet they dominated every facet of the political system, which yielded to their interests. To preserve the world they had always known from any change, they clung to the past, with disastrous consequences not long in coming. As the historian Gordon Wood writes, "By the 1820s the South, which at the time of the Revolution had thought of itself as the heart and soul of the nation, had become a bewildered and beleaguered slave-ridden minority out of touch with the tales of reform and free enterprise that now dominated the country."[26]

In his racial views, Washington might have agreed with what Abraham Lincoln said in his debate with Stephen Douglas:

> There is no reason in the world why the negro is not entitled to all the natural rights enumerated in the Declaration of Independence, the right to life, liberty, and the pursuit of happiness. I hold that he is as much entitled to these as the white man. I agree with Judge Douglas that he is not my equal in many respects—certainly not in color, perhaps not in moral or intellectual endowment. But in the right to eat the bread, without the leave of anybody else, which his own hand earns, he is my equal and the equal of Judge Douglas and the equal of every living man.[27]

The error of the founders, including Washington, regarding slavery, had to be undone—and Lincoln undid it. Both Washington and Jefferson had a premonition of what might come if slavery were not

abolished. Washington stated bluntly, "I can clearly foresee that nothing but the rooting out of slavery can perpetuate the existence of our
union." There is strong evidence that slavery had pushed George
Washington to a political breaking point. During his presidency the
preeminent Founding Father made the startling, indeed, amazing, remark that if the Union split apart into North and South, "he had
made up his mind to remove and be of the Northern." He made the
comment to his secretary of state, Edmund Randolph; it was recorded
by Jefferson.[28] Both Washington and Jefferson feared a calamity. Jefferson famously said, "I tremble for my country when I reflect that
God is just: that His justice cannot sleep forever."[29] When Washington confided to Humphreys his "regret" over slavery, he invoked "the
justice of the Creator," an invocation Lincoln echoed three score and
sixteen years later:

> Fondly do we hope—fervently do we pray—that this mighty scourge
> of war may speedily pass away. Yet, if God wills that it continue, un-
> til all the wealth piled by the bond-man's 250 years of unrequited toil
> shall be sunk, and until every drop of blood drawn with the lash shall
> be paid by another drawn with the sword, as was said 3,000 years ago,
> so still it must be said "the judgments of the Lord, are true and righ-
> teous altogether."[30]

Notes

A NOTE ON QUOTATIONS AND SOURCES

Quotations from Washington's correspondence have been taken whenever possible from the authoritative edition, *The Papers of George Washington* (cited as *Papers of GW*), which is still in process as this book is being written, with forty-three volumes in print. The editors of the *Papers* have attempted to publish every item written and received by Washington, preserving the original spelling, grammar, and punctuation. The *Papers* volumes, edited by W. W. Abbot, Dorothy Twohig, Philander D. Chase, et al., are arranged chronologically in five series: Colonial, Revolutionary War, Confederation, Presidential, and Retirement. The thirty-nine-volume John C. Fitzpatrick edition of *The Writings of George Washington* (cited as *Writings of GW*), published in 1931–44, is limited to Washington's own writings and is less accurate in its transcriptions. With one exception citations of Washington's diaries refer to the six-volume *Diaries of George Washington* (*Diaries of GW*), edited by Donald Jackson and Dorothy Twohig, rather than to the Fitzpatrick edition.

Occasionally quotations have been taken from an original Washington manuscript in the Library of Congress. Remarkably, the Library of Congress Website makes available images of every Washington item in its collection, often with transcriptions from Fitzpatrick (http://memory.loc.gov/ammem/gwhtml/gwhome.html). Citations of items in the *Papers*, except references to editorial notes, are by date rather than page number to enable ready cross-reference to Fitzpatrick and the LC site. The entire Fitzpatrick edition of the *Writings* is available online in a searchable format (http://etext.virginia.edu/washington/fitzpatrick). The Website of *The Papers of George Washington* (http://gwpapers.virginia.edu) reproduces certain key documents, provides indexes to the volumes in print, and offers a number of articles, maps, and other resources about Washington. The Mount Vernon Website (http://www.mountvernon.org) also offers research articles and finding aids to its collection.

INTRODUCTION: THE GENERAL'S DREAM

1. Joseph Fields, ed., *"Worthy Partner": The Papers of Martha Washington* (Westport, Conn.: Greenwood Press, 1994), pp. 321–22. The original letter has not been located; Fields derives the text from Benson J. Lossing, *Mary and Martha: The Mother and the Wife of George Washington* (New York: Harper & Brothers, 1886), pp. 324–26.

2. *The Papers of George Washington*, W. W. Abbot, Dorothy Twohig, Philander D. Chase, et al., eds. (Charlottesville: University Press of Virginia, 1980–), Retirement Series, 4:479.

3. *Mount Vernon: A Handbook* (Mount Vernon, Va.: Mount Vernon Ladies' Association, 1985), p. 81.

4. Patrick Henry quoted in David Brion Davis, *The Problem of Slavery in the Age of Revolution* (Ithaca, N.Y.: Cornell University Press, 1975), p. 196; Jefferson to Edward Bancroft, January 26, 1789, quoted in Lucia Stanton, "Those Who Labor for My Happiness," Peter Onuf, ed., *Jeffersonian Legacies* (Charlottesville: University Press of Virginia, 1993), p. 147.

5. David Humphreys, *David Humphreys' "Life of General Washington,"* Rosemarie Zagarri, ed. (Athens: University of Georgia Press, 1991), p. 78.

6. Quoted in John Corbin, *The Unknown Washington* (New York: Scribner, 1930), title page, p. 24; Abigail Adams and Nelly Custis quoted in Richard N. Smith, *Patriarch* (Boston: Houghton Mifflin, 1993), pp. 377, 25.

7. Sally Foster Otis to Mrs. Charles W. Apthorp, January 13, 1801, quoted in Allan C. Greenberg, *George Washington, Architect* (London: Andreas Papadakis, 1999), p. 17; Henry Wiencek, *Mansions of the Virginia Gentry* (Birmingham, Ala.: Oxmoor House, 1988), p. 12.

8. David Hackett Fischer, *Albion's Seed: Four British Folkways in America* (New York: Oxford University Press, 1989), pp. 268–69.

9. *Papers of GW,* Colonial Series, vol. 1, GW to John Augustine Washington, May 31, 1754.

10. Clifford Dowdey, *The Virginia Dynasties: The Emergence of "King" Carter and the Golden Age* (Boston: Little, Brown, 1969), p. 343.

11. Wendell Garrett, ed., *George Washington's Mount Vernon* (New York: Monacelli Press, 1998), p. 60.

12. Mac Griswold, *Washington's Gardens at Mount Vernon* (Boston: Houghton Mifflin, 1999), p. 95.

13. Douglas Southall Freeman, *George Washington: A Biography,* New York: Scribner, 1948–57), 1:xv.

1. HOME GROUND

1. Wiencek, *Mansions of the Virginia Gentry,* p. 14.

2. Paul K. Longmore, *The Invention of George Washington* (Charlottesville: University Press of Virginia, 1999), p. 10.

3. Freeman, *George Washington*, 1:89.

4. Fischer, *Albion's Seed*, pp. 305, 224; Rhys Isaac, *The Transformation of Virginia 1740–1790* (Chapel Hill: University of North Carolina Press, 1982), p. 145; Fischer, *Albion's Seed*, p. 222.

5. Louise Pecquet du Bellet, *Some Prominent Virginia Families* (Baltimore: Genealogical Publishing Company, 1976), p. 776.

6. Ralph Waldo Emerson, *Representative Men*, 1850, electronic resource, http://etext.lib.virginia.edu/toc/modeng/public/EmeRepr.html, p. 634.

7. Martin H. Quitt, "The English Cleric and the Virginia Adventurer," in Don Higginbotham, ed., *George Washington Reconsidered* (Charlottesville: University Press of Virginia, 2001), pp. 15ff.

8. Isaac, *Transformation of Virginia*, p. 29.

9. *Papers of GW*, Colonial Series, vol. 8, GW to John Posey, June 24, 1767; Fischer, *Albion's Seed*, p. 378.

10. Fischer, *Albion's Seed*, pp. 374–78.

11. Carol Berkin, *First Generations: Women in Colonial America* (New York: Hill and Wang, 1996), p. 8.

12. Freeman, *George Washington*, 1:15ff.

13. Quoted in Fischer, *Albion's Seed*, p. 224.

14. George Washington, "Forms of Writing, and The Rules of Civility and Decent Behavior in Company and Conversation," Library of Congress, Manuscript Division, George Washington Papers, 1741–99: Series 1 Exercise Books, Diaries, and Surveys; Subseries A Exercise Books.

15. Grizzard, Frank E., Jr., *George Washington: A Biographical Companion* (Santa Barbara, Calif.: ABC-CLIO, 2002), pp. 326–27.

16. George Washington Parke Custis, *Recollections and Private Memoirs of Washington*, Benson J. Lossing, ed. (New York: Derby & Jackson, 1860), p. 129.

17. Ibid., p. 131.

18. Mason L. Weems, *The Life of Washington*, Marcus Cunliffe, ed. (Cambridge, Mass.: Harvard University Press, 1962), pp. xxxvii, 12. Cunliffe examines the evidence carefully and cannot condemn the cherry tree story: "The cherry-tree incident could have happened to any small boy let loose with a hatchet; the unforgivable offense, in critics' eyes, was to moralize about it."

19. Custis, *Recollections*, pp. 132–34.

20. Ibid., p. 122.

21. C. C. Haven, *Thirty Days in New Jersey Ninety Years Ago*, quoted in Richard Brookhiser, *Founding Father: Rediscovering George Washington* (New York: Free Press, 1996), p. 30.

22. James Blair, quoted in "Virginia Gleanings in England," *Virginia Magazine of History and Biography* 20 (1912): 373; see Fischer, *Albion's Seed*, p. 318.

23. Fischer, *Albion's Seed*, p. 312.

24. Ibid., p. 318.

25. Ibid., p. 317.

Notes to Pages 35–45

26. Quoted in Brookhiser, *Founding Father,* p. 122.

27. Ibid., p. 123.

28. Quoted in Longmore, *Invention of George Washington,* p. 174.

29. Fischer, *Albion's Seed,* p. 317; *Cato, A Tragedy,* by Joseph Addison, in Ricardo Quintana, ed., *Eighteenth Century Plays* (New York: Modern Library, 1952).

30. Quoted in Benson J. Lossing, *George Washington's Mount Vernon* (New York: Fairfax Press, 1977; reprint of *The Home of Washington,* 1870), p. 368.

31. Fischer, *Albion's Seed,* p. 316.

32. James Thomas Flexner, *George Washington,* 4 vols. (Boston: Little, Brown, 1965–72), 4:493.

33. *Papers of GW,* Colonial Series, vol. 3, GW to Robert Dinwiddie, April 27, 1756.

34. *The Writings of George Washington from the Original Manuscript Sources, 1745–1799,* John C. Fitzpatrick, ed., 39 vols. (Washington, D.C.: United States Government Printing Office, 1931–44), 16:313–14, GW to Robert Howe, September 20, 1779.

35. *Writings of GW,* 21:295, GW to Armand Louis de Gontaut Brione, Duc de Lauzun, February 26, 1781.

36. Julian Ursyn Niemcewicz, *Under Their Vine and Fig Tree,* Metchie J. E. Budka, ed. and trans. (Elizabeth, N.J.: Grassman Publishing, 1965), pp. 86–87.

37. *Writings of GW,* 35:296–98, GW to Joseph Whipple, November 28, 1796.

38. Humphreys, *Life of General Washington,* p. 6.

39. Philip D. Morgan, *Slave Counterpoint: Black Culture in the Eighteenth-Century Chesapeake & Lowcountry* (Chapel Hill: University of North Carolina Press, 1998), p. 9 n. 12; Winthrop Jordan, *White Over Black: American Attitudes Toward the Negro 1550–1812* (Chapel Hill: University of North Carolina Press, 1968), p. 80; Fischer, *Albion's Seed,* p. 388.

40. Scott L. Malcomson, *One Drop of Blood: The American Misadventure of Race* (New York: Farrar, Straus and Giroux, 2000), pp. 36–37; Fischer, *Albion's Seed,* p. 387.

41. William Waller Hening, ed., *The Statutes at Large; Being a Collection of All the Laws of Virginia, from the First Session of the Legislature, in the Year 1619,* 13 vols. (Richmond, 1819–23), 2:260.

42. Ibid., 2:490.

43. Morgan, *Slave Counterpoint,* pp. 8–9, 13.

44. Ibid., p. 12; Fischer, *Albion's Seed,* p. 388 n. 14.

45. Pierre Marambaud, *William Byrd of Westover 1674–1744* (Charlottesville: University Press of Virginia, 1971), pp. 168–69.

46. Jordan, *White Over Black,* p. 82.

47. Marambaud, *William Byrd,* pp. 170–71.

48. Ibid., pp. 170–71, 167.

49. Ibid., p. 173; Morgan, *Slave Counterpoint,* p. 61, table 10.

366

50. Freeman, *George Washington,* 1:88–89; *Thomas Jefferson's Farm Book,* Edmund Morris Betts, ed. (Princeton: Princeton University Press, 1953), p. 46.

51. Morgan, *Slave Counterpoint,* p. 81; Freeman, *George Washington,* 1:88–89; Grizzard, *George Washington,* pp. 326–27.

52. Custis, *Recollections,* p. 15.

53. Freeman, *George Washington,* 1:84.

54. Daniel Meaders, *Dead or Alive: Fugitive Slaves and Indentured Servants Before 1830* (New York: Garland, 1993), p. 60.

55. Freeman, *George Washington,* 1:90.

56. Morgan, *Slave Counterpoint,* p. 282.

57. Ibid., pp. 356–57.

2. ON THE BORDERLAND

1. Custis, *Recollections,* pp. 127–28.

2. Westmoreland County Orders, May 31, July 28, September 29, November 29, 1732; February 27, March 29, May 29–30, September 26, November 28–29, 1733; Library of Virginia, Richmond.

3. Westmoreland County Orders, March 26, 1751.

4. Hening, *Statutes at Large,* 3:87, 4:133.

5. Westmoreland County Orders, May 26, 1752; Anita Wills, "In the Planter's House: Three Generations of Servants to George Washington's Family," African American Genealogical Society of Northern California (AAGSNC), http://www.aagsnc.org/columns/jan99col.htm; James Laray and Robert M. Dunkerly, "Remembering a Servant Family: The Bowdens and Popes Creek Plantation," *White House Studies* 1, no. 2:268.

6. Wills, "In the Planter's House."

7. Kathleen M. Brown, *Good Wives, Nasty Wenches, and Anxious Patriarchs: Gender, Race, and Power in Colonial Virginia* (Chapel Hill: University of North Carolina Press, 1996), pp. 187ff.

8. Tommy L. Bogger, *Free Blacks in Norfolk, Virginia, 1790–1860: The Darker Side of Freedom* (Charlottesville: University Press of Virginia, 1997), pp. 14–17.

9. Wills, "In the Planter's House."

10. Flexner, *George Washington,* 1:41.

11. Freeman, *George Washington,* 1:198–99.

12. Flexner, *George Washington,* 1:23–24.

13. Brookhiser, *Founding Father,* pp. 110–11.

14. Flexner, *George Washington,* 1:42.

15. *The Diaries of George Washington,* Donald Jackson and Dorothy Twohig, eds., 6 vols. (Charlottesville: University Press of Virginia, 1976–79), 1:18.

16. Flexner, *George Washington,* 1:37.

17. *Diaries of GW,* 1:33.

18. W. W. Abbot, *The Young George Washington and His Papers,* lecture presented at the University of Virginia, February 11, 1999 (Charlottesville: University of Virginia Press, 1999), pp. 11–15; Grizzard, *George Washington,* p. 85; Mary V. Thompson, "'Admiring the . . . Richness of the Land': George Washington and the Frontier," unpublished research paper, Mount Vernon, passim; John E. Ferling, "School for Command: Young George Washington and the Virginia Regiment," *Washington and the Virginia Backcountry,* Warren R. Hofstra, ed. (Madison, Wis.: Madison House, 1998), pp. 199–217.

19. *Diaries of GW,* 1:119–28.

20. Ibid., 1:144, 132; Grizzard, *George Washington,* pp. 85–86.

21. *Diaries of GW,* 1:132; Thompson, "Admiring the Richness," p. 26; Grizzard, *George Washington,* pp. 116, 118.

22. Grizzard, *George Washington,* p. 351.

23. Ibid., p. 118.

24. Ibid., pp. 33–35; *Papers of GW,* Colonial Series, vol. 1, GW to John Augustine Washington, July 18, 1755.

25. *Papers of GW,* Colonial Series, vol. 4, GW to Richard Washington, April 15, 1757.

26. Ibid.

27. Ibid., vol. 6, "George Mercer to a friend," 1760.

3. THE WIDOW CUSTIS

1. Niemcewicz, *Under Their Vine,* p. 103; Flexner, *George Washington,* 1:191, 230.

2. *Papers of GW,* Colonial Series, 6:202–09 n.

3. Custis, *Recollections,* pp. 449–502; LC, GW Papers, Series 5 Financial Papers, 1750–72, Ledger Book 1 (also known as Ledger A), p. 38.

4. Fields, *Papers of Martha Washington,* pp. xx–xxi; Freeman, *George Washington,* 2: picture caption after p. 299.

5. James B. Lynch, Jr., *The Custis Chronicles: The Virginia Generations* (Camden, Maine: Picton Press, 1997), p. 38.

6. Fields, *Papers of Martha Washington,* p. 90.

7. Fischer, *Albion's Seed,* p. 318.

8. Lynch, *Custis Chronicles,* p. 39.

9. Ibid.

10. Fischer, *Albion's Seed,* p. 320.

11. Ibid.; Lynch, *Custis Chronicles,* pp. 50–51.

12. Fields, *Papers of Martha Washington,* p. 424–25; Lynch, *Custis Chronicles,* pp. 102, 6, 54.

13. Fischer, *Albion's Seed,* p. 292.

14. Lynch, *Custis Chronicles,* p. 107.

15. Ibid., p. 95; Philip D. Morgan, "Interracial Sex in the Chesapeake," *Sally Hemings and Thomas Jefferson: History, Memory, and Civic Culture,* Jan Ellen

Lewis and Peter S. Onuf, eds. (Charlottesville: University Press of Virginia, 1999), pp. 52–55.

16. Lynch, *Custis Chronicles,* p. 2; Jo Zuppan, "Father to Son, Letters from John Custis IV to Daniel Parke Custis, *Virginia Magazine of History and Biography,* January 1990, p. 99.

17. Lynch, *Custis Chronicles,* p. 101.

18. Ibid., pp. 96–97.

19. Freeman, *George Washington,* 2:294–95.

20. Ibid., 2:293.

21. Lynch, *Custis Chronicles,* p. 112.

22. Freeman, *George Washington,* 2:291–94.

23. Custis, *Recollections,* p. 20 n.

24. Lynch, *Custis Chronicles,* p. 87.

25. Ibid., p. 100; Fields, *Papers of Martha Washington,* p. 440 n. 93.

26. "Diary of John Blair," *William and Mary Quarterly* 7, no. 3 (January 1899): 152; Communication from Dr. David Stone, UVA School of Medicine.

27. Morgan, "Interracial Sex in the Chesapeake," pp. 53–54.

28. Custis, *Recollections,* p. 20 n; Henry Wiencek, *The Hairstons: An American Family in Black and White* (New York: St. Martin's Press, 1999), pp. 94–98.

29. Freeman, *George Washington,* 2:293; Flexner, *George Washington,* 1:189.

30. *Papers of GW,* Colonial Series, vol. 6, GW to John Alton, April 5, 1759.

31. Freeman, *George Washington,* 3:19–22; *Papers of GW,* Colonial Series, vol. 6, GW to Robert Cary & Company, May 1, 1759.

32. *Papers of GW,* Colonial Series, 6:81–93, 202–09.

33. Fischer, *Albion's Seed,* p. 381.

34. *Papers of GW,* Colonial Series, vol. 6, GW to Richard Washington, September 20, 1759.

35. Custis, *Recollections,* pp. 163, 165–171.

36. Fields, *Papers of Martha Washington,* p. 126; *Papers of GW,* Colonial Series, vol. 6, p. 282.

37. Lynch, *Custis Chronicles,* pp. 131–32.

38. Washington, D.C., Land Records, Liber H, #8, p. 382, Recorder of Deeds.

39. *Special Report of the Commissioner of Education on the Condition and Improvement of Public Schools in the District of Columbia,* 41st Congress, 2d Session, Ex. Doc. No. 315, submitted to the Senate June 1868 and to the House June 1870 (Government Printing Office, 1871), pp. 203–04.

40. *Diaries of GW,* 1:222.

4. A LIFE HONORABLE AND AMUSING

1. *Diaries of GW,* 1:245.

2. *Papers of GW,* Colonial Series, vol. 6, GW to Robert Cary & Company, August 10, 1760.

3. Freeman, *George Washington*, 3:53, 54, 63.

4. *Papers of GW,* Colonial Series, vol. 7, GW to Robert Cary & Company, September 27, 1763; GW to Robert Stewart, April 27, 1763.

5. *The Diaries of George Washington 1748–1799,* John C. Fitzpatrick, ed. 4 vols. (Boston: Houghton Mifflin, 1925), 1:27–28.

6. Freeman, *George Washington*, 3:44.

7. T. H. Breen, *Tobacco Culture: The Mentality of the Great Tidewater Planters on the Eve of Revolution* (Princeton, N.J.: Princeton University Press, 1985), p. 127.

8. Ibid., p. 129.

9. Ibid., pp. 130–31.

10. Freeman, *George Washington*, 3:48.

11. Breen, *Tobacco Culture*, pp. 129–30.

12. *Papers of GW,* Colonial Series, vol. 8, GW to Robert Cary & Company, June 6, 1768.

13. Ibid., Invoice from Robert Cary & Company, September 28, 1768.

14. Lorena S. Walsh, "Slavery and Agriculture at Mount Vernon," *Slavery at the Home of George Washington,* Philip J. Schwarz, ed. (Mount Vernon, Va.: Mount Vernon Ladies' Association, 2001), p. 56.

15. Breen, *Tobacco Culture*, p. 128.

16. Freeman, *George Washington,* 3:64–65; LC, GW Papers, Ledger Book 1 (Ledger A), p. 36.

17. *Papers of GW,* Confederation Series, vol. 6, GW to Alexander Spotswood, February 13, 1788; Presidential Series, vol. 1, GW to Arthur Young, December 4, 1788.

18. Flannery O'Connor, *The Complete Stories* (New York: Noonday Press, Farrar, Straus and Giroux, 1971), p. 321.

19. Fritz Hirschfeld, *George Washington and Slavery: A Documentary Portrayal* (Columbia: University of Missouri Press, 1997), p. 33; Bernhard Knollenberg, *George Washington: The Virginia Period 1732–1775* (Durham, N.C.: Duke University Press, 1964), p. 90.

20. *Diaries of GW,* 1:232–34.

21. *Papers of GW,* Colonial Series, vol. 5, Humphrey Knight to George Washington, September 2, 1758.

22. Knollenberg, *George Washington*, pp. 85, 123–34.

23. *Diaries of GW,* 2:83.

24. *Papers of GW,* Retirement Series, vol. 1, GW to James McHenry, May 29, 1797.

25. Ibid., Presidential Series, vol. 1, GW to John Fairfax, January 1, 1789.

26. *Writings of GW,* 33:11–12, GW "To the Overseers at Mount Vernon."

27. *Diaries of GW,* xvii.

28. Quoted in Jean B. Lee, "Mount Vernon Plantation: A Model for the Republic," *Slavery at the Home of George Washington,* p. 13; Walsh, "Slavery and Agriculture," p. 57; *Diaries of GW,* 1:xvii.

29. Hirschfeld, *George Washington and Slavery,* p. 32; Walsh, "Slavery and Agriculture," pp. 56–59.

30. *Papers of GW,* Colonial Series, vol. 7, Advertisement for Runaway Slaves, August 11, 1761; Robert F. Dalzell, Jr., and Lee Baldwin Dalzell, *George Washington's Mount Vernon: At Home in Revolutionary America* (New York: Oxford University Press, 1998), p. 130.

31. *Papers of GW,* Colonial Series, vol. 9, James Hill to GW, February 5, 1773.

32. Ibid., vol. 7, pp. 67–68.

33. *Diaries of GW,* 1:309.

34. E-mail communication from Frank Grizzard.

35. Interview with Jinny Fox, January 2002.

36. *Papers of GW,* Colonial Series, vol. 9, James Hill to GW, August 30, 1772.

37. *Writings of GW,* 33:188–95, GW to William Pearce, December 18, 1793; 33:252–56, GW to Pearce, January 26, 1794; LC, GW Papers, Pearce to GW, Plantation Report, February 1, 1794.

38. *Writings of GW,* 33:195–207, GW to Pearce, December 22, 1793.

39. *Writings of GW,* 33:309, GW to Pearce, March 30, 1794.

40. Mary V. Thompson, "And Procure for Themselves a Few Amenities: The Private Life of George Washington's Slaves," *Virginia Cavalcade* 48, no. 4 (Autumn 1999): 183.

41. *Writings of GW,* 33:132–33, GW to Henry Lee, October 16, 1793; *Papers of GW,* Presidential Series, vol. 9, GW to Charles Vancouver, November 5, 1791.

42. *Writings of GW,* 34:501–02, GW to Pearce, March 20, 1796.

43. Quoted in Mary V. Thompson, "'I Never See That Man Laugh to Show His Teeeth': Relationships between Blacks and Whites at George Washington's Mount Vernon," unpublished research paper, Mount Vernon, pp. 3–4.

44. *Papers of GW,* Colonial Series, vol. 9, GW to Daniel Jenifer Adams, July 20, 1772; Hirschfeld, *George Washington and Slavery,* pp. 12, 18.

45. *Papers of GW,* Colonial Series, vol. 9, GW to Gilbert Simpson, February 23, 1773; Simpson to GW, July 1773.

46. Brenda E. Stevenson, *Life in Black and White: Family and Community in the Slave South* (New York: Oxford University Press, 1996), pp. 209–12.

47. Dalzell and Dalzell, *George Washington's Mount Vernon,* pp. 132–34.

48. LC, GW Papers, Ledger Book 1 (Ledger A), pp. 37, 230; *Papers of GW,* Revolutionary Series, vol. 2, Lund Washington to GW, November 24, 1775; Colonial Series, 10:137, 138 n. 2, "List of Tithables," c. July 1774; Retirement Series, 4:528, "Negros Belonging to George Washington."

49. *Papers of GW,* Colonial Series, vol. 9, James Hill to GW, July 2, 1773.

50. Anne Gorham, "The People Shall Be Cloathed," unpublished research paper, Mount Vernon.

51. *Papers of GW,* Retirement Series, 4:463–64.

52. *Papers of GW,* Colonial Series, vol. 9, James Hill to GW, August 30, 1772; Hill to GW, July 1773; Hill to GW, December 13, 1772.

53. *Writings of GW,* 32:366, GW to Whiting, March 3, 1793.

54. *Papers of GW,* Colonial Series, vol. 9, James Hill to GW, February 5, 1773; Hill to GW, May 11, 1773.

55. *Writings of GW,* 33:193, 309, GW to William Pearce, December 18, 1793, March 30, 1794.

56. *Writings of GW,* 33:188–95, GW to William Pearce, December 18, 1793; 33:308–10, GW to Pearce, March 30, 1794.

57. *Papers of GW,* Colonial Series, vol. 7, Cash Accounts: January 1762, August 1763, April 1766, May, August 1766, June 1767; Lund Washington to GW, March 30, 1767.

58. Nan Netherton, Donald Sweig, Janice Artemel, Patricia Hickin, and Patrick Reed, *Fairfax County, Virginia: A History* (Fairfax, Va.: Fairfax County Board of Supervisors, 1977), pp. 66–67.

59. Fairfax County Orders, November 21, 1771, Library of Virginia.

60. Fairfax Parish Vestry Book, November 27, 1766, November 28, 1768, Library of Virginia.

61. Fairfax County Orders, November 21, 1771.

62. Ibid., December 23, 1770, November 22, 1768, October 24, 1769, July 1765; August 23, 1765, May 20, 1766.

63. Fairfax County Minute Book, October 21, 1765, Library of Virginia.

64. Fairfax County Orders, February 20, 1770.

65. Ibid., February 20, 1770, March 19, 1770.

66. Ibid., May 21, 1770, November 21, 1770, March 19, 1771.

67. Ibid., February 21, 1769, December 19, 1769.

68. Quoted in Kathleen M. Brown, *Good Wives, Nasty Wenches, and Anxious Patriarchs: Gender, Race, and Power in Colonial Virginia* (Chapel Hill: University of North Carolina Press, 1996), p. 367.

69. *Papers of GW,* Colonial Series, vol. 8, Cash Accounts, October 1767, May 1768; LC, GW Papers, Ledger 1, p. 261.

70. Ibid., vol. 7, Cash Accounts, June 1766; GW to Joseph Thompson, July 2, 1766.

71. *Writings of GW,* 32:366, GW to Whiting, March 3, 1793.

5. A SCHEME IN WILLIAMSBURG

1. *Diaries of GW,* 2:190; *Papers of GW,* Colonial Series, vol. 8, Cash Accounts: November, December 1769; GW to Robert Cary & Company, August 20, 1770.

2. *Diaries of GW,* 2:58–59, 193–203; Jane Carson, "Plantation Housekeeping in Colonial Virginia" (Williamsburg, Va.: Colonial Williamsburg Foundation, 1974), microform, p. 69; Mary R. M. Goodwin, "Washington in Williamsburg" (Williamsburg, Va.: Colonial Williamsburg Foundation, 1954), microform, n.p.

3. Carl Bridenbaugh, *Seat of Empire: The Political Role of Eighteenth-century Williamsburg,* (Williamsburg, Va.: Colonial Williamsburg Foundation, 1950), p. 32.

4. Flexner, *George Washington*, 1:236–37, 267.

5. *Diaries of GW*, 2:196.

6. Henry Wiencek, *The Smithsonian Guides to Historic America: Virginia and the Capital Region* (New York: Stewart, Tabori & Chang, 1989), pp. 188–89.

7. William Clinton Ewing, *The Sports of Colonial Williamsburg* (Richmond: Dietz Press, 1937), pp. 11, 13–14.

8. Dowdey, *Virginia Dynasties*, p. 175.

9. Elizabeth Cometti, *Social Life in Virginia During the War for Independence*, Edward M. Riley, ed. (Williamsburg, Va.: Virginia Independence Bicentennial Commission, 1978), p. 12; Isaac, *Transformation of Virginia*, p. 99.

10. Landon Carter, *The Diary of Colonel Landon Carter of Sabine Hall, 1752–1778*, Jack P. Greene, ed., 2 vols. (Richmond: Virginia Historical Society, 1987), 2:618, August 21, 1771.

11. Ewing, *Sports of Colonial Willamsburg*, pp. 17–20.

12. Cometti, *Social Life in Virginia*, p. 19; Ewing, *Sports of Colonial Williamsburg*, p. 33.

13. Ewing, *Sports of Colonial Williamsburg*, p. 3; Isaac, *Transformation of Virginia*, pp. 99–100.

14. Humphreys, *Life of General Washington*, p. 62; Gretchen Schneider, "Public Behavior at the Governor's Palace, A Look at Eighteenth-century Gentle Persons" (Williamsburg, Va.: Colonial Williamsburg Foundation, 1981) microform, pp. 14–15.

15. Schneider, "Public Behavior," pp. 17–18.

16. Ibid., pp. 3–14.

17. Humphreys, *Life of General Washington*, p. 60.

18. Michael Olmert, *Official Guide to Colonial Williamsburg* (Williamsburg, Va.: Colonial Williamsburg Foundation, 1985), p. 43.

19. Wiencek, *Virginia and the Capital Region*, 196; Bridenbaugh, *Seat of Empire*, pp. 29, 32; Wiencek, *Mansions of the Virginia Gentry*, p. 14 caption.

20. *Papers of GW*, Colonial Series, vol. 8, Cash Accounts, May 1769, p. 194 n. 10; Carson, "Plantation Housekeeping," p. 20; Breen, *Tobacco Culture*, pp. 208–09; Purdie & Dixon's *Virginia Gazette*, July 23, 1767, October 27, 1768.

21. *Papers of GW*, Colonial Series, vol. 8, GW to Jonathan Boucher, May 30, 1768; December 16, 1770.

22. Ibid., Boucher to GW, May 21, 1770.

23. Ibid., Boucher to GW, November 19, 1771; vol. 9, Boucher to GW, January 19, 1773; Knollenberg, *George Washington*, p. 175 n. 26.

24. Custis, *Recollections*, pp. 34–35.

25. Fields, *Papers of Martha Washington*, p. 147.

26. *Papers of GW*, Colonial Series, vol. 8, GW to Boucher, July 27, 1769.

27. *Diaries of GW*, 2:194–95; Lynch, *Custis Chronicles*, pp. 133–34.

28. *Diaries of GW*, 2:199–200.

29. *Papers of GW*, Colonial Series, vol. 9, GW to Burwell Bassett, June 20, 1773.

30. Freeman, *George Washington*, 3:130.

31. Flexner, *George Washington*, 1:250–51.

32. Netherton et al., *Fairfax County*, p. 69.

33. Knollenberg, *George Washington*, p. 101.

34. Ibid., pp. 101–2.

35. Ibid. Much of this section on Washington's elections is based on the analysis of Paul Longmore in *The Invention of George Washington*, pp. 56–67.

36. Longmore, *Invention of George Washington*, pp. 64–65.

37. Bridenbaugh, *Seat of Empire*, pp. 7, 36.

38. Ibid., pp. 2–3, 6, 7.

39. Ibid., p. 17.

40. Ibid., p. 10.

41. Edmund S. Morgan, "Slavery and Freedom: The American Paradox," *Journal of American History* 59, no. 1 (June 1972): 29.

42. Ibid., pp. 22–24.

43. Ibid., pp. 6, 27–29.

44. Longmore, *Invention of George Washington*, pp. 73–74.

45. Netherton et al., *Fairfax County*, p. 84.

46. Bridenbaugh, *Seat of Empire*, p. 13; Freeman, *George Washington*, 3:113–23.

47. *Papers of GW*, Colonial Series, vol. 10, GW to Bryan Fairfax, August 24, 1774.

48. Freeman, *George Washington*, 3:169–70; Dumas Malone, *Jefferson the Virginian* (Boston: Little, Brown, 1948), pp. 94–95.

49. Longmore, *Invention of George Washington*, p. 80.

50. John E. Ferling, *The First of Men: A Life of George Washington* (Knoxville: University of Tennessee Press, 1988), p. 97.

51. *Papers of GW*, Colonial Series, vol. 8, GW to George Mason, April 5, 1769.

52. Freeman, *George Washington*, 3:208 n. 151.

53. *Papers of GW*, Colonial Series, vol. 7, GW to Robert Cary & Company, August 10, 1764; Longmore, *Invention of George Washington*, p. 72.

54. Rind's *Virginia Gazette*, June 1, 1769; Woody Holton, *Forced Founders: Indians, Debtors, Slaves, and the Making of the American Revolution in Virginia* (Chapel Hill: University of North Carolina Press, 1999), pp. 82–84; Isaac, *Transformation of Virginia*, p. 251.

55. Paul Finkelman, *Slavery and the Founders: Race and Liberty in the Age of Jefferson* (Armonk, N.Y.: M.E. Sharpe, 2001), p. 137.

56. Ibid., p. 139.

57. Ibid., pp. 137–39; http://www.loc.gov/exhibits/jefferson/images/vc36p1.jpg: *Howell v. Netherland*, April 1770, *Reports of Cases Determined in the General Court of Virginia* (Charlottesville, 1829), pp. 90–93.

58. Bruton Parish Register, Births and Baptisms, Swem Library Special Collections, College of William and Mary, Williamsburg, Va., pp. 53–65.

59. Thomas N. Ingersoll, "'Releese us out of this Cruell Bondegg': An Appeal

From Virginia in 1723," *William and Mary Quarterly,* 3d. ser., 51, no. 4 (October 1994): 777–82.

60. Dan Eggen, "A Taste of Slavery Has Tourists Up in Arms: Williamsburg's New Skits Elicit Raw Emotions," *Washington Post,* July 7, 1999, Final Edition, p. A1.

61. *Colonial Williamsburg Interpreter* 20, no. 2 (Summer 1999): 29–30.

62. Ibid., p. 29.

63. Ibid.

64. Michael Kammen, *Mystic Chords of Memory: The Transformation of Tradition in American Culture* (New York: Knopf, 1991), p. 366.

65. Freeman Tilden, *Interpreting Our Heritage* (Chapel Hill: University of North Carolina Press, 1977), p. 12.

66. Ibid., pp. 12, 36.

67. Leon F. Litwack, "Forgotten Heroes of Freedom," *Atlantic Monthly,* November 1999, p. 116.

68. Mark R. Wenger, *Carter's Grove: The Story of a Virginia Plantation* (Williamsburg, Va.: Colonial Williamsburg Foundation, 1994), p. 16.

69. Henry Wiencek, *Plantations of the Old South* (Birmingham, Ala.: Oxmoor House, 1988), p. 15.

70. Helen Jones Campbell, *Diary of a Williamsburg Hostess* (New York: Putnam, 1946), p. 4.

71. Ibid., p. 26.

72. Eliza Baker, "Memoirs of Williamsburg, Virginia," report taken by Elizabeth Hayes of a conversation between Eliza Baker and the Reverend Dr. W.A.R. Goodwin, May 4, 1933, Dr. W.A.R. Goodwin Records, Colonial Williamsburg Archives, Williamsburg, Va.

73. Kammen, *Mystic Chords,* pp. 368, 552.

74. Christy Coleman Matthews, "A Colonial Williamsburg Revolution," *History News* 54, no. 2 (Spring 1999): 6; James Oliver Horton, "Presenting Slavery," *Public Historian,* Fall 1999, pp. 19ff.

75. *Colonial Williamsburg Interpreter* 20, no. 2 (Summer 1990): 30.

76. Rind's *Virginia Gazette,* April 14, 1768, October 19, November 23, 1769.

77. The other raffle managers who sat in the First Continental Congress were Richard Henry Lee, Benjamin Harrison, and Edmund Pendleton.

78. *Papers of GW,* Colonial Series, vol. 8, Guardian Accounts, May 1769, Cash Accounts, June 1770; David John Mays, *Edmund Pendleton, 1721–1803: A Biography,* 2 vols. (Cambridge, Mass.: Harvard University Press, 1952), 1:144, 182, 205–06, 335 n. 152; Freeman, *George Washington,* 3:111, 192–93.

79. Freeman, *George Washington,* 3:165–76; Malone, *Jefferson the Virginian,* pp. 95–96; Breen, *Tobacco Culture,* pp. 103–05.

80. Knollenberg, *George Washington,* p. 103; Holton, *Forced Founders,* pp. 79–82; Freeman, *George Washington,* 3:264–65.

81. Rind's *Virginia Gazette,* October 19, 1769.

82. Freeman, *George Washington,* 3:240 no. 64.

83. Malone, *Jefferson the Virginian,* pp. 63–64.

84. Rind's *Virginia Gazette,* November 2, 1769.

85. Rind's *Virginia Gazette,* October 13, 1768, advertisement for a sale on the 31st; Malone, *Jefferson the Virginian,* p. 97.

86. Mays, *Edmund Pendleton,* 1:335 n. 169.

87. Karen E. Sutton and Kathy Thompson, "Corrected Research Plan for 'Forever Here,' Williamsburg, Virginia, Slave Descendants Oral History Project, February 11, 2000," unpublished research report, pp. 19–20.

88. *Papers of GW,* Revolutionary Series, vol. 2, Lund Washington to GW, December 3, 1775.

89. Jefferson quoted in Ferling, *First of Men,* p. 257.

6. "SO SACRED A WAR AS THIS"

1. Sidney Kaplan and Emma Nogrady Kaplan, *The Black Presence in the Era of the American Revolution* (Amherst: University of Massachusetts Press, 1989), pp. 17–19.

2. Benjamin Quarles, *The Negro in the American Revolution* (Chapel Hill: University of North Carolina Press, 1996), p. xxix; Philip D. Morgan and Andrew J. O'Shaughnessy, "Arming Slaves in the American Revolution," from a forthcoming work edited by Christopher L. Brown and Philip D. Morgan on arming slaves from antiquity to the modern era, to be published by Yale University Press; I am grateful to Professor Morgan for allowing me to consult the manuscript (unpaginated).

3. Kaplan and Kaplan, *Black Presence,* p. 34.

4. Brookhiser, *Founding Father,* pp. 177, 179; Pete Maslowski, "National Policy Toward the Use of Black Troops in the Revolution," *South Carolina Historical Magazine* 73 (1972): 3.

5. Otis quoted in Gary B. Nash, *Race and Revolution* (Madison, Wis.: Madison House, 1990), p. 8.

6. Adams quoted in Kaplan and Kaplan, *Black Presence,* p. 15.

7. GW quoted in Ferling, *First of Men,* p. 103.

8. Ibid., pp. 86–87.

9. Knollenberg, *George Washington,* p. 108.

10. Flexner, *George Washington,* 1:322, 324, 326.

11. Ibid., 1:324–25, 327.

12. Ibid., 1:328.

13. Netherton et al., *Fairfax County,* pp. 105, 107.

14. *Papers of GW,* Colonial Series, vol. 10, GW to George William Fairfax, May 31, 1775.

15. Flexner, *George Washington,* 1:331.

16. Ibid., 1:334, 342–43.

17. *Papers of GW,* Revolutionary War Series, vol. 1, GW to Martha Washington, June 18, 1775.

18. Flexner, *George Washington,* 1:344–45.

19. Ferling, *First of Men,* p. 124.

20. *Papers of GW,* Revolutionary War Series, vol. 1, GW to Richard Henry Lee, July 10, August 29, 1775; GW to Lund Washington, August 20, 1775; Ferling, *First of Men,* p. 127.

21. Ferling, *First of Men,* p. 127.

22. John Shy, *A People Numerous and Armed: Reflections on the Military Struggle for American Independence* (Ann Arbor: University of Michigan Press, 1990), pp. 126–27, 305 n. 19.

23. Quarles, *Negro in the American Revolution,* p. 72; Philip S. Foner, *Blacks in the American Revolution* (Westport, Conn.: Greenwood Press, 1975), pp. 96, 175.

24. Morgan and O'Shaughnessy, "Arming Slaves"; Shy, *A People Numerous and Armed,* pp. 36–37.

25. Morgan and O'Shaughnessy, "Arming Slaves."

26. Shy, *A People Numerous and Armed,* pp. 126–27.

27. Kaplan and Kaplan, *Black Presence,* p. 21.

28. Ibid., p. 19.

29. John C. Dann, ed., *The Revolution Remembered: Eyewitness Accounts of the War for Independence* (Chicago: University of Chicago Press, 1980), pp. 27–28.

30. Maslowski, "National Policy," p. 2.

31. *Papers of GW,* Revolutionary War Series, vol. 1, GW to John Hancock, July 10–11, 1775, Council of War, July 9, 1775.

32. Maslowski, "National Policy," p. 2.

33. Swett quoted in Quarles, *Negro in the American Revolution,* p. 14; *Papers of GW,* Revolutionary War Series, vol. 2, Council of War, October 8, 1775.

34. *Papers of GW,* Revolutionary War Series, vol. 2., General Orders, November 12, 1775.

35. Dann, *Revolution Remembered,* pp. 392–93.

36. Maslowski "National Policy," p. 4; Quarles, *Negro in the American Revolution,* pp. 19–32.

37. *Papers of GW,* Revolutionary War Series, vol. 2, GW to Richard Henry Lee, December 26, 1775; Maslowski, "National Policy," p. 4.

38. *Papers of GW,* Revolutionary War Series, vol. 2, GW to Lund Washington, December 3, 1775.

39. Ibid., General Orders, December 30, 1775.

40. Ibid., GW to John Hancock, December 31, 1775.

41. Arabus case quoted in *Hartford Courant:* http://courant.ctnow.com/projects/bhistory/arabusa.htm; Quarles, *Negro in the American Revolution,* p. 184; Ferling, *First of Men,* p. 132.

42. Quarles, *Negro in the American Revolution,* pp. 16–17.

43. *Papers of GW*, Revolutionary War Series, vol. 2, Phillis Wheatley to GW, October 26, 1775.

44. Ibid.

45. Sparks quoted in William H. Robinson, *Critical Essays on Phillis Wheatley* (Boston: G.K. Hall, 1982), p. 52.

46. *Papers of GW*, Revolutionary War Series, vol. 3, GW to Joseph Reed, February 10, 1776.

47. Memoir of Margaretta Matilda Odell, quoted in William H. Robinson, *Phillis Wheatley and Her Writings* (New York: Garland, 1984), p. 431.

48. Charles W. Akers, "Our Modern Egyptians," *Journal of Negro History*, July 1975, p. 398; Kaplan and Kaplan, *Black Presence*, p. 182.

49. Robinson, *Phillis Wheatley and Her Writings*, pp. 19, 433.

50. Henry Louis Gates, Jr., "Mister Jefferson and the Trials of Phillis Wheatley," 31st Jefferson Lecture in the Humanities, March 22, 2000, Washington, D.C., n.p.; *The Poems of Phillis Wheatley*, Julian D. Mason, Jr., ed., rev. ed. (Chapel Hill: University of North Carolina Press, 1989), p. 53.

51. Akers, "Our Modern Egyptians," pp. 406–07.

52. Frank Shuffelton, "On Her Own Footing: Phillis Wheatley in Freedom," *Genius in Bondage: Literature of the Early Black Atlantic*, Vincent Carretta and Philip Gould, eds. (Lexington: University Press of Kentucky, 2001), p. 187.

53. *Papers of GW*, Revolutionary War Series, vol. 3, GW to Phillis Wheatley, February 28, 1776.

54. Robinson, *Phillis Wheatley and Her Writings*, p. 52.

55. Jefferson quoted in Mason, *Poems of Phillis Wheatley*, p. 30.

56. Walter H. Mazyck, *George Washington and the Negro* (Washington, D.C.: Associated Publishers, 1932), pp. 44–45.

57. Hirschfeld, *George Washington and Slavery*, pp. 90–91; Grizzard, *George Washington*, pp. 347–49.

58. Shy, *A People Numerous and Armed*, p. 127; Don E. Fehrenbacher, *The Slaveholding Republic: An Account of the United States Government's Relations to Slavery* (New York: Oxford University Press, 2001), pp. 18–19; Morgan and O'Shaughnessy, "Arming Slaves."

59. Foner, *Blacks in the American Revolution*, p. 186.

60. Mark M. Boatner III, *Encyclopedia of the American Revolution* (New York: David McKay, 1966), pp. 647–57; David McCullough, "What the Fog Wrought," *What If? The World's Foremost Military Historians Imagine What Might Have Been*, Robert Cowley, ed. (New York: Putnam, 1999), p. 193.

61. McCullough, "What the Fog Wrought," p. 197.

62. Ibid., p. 199.

63. Kaplan and Kaplan, *Black Presence*, p. 46.

64. Hirschfeld, *George Washington and Slavery*, p. 148.

65. Ibid., pp. 148–49; Boatner, *Encyclopedia of the American Revolution*, p. 424.

66. John Chester Miller, *The Wolf by the Ears: Thomas Jefferson and Slavery* (Charlottesville: University Press of Virginia, 1991), p. 38.

67. Ibid., pp. 47, 57, 58.

68. Gregory D. Massey, *John Laurens and the American Revolution* (Columbia: University of South Carolina Press, 2000), p. 133.

69. Ibid., p. 89.

70. Ibid., pp. 8–11; Edward Ball, *Slaves in the Family* (New York: Farrar, Straus and Giroux, 1998), pp. 190–91.

71. Massey, *John Laurens*, p. 93.

72. Quarles, *Nergo in the American Revolution*, p. 60; Massey, *John Laurens*, pp. 93–95.

73. Massey, *John Laurens*, p. 63; Maslowski, p. 7.

74. Maslowski, "National Policy," p. 8.

75. Massey, *John Laurens*, pp. 96–97.

76. Marshall Smelser, *The Winning of Independence* (Chicago: Quadrangle Books, 1972), pp. 269–70.

77. Massey, *John Laurens*, pp. 130–31.

78. Grizzard, *George Washington*, p. 144; Massey, *John Laurens*, p. 125.

79. Harold C. Syrett, ed., *The Papers of Alexander Hamilton*, 27 vols. (New York: Columbia University Press, 1961–87), 2:17–18, Hamilton to John Jay, March 14, 1779.

80. *Writings of GW,* 14:267 n, Laurens to GW, March 16, 1779.

81. Ibid., 14:267, GW to Laurens, March 20, 1779.

82. Ibid., 10:400, GW to The Committee of Congress with the Army, January 29, 1778.

83. *Writings of GW,* 14:147–49, GW to Lund Washington, February 24, 1779.

84. Hirschfeld, *George Washington and Slavery*, pp. 27–28; LC, Ledger Book 2 (Ledger B), p. 156.

85. http://memory.loc.gov/ammen/amlaw/lwjc.html—*Journals of the Continental Congress, 1774–89,* 18:385–89, March 29, 1779.

86. Massey, *John Laurens*, p. 133.

87. Quarles, *Negro in the American Revolution*, pp. 63–64.

88. Massey, *John Laurens*, p. 156.

89. Foner, *Blacks in the American Revolution*, p. 64.

90. Quarles, *Negro in the American Revolution*, pp. 64–65; Foner, *Blacks in the American Revolution*, pp. 64–65.

91. Foner, *Blacks in the American Revolution*, p. 64; Massey, *John Laurens*, p. 208; William W. Freehling, "The Founding Fathers and Slavery," *American Historical Review* 77, no. 4 (February 1972): 84; Finkelman, *Slavery and the Founders*, p. 143.

92. *Papers of GW,* Revolutionary War Series, vol. 3, GW to Burwell Bassett, February 28, 1776.

93. GW quoted in Thomas Fleming, *Liberty! The American Revolution* (New York: Viking, 1997), p. 200.

94. James McHenry quoted in Gerald Edward Kahler, "Gentlemen of the Family: General George Washington's Aides-de-Camp and Military Secretaries," M.A. thesis, University of Richmond, 1997, p. 84.

95. Shy, *A People Numerous and Armed*, p. 161.

96. Boatner, *Encyclopedia of the American Revolution*, pp. 400, 426–30; Flexner, *George Washington*, 2:237.

97. Boatner, *Encyclopedia of the American Revolution*, p. 1137.

98. Ibid., pp. 1056–57, 1137.

99. Patricia L. Hudson and Sandra L. Ballard, *The Smithsonian Guide to Historic America: The Carolinas and the Appalachian States* (New York: Stewart, Tabori & Chang, 1989), pp. 83–87.

100. Boatner, *Encyclopedia of the American Revolution*, pp. 1034–37, 1152–55, 1029, 1152.

101. *Diaries of GW*, 3:356.

102. Kaplan and Kaplan, *Black Presence*, p. 34; Quarles, *Negro in the American Revolution*, p. xxviii.

103. Catherine Read Williams, *Biography of Revolutionary Heroes; Containing the Life of Brigadier General William Barton, and Also, of Captain Stephen Olney* (New York: Wiley & Putnam, 1839), p. 276.

104. Freeman, *George Washington*, 5:370.

105. Robert A. Selig, "Storming the Redoubts," *MHQ: The Quarterly Journal of Military History* 8, no. 1 (Autumn 1995): 18–27; Burke Davis, *The Campaign That Won America: The Story of Yorktown* (New York: Eastern Acorn Press, 1997), pp. 225–29; Williams, *Biography of Revolutionary Heroes*, pp. 273–79; Brendan Morrissey, *Yorktown 1781: The World Turned Upside Down* (Oxford, England: Osprey, 1997), pp. 64–71; Henry P. Johnston, *The Yorktown Campaign and the Surrender of Cornwallis 1781* (New York: Eastern Acorn, 1981), pp. 140–47.

106. Freeman, *George Washington*, 5:372; Johnston, *Yorktown Campaign*, p. 147.

107. Robert A. Selig, "A German Soldier in America, 1780–1783: The Journal of Georg Daniel Flohr," *William and Mary Quarterly* 50, no. 3 (July 1993): 575–90; Selig, "The Revolution's Black Soldiers," *Colonial Williamsburg* 19, no. 4 (Summer 1997): 15–22 (online: www.AmericanRevolution.org).

108. Johann Ewald, *Diary of the American War: A Hessian Journal*, Joseph P. Tustin, ed. (New Haven: Yale University Press, 1979), pp. 335–36; Elizabeth A. Fenn, *Pox Americana: The Great Smallpox Epidemic of 1775–82* (New York: Hill and Wang, 2001), p. 130.

109. Fenn, *Great Smallpox Epidemic*, p. 130.

110. Selig, "The Revolution's Black Soldiers."

111. Condemned slave quoted in Malcomson, *One Drop of Blood*, p. 187.

7. A DIFFERENT DESTINY

1. *Writings of GW*, 21:385, GW to Lund Washington, March 28, 1781; Flexner, *George Washington*, 2:445–47.

2. "A Poem on the Death of General Washington," quoted in Hirschfeld, *George Washington and Slavery*, p. 72.

3. Ellen Gibson Wilson, *The Loyal Blacks* (New York: Capricorn Books, 1976), p. 52.

4. *Dictionary of American Negro Biography*, Rayford W. Logan and Michael R. Winston, eds. (New York: Norton, 1982), pp. 16–17; John Salmon, "A Mission of the Most Secret and Important Kind: James Lafayette and American Espionage in 1781," *Virginia Cavalcade*, Autumn 1981, pp. 78–85.

5. Salmon, "Mission of the Most Secret," p. 80.

6. Ibid., pp. 82–85.

7. Massey, *John Laurens*, pp. 165–66, 201, 211, 287 n. 59.

8. Wilson, *Loyal Blacks*, p. 48, 59 n. 23.

9. Ibid., p. 43.

10. Ibid., pp. 43, 49; Quarles, *Negro in the American Revolution*, pp. 167–81.

11. Wilson, *Loyal Blacks*, p. 49.

12. *Writings of GW*, 26:370, GW to Governor Benjamin Harrison, April 30, 1783.

13. Wilson, *Loyal Blacks*, pp. 52–55; Quarles, *Negro in the American Revolution*, pp. 168–69; *Writings of GW*, 26:401, GW to Harrison, May 6, 1783.

14. Wilson, *Loyal Blacks*, pp. 55–56.

15. Ibid., pp. 56–57; Wiencek, *Hairstons*, p. 48.

16. Wilson, *Loyal Blacks*, p. 41; Selig, "The Revolution's Black Soldiers."

17. Mary Beth Norton, "The Fate of Some Black Loyalists of the American Revolution," *Journal of Negro History* 58, no. 4 (October 1973): 404–09; Wilson, *Loyal Blacks*, pp. 41–42, 47.

18. Lamin Sanneh, *Abolitionists Abroad* (Cambridge, Mass.: Harvard University Press, 1999), p. 98; Wilson, *Loyal Blacks*, pp. 383–96.

19. Hirschfeld, *George Washington and Slavery*, pp. 122–23.

20. Lafayette quoted in Lloyd Kramer, *Lafayette in Two Worlds* (Chapel Hill: University of North Carolina Press, 1996), p. 201; *Mount Vernon: A Handbook*, p. 50.

21. Lafayette quoted in Hirschfeld, *George Washington and Slavery*, p. 121; Lafayette to John Adams, February 22, 1786, quoted in Lafayette College Website: http://ww2.lafayette.edu/~library/special/specialexhibits/slaveryexhibit/onlineexhibit/lifetimepassion.htm.

22. Kramer, *Lafayette in Two Worlds*, p. 218.

23. *Writings of GW*, 26:300, GW to Marquis de Lafayette, April 5, 1783.

24. *Papers of GW*, Confederation Series, vol 2., William Gordon to GW, August 30, 1784; ibid., vol. 3, Lafayette to GW, July 14, 1785, February 6, 1786; Peter Buckman, *Lafayette* (London: Paddington Press, 1977), pp. 122–23.

25. *Papers of GW*, Confederation Series, vol. 4, GW to Lafayette, May 10, 1786.

26. Buckman, *Lafayette*, p. 123; Dorothy Twohig, "'That Species of Property': Washington's Role in the Controversy Over Slavery," http://gwpapers.virginia.edu/articles/slavery/index.html, also in *George Washington Reconsidered*, Don Higginbotham, ed. (Charlottesville: University Press of Virginia, 2001).

27. Jefferson quoted in Shy, *A People Numerous and Armed*, p. 24; *Papers of GW*, Confederation Series, vol. 4, GW to John Jay, August 15, 1786.

28. *Writings of GW*, 28:503, GW to the Secretary for Foreign Affairs, August 1, 1786; ibid., 29:51, GW to James Madison, November 5, 1786; Ferling, *First of Men*, pp. 348–52, 355.

29. Hirschfeld, *George Washington and Slavery*, p. 171.

30. Farrand quoted in Hirschfeld, *George Washington and Slavery*, p. 172.

31. Ferling, *First of Men*, p. 357.

32. *The Records of the Federal Convention of 1787*, Max Farrand, ed., searchable by key words in the quotations at http://memory.loc.gov/ammem/amlaw/lwfr.html.

33. Ibid.

34. Morgan, *Slave Counterpoint*, p. 62.

35. Joseph Ellis, *Founding Brothers: The Revolutionary Generation* (New York: Knopf, 2000), p. 94; Twohig, "That Species of Property."

36. *Records of the Federal Convention.*

37. Ibid.

38. *Papers of GW*, Confederation Series, vol. 4, GW to Lafayette, May 10, 1786.

39. Ibid., vol. 3, GW to James McHenry, August 22, 1785.

40. Hirschfeld, *George Washington and Slavery*, p. 177.

41. GW's Letter to Congress, September 17, 1787, in *Records of the Federal Convention.*

42. Ellis, *Founding Brothers*, p. 119; *Papers of GW*, Confederation Series, vol. 6, GW to Lafayette, February 7, 1788: GW actually wrote, "It appears to me, then, little short of a miracle, that the Delegates from so many different States . . . should unite in forming a system of national Government."

43. LC, Thomas Jefferson Papers Series 1, General Correspondence, Thomas Jefferson to Walter Jones, January 2, 1814, http://memory.loc.gov/ammem/mtjhtml/mtjhome.html.

44. Butler quoted in Ferling, *First of Men*, pp. 362–64.

45. Humphreys, *Life of General Washington*, p. 78.

46. Ibid., p. xxii. Rosemarie Zagarri, editor of the Humphreys biography, concludes that the "direct quotes and paraphrases of private conversations" most likely date between the fall of 1788 and April 1789.

47. *Writings of GW*, 33:385, GW to Tobias Lear, May 6, 1794.

48. Ibid., 14:147–49, GW to Lund Washington, February 24, 1779.

49. Ellis, *Founding Brothers*, pp. 85, 97, 99.

50. Ibid., pp. 117–18.

51. *Writings of GW*, 31:28–30, GW to David Stuart, March 28, 1790.

52. Ibid., 33:78–79, 174–83, GW to Arthur Young, September 1, December 12, 1793.

53. Ibid., 31:49 n. 93, Stuart to GW, March 15, 1790; GW to Stuart, June 15, 1790.

54. Ibid., 34:47, GW to Alexander Spotswood, November 23, 1794.

55. Humphreys, *Life of General Washington*, p. 54.

8. "A SORT OF SHADOWY LIFE"

1. Virginius Dabney, *Liberalism in the South* (Chapel Hill: University of North Carolina Press, 1932), pp. 76–77.

2. Chesnut quoted in Donna Lucey, *I Dwell in Possibility: Women Build a Nation 1600–1920* (Washington, D.C.: National Geographic, 2001), p. 86.

3. Carter quoted in Lucey, *I Dwell in Possibility*, p. 90.

4. Mrs. Edward Carrington, "A Visit to Mount Vernon," *William and Mary Quarterly*, April 1938, p. 201.

5. Interview with Mary V. Thompson, Research Specialist, Mount Vernon Ladies' Association.

6. Marcia Carter to Mount Vernon Ladies' Association, January 7, 1981, Mount Vernon Curatorial Records, Washingtoniana Unowned.

7. Marcia Carter to Mount Vernon Ladies' Association, January 21, 1981.

8. Album, Elizabeth L. Van Lew, Virginia Historical Society, Richmond; e-mail communication from Professor Elizabeth R. Varon, Wellesley College.

9. John Parke Custis to Martha Washington, July 5, 1773, quoted in *Papers of GW*, Colonial Series, 9:266 n. 2; Knollenberg, *George Washington*, pp. 76, 174 n. 17.

10. John Parke Custis to GW, August 8, 1776, quoted in Custis, *Recollections*, p. 537.

11. Lossing, *Mary and Martha*, pp. 150–51 n.

12. Ellen McCallister Clark, *Martha Washington: A Brief Biography* (Mount Vernon, Va.: Mount Vernon Ladies' Association, 2002), p. 39; Lynch, *Custis Chronicles*, pp. 155, 158.

13. Ann's husband had the last name of Costin and an unknown first name. Since they were slaves, their marriage was extralegal and no official record of it was kept. There is no mention of a Costin in Mount Vernon's records, but GW seldom recorded surnames of slaves and, furthermore, slaves often kept their surnames private. The Costin name appears in records of Accomack County on the Eastern Shore of Virginia, where the Custis family had property, suggesting that Ann's husband was a Custis slave with roots on the Eastern Shore. The marriage ended either by death or by separation; Ann later used the surname Holmes, apparently from a second marriage. For Law's emancipations, see Washington, D.C., Land Records, Liber H, #8, p. 382; Liber R, #17, p. 288.

14. Thomas Law to Mrs. Tucker, July 1, 1829, Papers of Thomas Law, Tracy W. McGregor Library, 1803–34, Accession #2801, Albert H. Small Special Collections Library, University of Virginia, Charlottesville, Va.

15. Law to Charles Rumbold, January 10, 1832, Papers of Thomas Law.

16. Donald M. Sweig, "'Dear Master': A Unique Letter from West Ford Discovered," *Fairfax Chronicles* 10, no. 2 (May–July 1986): 1–5.

17. Eugene A. Foster et al., "Jefferson Fathered Slave's Last Child"; Eric S. Lander and Joseph J. Ellis, "DNA Analysis: Founding Father," both in *Nature* 396, no. 6706 (November 5, 1998), pp. 27, 13; Foster et al., "The Thomas Jefferson Paternity Case," *Nature* 397, no. 32 (January 7, 1999), p. 32; Thomas Jefferson

Memorial Foundation Research Committee, *Report on Thomas Jefferson and Sally Hemings* (Charlottesville, Va.: Thomas Jefferson Memorial Foundation, 2000), p. 10. The West Ford story had garnered some publicity earlier: Robert Jackson, "George Washington in Family Apple Tree, Black Sisters Say," *Rocky Mountain News* (Denver), November 4, 1996, p. 24A; Lucy Howard and Carla Koehl, "Tracing a Very Familiar Face?" *Newsweek,* November 25, 1996, p. 8. The story gained much wider currency in the wake of the Jefferson-Hemings controversy.

18. Nicholas Wade, "After Jefferson, a Question About Washington and a Young Slave," *New York Times,* July 7, 1999, p. A12; Reed Irvine, "Mainstream Media Allows Smear of Washington, But Not Bill Clinton," August 9, 1999, via LexisNexis search; Richard Brookhiser, "Father of His Country, Only; George Washington Faces a Bad Rap," *National Review* 51, no. 15 (August 9, 1999): 28.

19. [Benson J. Lossing,] "Mount Vernon As It Is," *Harper's New Monthly Magazine* 18, no. 106 (March 1859): 444–45; Lossing, *George Washington's Mount Vernon,* pp. 352–53.

20. Description of West Ford in free register quoted in Henry S. Robinson, "Who Was West Ford?" *Journal of Negro History* 66, no. 2 (Summer 1981): 171.

21. Linda Allen Bryant, *I Cannot Tell a Lie: The True Story of George Washington's African-American Descendants* (San Jose: Writer's Showcase, 2001), p. 411; *Illinois State Register* (Springfield), January 17, 1937. The Website westfordlegacy.com contains an archive of articles and other information about West Ford.

22. J. A. Rogers, *Sex and Race: A History of White, Negro, and Indian Miscegenation in the Two Americas,* 3 vols. (St. Petersburg, Fla.: Helga M. Rogers, 1942), vol. 2: *Sex and Race: The New World,* p. 222.

23. Thomas Grubisich, "Register of Freed Slaves Bares Fairfax County 'Roots,'" *Washington Post,* February 8, 1977, p. B1.

24. Judith Saunders Burton, "A History of Gum Springs, Virginia: A Report of a Case Study of Leadership in a Black Enclave," Ed.D. dissertation, Vanderbilt University, 1986, p. 21.

25. Wade's *New York Times* article states, "the cousins say that they have known one another only since 1994," but Bryant's book (*I Cannot Tell a Lie,* pp. 397–98) suggests that the Allens and Burton made contact by telephone in 1985 after the *National Enquirer* published an article about West Ford that mentioned Burton.

26. *Frontline,* May 6, 2000; Jeremy Manier, "Father of Our Country May Have Been a Dad: Family from Peoria Is Pursuing Genetic Link to Washington," *Chicago Tribune,* March 26, 2000, p. 1; CBS *Sunday Morning,* February 29, 2000.

27. Grizzard, *George Washington,* pp. 179–80, 328–29, 331; Gerald T. Dunne, "Bushrod Washington and the Mount Vernon Slaves," *Yearbook 1980,* Supreme Court Historical Society, pp. 25–29.

28. Bushrod Washington's will quoted in Robinson, "Who Was West Ford?," p. 170.

29. John Terry Chase, *Gum Springs: The Triumph of a Black Community* (Fairfax, Va.: Heritage Resources Program of the Fairfax County Office of Comprehensive Planning, 1990), p. 13; Burton, "History of Gum Springs," pp. 14–16; Robinson, "Who Was West Ford?," p. 170.

30. List of Tithables and Taxable Property taken by order of the Westmoreland County Court of March 28, 1786, filed June 27, 1786 (I am grateful to Prof. Philip J. Schwarz, Virginia Commonwealth University, for providing me with a transcription of this document). The 1831 Fairfax County register of free blacks states Ford's age as forty-seven, suggesting a birth date in 1784; the register entry dated 1839 gives his age as fifty-four, for a birth date of 1785; Lossing's *Harper's* article stated vaguely that in 1858 (the year of the interview) Ford was in his seventy-second year, for a birth date of 1786 or 1787; Ford's 1863 obituary in the *Alexandria Gazette* puts his age at seventy-nine for a birth date in 1784. Hannah Washington's will is recorded in Westmoreland County Deeds and Wills, Book 20, April 26, 1801, p. 211; the clause relating to West Ford is quoted in Robinson, "Who Was West Ford?," p. 167; Robinson's transcription omits a crucial phrase: "my dear husband left me in his will the following slaves to dispose of *as I chose at my death provided I gave them to our own children* the slaves are as follows. . . ." (emphasis added). Miriam Caravella, "The Black Heirs of George Washington," 1975, unpublished research report, author's collection.

31. John W. Wayland, *The Washingtons and Their Homes* (Baltimore: Genealogical Publishing, 1998; reprint of 1944 edition), pp. 122–25.

32. Westmoreland County Deeds and Wills, Book 18, pp. 6–10. The version of John Augustine Washington's will in the county's book is not the true original of the will; it is a copy made by county clerks from the original sheaf of papers in the testator's handwriting, which was presented to the court by Bushrod and Corbin. The will was recorded in a confusing way. It has two parts: the 1784 will on pp. 6–8 and the 1785 codicil on p. 9 (p. 10 is an appendix stating that bond was posted). Pages 6–8 present an apparently seamless document written all at once, but p. 9 makes it clear that the testator added interlineations to the original 1784 document in 1785. After inserting phrases between the lines, John Augustine wrote the codicil attesting to the authenticity of the additions. When the clerks copied the document, they incorporated the insertions without identifying them as such. Wayland copied the text from pp. 6–8 and made only passing reference to the codicil. Thus his published version is misleading as to the chronology of the will's composition.

33. William Faulkner, *Go Down, Moses* (New York: Vintage, 1990), pp. 250, 254.

34. Wayland, *The Washingtons and Their Homes*, pp. 122–23.

35. Hannah's will quoted in Robinson, "Who Was West Ford?," p. 167.

36. Mount Vernon's research on this point is cited in Wade, "After Jefferson, a Question."

37. *Papers of GW*, Confederation Series, vol. 3, John Augustine Washington to GW, July 17, 1785.

38. *Papers of GW,* Confederation Series, vol. 2, John Augustine Washington to GW, July 1784, alludes to Corbin's July 1784 visit to Mount Vernon. It is unlikely that GW would have engaged in an illicit sexual encounter when his wife might discover it. In October 1784 Martha was confined to bed with a severe illness: on his return to Mount Vernon from his trip in early October, the general found "a very sickly family . . . Mrs Washington has been very unwell—Miss Custis very ill": ibid., GW to William Gordon, November 3, 1784.

39. Lucey, *I Dwell in Possibility,* p. 114; Alex Bontemps, "Seeing Slavery: How Paintings Make Words Look Different," www.common-place.org, vol. 1, no. 4, July 2001.

40. Visiting officer, William North, quoted in Flexner, *George Washington,* 3:24; former slave, Rev. Ishrael Massie, quoted in Charles L. Perdue, Jr., et al., eds., *Weevils in the Wheat: Interviews with Virginia Ex-Slaves* (Charlottesville: University Press of Virginia, 1992), p. 207.

41. *Writings of GW,* 34:501–02, GW to William Pearce, March 20, 1796.

42. *Papers of GW,* Presidential Series, vol. 1, GW to Arthur Young, December 4, 1788.

43. *Diaries of GW,* 5:439. The family resemblance is indeed startling: in Wade's *New York Times* article ("After Jefferson, a Question") Philander Chase, editor of the George Washington papers, is quoted as saying, "If you compare pictures of West Ford with Bushrod Washington they look a lot alike."

9. THE GREAT ESCAPE

1. Jack D. Warren, Jr., *The Presidency of George Washington* (Mount Vernon, Va.: Mount Vernon Ladies' Association, 2000), p. 1; Flexner, *George Washington,* 3:173; Peter R. Henriques, *America's First President: George Washington* (Fort Washington, Pa.: Eastern National, 2002), p. 38.

2. Freeman, *George Washington,* 6:165.

3. Henriques, *America's First President,* pp. 43–44; Ellis, *Founding Brothers,* pp. 120–121.

4. Brookhiser, *Founding Father,* pp. 73–75.

5. Evelyn B. Gerson, "A Thirst for Complete Freedom: Why Fugitive Slave Ona Judge Staines Never Returned to Her Master, President George Washington," M.A. thesis, Extension Studies, Harvard University, June 2000, p. 53.

6. Ibid., p. 58.

7. Hirschfeld, *George Washington and Slavery,* p. 72.

8. Gerson, "Thirst for Complete Freedom," pp. 65–66; Custis, *Recollections,* p. 422–24.

9. Flexner, *George Washington,* 4:432. Flexner believes a runaway servant named John Cline was a slave, but no slave by that name appears in GW's records.

10. *Writings of GW,* 37:573–74, GW to Tobias Lear, April 12, 1791.

11. LC, GW Papers, Tobias Lear to GW, June 5, 1791.

12. Henriques, *America's First President,* p. 45; Brookhiser, *Founding Father,* p. 76.

13. Brookhiser, *Founding Father,* p. 76.

14. Warren, *Presidency of George Washington,* p. 13; Henriques, *America's First President,* p. 46.

15. Hirschfeld, *George Washington and Slavery,* p. 191.

16. Ibid., pp. 176–77.

17. Finkelman, *Slavery and the Founders,* p. 99.

18. Edward Lawler, Jr., "The President's House in Philadelphia: The Rediscovery of a Lost Landmark," *Pennsylvania Magazine of History and Biography* 126, no. 1 (January 2002): 5–96; Stephan Salisbury and Inga Saffron, "Echoes of Slavery at Liberty Bell Site," *Philadelphia Inquirer,* March 24, 2002; Stephan Salisbury, "Proposed Wording on Slave Quarters Draws Fire," *Philadelphia Inquirer,* October 31, 2002; Dinitia Smith, "Slave Site for a Symbol of Freedom," *New York Times,* April 20, 2002; Associated Press, "Dispute As Slavery Is Not Mentioned," November 1, 2002; www.ushistory.org/presidentshouse; Stephen Mihm, "Liberty-Bell Plan Shows Freedom and Slavery," *New York Times,* April 23, 2003, p. G22.

19. Gerson, "Thirst for Complete Freedom," p. 75 n. 101.

20. Ibid., p. 82.

21. Ibid., p. 87.

22. "Washington's Runaway Slave," *Granite Freeman* (Concord, N.H.), May 22, 1845, p. 1.

23. *Writings of GW,* 35:201, GW to the Secretary of the Treasury, September 1, 1796.

24. Fields, *Papers of Martha Washington,* p. 287; Gerson, "Thirst for Complete Freedom," p. 112; "Washington's Runaway Slave," *Granite Freeman,* p. 1.

25. LC, GW Papers, Joseph Whipple to Oliver Wolcott, Jr., September 10, 1796; *Writings of GW,* 35:201, GW to the Secretary of the Treasury, September 1, 1796.

26. LC, GW Papers, Whipple to Wolcott, October 4, 1796.

27. Ibid.

28. Ibid.

29. Ibid.

30. *Writings of GW,* 35:296–98, GW to Joseph Whipple, November 28, 1796.

31. Ibid.

32. "Washington's Runaway Slave," *Granite Freeman,* p. 1.

33. Gerson, "Thirst for Complete Freedom," pp. 93–95.

34. Gerson, "Thirst for Complete Freedom," p. 147.

35. LC, GW Papers, Bartholomew Dandridge to GW, June 1, 1796; *Writings of GW,* 35:135, GW to John Dandridge, July 11, 1796.

36. *Writings of GW,* 35:296–98, GW to Joseph Whipple, November 28, 1796.

37. LC, GW Papers, Joseph Whipple to GW, December 22, 1796.

38. Ibid.

39. Ibid.

40. *Papers of GW,* Retirement Series, vol. 4, GW to Burwell Bassett, Jr., (August 11), 1799.

41. Gerson, *"Thirst for Complete Freedom,"* pp. 109–11.

10. MRS. PETER'S PATRIMONY

1. Armistead Peter, *Tudor Place* (Georgetown [Washington, D.C.], 1969), p. vii.

2. Peter, *Tudor Place,* pp. ix, 38, 40, 50; Sarah Booth Conroy, "Washington's Granddaughter Slept Here," *Washington Post,* June 5, 1988, p. F1.

3. Peter, *Tudor Place,* pp. 75, 79.

4. Account Book of Thomas Peter, MS-2, Thomas and Martha Custis Peter Papers, Box 1, Folder 19, Tudor Place Manuscript Collection.

5. The slaves Arbour, Toney, and Dinah appear in GW's farm records; members of the Twine family are mentioned in his records, a letter, and his will.

6. *Writings of GW,* 34:452, GW to David Stuart, February 7, 1796; LC, GW Papers, David Stuart to GW, February 25, 1796 (I am grateful to the editors of the *Papers* for providing an accurate transcription of this crucial, unpublished letter).

7. *Writings of GW,* GW to William Pearce, January 27, 1796.

8. GW quoted in Warren, *Presidency of George Washington,* p. 88; Todd Estes, "The Art of Presidential Leadership: George Washington and the Jay Treaty," *Virginia Magazine of History and Biography* 109, no. 2 (2001): 127–58.

9. The letters between GW and Stuart reveal that even GW did not understand the legal technicalities of the division of the Custis slaves, a transaction made extremely complex by ambiguities in a 1778 contract between Jacky Custis and the Washingtons (Lynch, *Custis Chronicles,* pp. 147–48) and by a 1785 change in Virginia's inheritance laws (I am grateful to Mary Thompson for information on the 1785 legal revision). *Papers of GW,* Retirement Series, vol. 1, GW to Samuel Stanhope Smith, May 24, 1797; Lynch, *Custis Chronicles,* pp. 229–31. G.W.P. Custis had children with slaves: Lynch, *Custis Chronicles,* p. 5, Thompson, "'I Never See That Man Laugh'," pp. 39–41.

10. *Writings of GW,* 34:500, GW to William Pearce, March 20, 1796.

11. THE JUSTICE OF THE CREATOR

1. Flexner, *George Washington,* 4:339.

2. Niemcewicz, *Under Their Vine,* 102–3.

3. Ibid., p. 84.

4. Ibid., p. 92.

5. Ibid., p. 93.

6. Ibid., pp. 87–88.

7. Ibid., p. 103.

8. Louis Philippe, *Diary of My Travels in America,* translated from the French by Stephen Becker (New York: Delacorte Press, 1977), pp. 32–33. A visitor to Mount Vernon in 1833 made a similar observation: "Among the females was a Mulatto so light as to show the red in her cheeks, very modest and intelligent.

The blood of some offshoots of the W. family no doubt ran in her veins": Tap. Wentworth to John S. Burleigh, March 12, 1833, Mount Vernon Collection, A-259, M-1294.

9. Parkinson quoted in Hirschfeld, *George Washington and Slavery:* 58.

10. *Writings of GW,* 34:193, GW to William Pearce, May 10, 1795; ibid., 32:277, GW to Anthony Whiting, December 23, 1792.

11. *Writings of GW,* 34:379, GW to Pearce, November 29, 1795; ibid., 34:12, GW to Pearce, November 2, 1794; ibid., 31:465, GW to Oliver Evans, January 25, 1792; ibid., 34:145, GW to Pearce, March 15, 1795.

12. *Writings of GW,* 33:196, GW to Pearce, December 22, 1793; Anthony Whiting to GW, January 16, 1793, quoted in Mary V. Thompson, "'A Mean Pallet': Housing of the Mount Vernon Slaves," unpublished research report, Mount Vernon, p. 11; *Writings of GW,* 33:177–78, GW to Arthur Young, December 12, 1793; *Papers,* Revolutionary War Series, vol. 2, Lund Washington to GW, December 10, 1775.

13. Niemcewicz, *Under Their Vine:* 104; LC, David Stuart to GW, February 25, 1796.

14. Fairfax County Will Book H, pp. 180–81.

15. GW's remarks to John Bernard quoted in Hirschfeld, *George Washington and Slavery,* p. 78.

16. *Papers of GW,* Retirement Series, vol. 4, GW to Lawrence Lewis, September 20, 1799; ibid., GW to Robert Lewis, August 17, 1799.

17. Fields, *Papers of Martha Washington,* pp. 272–73, 321–22; Flexner, *George Washington,* 4:149. The authenticity of the dream letter has been challenged by the Washington scholar Peter Henriques, who points out several questionable elements, including reference to "the summer house," a structure that did not exist at Mount Vernon in Washington's time: Peter R. Henriques, *The Death of George Washington: He Died As He Lived,* Mount Vernon: Mount Vernon Ladies' Association, 2000, p. 77, n. 23. I believe the dream's occurrence is factual. Lossing derived much of his information from G.W.P. Custis and his daughter, Mary Custis Lee, the wife of Robert E. Lee. It is likely that the story was passed orally from Martha to her Custis descendants, who conveyed it to Lossing, who framed the story in a fictitious letter as a literary device, adding sentimental details. Lossing's text appears in *Mary and Martha,* pp. 324–26. The editor of MW's letters, Joseph E. Fields, guardedly accepted its authenticity. The letter illustrates the difficulty of evaluating an apparently garbled and edited oral history and the danger of discarding it because of inconsistencies. Similarly, Freeman wrestled with evaluating the historical value of G.W.P. Custis's memoir of Washington. Referring to a story in Custis's *Recollections,* which had been challenged: "[It] is florid and is somewhat overwritten but it is the testimony of Mrs. Washington's grandson and it either must have come from her or must have been invented. . . . In all probability it was told Parke Custis by Mrs. Washington. . . . [A] long lapse of time bars Custis's story as historical evidence of a sort to be accepted in all detail but does not necessarily brand it as evidence to be disregarded alto-

gether. Known facts are in part confirmatory." (Freeman, *George Washington,* 2:402–3.) Likewise, the disputed dream letter mentions an illness Martha is known to have suffered in September 1799.

18. Henriques, *The Death of GW,* passim; White McKenzie Wallenborn, M.D., "George Washington's Terminal Illness: A Modern Medical Analysis of the Last Illness and Death of George Washington," http://gwpapers.virginia.edu/articles/wallenborn/index.html.

19. Clark, *Martha Washington,* pp. 52–53.

20. Custis, *Recollections,* pp. 157–58; *The Last Will and Testament of George Washington and Schedule of His Property: To Which Is Appended the Last Will and Testament of Martha Washington,* John C. Fitzpatrick, ed., Mount Vernon: Mount Vernon Ladies' Association, 1992, p. 61; John P. Riley, "Written with My Own Hand: George Washington's Last Will and Testament," *Virginia Cavalcade,* vol. 48 no. 4, Autumn 1999, pp. 171–72; Edward Coles to James Madison, January 8, 1832, Edward Coles Papers, Princeton University Library. No descriptive account of the emancipation of GW's slaves has been found. Mary V. Thompson writes, "In December 1800, Martha Washington signed a deed of manumission for her deceased husband's slaves, a transaction which is recorded in the abstracts of the Fairfax County, Virginia, Court Records. They would become free on January 1, 1801": Mary V. Thompson, "'The Only Unavoidable Subject of Regret': George Washington and Slavery," np, http://mountvernon.org/library/research/Regret.html.

21. LC, Thomas Jefferson to John Holmes, April 22, 1820.

22. Thomas Jefferson, *Notes on the State of Virginia* [electronic resource], Charlottesville: University of Virginia Library, Electronic Text Center, 1993, transcribed from: *Writings,* selected [and edited] by Merrill D. Peterson, New York: Literary Classics of the U.S., Library of America 1984, Query XIV, p. 192, http://etext.lib.virginia.edu/toc/modeng/public/JefBvo21.html.

23. Ellis, *Founding Brothers,* p. 105; LC, Thomas Jefferson to James Monroe, June 12, 1796.

24. LC, GW to Sir John Sinclair, December 11, 1796.

25. Jordan, *White Over Black:* 320–21.

26. Netherton et al., pp. 33, 35; Gordon Wood, "Early American Get-Up-and-Go," *New York Review of Books,* June 29, 2000.

27. First Lincoln vs. Douglas Debate, August 21, 1858, Ottawa, Illinois, http://www.oberlin.edu/history/GJK/H103syl/HouseDivided.html.

28. Julian P. Boyd et al., eds., *The Papers of Thomas Jefferson,* 30 vols. (Princeton, N.J., and Oxford: Princeton University Press, 1950–), 28:568, "Notes of a Conversation with Edmund Randolph," dated by the editors "after 1795."

29. Jefferson, *Notes,* Query XVIII, p. 227.

30. Second Inaugural Address of Abraham Lincoln, March 4, 1865, quoted in The Avalon Project at Yale Law School, http://www.yale.edu/lawweb/avalon/presiden/inaug/lincoln2.htm.

Acknowledgments

The writing of this book would have been impossible without the cooperation of the staff at Mount Vernon and the editors of the George Washington papers. From the outset both institutions welcomed my inquiries and offered freely of their expertise, despite the sensitive nature of the topic. I drew heavily on their resources and advice, but the conclusions stated in this book are my own and do not necessarily reflect the thinking of the Mount Vernon staff or the editors of the papers.

I owe a very deep debt to Mary Thompson, research specialist for the Mount Vernon Ladies' Association, who probably knows as much about life at Mount Vernon as any living soul and generously shared research and insights gathered over many years. I am grateful to James C. Rees, executive director, for his support, and to Dennis Pogue, associate director, for meeting with me at the start of the project and lending advice throughout. I thank Mount Vernon's librarian, Barbara McMillan, for guiding me through the Washington collections, and Dawn Bonner for her gracious help gathering illustrations. In the field, Jinny Fox and Mike Robinson shared their research into eighteenth-century agriculture and made Mount Vernon's daily routines come alive.

Philander Chase and Frank Grizzard opened the doors of the George Washington papers project to me. I spent many delightful hours on the fifth floor of Alderman Library in discussions with them, Beverly Runge, David Hoth, James Guba, and Beverly Kirsch. I am particularly grateful to Phil and Frank for allowing access to the project's invaluable collection of ancillary research materials and for providing transcriptions of crucial documents. I thank Jennifer Stertzer and the other staff members of the Washington papers for the many courtesies they extended. Bill Abbot, former editor of the papers, shared his insights on Washington's character and on the singular importance of the Custis family.

I am grateful to the family historians who shared their research with me. My deep thanks to Judith Saunders Burton and Ruby Saunders for their guidance on the West Ford story, to Anita Wills for inviting me to the Bowden reunion, to Karen E. Sutton for sharing her research and taking me through Christ Church, to Dr. Harry Carter for his help with the Custis/Costin line, and to ZSun-nee Matema for information about her forebears. The Latané family graciously opened Blenheim to me and shared important documents—the fabled Washington hospitality endures.

I thank Harvey Bakari, Lorraine Brooks, Kathy Thompson, Linda Rowe, and Aaron Wolf of Colonial Williamsburg; Wendy Kail, archivist at Tudor Place; Brent Tarter at the Library of Virginia for his archival help and expert advice; and Dr. David Stone of UVA. I am indebted to Evelyn Gerson for her fascinating study of Ona Judge.

My research got under way during a resident fellowship at the Virginia Foundation for the Humanities, where I thank Robert Vaughan, Roberta Culbertson, John d'Entremont, Holly Shulman, Jerome Handler, and Gail Shea. Additional thanks go to Shaye Areheart, Philip Morgan, Philip J. Schwarz, Anthony A. Iaccarino, Liz Varon, Rosemarie Zagarri, Martha J. King, Greg Massey, Vernon Edenfield, Amy Muraca, Jervis Hairston, Jane Colihan, Dorinda Evans, Merle and Rose Marie Aus, Brian and Mary McGinn, and Senator Nat W. Washington. From start to finish I was utterly dependent on the superb staff and facilities of the Library of Congress and the University of Virginia's Alderman Library. It is easy to take such institutions for granted.

My demanding agent and sympathetic friend, Howard Morhaim, poked, prodded, and shaped this project from the start with his usual sharp insight and tenacity. In some ways this book had its genesis in a chance meeting in Mississippi with Elisabeth Sifton several years ago; a benign fate brought my proposal to her desk at just the right moment. Using hammer and nails where needed, and a scalpel elsewhere, she fixed what was broken while always offering encouragement. There are giants among us still. I am grateful to Danny Mulligan for his heavy lifting and cheerful e-mails as deadlines loomed, and to Robert C. Olsson for his splendid, lovely design. Thanks to my friend Stow Lovejoy for his advice on inheritance law, to David Mielke for his hospitality, and to my parents for their ardent support.

I have dedicated this book to my son, Henry ("the Next"), who shows ominous signs of having the writing gift in large measure. My wife, Donna, once again read every page through every draft, always making things better. Both endured the travails of composition without audible complaint—but they too are writers, so they know what it's like. To both, my love always. I close with an old Virginia toast, heartfelt: "God bless General Washington."

Charlottesville
June 2003

Index